High Places

INTERNATIONAL LIBRARY OF HUMAN GEOGRAPHY

1. *Egypt: An Economic Geography*
Fouad N. Ibrahim and Barbara Ibrahim
978 1 86064 547 1

2. *The Middle East Water Question: Hydropolitics and the Global Economy*
Tony Allan
978 1 86064 582 2

3. *Cultural Geography: A Critical Dictionary of Key Concepts*
David Atkinson, Peter Jackson, David Sibley & Neil Washbourne (eds)
978 1 86064 703 1

4. *The Cognition of Geographic Space*
Rob Kitchin and Mark Blades
978 1 86064 704 8

5. *Picturing Place: Photography and the Geographical Imagination*
Joan M. Schwartz and James R. Ryan
978186064 751 2

6. *Pink Ice: Britain and the South Atlantic Empire*
Klaus Dodds
978 1 86064 769 7

7. *Human Capital: Population Economics in the Middle East*
I. Sirageldin (ed.)
978 1 86064 795 6

8. *Culture and Space: Conceiving a New Cultural Geography*
Joel Bonnemaison
978 1 86064 907 3

9. *Globalization and Identity: Development and Integration in a Changing World*
Alan Carling (ed.)
978 1 85043 848 9

10. *Challenging the NGOs: Women, Religion and Western Dialogues in India*
Tamsin Bradley
978 1 84511 152 6

11. *Traditional Buildings: A Global Survey of Structural Forms and Cultural Functions*
Allen Noble
978 1 84511 305 6

12. *Geography and Vision: Seeing, Imagining and Representing the World*
Denis Cosgrove
978 1 85043 846 5

13. *Muslims on the Map: A National Survey of Social Trends in Britain*
Serena Hussain
978 1 84511 471 8

14. *The World Water Crisis: The Failures of Resource Management*
Stephen Brichieri-Colombi
978 1 84511 753 5

15. *High Places: Cultural Geographies of Mountains, Ice and Science*
Denis Cosgrove and Veronica della Dora (eds)
978 1 84511 616 3

High Places

Cultural Geographies of Mountains, Ice and Science

Edited by
Denis Cosgrove and Veronica della Dora

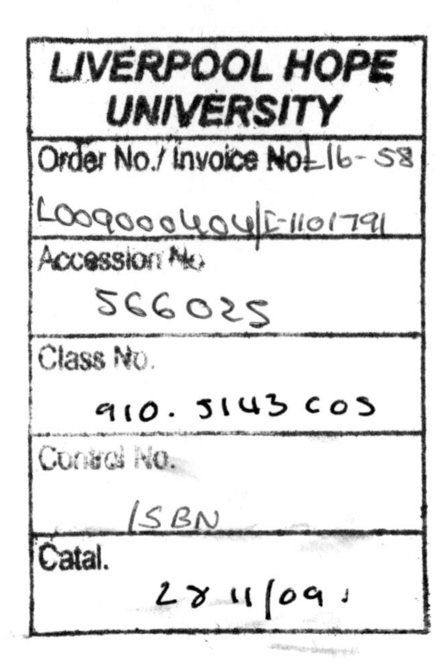

Published in 2009 by I.B.Tauris & Co Ltd
6 Salem Road, London W2 4BU
175 Fifth Avenue, New York NY 10010
www.ibtauris.com

In the United States and Canada distributed by Palgrave Macmillan,
a division of St. Martin's Press, 175 Fifth Avenue, New York NY 10010

International Library of Human Geography: 15

ISBN 978 1 84511 616 3 (Hb)
ISBN 978 1 84511 617 0 (Pb)

A full CIP record for this book is available from the British Library

A full CIP record for this book is available from the Library of Congress Library of Congress catalog card: available

Typeset in Caslon by Stilman Davis
Printed and bound in Great Britain by TJ International Ltd, Padstow, Cornwall

Contents

Illustrations

Acknowledgements

We would like to thank Felix Driver for his critical comments and helpful suggestions on previous versions of the manuscript, David Stonestreet for his support and all those who helped in the production of the volume, in particular Stilman Davis and Jayne Hill. We would also acknowledge the sources of the photographs used in this book with grateful thanks.

Contributors

Michael T. Bravo is Head of the Circumpolar History and Public Policy Group at the Scott Polar Research Institute, University of Cambridge. He has edited *Narrating the Arctic* (2002) with Sverker Sörlin, as well as numerous articles on the history of scientific travel and empire.

Denis Cosgrove was Alexander von Humboldt Professor of Geography at the University of California, Los Angeles until his death in the summer of 2008. His recent books include *Geography and Vision* (2008), *Apollo's Eye: A Cartographic Genealogy of the Earth in the Western Imagination* (2001), and as editor, *Mappings* (1999).

Bernard Debarbieux is Professor of Geography at the University of Geneva (Switzerland). He has published widely on scientific knowledge, social perception and political uses of mountains. His recent books include *Ces territorialités qui se dessinent*, with Martin Vanier (2001).

Veronica della Dora is Lecturer in Geography at the University of Bristol. She has published on visual and textual representations and their role in shaping geographical imaginations of the eastern Mediterranean. She is currently completing a monograph on Western and post-Byzantine depictions of Mount Athos.

J. Nicholas Entrikin is Professor of Geography at University of California, Los Angeles and Acting Dean of the International Institute. His research and teaching interests include geographical theory and cultural/political geography, with regional focus on North America and Europe. He is the author of *The Betweenness of Place* (1991) and the co-editor (with John Agnew) of *The Marshall Plan Today: Model and Metaphor* (2004).

William L. Fox has published numerous books on cognition and landscape. His most recent books are *Driving to Mars* (2006) and *Climbing Mount Limbo: Essays on the Edge of Land and Language* (2008). He is currently working on a book about how we see the world from above, as well as on another with Denis Cosgrove about photography and flight.

Heather Frazar is an independent scholar and visual artist based in Los Angeles. In 2005 she earned a master's degree in cultural geography from the University of California, Los Angeles. Her work focuses on the materiality and aesthetics of science, including a recent video piece entitled, *Core Matters* (or GISP2 chronologies).

Jong-Heon Jin is a Research Fellow of the Institute for Korean Regional Studies at Seoul National University. His chapter on symbolic landscape in Korea appeared in *Critical Approaches to Korean Geography* (2007).

K. Maria D. Lane is an Assistant Professor of Geography at the University of New Mexico. She has published on the geographical dimensions of late-nineteenth-century Mars science and is currently preparing a monograph for the University of Chicago Press titled *Geographies of Mars*.

Richard C. Powell is Lecturer in Geography at the University of Liverpool. He has published on the geographies of scientific practice and the cultural politics of the circum-polar Arctic. He is currently completing an ethnographic monograph on post-1945 environmental science in the Canadian Arctic.

Gilles Rudaz is a Post-Doctoral Scholar in the Environmental Policy and Planning Group, Department of Urban Studies and Planning, Massachusetts Institute of Technology. He has published on mountain lobbies and networks, and edited *Mountains of Europe: Stakeholders, Legitimization, Delineation* (2004), a thematic issue of the *Journal of Alpine Research*.

John Wylie is Senior Lecturer in Cultural Geography in the School of Geography, Archaeology & Earth Resources, University of Exeter. His research focuses on issues of landscape, embodiment, affectivity and perception in various contemporary and historical contexts. He is the author of *Landscape* (2007).

Kathryn Yusoff is a Lecturer in Human (and Nonhuman) Geography at the University of Exeter, Cornwall. Her research interests include exploring the aesthetics of environmental change and re-thinking visual culture in relation to emerging technologies of vision. She recently curated *POLAR: The Art & Science of Climate Change* and edited the book *BIPOLAR* (2008, The Arts Catalyst). Kathryn is currently working on the project 'The political aesthetics of climate change'.

1

Introduction

High Places

Denis Cosgrove and Veronica della Dora

> The physical landscape is baffling in its ability to transcend whatever we would make of it. It is absolute in its expression as turns of the mind, and larger than our grasp; and yet it is still knowable.[1]

High places take many forms. Topographically, mountain peaks and ranges and high plateaus are elevated above sea level or surrounding plains; polar regions are geographically elevated according to the global measure of latitude that rises towards the earth's poles. Sacred locations, often but not always physically elevated, are 'high' principally because they have been set apart by the faithful as being closer to divinity. Indeed the biblical expression 'the high places' is an English rendering of the Hebrew *bamot*, which denoted a place marked for worship by an altar, a stone stele, or a wooden post. Height, then, is much more than a question of scale or altitudinal measure, just as place is much more than geographical location; it denotes a relationship between location and human experience. Connected, as height and place have consistently been across cultures and faiths, for example in the Western concept of Sublime or Chinese ideas of the mountain as an originating 'place of places', high places make for complex and fascinating geographies, both material and imaginative. As a collection of essays, *High Places* can be situated within a rapidly expanding literature that seeks to re-conceptualise what Lewis and Wigen have called 'metageographies', i.e. large-scale classificatory labels through which we frame geographical knowledge. In this sense, *High Places* complements recent works such as Felix Driver and Luciana Martins' collection on the tropics,[2] or the *Journal of Historical Geography*'s special issues on islands and oceans.[3] It also adds to already existing literature on cultures of science in extreme environments.[4]

Figure 1.1 View of Mount Athos, Greece (photograph by Monk Apollò, Docheiariou Monastery, 2006).

Introducing this collection of studies devoted to high places we consider their material and metaphorical aspects and the ways in which the two dimensions of altitude and latitude interplay. We begin by addressing a conventionally 'spiritual', 'Christianised' and Western vision of high places, but move towards a more polyvocal approach through the exploration of cultures of science-making and cognition in these regions. For the sake of clarity and structure we have divided our discussion into sections. The first of these considers how topographic and latitudinal height have been brought together in geographical writing, especially in relation to the concept of the sublime that framed both mountain and polar regions during the era of Western exploration and colonisation of the globe. Next we comment on how an expanded concept of place permits more complex and subtle geographies of such areas to be written today. A section on mapping of and in high places examines the complex relations between representation and materiality there, while our comments on the body respond not only to a growing geographical recognition of the human body as the site where nature and culture come together and are inscribed, but also to the special demands that high mountain and polar regions make on an organism that evolved physically in much warmer parts of the earth. In a final theoretical section on cognition, knowledge and science making in high places we recognise the enduring role that they have played in Western environmental and ethnographic science and the ways that this connects quite diverse peoples and places while sustaining in some respects a colonial relationship that in geopolitical terms has passed. These themes are *foci* of the book's individual studies, whose organisation and principal concerns we summarise in the final section of this introduction.

Height

The high places considered in this collection are defined by either high altitude or high latitude: they are mountain ranges and peaks, or polar regions (i.e. those lying beyond 66' 32" north and south latitudes): places of rock, snow and ice. Such locations share various climatic, geomorphic and biotic characteristics, including low mean and absolute temperatures, regular snowfall and ice formation and high winds, with consequent glacial and aeolian processes shaping their landforms, and a limited range of flora and fauna whose adaptation to climatic conditions renders them unfamiliar and even invisible to eyes accustomed to more 'temperate' environments. These shared physical conditions account in large measure for the grouping of high mountains and polar regions in conventional geographical study. It was a commonplace of modern physical geography in the nineteenth and twentieth centuries that the altitudinal belts of tropical mountains such as Chimborazo or Kilimanjaro allowed the climatic belts of the globe to be observed and studied over the limited space of a few miles, and within sight of the equator, and this was reflected in maps of world climate and 'natural' regions by geographers such as Köppen and Herbertson.[5] Today, both polar ice sheets and mountain glaciers are treated scientifically as equally significant, as barometers of global climate change. In fact, even from the perspective of physical geography alone, the differences between high latitudes and high altitudes can be as great as their similarities. Low-latitude high mountains such as the tropical examples just mentioned, with their regular diurnal and unvarying seasonal cycles of day and night experience very different annual insolation from polar regions with their annual shifts between light and dark, while in temperate high mountains aspect plays a role not parallelled in polar regions. Mountain glaciers behave differently from continental ice sheets. Vast areas of the Arctic are low-lying plains, and even the Antarctic continent – although a 'high place' in that it boasts the highest mean altitude of any continent – has limited regions of the high-angled slopes typical of mountains in any part of the world.

While physical geography alone might argue against collecting high altitudes and high latitudes under a single rubric, human geography is more accommodating. Both environments are characterised by sparse and largely impermanent human settlement, their physical landscapes for the most only moderately transformed by human occupance. High places fall into what the early twentieth-century geographer H.J. Fleure termed 'regions of difficulty': areas of scant resources for dense human occupation that 'refuse sensible increment even to prolonged effort'.[6] Fleure's perspective was of course typical of those whose individual experience and cultural resources are not designed to accommodate daily life in such spaces, as John Wylie's comparison of Amundsen's and Scott's contrasting experiences 'on ice' deftly reveals. And as Gilles Rudaz points out in his discussion here of Alpine

Figure 1.2 View of Croagh Patrick, Ireland (courtesy of Alan Reevell).

mountain dwellers, even such generalising terms as 'mountains', let alone comparative and globalised terminology as Fleure's, do not figure in the place perceptions of native dwellers, who use more localised toponyms. Michael Bravo's study reveals clearly that Inuit and others whose individual lives, communities and cultures have been framed by dwelling at high latitudes, regard the idea of living on those margins of survival (as figured by those from more temperate zones) as quite bizarre.

It is of course precisely the interplay between the generalising cultural visions and environmental interpretations of outsiders and visitors, and the localised knowledge and experience of insiders and dwellers that can make geography a compelling subject of study. All geographical writing is inflected by the expectations, needs and desires of its authors and never wholly subject to empirical specifics. At the same time, however, meanings are not simply imposed on territory, but they rather work through its material specificities. The human connection with high places is a two-way physical and imaginative dialogue in which geographical knowledge is continuously built and destabilised, shaped and reshaped. The landscapes of high places have commonly evoked in those arriving from more 'temperate regions' (the layered meanings of that phrase itself give clues to their likely interpretation of non- or in-temperate places) feelings of awe, reverence, but also displacement and anxiety. Nineteenth century exploration and colonialist discourse figured high places as spaces of muscular and masculine challenge, of competitive adventure, and unearthly, intense, sometimes even spiritual experience, as well as of intense scientific curiosity. For the outsider, there is little of the homely about these regions, little of dwelling. And their 'un-homely' physicality has played an active role in the processes of their geographical signification. Local experience and knowledge differ of course, but only very recently have voices domesticated within high places gained an audience in the wider world and entered into a more balanced dialogue with the 'formal' scientific knowledge of visitors. Gilles Rudaz, Richard Powell and Michael Bravo all seek to bring those voices into this volume.

The outside vision of high places, whether mountainous or polar, renders them as liminal, inaccessible and pure. The presence of snow and ice as landscape elements in themselves and in their capacity to blanket and mask more durable landforms, the obscurity and evanescence of mist and cloud, together with the disorientation these can produce, and the physical rigours of ascent and traverse for those whose technologies of movement have been shaped in different environments, all reinforce associations of high places with physical and moral demands, with moral purification, eschatology and transcendence. Jagged rock and ice, snowdrift and freezing mist, intermittently clearing to reveal forms of unparalleled clarity, are among the standard geographical tropes of high places, whose imaginative power is reinforced by distance from permanent habitation, intense cold, unrelenting wind, physical isolation and discomfort, distorted vision, physical danger and death. Mountain peaks viewed from a distance, polar ice sheets, icebergs and windswept, white plains seen from the deck of a ship or from the air combine line, form and colour into powerful landscape images for which the conventional aesthetic language is that of the 'sublime'.

The idea of the sublime is complex and multilayered, and the literature seeking to specify and explicate it is too large and sophisticated for us to do it justice here, but it is worth recording that the Greek word used by Longinus in the earliest discussion of the sublime as a poetic and literary form is *ypsos*, literally meaning 'height'. Longinus associates the sublime with high passion and its bodily effects and expression, especially terror. The Latin word from which the English 'sublime' is derived, also denotes 'high' or 'exalted', so that as a term of rhetoric 'sublimity' referred to metaphors that encouraged the visceral sense of awe, terror and humility in the face of immensity that we associate with vertigo – fear induced by height. When attributed in Christian thought to the experience of the divine especially, transcendent height was always an element of the sublime. It was in eighteenth-century England, and in direct association with experience of the Alps in the Grand Tour and the fascination with landscape aesthetics, that the sublime became contrasted to 'the beautiful' and attached specifically to the embodied, aesthetic experience of specific kinds of natural places.[7] Such places were characterised by irregular forms, vertiginous contrasts of height and depth, precipitous ledges and slopes, and perhaps intensities of heat or cold that gave the human body an agreeable frisson of terror. In an age when Europeans – educated in the fashionable philosophical and literary language of the beautiful and the sublime – systematically explored and recounted the globe's mountain and polar regions, it is unsurprising that they drew repeatedly on the aesthetic theory and literary language of the sublime to describe such high places.[8] Sublime language and its graphic equivalent of stock images have endured, at least in the popular imagination of outsiders, up to our own days. In the twenty-first century high places are no longer regarded merely as adventure playgrounds in which to experience the conventional pleasures and trials of the sublime. They are increasingly treated as uniquely precious locations for human survival, barometers of environmental and social vulnerability, spaces of scientific study and cultural, geopolitical and environmental contestation. However, as a number of these essays sometimes explicitly reveal, these concerns still draw upon and contribute to an aesthetic reservoir best described by the parameters of sublime landscape. As William Fox suggests, the psychological responses conventionally associated with the sublime may yet prove to have physiological foundations.

Place

So far our focus has been on the first part of the term high places, on their most characteristic dimension. But the characteristics of 'place' demand some reflection. For geographers, place denotes something much more than pure location in physical space or indeed natural and topographic features. Places do have a location, some form of physical presence, to be sure, but they are also the expression and the necessary medium of social processes, they represent a gathering of humans together with the material, social, political and symbolic appropriation of space that such a gathering always entails.[9] Humans do not need to be physically present to create and sustain place. Barring a tiny number of scientific outposts, the continent of Antarctica remains empty of human presence, but its existence on maps, in explorers' reports, in scientific and literary publication, in photographs, movies and paintings make it a significant place on the globe. The history of exploration efforts, the application across its surface of political boundaries and toponyms, and the presence of those research stations and camps, all contribute to create a texture of places within its designated continental space. Estonia's current desire to establish a scientific presence on Antarctica in order to demonstrate its significance as a scientific nation, and the conquest of Everest by an Estonian group of mountaineers in 2003 on the fiftieth anniversary of the first ascent and the year of the country's accession to the European Union, widely celebrated in the national press, are examples of the continued significance of high places in framing narratives of national identity.[10] Places have complex and overlapping existences within geographic space whose meanings and significance are commonly the subject of struggle and contestation.

Applying these insights to the term 'high places' implies that something in the elevation of mountain and polar regions contributes significantly to their social form and order and that they share through the physical fact of elevation some social characteristics. In the past, as H.J. Fleure's designation implies, the geographer would have searched for common social morphologies in inhabited polar and mountain regions: seasonal migratory activities, hunting and herding economies for example, and sought to connect these to common features of their physical environments. The environmental determinism (although Fleure would have rejected such a designation) explicit or implicit in such study is unacceptable today, not only on theoretical grounds, but because it is based on too broad an understanding and interpretation of human life and landscape in such regions. Superficial parallels between reindeer herders in northern Scandinavia and llama herders in the Andean cordillera for

Figure 1.3 Ceremonial South Pole marker (courtesy of Alberto Bolatto).

example do not take us very far in understanding the complex interconnections between physical environments, natural ecosystems, domestication and social organisation within the respective communities.

Yet to employ the term 'high places' denotes a commonality between designated regions on the globe that is more than purely physical. Given that the place making activities of those whose lives and cultures have been formed in these various regions are as varied as those of other human groups, whence does the common designation spring? Once again, the designation of a high place comes from outside of the society which has made the high place its home; it is an imaginative act, the outsider's attribution of common characteristics and meanings that shape diverse locations into comparable places. While rejecting the environmental theories that originally gave rise to the concept of high places we cannot escape the intellectual heritage that has shaped both the representation of mountain and polar regions across the globe and the embodied practices to which such representations have given rise and which in turn have reinforced them. At the same time, the studies here draw upon sophisticated meanings of place that seek to embrace the complex social processes involved in their designation, description and interpretation.

Mapping high places

Physically or imaginatively, high places mark the ends of the earth. They do so in different ways. Firmly grounded in the earth, territorially bounded, and yet stretching towards heaven, mountains, for example, have represented sites of revelation in many different faiths, points of junction between the immanent and the transcendent: what Mircea Eliade long ago called *axes mundi*. In the Christian tradition, the pyramidal silhouettes of the sacred mountains Mount Athos in Greece and Croagh Patrick in Ireland [Figs 1.1 and 1.2] looming over the sea at the opposite ends of Europe might be considered emblematic. Thanks to their majesty and well-defined profiles, high mountain peaks are primary geographical objects in the landscape to capture the human gaze. In their metaphorical use, mountains seem to help us grasp the ungraspable and visualise the indefinite. Walter Benjamin used a mountain range to describe his 'auratic experience', while Frederick Nietzsche gave visual shape to 'the modern spirit' in the form of an erupting volcano.[11] Even in everyday speech, who has never complained about being buried under 'a mountain of work', or aimed to reach 'the top'? Nor is this purely a Western metaphor: in Chinese thinking, mountains are the bones that comprise the very structure of the earth; 'more dramatically or completely than any other natural thing, a mountain is ... a place for the interplay of such basic forces as *ch'i* and *li*, *yin* and *yang*. It is also the primary place of authentic wilderness. In short, a mountain is a place of places – a place from which other places originate: 'the originating host of all the guest places in a given landscape'.[12] Chinese landscape paintings seek to 'map' the resonance of such places.

We talk metaphorically too about 'opposite poles' to 'map' contrasting extremities in people's personalities, or in polemical arguments. Yet geographically the notion of the poles as 'the ends of the earth' is more arbitrary and complex to define than visible mountain peaks. Sometimes named 'the third pole', Mount Everest is a well-defined, visible, physical place – differentiated by humans from the surrounding range of similar peaks by reason of its unique height. As places, the North and South Poles, by contrast, are more abstract, geometric, spatial concepts. Indeed, the earth has various Poles: magnetic, geodetic and geographic. The geographical poles are defined by the earth's axis of rotation, and thus by astronomical principles and the invisible laws of physics, rather than by physical geographical appearance, while the magnetic poles are migratory over time and thus difficult to determine and mark precisely. Unlike mountains, the geographical poles need scientific instruments (or human markers) in order to be rendered visible in the landscape.

Visible or invisible, latitudinal or altitudinal, high places are similarly challenging to those trying to 'map' them formally and thus encompass them within the remit of secular science. Practically, the mobility of ice sheets and glaciers, and of steep slopes and screes, as well as the shifting and often obscured boundaries between land and sea in polar regions or between horizon and sky in high mountains, challenge the cartographic desire for stable lines on the map. Speaking more theoretically, for all the claims to scientific objectivity associated with it, mapping is a process that is as much physical as it is imaginative. It involves physical

Figure 1.4 Greek-Orthodox chapel at the top of Mount Sinai.

interaction with the territory, but also the ability to contemplate it from a distance. The Western discourse of mapping is above all one of visibility, depending on the ability to see and measure location and distance and yielding in the map itself a visible representation of the surveyed place. High places represent peculiar challenges to the idea of visibility, as William Fox's study reveals. In high mountains the influence of altitude on the body can place great demands on accurate recording of scientific data, as von Humboldt's scientific work in the high Andes made so apparent in bleeding lips and strained eyes, while steepness of slope challenges such graphic techniques as relief shading or contours to represent altitude on maps.[13] When British surveyors from the Falkland Islands Dependency Survey tried to map the Antarctic spaces of Graham Land in the early 1950s, using aerial-survey techniques developed in the war theatres of Western Europe and South Asia that they believed would radically ease and speed their work, they were often stymied by the same problems of mist and fog, magnetic variation and mirage that had faced their maritime predecessors in polar regions, while the need for 'ground truthing' – terrestrial survey to fix aerial traverses to geodetic points – remained a physically challenging necessity.[14] Indeed the 'final' mapping of Antarctica was achieved only in 1997 when the Canadian Space Agency (CSA) and NASA published a composite mosaic of photographic traverses based on satellite imagery.

In its broader, less purely technical sense, mapping is a cognitive process that helps us make sense of the world in our everyday lives. All mapping rests on selectivity and on the imposition of markings, boundaries and meanings that inscribe the natural world but are not inherently 'natural'. For this reason, mapping is always a potentially contested cultural practice. If the boundary between the solid rock of a mountain ridge and the sky above marks a stark contrast to the eye, then the boundary of the 'ends of the earth' can be set. To trace those same limits on the map or on a satellite picture represents a cultural – often a political – choice, as Bernard Debarbieux and Jong-Heon Jin reveal in the very different contexts of mapping mountain chains in the Western and Korean cartographic traditions.

The work of identification, or 'pinning down on the map', a specific point-location of or in high places is no less problematic than setting boundaries or defining the limits of geographical objects. It was not until the eighteenth century that the mathematician Leonhard Euler predicted a 'slight wobbling' of the terrestrial axis, and not until recent times that scientists recorded a consistent movement of the southern polar ice sheet (roughly ten metres per year). By a strange paradox, the poles (the points of origin of the meridians and of our modern grid of certainties) thus escape the implications of fixedness suggested by survey and mapping. Also, the gathering of longitude lines towards the poles renders the graticule, so useful in transferring locations from ground to map over most of the global surface, of decidedly limited value. Even fixed 'taken-for-granted' mountain-landmarks are not always obvious to identify. Unlike the dramatic cones of Mount Athos and Croagh Patrick that rise above the level surface of the immediately adjacent sea, or Mounts Ararat and Kilimanjaro whose snowy peaks tower over surrounding highlands, Mount Sinai, the most famous and 'holiest' of all Biblical mountains, for example, does not stand out against the horizon, nor does it have any striking physical individuality. Surpassed by almost 400 metres by the nearby Mount Catherine, the Mountain of Moses is virtually impossible for 'non-expert' eyes to single out from the intricate Upper Sinai massif. Its identification has long been contested, with a number of 'competing peaks' laying claim to the title. The small chapel and mosque now perched on a specific peak provide landmarks no more reassuring than the South Pole marker on the white wastes of the Antarctic ice sheet [Figs. 1.3 and 1.4]. The former has been determined by careful research on text and territory, the latter by geophysical and mathematical calculation. The chapel and mosque on the Mountain of Moses and the South Pole marker, in their different ways, celebrate mapping achievements.

The body in high places

Both altitudinal and latitudinal high places are characterised by physical conditions that place extreme demands on the human body. These are environments in which the body is forced into visceral struggle with the matter of landscape, to protect itself from the numbing effects of extreme cold, the searing bite of wind chills, the disorientation and blinding effects of snow and the blood thinning and sickening effects of low pressure and high altitude. Accommodation to these features of the physical environment is apparent in the material culture, the social *mores* and the language of peoples inhabiting them, as Michael Bravo's discussions with Inuit people make clear. On the other hand, senses accustomed to the physical environment of temperate places are shocked and alternately sharpened and dulled by these immediately physical aspects of high places, and those encounters are inevitably reflected in narratives and other representations of such encounters and the geographical assumptions to which they give rise.

The imaginative sublimity of high places may be linked to the physical process of *sublimation* – the transformation of solid ice and snow into vapour, for example, without passage through an intermediate liquid state. This phenomenon occurs only at sub-zero temperatures, so this can occur naturally in high places. Sublimation can have direct physical impacts on the human body. In the midst of a polar blizzard, or of a mountain climb, the body is rendered porous to the elements. In this sense, it also metaphorically experiences another sort of sublimation: through the tactile contact with rock, or through its becoming one with the wind and the snow. It is against such elemental harshness that physical endurance is tested, giving rise to complex discourses, inflected by cultural assumptions about gender, class and ethnicity.

In nineteenth and early twentieth-century literature of western exploration, mountain and polar landscapes were usually described in Manichean terms: extreme and austere, painted in black and white, arenas in which human values were also polarised.[15] High places were figured not only as geographical *terrae incognitae* to explore, but spaces for a sort of Stoic self-reflection – for an inner exploration through physical distancing from the inhabited world. If mountaintops had traditionally provided a visually powerful metaphor for Cartesian detachment from the world at their feet, the continuous bodily confrontation with injury and death during the ascent could also offer a different, more distanced perspective on everyday 'human affairs'. This remove was sought by travellers into these regions long after the heroic period of first exploration and 'discovery' was over. Peter Matthiessen's 1970s search for the 'snow leopard' among the ravines and flapping prayer flags of Tibet's high plateau is figured as much as an exploration for self and relationship as a quest for the physical presence of the rare creature itself.[16] Like ancient Greek heroes travelling to the Pillars of Hercules, mountaineers and polar explorers of the 'heroic' age of Western exploration achieved a sort of super-human status by reaching the 'ends of the earth', although this could sour if their motives were detected as less than pure, defiled by the desire for money or fame.[17] Any detachment from the world, of course, was only temporary. It was through the transitory physical experience of high places, especially when marked permanently on the body in the form of scars or lost limbs and faculties, that heroic values could be brought back 'home' and circulated through the great metropolises of Europe and North America. In this sense, the tempering, masculine qualities attributed to high places and their elemental landscapes served as signs of the authority of science and a moral counterpart to the supposedly effeminate Tropics and their 'corrupting' corporeal influences.[18]

The environmental extremes of high places have also intrigued scientists studying human psychological and physiological responses to challenging, physical conditions. Usually remote, potentially dangerous, alternatively nerve-racking and enervating, high places might lead to depression, despair, or physical sickness, but they could also encourage group cohesion. If acclimatisation to the Tropics was mainly a nineteenth-century concern, acclimatisation to high places remains an object of scientific investigation today. In 1982, Peter Hackett, a University of Colorado researcher on high altitude physiology and methods for coping with life-threatening conditions, established a still-working laboratory on a 14,000-feet-high glacier on Mount Denali, the coldest place in Alaska and indeed on the whole North American continent. This cluster of 12 by 14 foot plastic shells is used by Hackett and a small group of colleagues two months each year to study the human body's reactions to high altitudes and extreme conditions. Over the years, the lab has been also been used by NASA to explore the dynamics of a small isolated technical group, given the similarity between the lab's conditions with those travelling to the ultimate high places on the space shuttle and International Space Station.[19] In *Driving to Mars*, William Fox describes a similar scientific research location – the Haughton Crater of Devon Island in the Canadian High Arctic, the largest uninhabited island on earth. Each July a score of scientists camp in the twelve-mile-wide, 1,000-foot-deep crater in order to conduct experiments in an environment that is the closest available on our planet to that of Mars.[20]

Science making in high places

Contemporary laboratories located on glaciers and in the polar regions continue a long tradition of regarding high places as privileged arenas for science making. Their scientific significance seems to increase in direct proportion to their remoteness – physical and imaginative – from what Bruno Latour has called 'centres of calculation' in the metropolitan regions of the earth's densely populated, more temperate regions. Just as physical isolation has been seen by people of faith as a pre-condition for the human search for 'truth', so it remains the same for those whose quest is scientific rather than religious. The early Christian hermit's search for a contact with God on lofty mountain peaks was preceded by the ancient natural philosophers' desire for a no less transcendent contact with the stars, with rare herbs, with nature's truths. Like polar explorers and holy ascetics, by setting themselves apart from the world through their ascent of high mountain summits, or by reaching the polar ends of the earth, entire generations of natural scientists gained a degree of authority simply from the location of their field activities. As Maria Lane shows in her chapter, it is through their physical access to remote mountaintops that late nineteenth-century American astronomers, for example, were able to legitimise their scientific enterprises, and to gain legitimacy among their colleagues. In this sense, awe-inspiring high places have 'sublimated' the astronomer's status in the eyes of modern society.

As privileged sites for observatories and laboratories, high places have often been conceptualised as large-scale laboratories in themselves. High places and laboratories have been seen to share such characteristics as 'sterility' (in the sense of 'pure', uncontaminated environments), and 'distance' in the sense of separation from the rest of the world. These features were deemed necessary to fulfill the requirements for what was conceived as scientific 'objectivity'. Thus, the only permanent settlements permitted on Antarctica are 'research' laboratories and bases, in spite of the fact that their occupants and activities can be as environmentally damaging as any tourist camp. Or consider Heather Frazar's compelling descriptions of the parallels between the surface of the Greenland Ice Sheet and the National Ice Core Laboratory in Denver, CO. Thanks to their environmental characteristics, high places have also been considered able to disclose the most recondite secrets of our planet's history. Nineteenth-century Scottish physicist James Forbes envisaged glaciers as 'endless scrolls, as streams of time engraved with the succession of events', just like geologists of his time regarded mountains as 'archives of the earth' – the 'great stone book'.[21] A century and a half later, as Frazar shows, scientists are piercing Greenland's ice to map earth's climatic changes on a 'pristine' three-kilometre-long ice core, used to construct a literal archive.

The scopes and modalities of science making in high places vary. The Humboldtian conceptualisation of a mountain-peninsula such as Mount Athos, with its well-defined altitudinal belts and coastal boundaries, as described in Veronica della Dora's chapter, is very different from science making on the polar ice cap. They are visually and cognitively different: in the former case the scientist is offered the chance to grasp the mountain's unity in diversity with a single gaze from afar. In the latter, as William Fox and Kathryn Yusoff show, the gaze can often quite simply get lost. And yet, the mental processes that identify Mount Athos and the Antarctic continent as discrete geographical objects and natural scientific oases rest on similar principles and have similar ethical implications. The 'isolation' of these features produces complex meta-geographies of purity within a broader ecological discourse of environmental threat; it produces, in other words, a series of seemingly uncorrupted islands within an impure world. Represented in popular geographical imagination as a universal heritage to be safeguarded, high places thus transform physical regions into mental regions of individual (ecological) conscience. At the same time, while increasingly internationalised through such initiatives as the Antarctic Treaty, the 'twinning' of high mountain communities and the internationally-designated 'years' devoted to their formal study and conservation,[22] high places remain pre-eminently spaces for science. Ironically, the imperatives of 'science' frequently seek to maintain an inaccessibility challenged by modern communications by denying access to non-scientific visitors: the most recent shift in the politics of extremity and height.

Finally, science making in high places is inflected by ethnographic encounter, perhaps more often than is readily acknowledged by scientists themselves. Both Bravo and Powell point to the role of polar scientists today as the unintentional inheritors of the colonialist and sometimes racialist attitudes that governed the encounter between temperate and Inuit peoples well into the late twentieth century. While the wholly exploitative attitudes and conduct of many earlier polar explorers and scientists towards local dwellers – on whose knowledge base and skills those outsiders, of course, depended – have gone, the tensions and misunderstandings of encounter continue to shape practices of knowledge making in high places.[23]

Structure and contents of the book

This collection explores various ways in which high places become meaningful, and how, through various significations, their landscapes migrate and circulate. We have grouped the essays into two parts. Part 1 is devoted to studies of cognition and formal science in high places, framed by individuals and groups who come from 'outside', and for whom such places are generally viewed as distant, marginal and difficult. In this sense these essays could be said to adopt a classic geographical perspective, although they draw upon novel modes of geographic theory and method in treating spaces and places. Part 2 considers knowledge of high places from the point of view of the natives, or the 'insiders'. It gives voices to those who inhabit such locations and who have conventionally been excluded from the geographic except on terms dictated by others. As each of the contributors makes abundantly clear, such knowledge derived from 'the inside' cannot be considered distinct or opposed in some way to 'scientific' knowledge, but it is in constant negotiation with external knowledge, to which it actively contributes. Each type of knowledge pressures the other in framing a constantly evolving understanding of the geography of high places in all its aspects.

Part 1 comprises seven essays. Three are devoted to high latitudes and three to high altitudes. These essays are introduced by a piece by William Fox, which explores problems of cognition and (dis)orientation in both types of environments through personal, embodied experiences on Mount Erebus and Pico de Orizaba (central Mexico), respectively the highest volcanoes in the Antarctic continent and the fourth highest in the northern hemisphere. Themes of cognition, disorientation and embodiment are also pursued in John Wylie and Katherine Yusoff's chapters. Weaving a personal story of archival research at the University of Cambridge's Scott Polar Research Institute with the stories of Scott and Amundsen's expeditions taken from the explorers' diaries, Wylie's account unfolds in a complex and mobile intertwining of subjectivity and materiality specific to the Antarctic continent, that also move beyond it. For Yusoff, nineteenth-century knowledge of the Antarctic lay in a fluid zone between fact and fiction. Her chapter discusses examples from the charge of 'immoral mapping' made against American explorer Charles Wilkes in 1840 for the designation in his reports of land where none was later to be found, tracing the origins of his expedition to the truly speculative geographies of Symmes' Hollow Earth theory. As Yusoff shows, mirages, even utopian visions, are always to a degree geographically grounded in the material specificities of high-latitude geographies. In Heather Frazar's chapter, high-latitude materialities are quite literally taken 'out of place', and turned into valuable 'scientific objects' able to unfold and circulate in stories that transcend high places' locational specifics, as the GISP2 ice core project demonstrates. In this sense, from untamed places of deception, high places can turn into places for 'scientific domestication'. Similar narratives run through the three mountain chapters. The conceptual domestication of mountains, as Bernard Debarbieux shows, is overwhelmingly an Enlightenment project, one dictated by the desire to read order in the complex 'text of nature'. At the same time, it is also a project encompassing different, often contrasting, discourses and sets of practices: from the normative, theoretical and distanced conception promoted by cabinet scholars, like Buache, to the empirical work of von Humboldt. This latter tradition, grounded in fieldwork and reconnaissance processes, would open the way to the later successes in geology and botany, validating direct experience of the mountain environment in the construction of scientific knowledge. Veronica della Dora's chapter shows how the 336-square-kilometre mountain-peninsula of Mount Athos, a monastic republic and 'naturally bounded' high place in northern Greece, has been conceptualised as a large botanical garden in different scientific traditions, from the sixteenth-century, pre-Linnaean taxonomies to the early twentieth-century ecological theories. Thanks to Athos' internal floristic variety, panoptic conformation, and self-enclosed cartographic nature, the peninsula has long 'mattered' as a place for science making, becoming for botanists a floristic sanctuary. The idea of mountains as scientific laboratories/observatories is taken further by Maria Lane in her exploration of late-nineteenth-century North American high-altitude astronomy. Lane's study reveals how wild, lofty peaks are not only domesticated through scientific practice and the establishment of astronomical observatories, but actively participate in the social legitimisation of the astronomer himself as a scientific figure. Furthermore, the astronomer's status is affirmed through his act of climbing and his kinetic interaction with specific high-altitude milieus.

Four essays comprise Part 2 of the collection, each in its way giving voice to those who variously 'inhabit' high places and their negotiations with visitors of diverse stripes: scientists, tourists, and state and other 'flatlanders' or 'temperate' types. Gilles Rudaz examines the ways in which those dwelling in, and making their living from, Alpine mountain places have come to adopt from such outsiders the designation of 'mountain' as a geographical and environmental classification and have used complex relations of dependence and independence to negotiate their own material interests. Rudaz makes it very clear that there is no single voice within Alpine communities, but that negotiations and conflicts occur among mountain dwellers as well as with territorial outsiders. Michael Bravo's exploration of the complex and never fully-mastered skills of observation and bodily sensation used by Inuit hunters and fishers on the sea ice along the shores of Baffin Island are also in constant negotiation with forms of knowledge available with increasing facility from outside, such as weather forecasts and global positioning systems. His study is also a personal account of negotiations between scientific discourse – increasingly practised among Inuit individuals – and traditional knowledge, and the questions of language and the cartographic representation these encounters entail.

Richard Powell's account of the Canada Day celebrations at Resolute in the Canadian High Arctic – since the 1950s, a scientific base and a federally created Inuit settlement – offers another perspective on the sometimes tense, sometimes humorous relations between scientists visiting from temperate regions and Inuit inhabitants of this very high latitude place. Living in largely separate spaces within Resolute, the contacts between Inuits and the visitors, who were regarded suspiciously as representatives of a paternalist, if not colonialist, Federal government, coincide and occasionally collide in such everyday practices as casual labour and recreation, but on Canada Day – something of an awkward celebration in much of Canada – the inhabitants of the still recently designated Nunavut, proclaim their allegiance to a greater territory while in a carnivalesque fashion 'turn upside down' everyday relations of power and authority.

Deploying alternative epistemologies to challenge colonialist intellectual structures is the subject of Jin Jong-Heon's study of the revival of Paektudaegan, a unique Korean mode of mountaineering that involves walking ridgeway watersheds rather than scaling peaks. Jin shows how the practice relates to a mode of geographical science and cartography that predated the modernisation of Korea initiated in the late nineteenth century. In the early twentieth century Japanese colonial science, drawing on European concepts, redrew the map of Korean mountains, thus breaking a system that corresponded to a long-standing cosmological model of Korean national territory. Debates over the scientific status of *pung-su*, the geomantic model that underpins Paektudaegan, and the embodied practice itself, reveal continuing ideological tensions in a divided and post-colonial Korea.

High Places presents multiple and refracted geographies of polar and mountain regions, revealing something of the always contingent, contested and mobile nature of scientific knowledge, and its necessary engagement with the lives, experiences and understanding of those who dwell in such places.

Part 1

Science and Formal Knowledge in High Places

2

Walking in Circles

Cognition and Science in High Places

William L. Fox

After the hurricane, the air at 12,447 feet is preternaturally still. It is midnight in late December, and a column of steam rises a thousand feet in the air above the crater rim at my feet. The temperature here at the summit of Antarctica's Mount Erebus is about thirty degrees below zero. Six hundred feet down, where one of the world's three actively convecting lava lakes pulses with magma, it's about 1,400°F. Several of us have driven up to the bottom of the summit cone on snowmobiles from a camp at 11,000 feet, where we've been pinned down by the storm for several days. From there it was a short but steep hike five hundred feet up slopes of volcanic ash and feldspar. Volcanic bombs ranging in size from baseballs to sofas dot the landscape around us, remnants of the almost daily eruptions.

Next to me Bill McIntosh, a volcanologist from New Mexico Institute of Mining and Technology, chips away at the ice on a video camera lens with a knife blade. He has to be careful as it's only a hardened plastic eye. The steam, a potent brew of hydrochloric and sulfuric acids rushing upwards an arm's length away, used to corrode the old glass optics into opacity within weeks. Once he's finished, we'll make our way carefully around the rim to where Jesse Crain is dismantling the equipment she's kept up here to analyse the volcanic gases. We're at −77 degrees latitude, less than nine hundred miles from the South Pole, and the field season never lasts more than six weeks. This year the weather has been unusually severe, and this last storm has obliterated much of the volcano team's communication equipment after only a month. They'll start pulling the camp down as soon as it's possible to get a helicopter into camp, probably tomorrow.

Behind me the sun revolves over the Transantarctic Mountains, which lie across the frozen Ross Sound. This is the middle of the Austral summer, so the sun won't go down for three months yet. I turn around and lean back on my ice ax. For just a moment I push back the fur-rimmed hood on my parka, take off my glacier glasses, unwrap the neoprene face mask, and pull down my fleece neck gaiter. Sunlight bathes my unprotected face. I smile. It feels warm. Sixty seconds, ninety . . . two minutes. I'm losing sensation on my nose, my cheekbones. Time to rewrap. I've already been frostbitten once on the mountain while setting out safety lines during the blizzard so people could find their way from tents into the work hut. It turned out to be a one-way trip; most of the tents collapsed in the storm and we slept on the floor and tables of the small lab. The previously frozen parts of my face are peeling and itch like crazy.

Bill's finished and we begin our walk around this quadrant of the crater, picking up Sarah Krall along the way. Sarah has been to the Antarctic for seventeen seasons and actually has one of the crags on Erebus named after her. She's been collecting 'Pele hair' in a small glass vial. The tiny strands of fused ash must have drifted down out of the steam since the hurricane, landing on the snow after the most recent event in the crater.

* * *

For almost two decades I have been writing about cognitive dissonance in isotropic spaces, which is to say I write about how we get lost in spaces that appear much the same in all directions. I do this in order to understand how human cognition interacts with land as we transform it into landscape, or how we take what we consider to be an empty space and turn it into *place*. The ideal environments for this study are extreme ones where there are few trees or recognisable features with which we can orient and scale ourselves. The history of exploration can show how place is made from what were taken to be empty spaces, for that activity converted terrain into territory, *terra incognita* into *terra nostra* as it were. I seek out environments that are as different as possible from the forests and savannahs where we evolved as a species, because that is where the process of converting land into landscape is naturally the most difficult for us. I started working in the deserts of the American Southwest and where the Tibetan Plateau abuts the Himalaya, and then in both the Arctic and Antarctic. Increasingly, I sought out vantage points at high altitudes and in high latitudes. These great spaces offer opportunities to experience first hand that point where our natural navigational abilities begin to fail catastrophically – a point where it becomes essential to deploy cultural means, such as cartography, in order to proceed with any degree of success, much less comfort. It doesn't hurt that such places also have fewer and more clearly defined layers of cartography, art, architecture and narrative left behind as evidence of the transformative process.

This is why I'm standing on top of the southernmost active volcano in the world and thinking about the other volcanoes I've climbed up, clambered down into, and walked across. They are barren and, because they are at least roughly circular, they force me to confront what it means to walk somewhere and yet get nowhere, which is very much a physical analog for a mind trying to understand its own cognitive processes without the advantage of being able to stand outside itself.

* * *

The most extreme environment on Earth is the Antarctic, famously the world's coldest, windiest, and most remote continent. Because of its remoteness, and the fact that it is perpetually encircled by circumpolar hurricanes, we managed to map the entire surface of Mars twenty-five years before we captured a complete aerial perspective of the Antarctic in 1997. Furthermore, the topographical maps of the Antarctic produced by the United States Geological Survey offer to us a singular piece of what most people suppose to be only legend these days, true *terra incognita*. Climb the Transantarctic Mountains, which separate West Antarctica from the high plateau of the East Antarctic, and open the map to compare it with the view before you. This is where the big ice starts, a sheet that stretches away to the South Pole and proceeds unencumbered to the other side of the continent. Open up your 'topo' map to see what lies in front of you. Here are the mountains, steeply contoured in black lines. To the north and behind you stretch the Dry Valleys, anomalously ice-free terrain where it has not rained in more than two million years. To the south and in front of you the map shows the mountains meeting the ice sheet, and then . . . . . a dotted line. 'Line of completion', it says. Beyond it, the top half of the map is blank, the only place on our planet where that remains the case, and one of the few places on land where the visual appearance of land and map are congruent. Flat white.

Consider three more circumstances. The Antarctic has simultaneously the highest and lowest average elevations of any continent. You can stand on the East Antarctic plateau at 10,000 feet, yet the ice beneath your feet – which is more than two miles thick – is so heavy that the bedrock is below sea level. And it's moving, that ice. The marker at the South Pole must be relocated more than thirty feet each year as the ice sheet flows steadily toward South America. Finally, the freezing of the sea ice each winter doubles the size of the continent, the largest single seasonal event on the planet. So the Antarctic is not only the space most estranged from our senses, its very surface is plastic. The Antarctic is so isotropic, so impossible to map consistently over time, that even that supreme cultural extension of our neurophysiology, our ability to map, is compromised.

People have been visiting the Antarctic continent and attempting to understand it since it was first sighted in 1820. James Ross, in search of the magnetic South Pole, sailed into what we now call the Ross Sea in 1841 and was confronted by a slab of ice a thousand feet thick. The Ross Ice Shelf, attached to the continent but floating on the sea, is the size of France and the largest single piece of ice in the world. His crew was presented with a vertical face three times the height of their ships' masts. They were unable to breach this formidable 'Great Ice Barrier', but they did discover Ross Island, from which early the next century Scott and Shackleton would launch their attempts to reach the South Pole. Much to the astonishment of Ross and his men, the summit of the large mountain that rose from the centre of the island was smoking. They spied a glow on its slopes that could only be caused by lava. If they were perplexed and confounded by the virtually infinite ice shelf, at least they could fasten their vision to a vertical landmark comparable to other mountains in the world.

The story helped inspire Jules Verne to write *Journey to the Centre of the Earth* (although he substituted an Icelandic volcano for the entrance), and ever since the peak has been a central trope in Antarctic literature, beginning with Edgar Allen Poe and H.P. Lovecraft through contemporary science fiction writers. The idea that an opening deep into the Earth would exist so close to its axis of rotation was an irresistible one to nineteenth century audiences, evidence of a geographical symmetry so profound that surely it had to signify the revelation of a great mystery. The first people to climb the mountain were the members of a team led by Shackleton in 1908. Peering down into its crater, they discovered a lake of slowly pulsing lava at its bottom. It was as if they had found a way to examine the circulatory system of the planet, and that is precisely why a team of volcanologists from New Mexico Tech now inhabits its upper slopes for a month each Austral summer.

To stand on the rim of the uppermost crater on Erebus requires that you grapple directly with all the challenges offered up to our perceptual abilities at both high latitudes and high altitudes. You experience in person the intimate metaphorical relationships among compass, sundial and clock face as the sun circles overhead. Not only is the space around you almost incomprehensible, but time seems to have slipped its anchor. The relative orbits require a calculus that the mind is ill-equipped to provide. If you have a Global Positioning System unit, which is able to ignore the magnetic forces that would otherwise incapacitate the needle of a compass, you can orient yourself to some extent on a map. It is only through the extension of our body's senses via instrumentation that we can figure out where we are. It is, in short, an ideal setting in which to tease out how we create places – human geography.

* * *

The circular nature of the crater on Erebus is very much like that of Pico de Orizaba in central Mexico, but the difference in latitude is instructive. Unlike climbing Mount Erebus, to walk up the Jamapa Glacier on the north slope of Orizaba is to execute a much more easily understood geometry upon the face of the Earth. At 18,450 feet, Orizaba is the third highest peak in North America and the fourth highest volcano in the northern hemisphere. Orizaba is a 'stratovolcano', the most common kind found on the globe, as is Erebus. Like most of the volcanoes in this category, Orizaba is a composite structure formed by alternating layers of ash and lava, a conical mountain that gravity has forced toward symmetry. The classic example, and one celebrated in a variety of aesthetic forms, is Japan's Mount Fuji. As with most stratovolcanoes, Orizaba features a crater at its summit with numerous vents located on the inside, as well as on the flanks, of the mountain. Of the world's 1,511 known volcanos, 699 of them fall into this category. Most of the volcanoes found around the Pacific 'Ring of Fire', including the Cascades in the Pacific Northwest and the volcanoes of Mexico and

South America, are stratovolcanoes. They also happen to be the most deadly kind: one need only think of Vesuvius, Mount Etna and Mount St. Helens.

To climb Orizaba you leave the Piedra Grande Hut at 14,000 feet at midnight, thus ensuring firm ice to climb and a descent before the afternoon clouds move in. This also provides you, given a clear sunrise, a chance to watch the mountain's shadow stretch out as a perfect triangle forty miles across the plains to the western horizon, a dark pointer that terminates where blue earth and orange sky meet. Every mountain, no matter its shape, will have its shadow optically reduced by sunlight into a symmetry, forming an arrow of time.

The summit of Orizaba is a barren stockade of rock, the rim of a steep-walled stony pit hundreds of feet deep that could be called the Crater of Doom. The rocks on top are actually hot in places, offering relief from the below-freezing temperatures, and despite the sulfurous odours they provide a pleasant place from which to contemplate the earth below. You are only 19° north of the equator, and the climate in the valleys below is temperate. The fields of Veracruz surround the forested lower slopes like a patchwork quilt, an anthropomorphic regularity that flows with the contours of the terrain. To the east is the Gulf of Mexico, visible on a clear day, and to the west the Pacific, invisible yet palpable. Some thirty-five miles distant stands the slightly lesser summit of Popocatépetl. A similar distance beyond it is Mexico City with its twenty million people. 'Popo' is smoking, and you wonder if the pyroclastic and debris flows for which these mountains are known would now reach the suburbs. All these aspects of the landscape are relatively easy to see, to imagine, to encompass mentally.

Climbers pay close attention to numbers. Enumeration allows us to rank our achievements within a hierarchical matrix of elevation above sea level, difficulty of route, how many times the peak has been climbed before and by whom. These numbers are an attempt to quantify the experience, to place it within a multitude of contexts – historical, geological, geographical. In spite of the numbers it is a matter of art as much as science, and the satisfaction of climbing Orizaba is as much derived from securing yourself in time and space as it is from attaining the summit above 18,000 feet. The contrast with the experience of being on Mount Erebus is acute. Here in Mexico the progress of the sun fits the expectations of a hominid that evolved in the temperate savannah of low and middle latitudes. The far features of the landscape fade predictably into the blue end of the spectrum according to their distance. We can place ourselves without having to decode signals from satellites orbiting the planet, signals requiring the use of an atomic clock that is accurate to one second per million years, the current scientific standard.

We locate ourselves in space by coding one or more of four kinds of information. The easiest, and one first adopted by children, is clue learning – we remember where one object is in reference to another object. That's why, even as adults, we tend to put the car keys down in the same place every time when we enter the house. Change your habit and see how hard you have to work to find your keys. The second is place learning, which we do by memorising the distance and direction of landmarks. That's often how we keep track of where we parked the car. Both of those types of learning are founded upon external references. The other two ways of coding space are driven by internal, viewer-oriented means. Response learning works by remembering motor movements. Getting up to go to the bathroom in the middle of a dark night is a common example. You are able to accomplish this manouevre because you know from experience how many steps and turns it takes to get there. The fourth and most sophisticated method, and our most powerful navigational tool, is dead reckoning. We code where we are in reference to the distance and direction of landmarks, and then constantly update the information. It's a workable system in most environments, including on Orizaba.

* * *

And that is why, lumbering along in my parka at the edge of the crater on Mount Erebus, I find myself happily perplexed. All craters have the potential to allow disorientation into our lives because they are circular, and we tend to navigate whenever possible in straight lines, preferably those oriented in line with or at right angles to the path of the sun – the cardinals of north, south, east and west. The circular pits that are flush with the ground are the easiest to handle. I'm thinking of Meteor Crater in Arizona and the Sedan Crater on the Nevada Test Site, the latter excavated by an atomic blast as a test to see if nuclear devices could be used for construction purposes. Both craters have viewing stands which anchor the visitor firmly in one direction. The potential disorientation is further mitigated by interpretive devices, such as plaques pointing out local features. Even when leaving behind these architectural constructs and walking around the craters, you remain oriented by vertical features that surround you, primarily peaks that define the horizon.

Volcanic craters – the ones I've explored, from those as small as Ubehebe, which rises only a few hundred feet above the floor of Death Valley National Park, to monsters such as Haughton Crater on Devon Island in the Canadian High Arctic, which is 12 miles across and 1,000 feet deep – loosen our ability to maintain our orientation significantly. The very elevation that allows us to encompass a larger view of the world necessarily distances us from it, thus abstracting the local geomorphology and landmarks. We lose our sense of scale. When you traipse around their rims, as Bill McIntosh reminded me, you have a hard time projecting how long it's going to take you to get back to your starting point, a problem of 'supersymmetry', as he puts it. It's always a lot closer or a lot farther away than you thought. Orizaba looked huge to me, but a circuit could be done around it in less than an hour.

The upper crater of Mount Erebus is about 2,133 feet across, so its circumference is roughly a mile and a third. If I hadn't looked up those figures, which were produced by an instrumented survey, I would have no idea how large it is. Furthermore, even though I can sort of peg the direction of the South Pole by looking down the Transantarctics, because the sun has neither risen nor set since I arrived in November, I can't easily tell where east and west are. One can complicate matters on Erebus by walking in the cloud rising out of the crater … well, you see. Or rather, you don't. Craters are disorienting precisely because there is no sense of squaring off with the landscape.

Mount Erebus rises behind the largest American research base on the continent, McMurdo Station. The 1,100 or so people working in town during the Austral summer don't pay much attention to east and west, and only nominally to north and south. What you pin your sense of direction to is the volcano with its plume of steam rising thousands of feet above its summit. The opposite is true when you are on top of the summit looking down. Even when standing still you feel as if you're on a revolving carousel.

Although Mount Erebus is a stratovolcano, it provides a very different kind of experience than Orizaba. Its rim is white, icy, visually indeterminate as to width and depth. So is the landscape below. Much of the sea ice has melted out this December, and even the relatively permanent Ross Ice Shelf is shedding pieces. A section 183 miles long by 23 miles wide broke off two summers ago and drifted off what satellite photos define as the north of Ross Island. The storm winds of the last few days have pushed it several miles to what might be called the west. They simply shoved along a piece of ice the size of Connecticut until it grounded on the sea bottom. The iceberg, designated B-15 and the largest ever recorded, is so large that even from this elevation I can't see its far end.

Erebus and Ross Island are surrounded on three sides by a flat white plain of ice. From this altitude the Ross Ice Shelf and the frozen sea ice appear virtually identical, although in certain conditions of low light it's possible to discern a faint line where they meet. Only the Transantarctics provide any sense of horizon. Even then, when I try to point directly south, I'm guessing to some degree.

To summarise, then. The cues we are given are inscrutable, as neither distance nor direction of nearby and far landmarks are easily determined. Unlike standing on Orizaba, we have no geometry stretched out on the plains below us, either natural or that imposed by humans, to provide clues as to scale and direction. We don't know where we are in relationship to other things, so our external spatial reasoning is severely challenged. Furthermore, we have few chances to memorise a walked path in the Antarctic, much less on Mount Erebus, and dead reckoning across a blank sheet of ice here is extremely difficult. Our internal gyroscope just doesn't have much to go on visually. Furthermore, there is no native population here to transmit to us knowledge of how to navigate under such conditions, as there are with the Inuit and other native peoples in the Arctic.

* * *

As we approach Jesse and her instruments, I bend to pick up an Erebus crystal the size of my finger. The rhomboidal feldspar crystals are only found on two extinct African volcanoes, Mount Kenya and Kilimanjaro, and on Erebus, the single place where they are currently being created. They start out as small nuggets in the magma below, adding layers each time they circulate up to the lava lake until they are thrown out during one of the eruptions, encased in the hot gooey lava bombs that splat on the rim and down the slopes. The bombs, some of which can be as large as mini-vans, cool quickly. – Bill once stuck an ice ax into one and he says the black glass pulled like taffy as he extracted the shaft of the climbing tool. – The bombs crumble quickly in the extreme Antarctic environment, leaving behind only the crystals. In my hand is a rare red one, a crystal that was thrown out, cooled, and then ended up back in the crater to be heated once again before being thrown out one last time to the rim. The rarest of the rare. I put it in my pocket.

* * *

Another rare thing – I wish I had a camera with me because of ... The moment passes as I catch my breath. I find myself once again glad that I am not encumbered with one. The Center for Land Use Interpretation in Los Angeles had sent a camera with me on this trip, but one morning while attempting to document a geology experiment in the Transantarctics, I heard a crunching sound as I was winding the film. That would be the frozen celluloid destructing inside the camera, I realised. After that I left the camera in my room at McMurdo. No wonder all the scientists here started carrying digital cameras as soon as feasible.

My deep-seated ambivalence toward cameras actually began with a hike on another volcano many years ago. In the fall of 1967 I walked across part of the Kiluea caldera on the Big Island of Hawaii. I had been offered a chance to submit some pictures to a postcard company, and spent the entire walk looking through the lens of the camera. The surface of the ground was so hot that the bottoms of my tennis shoes were fused when I reached the other side. Two weeks later an eruption buried the track. Where I had once walked was erased from the surface of the planet and I could remember almost nothing of the experience; my memory had been short-circuited by my looking through a view-finder. I have ever since regretted not having really seen a place that no longer exists.

* * *

So here I am, at Jesse's station, peering intermittently through the toxic steam at the far wall of the Erebus crater where the rocks are a startling yellow. This is the only place I've seen that colour appearing naturally on the continent. It's dead quiet, the wind nonexistent, which in itself is disturbing. That's one way the Inuit keep a sense of direction, the pressure of wind on their bodies, and the same is true here in a whiteout. Of course, you have to know where you are in the weather cycle, as polar winds come from one direction before a storm, rotate 90 degrees during it, and end up in the opposite direction afterwards. That means even the sastrugi, the small ridges carved on the ice by wind which are also used for navigation, must be read with care.

* * *

When I lecture about the art history of the Antarctic, I start with a painting by Claude Lorrain from the 1640s, *The Rest on the Flight into Egypt*. I do this to show several things, among them what the Antarctic is not, but also an ideal representation of the environment in which humans evolved, the kind in which we know instinctively how to navigate. The scene is framed by dark foliage on either side, Mary and her companions resting on the ground. Behind them in the painting's middle-ground is a lake upon which a small boat floats. In the background is a mountain range fading blue with distance.

The artist team of Komar and Melamid, two young Russian painters, escaped from the Soviet Union in the late 1970s and set up shop in New York City, expecting to paint and sell abstract art, precisely the sort of thing they had been forbidden to make in Russia. To their surprise, although they now had the freedom to paint like Jackson Pollock, few patrons were interested in such work. Eventually they decided to survey people to see what kind of paintings they wanted to buy. The result of what later became a famous conceptual art project was a painting that featured dark foliage in the foreground, a water feature in middle distance, preferably some figures of recognisable historical import nearby and mountains in the distance. Claude would have been gratified. Over the course of several years they repeated this experiment in countries around the world, discovering that most children and many adults in foreign lands, even those not familiar with the Western tradition of landscape painting, preferred this scheme.

Geographers, such as Jay Appleton, call this a conceal-and-reveal landscape, or one with prospect-and-refuge. You have foliage to hide behind and not be seen while you can spy on what's around you, preferably game animals you can hunt at the waterhole. It is our ancestral savannah, the temperate environment of rolling hills dotted with trees and brush in which we evolved. Furthermore, it's also the scheme around which many living rooms and landscape designs are arranged. Drapes frame the picture window through which you circumspectly view a front lawn that slopes to the street, the contemporary waterhole – if you are lucky or rich enough, beyond that is a long view.

We settle preferentially in environments naturally organised in this fashion when we can find them, but manufacture them when we cannot. It gives us comfort to be in a landscape where we know the length of our limbs in comparison to the limbs of the trees, where we can envision ourselves climbing up if need be in order to avoid something higher on the food chain than we are. We tend to abandon the conceal-and-reveal scheme only when comfortable enough with our circumstance to do so. Overall, we continue to prefer the presence of our inherited predisposition for visual cues even when the nearest predator is locked up in a zoo.

* * *

There is only one standing forest in the Antarctic (if you don't count the fossil remains of the tree fern *Glossopteris* found exposed on a cliff in the Transantarctics). It is the 145 telephone poles at McMurdo. The National Science Foundation has talked about burying the cables and eliminating the pressure-treated trunks of yellow pine, but architects brought in to deal with town planning promptly counter with proposals for ceremonial flagpoles. They know that the vertical structures scaled to humans provide a degree of psychological comfort. The visibility of the telephone poles provide a handy way to measure how bad the weather is outside, as anyone who has worked there will tell you.

Walking around Mount Erebus provokes such thoughts because the normative markers by which we measure our place in the world have been eliminated. Take the atmospheric perspective that makes the appearance of far mountains shift increasingly downward into the blue portion of the spectrum as light is increasingly scattered over distance. Our species is adapted to a climate where there is enough moisture in the air to make mountains ten miles away start to shift in atmospheric perspective, as in fact they do around Pico de Orizaba. Leonardo Da Vinci commented on the phenomenon in his notebooks and may have been the first artist to adopt it for a painting. If you look behind the Mona Lisa to the scenery, you'll see what I mean. In deserts the shift occurs much more slowly over distance. People driving from Los Angeles to Las Vegas, passing through the Mojave Desert, routinely wander away from their cars for what they think are short walks to nearby hills. Hours later, what are in actuality mountains remain miles away. Cognitive dissonance, the difference between what we expect to see and what we are actually seeing, is at play. Newcomers to McMurdo look across the Ross Sea and think they could cross-country ski to the foot of the hills in a day. The peaks rise more than 11,000 feet and are 60 miles away.

* * *

This evening, standing with Bill and Jesse and Sarah atop Mount Erebus when it is calm, everything seems so close, and yet the distance is huge. All of it. William Sutton, who helps run the Crary Laboratory in McMurdo, made a portrait of the mountain from out on the sea ice. He used a telephoto lens to compress the view, to foreshorten the distance and make the volcano appear taller than it is in reality – but this is exactly how it appears in our minds, whether we are looking at the peak or remembering its appearance. The view of the peak executed in 1841 by J.E. Davis from Ross' ship, The Terror, *did the same thing – foreshortened it so that readers would understand how prominently it loomed in the lives of the sailors. Herbert Ponting, the first professional photographer on the ice, who accompanied Scott on this fatal 1910 expedition, also used a telephoto when picturing Erebus and the Transantarctics, seeking to capture how prominent in, and critical to, our sense of place the landscape verticals were in the Antarctic.*

* * *

A Landsat 5 satellite image of the volcano was acquired in 1985 from approximately 440 miles above the Earth. It, too, is foreshortened. Assembled from data remotely sensed in four bands from the visible through infrared spectrum, it is primarily a thermal image. The data was assigned false-colour values in order to create a picture that reads like a photograph, and it works brilliantly. The peak appears as a cobalt and indigo cone bracketed on the right by the curvilinear clouds of a storm. In the centre of the land mass is a red dot that represents the heat radiated by the lava lake. Of all the images I have seen of Erebus made since that first one in 1841, none has struck me as being as true to my experience on the mountain as this one – yet it is by far the one most removed from human visual reality. First, the issue of colour. The picture was taken in late January during the Antarctic day, hence the scene would have been flooded with light, the mountain white, not blue. Second, the twenty-metre lava lake would have been completely invisible. What the scientists have done is compress the data – to foreshorten it – in order make visible the temperature differential. The fact that people deployed foreshortening across such a variety of media and time – in a painting, in photographs, and with an infrared image – is a fine example of how, when our evolved neurophysiology falls short of being able to process a scene, we use cultural means in order to augment it. In each case the dimensions of the mountain have been manipulated in order to bring it into a frame of reference we can more easily grasp. It is the conversion of an object into a comprehensible landmark within the white page of the Antarctic, yet one more step in converting that immense space into a place.

* * *

We finish stuffing Jesse's gear into our packs for the long walk down. There's less of it than there should be – her solar panel was blown away in the wind this year while last year a lava bomb burned through some of her gear. Measuring tools of all kinds, it appears, have a tough time on the summit. It is not just our natural senses that fail here – even instrumentation has its limits. We step off the rim and begin taking the long, stiff-legged strides volcanologists use to descend loose slopes of ash. It's warm enough work to unzip the parkas, and when I spy the snowmobiles I can almost fool myself into believing I'm back in the Sierra Nevada returning to a trailhead in winter. I stop to take a breath and far below is the fractured edge of the B-15 iceberg, a chunk of a world set adrift. The momentary illusion of being in a familiar landscape disappears, and leaves in its stead a trace of how the mind attempts to construct a place out of a high and cold space.

High Latitudes

3

The Ends of the Earth

Narrating Scott, Amundsen and Antarctica

John Wylie

For every myth told, there is another, unnameable, that is not told, another which beckons from the shadows, surfacing only through allusions, fragments, coincidences.[1]

Introduction (part one)

In November 1998 I travelled by train from Bristol to Cambridge, in order to spend some time working in the library and archives of Cambridge University's Scott Polar Research Institute. Even though I was by then in my mid-twenties, and had lived in England for several years, the journey still seemed to take me far into a foreign land, an altogether different place and time. Perhaps all train journeys have something of this quality about them. I was certainly quite conscious of being alone on this occasion, sitting in a corner of the carriage, isolated from both the other travellers and the autumn world outside. And I have never felt at ease in London, which I had to cross in order to pick up my connection to Cambridge. On that day, the city, with its fat, gothic-like buildings fastened tight together, and standing square-shouldered along the streets and avenues, and then the sharp movements of the throngs of commuters through the giddy vault of the train station – all of this seemed more than usually aggressive and alien.

Later, as the train curved north and eastward from London, the landscape outside progressively simplified, peeling itself away, brick by brick, layer by layer, until the view from the carriage took on an abstract quality: earth–horizon–sky. The ground itself gradually flattened out, like a bed-sheet billowing down onto a mattress, and the lustreless green of the late-autumn fields was only interrupted by the odd tree and farmhouse, and occasionally a shard of bare, brown earth. As afternoon lapsed into twilight, a mist rose and chilled over the plain, a spectral medium, as I thought, in which the whole world hung suspended. Everything was extraordinarily still and hushed.

As for myself, as the train continued on what now seemed like a journey to the very ends of the earth, I felt suddenly unaccountably nervous.

Roald Amundsen — Robert Falcon Scott

Even the names of their ships note a difference between them, a bifurcation of purposes and practices that would emerge in the spaces and trajectories they were shaping all the time as they went on. For Scott, the *Terra Nova* – a promise of a name: in its suggestions of annexation, mapping, and eventual assimilation, a declaration that Antarctica could become a territory among so many others in the imperial pantheon. For Amundsen, the *Fram* (Forwards) – more direct but more subtle, a restless need for movement, a point suborned to a line which 'transforms the serene identities of the soil into the speed with which they slip away into the distance'.[2]

9 September 1910

'Their very faces began to resemble notes of interrogation.'[3] Agitated, Amundsen surveys his crew. He stands upon the deck of the *Fram*, anchored off Madeira in the mid-Atlantic. Beside him, his second-in-command nails to the mast a map of the Antarctic, and then Amundsen begins to speak of his plans to attain the South Pole. It is a moment of rupture. A sudden, unforeseen translation of the geography of the earth. This map before their eyes, its etching of landfalls a record of the embraces of the ice, has changed everything.

'This is an expedition to the North Pole,' Amundsen had told them, the press, the world. Yet now they all agree to follow him southward. If it is a question of modelling what occurs upon the *Fram* as the crew agree upon their *volte-face*, then I would say: they have formed a pack, a multiplicity, and have 'disappeared from view'. Now there is no communication with the world beyond – for months perhaps, nobody knows. Their voyage south could be a deterritorialisation, appropriating again the smoothness of the sea, the fissures and hollows of space: the way it enfolds and hides and lets you re-weave a trajectory. For over 16,000 miles from Madeira, the Norwegians have no sight of land before reaching Antarctica.

29 November 1910

There are cheering crowds, a blizzard of Union Jacks as the *Terra Nova* steams south from the port of Lyttleton, New Zealand. Yet perhaps even as he stands to attention on the bridge, Scott is thinking of the telegram he has recently received from Amundsen, ('Am going South'), informing him that his cruise has been turned into a race.

His voyage thus far has been a register of different spaces, different priorities, from Amundsen's. It has been very much a self-consciously imperial venture. The *Terra Nova* has called at Cardiff, at Madeira, and thence to Cape Town, Melbourne and New Zealand. The diaries of Scott's officers are a record of civic receptions, banquets, speeches, sorties into the bush-lands behind the coast.

In this way the tack of the *Terra Nova* is a stitching – a practising of colonial space. The ship's landfalls, its inscriptions, are a re-affirmation of the reality of empire. An imperium straddling the globe perhaps needs such voyages in order to see the anchorage of its identity, or, rather, its tensile and multiple identities, its subsumption of the temperate, the torrid and the frigid within a dialectic of 'home' and 'abroad'. This is a dialectic which the *Terra Nova* now literally embodies as it heads for Antarctica. The echo from the colonial shores it has touched will resonate in other spaces, the headlands and promontories of the southlands marked by English names and habits.

But what are these habits, beyond the litany of official routine, the formal record? Is the *Terra Nova* a sort of time capsule, a type of 'English' adventurous comportment distilled and preserved in honey? The manners of a minor public school are mirrored by the officers' quarters. They fight. They frolic. 'We had a general rag, which means turning an individual's clothes inside out for some imaginary offence. This is known as "furling topgallant sails" ... the struggle lasted an hour or two, and half of us were nearly naked towards the finish. All in excellent fun and splendid exercise.'[4] It seems a reversion to 'boyishness', to the glory of the dormitory. On this ship, bodies may be displayed in riotous arrangements, may freely mingle. This exuberance both gleefully celebrates and comically rues the absence of girls:

Who doesn't like women?
I, said Captain Oates,
I prefer goats.[5]

Antarctica is never still, consisting as it does of 'phenomena of relative slowness and viscosity, or, on the contrary, of acceleration and rupture'.[6] One moves south, and the ice, in sheets, packs and bergs, comes north to embrace you: an eddying, labyrinthine embrace whose origins are traceable to vast inland reservoirs of ice. 'Within its ice the berg contains a frozen record of these terrains and a history of movement through them.'[7]

Both the *Terra Nova* and the *Fram* must pass through this 'pack' ice. They must learn to love the sensuality of its drift, to catch the sudden opening of 'leads', to avoid the currents which cause it to grip like a vice. They must be on the look-out, constantly, to find the signs reflected by the ice in the atmosphere: the glinting 'ice-blink' warning of a perilous fastness ahead, the darker 'water sky' holding the promise of open sea.

The *Terra Nova* spends three weeks enclosed by this ice: unlucky, perhaps, to catch the pack at its heaviest. But the *Fram* takes four days to complete its passage. Many of the crew have worked as Arctic sealers, spending whole seasons amidst the pack. There is on board an ice-pilot, Andreas Beck. 'He had that quality some Arctic skippers possess – that of being able to smell the ice. He seemed to know the ice by instinct, it talked a language he understood.'[8] The ship itself has been purposefully designed for the ice by one of Amundsen's mentors, Fridjtof Nansen. 'Bow, stern and keel – all were rounded off so that the ice should not be able to get a grip of her anywhere … the whole craft should be able to slip like an eel out of the embraces of the ice.'[9]

Introduction (part two)

Before leaving, I'd had to face questions as to whether it was still possible to discover something new in the well-grooved tale of Scott's and Amundsen's south polar voyages. There were lots of different possible answers, but still the best one came from Francis Spufford: 'the perpetual present tense in which the story takes place keeps hope helplessly alive.'[10] The story is always being told for the first time, always refracting the light in a slightly different way, we might say, on each occasion it is glossed and commented upon. In any case, this Antarctica is a wipe-clean surface, with all traces continually being erased. Putting this another way, it isn't so much about discovering new facts or features in this story as about finding a way to make it strange, re-present it, in other words, in an oblique and maybe even tendentious fashion, one in which different places, times and events are scored across and through each other.

5 – 15 January 1911

To speak of 'landing' upon Antarctica is to mislead. There is no clear boundary between sea and ice. There is the Barrier, a shelf of ice plugging a bay the size of France, which presents a high cliff-face along some 400 miles of sea. But the sea freezes, and the Barrier 'calves', so that one should not imagine a clear dividing line. Casting aside a habit of thought based upon such boundaries, and adopting one which valorises mobility and mutability, the principle of ceaseless interaction, is perhaps one way of dwelling in Antarctica. 'With no warning, there would come, suddenly and completely, a lull. And there would be a film of ice, covering the surface of the sea, come so quickly that all you could say was that it was not there before and it was there now.'[11]

Scott chooses to site his base on *terra firma*, on a cape of Ross Island at the Barrier's western edge, which he names Cape Evans. Here at least he finds himself within a familiar spatial idiom – capes and bays within the bowl of the western mountains. He prefers the solidity of rock to the suppleness of ice. The interactions of sea, ice and land in the bay around the base are sometimes opaque to him, a constant source of perplexity and unease. And so one of his motor-sledges sinks heavily through ice that was thought firm, and is lost.

Amundsen sites his base upon the Barrier itself: the first to do so. Here there is no land, no framing of capes, bays and surrounding hills into a familiar landscaped tableau, no perspective for the eye to seize and gauge the scene. Only ice, in a seemingly limitless sweep southward.

Now the two protagonists draw breath and reflect upon the task before them. To Scott, Antarctica presents itself as a unintelligible texturology. The aurora sums up what for him seems to be an essential ephemerality. It is 'the language of mystic signs and portents ... provocative of imagination. Might not the inhabitants of some other world controlling mighty forces thus surround our globe with fiery symbols, a golden writing which we have not the key to decipher?'[12] To Amundsen, the landscape is figured as a female body, something that one must couple with to understand, something with which coupling seems to be an imperative. 'It seems as if the princess is still sleeping in her shining castle. Will we be able to awaken her?'[13] Again he writes, 'Inviting and attractive the fair one lies before us. Yes we hear you calling and we shall come.'[14]

17 February 1911

There is barely time to lay depots to the south before winter sets in. The Great Ice Barrier forms the southern road both must take. It is in some ways a featureless landscape, displaying 'nothing of the beautiful, the pastoral, the picturesque or the sublime',[15] a white plain where, as Amundsen says, 'there are no shadows, and everything looks the same'.[16] This does not mean that it is static, or homogenous. It is different at every point. The elements of its composition are in constant flux. The horizon is a chimera: earth and sky, like sea and ice, form a zone of interaction rather than division. 'The surface is dusted with millions of infinitesimal mirrors and prisms.'[17] Thus there exists a multiplicity of light sources within the landscape: light emanates everywhere – distance, relation and aspect cannot be gauged. The scene is continuously transformed by the effects of mirages, both 'inferior' and 'superior'. Sometimes vision is bewitched by the 'castles in the air' of the *fata morgana* mirage, wherein 'curvature of light rays increases with height, causing part of the object to be lengthened vertically',[18] a phenomenon which makes the Transantarctic Mountains at the Barrier's end loom up like the battlements of fairytale castles. Sometimes the eye's range is extended by long-range visibility, where a coincidence of temperature gradient with the angle of the earth's curvature produces 'the equivalent of what would be seen on a flat earth. That is to say, the horizon will be infinitely far away'.[19] Yet more often the explorers will find themselves enshrouded by a uniform greyish-white haze, bereft of any horizonal effect, and they will fall victim to what is called 'empty field myopia', 'peering ahead with anxious eyes, and at intervals falling'.[20] The middle ground vanishes, leaving only the impossibly distant and the ready-to-hand. The landscape stretches and compresses, vision swirls between visibilities malevolently, and so the anchorage of one's habitual perspective must be abandoned. The surface, apparently flat, is corrugated by waves of sastrugi.[21] But there are no shadows, one cannot tell, footfalls become uncertain, hesitant. Amundsen writes: 'it is no easy matter to go straight on a surface without landmarks. Imagine an immense plain that you have to cross in thick fog; it is dead calm, and the snow lies evenly without drifts. What would you do?'[22]

We have perhaps become accustomed to thinking of Antarctica in terms of its unity; as an unbroken mass, an immensity, an unrelenting physicality. But think of the view in 1911. Little was known; a few scattered landfalls, the possibility of an interior. Antarctica was imagined within a different (northerly?) spatial order: archipelago. 'The state of things consists of islands sown in archipelagos on the noisy, poorly-understood disorder of the sea.'[23] Perhaps this is why Scott, returning from his depot journey, is so disconcerted to find that his crew have chanced upon Amundsen's base, 250 miles to the east. Now he is no longer a potential amidst a scattering; he is within known space, they have discovered each other.

Introduction (part three)

The Scott Polar Research Institute is situated on the southern edge of Cambridge town centre, not far in fact from the train station where I had arrived at nightfall the previous day. But I was staying with a friend who lived on the northern edge of town. My mornings thus began with a thirty-minute walk through town, a walk made tedious and sometimes challenging by the fact that its course ran for the most part along the long single street (I've forgotten its name) that runs through the centre of Cambridge. There was also the flatness of the terrain, which meant that I could see my turn-off ahead far in advance of arriving there, and, above all, there was the damp chilliness of the Fenland air.

In the course of these daily marches I formed the impression that the southern part of the town centre was less fashionable, certainly less grand, than the domey, churchy north of St. John's and Trinity College. The Institute itself had certainly not found an august situation. It squatted disappointingly behind a high hedge that seemed designed to serve as a sound-screen against the constant roar of the busy road onto which the building fronted, a link-road to the motorway favoured by lorries and coaches. The Institute cowered further beneath the much more massive forms of the chemistry laboratories which flanked it on two sides. The first time I saw it was disturbingly different – much smaller and much less pastoral – from the website photographs I had previously seen.

22 June 1911 – Midwinter Day

Scott's companions include two artists. The first of these is a photographer – the self-styled 'camera artist' Herbert Ponting – a man who found himself something of an outsider amongst the Cape Evans community. For his interest in Antarctica was almost wholly commercial – he frequently quarrelled with Scott about copyright and publication. His aim was to manufacture the most picturesque and thus most valuable studies. A conscious artifice of foreground and background and figures thus permeates his landscapes. The verb, 'to pont', meaning to stand (frozen) in a picturesque pose, took root in the expedition. Yet Ponting later wrote that he 'found the Antarctic a very disappointing region for photography'.[24] It lacked perspective, relief, contrast: it could not be captured graphically.

But this belief was certainly not shared by Scott's second artist, Edward Wilson. A devout and ascetic Christian, Wilson's paintings are suffused with a spiritual, other-worldly aura, 'a milky and tasteful pantheism'.[25] He attempted to combine an almost Franciscan worship of nature with the landscape idioms of the Romantic sublime. Yet these aesthetic and even ethical concerns were surmounted by a Ruskinesque emphasis upon accuracy of observation – a constant impulse towards *mimesis*.

Principles of Sketching:

Accuracy, by attention to small details and differences.
Methods, pen and ink is difficult for snow and sky and soft pencil is easier.
Outlines are the edges of shadows.
Perspective is not of much use in Antarctica.[26]

Science and art and sublimity – again and again Scott and his companions try to fuse them: '"Here you are," Birdie would say of a particularly uninteresting rock, "here's a gabbroid nodule impaled in basalt with felspar and olivine rampant."'[27] Climbing the Transantarctic Mountains en route to the Pole, Wilson will remark upon the 'magnificent ochreous reddish gneissic granite columnous crags'.[28]

The young Australian Griffith Taylor, in later years a celebrated geographer, likened his glaciological work to that of an antiquarian: 'In old Greek manuscripts one can sometimes discern traces of an older script half obliterated by the later writing – this M.S. is called a palimpsest. Just so in Antarctica – I think that beneath the largest outlet glaciers ... we can perceive the traces of an earlier erosion.'[29]

A few days later he will note in his diary that 'at lunch we had a great discussion on Browning and Tennyson ... Scott preferred Keats.'[30]

* * *

Amundsen too likes to stand and gaze upon the landscape. 'If only I could paint', he writes, 'if only I could.'[31] But he has no artists among his companions. Perhaps they are scientists and they are artists of a different type. Scott's is a science of coverage and observation and classification – almost a regional geography. His companions are meteorologists, geologists, biologists and glaciologists. Amundsen's are sailmakers, cobblers, carpenters and ironmongers. They spend their entire winter overhauling their equipment. Amundsen's diaries are devoted to the minutiae of ski-bindings, tent pegs, sledge-runners and fur clothing. 'We had two hundred and fifty reindeer skins prepared by the Eskimos ... I had watched their preparation myself ... we had forty ski poles, with ebonite points. The ski-bindings were a combination of the Huitfeldt and Hoyer-Ellefsen bindings.'[32] The champion skier Olaf Bjaaland systematically reduced the weight of the skis and sledges. The carpenter Jorgen Stubberud built and remorselessly planed the sledge-cases. Oscar Wisting sewed and dyed the tents. The dog-driver Sverre Hassel made dog whips. Theirs is a different science, at a stretch a nomad science, the forging of a landscape one might travel through rather than observe.

On midwinter day the Norwegians feast on 'the daintiest frozen polar dishes – reindeer meat, fish and reindeer tripes, garnished with blubber cut up in squares',[33] while to the west Scott records a sort of Blytonesque High Tea, 'a wondrous attractive meal ... with its garnishments a positive feast, for withal the table was strewn with dishes of burnt almonds, crystallised fruits, chocolates and such toothsome kickshaws'.[34] The diary of the scientist Frank Debenham, later director of the Scott Polar Research Institute, notes 'there is much talk in the air about scorbutics and anti-scorbutics, mostly in fun.'[35]

All through this long, cramped winter both expeditions are mostly confined to base. And the snow accumulates around their huts in ever-greater drifts. Each evening before the latest lecture on terrestrial magnetism, or ice physics, or the constitution of matter, Scott and his men are obliged to spend time in the cold and darkness clearing away the incessant ice. To the east, Amundsen's base is quickly completely submerged. He always wants to move with the ice, to use it, to mould his patterns with its own. He sees the futility in constant shovelling. He digs into the ice, carving a series of caves and tunnels, shaping ice-spaces, becoming icy.

Amidst these lectures, discussions and slide-shows at Cape Evans, Scott finds time for excursions to the various islands in the bay. A romantic, this pattern of movement is his vehicle of expression. In good light the bay offers a dislocating panorama, 'so clear that it was impossible to persuade oneself that much of what we looked at was in the far distance'.[36] He writes: 'Standing on the island today with a glorious view of mountains, islands and glaciers, I thought how very different must be the outlook of the Norwegians. A dreary white plain of the Barrier behind and an uninviting stretch of sea-ice in front. With no landmarks, nothing to guide if the light fails, it is probable that they venture but a very short distance from their hut. 'The prospects of such a situation do not smile on us'.[37]

Introduction (part four)

On that first morning I hovered uneasily and indecisively outside the entrance to the Institute, smoking several cigarettes in succession. At the front of the building, from a gate in a gap in the hedge, a short paved path led to an arched doorway. A sign on the gate, however, stated that visitors to the Institute should proceed through the chemistry car park to the side door. I followed these instructions, but felt unable to immediately enter the foyer of what was obviously a recent extension to the building on the east side, and, rolling another cigarette, walked back around to the front. The façade had a deserted, unused feeling, the many windows remained unlit in the late autumnal gloom, the doors were firmly shut. In a niche above the doorway sat a bust of Scott by his sculptress widow, his eyes frowning upon the grass below. Above his head, running across the entire length of the front, was a Latin inscription, quesivit aracana poli videt dei *('In seeking to uncover the secret of the Pole, he found the hidden face of God').*

What was most immediately apparent on first sight, however, was the scaffolding which covered much of the Institute's west side. Even from where I stood by the road the din of hammers and drills was audible, as if the road's noise had somehow infiltrated the building and was now clamorously engaged in dismantling it from the inside out. This noise would be my constant companion during two of my visits to the Institute, but not the third.

In fact I remember that, having finally entered the building, my attempt to introduce myself to the receptionist was cut short by the heart-shaking rumble of a drill. Inured to the noise, she stared at me severely, even, I thought, suspiciously. But then I was led upstairs to the library, and in the space of a few minutes given a brief tour, shown the computer catalogue and allocated a desk.

20 October 1911

Amundsen has adapted his sledging techniques from those of the Polar Inuit. On his previous (first ever) navigation of the Arctic North West Passage he spent over two years observing and practising their everyday strategems of polar dwelling. His published account of this time reads as if it were a training manual, written for his own benefit, for some unspecified future challenge. For example, regarding reindeer fur clothes, 'Both inner and outer anorak hang loosely outside the trousers and the air has free access all the way up the body. Inner and outer trousers are held up round the waist with a cord and hang free over the kamikks (boots), so the air can circulate freely. … Now I can move as I want to. Am always warm without sweating.'[38]

Thus he has forged a mobile synthesis: the assimilation of an indigenous art of dwelling, its translation into a hybrid art of voyaging, and its re-deployment within this specifically European adventure of exploration and discovery – this race to the Pole. Amundsen is better equipped, physically and mentally, to travel across the ice, than is Scott. His strategy for voyaging, dogs and skis, is based upon what Beau Riffenbaugh calls 'the creative interplay between skis and dogs and ice, proving that skis could be used to keep up with dogs and that dogs could be driven by men skiing instead of riding on sledges, so that bigger loads could be carried'.[39] 'I want the ski to be part of oneself,' Amundsen writes.[40]

The Norwegians travel fast, they have ample food, and 'the going is as good as it could possibly be'.[41] The landscape is produced as prosaic, everyday: 'the Antarctic becomes a sunny prairie where men are always vigorous and assured.'[42] This assurance is sustained by the remorselessness of their advance, an arrow superimposing itself upon the abstract geometry of latitude and longitude. Amundsen has a harsh disdain for the hyperbole of explorers. In a cold and bitter memoir he will write: 'exploration is a highly technical and serious profession … an adventure is merely an unwelcome interruption of hard labour, an adventure is merely a bit of bad planning'.[43] The horror of the unanticipated event leads to unyielding calculations. For example: 'I made the most careful estimate of the average weight of edible flesh of a dog and its food value. By these calculations I was able to lay out a schedule of dates upon which dog after dog would be converted from motive power into food'.[44]

Then, scouting for routes among the mountains at the Barrier's end which block the way to the Pole, they turn, and look back, this once becoming panoramic. 'Seeing the little dark speck down there – our tent – gave us a feeling of strength and power.'[45]

> [SEQUENCE: Using date captioned mapping device, show the respective journeys to and from the Pole, together with essential images of these two separate processes: Amundsen's shows speed, ease, organisation; Scott's, obduracy, will, correct passion. The Norwegians eat well, the British lick their mess tins].[46]

10 December 1911 – 'Nothing that Happens to our Bodies really matters'[47]

'Thank God the horses are now all done with and we begin the heavier work ourselves.'[48] Scott's advance upon the pole is like a striptease. Motor-sledges, dogs, ponies: all are displayed then cast aside, leaving only men and the landscape. So simple, then, to theorise. 'The male body's performance becomes the means by which a moral theatre is constructed in which the body ultimately disappears. The gendered physical body is replaced by moral character.'[49] After all, Scott had written that 'no journey done with dogs can approach the height of that fine conception which is realised when a party of men go forth with their own unaided efforts ... surely in this case the conquest is more nobly and splendidly won.'[50] More prosaically, and disregarding the overwhelming evidence to the contrary from the Arctic, plus the need to practice, he had written that 'a party on foot invariably beats a party of skis ... in the Antarctic regions there is nothing to equal the honest and customary use of one's legs.'[51]

So to conceive of the narrative of bodies and landscapes which this 'man-hauling' produces: figures are made to stand out starkly against suddenly passive backdrops, and a space is thus opened for a mode of comportment wherein embodiment is sustained by a dialectic of exaltation and denial. The body is exalted in its 'performance', and it becomes the epitome of Wilson's definition of polar exploration as a harmony of mind and body: 'The physical expression of the intellectual passion.'[52] Even in the 1930s, writers will seek to argue for the efficacy of man-hauling on the basis of a relation between an unfolding visible world and energised limbs: 'the men are elated, for each day they see more than eyes have ever seen before: new, towering ranges, great glaciers and icefalls ... of these the dog sees almost nothing.'[53] And equally, on the side of denial, and in accordance with the Christianised ascet-icism so oddly pervasive amongst this party, the killing labour of 'man-hauling' is a suitable mortification of the flesh.

However, this 'performance' is still a mockery: 'What shall we say of Scott and his comrades, who were their own dogs?' one of Amundsen's companions will later write.[54] To speak of exaltation and denial is to efface the caring for the self which the materiality of the Antarctic landscape demands. Each night in the tents, eyes blinded by the luminous intimacy of the landscape are treated with zinc sulphate and cocaine, then swaddled in rags and tea leaves. Frozen feet and hands are placed upon the warm chests and stomachs of consenting companions in a series of awkward embraces, unlikely arrangements of bodily parts. Antarctica demands, above all, that the frontiers of one's body be rigorously established and maintained.

> As one moves from perimeter to interior, so the proportion of ice relentlessly increases ... higher-order ice forms collectively compose the entire continent: the icebergs: tabular bergs, glacier bergs, ice islands, bergy bits, growlers, brash ice, white ice, blue ice, green ice, dirty ice; the sea ices: ice stalactites, pancake ice, frazil ice, grease ice, congelation ice, infiltration ice, undersea ice, vuggy ice, new ice, old ice, brown ice, rotten ice; the coastal ices: fast ice, shore ice, glacial ice-tongues, ice piedmonts, ice fringes, ice cakes, ice foots, ice walls, ice fronts, floating ice, grounded ice, anchor ice, rime ice, ice ports, ice shelves, ice rises, ice bastions, ice haycocks, ice lobes, ice streams; the mountain ices: glacial ice, valley glaciers, cirque glaciers, piedmont glaciers, ice fjords, ice layers, ice pipes, ice falls, ice folds, ice faults, ice pinnacles, ice lenses, ice aprons, ice fronts, ice slush; the ground ices: ice wedges, ice veins, permafrost; the polar plateau ices: ice sheets, ice caps, ice domes, ice streams, ice divides, ice saddles, ice rumples; the atmospheric ices: ice grains, ice crystals, ice dust, pencil ice, plate ice, bullet ice.[55]

Introduction (part five)

Throughout those days at the Institute I experienced levels of concentration and determination I've since struggled to ever recapture. Life took on a ritual, regimented quality. There was a café near the Institute, where each morning I would drink double espressos, smoke, and think about the work ahead. Two hours of reading and note-taking followed, before the tolling of a bell announced the Institute's morning coffee break. They always served good, strong filter coffee, far superior to the usual university common room instant. The bell had originally been mounted on the deck of Scott's ship, the Terra Nova.

I hardly ever spoke to anyone. At coffee in the morning and then again in mid-afternoon, I would weave quickly through the throng surrounding the serving-table and slip outside the foyer for a cigarette. At one and the same time I felt myself to be both too serious and too frivolous in comparison with the staff, students and researchers of the Institute. I felt at times like a secret agent on a covert mission, at every instant in danger of being uncovered (this exposure would consist of my inability to sum up concisely what my research involved, what I was doing there). Otherwise I felt a little absurd in my dark clothes and goatee, callow by contrast with the physical scientists who made up easily the majority of the Institute's staff, the men (nearly all men) who had been there, who were on their way there. There hadn't, throughout all my time in England, been that many occasions on which I'd felt marginal, inferior. But in truth I did not know what to make of the bluff, hail-fellow-well-met atmosphere they tended to exude. I say 'they' because all that remains with me now is a rather unfortunate impression, a meld of Gore-tex™ and beards and sonorous surnames.

At 90° S

The South Pole constructs its own particular mix of striation and smoothness, weaving and unweaving, for 'the two spaces in fact exist only in mixture.'[56] It is the conceptual outcome of the abstractions of latitude and longitude, a systematic ordering, a relentless convergence, a navigational proof. In a sense, the Pole is everywhere: 'lines of longitude surge around the Earth from the Pole like a nervous system. The nexus leaves its imprint all over the globe.'[57] Yet as a 'dimensionless' point it cannot be 'reached', and exhibits no static materiality. Its nature instead is incessant movement: one cannot be 'at' the pole without instantly and always moving in the direction of its opposite. The Pole thus inhabits a zone of ceaseless and dynamic symbiosis with its Other: North.

Amundsen wins the race. He reaches the vicinity of the Pole on 15 December 1911, recording in his diary that 'the day passed without any occurrence worth mentioning, and at three o'clock in the afternoon we halted, as according to our reckoning we had reached our goal.'[58] He then spends two days marking his position, hedging the Pole with dozens of flags. In this way, perhaps, his entire voyage may also be seen as a mixture of smoothness and striation. From the start he has been 'elusive' – a hidden trajectory across space, a tactical weaving and occupancy of landscape. Yet now at the Pole, for the first and last time, he decisively leaves a 'trace', a territorial mark beyond dispute. But in his diary he writes, 'I had better be honest and admit straight out that I have never known any man to be placed in such a diametrically opposite position to the goal of his desires. The regions around the North Pole – the North Pole itself – had attracted me from childhood, and here I was at the South Pole. Can anything more absurd be imagined?'[59]

Having left their trace, the Norwegians once again 'disappear'. No pictures survive of their return journey of 700 miles. Their route back to base is abundantly supplied – they have transformed the wilderness into arcadia, a cornucopia of seal meat, pemmican and chocolate. There is sometimes no need to navigate, for the dogs can smell the food ahead, the excreta of previous camps which they can digest for nourishment. The strict geometry of navigation is augmented by a more manifold sensual vector. To this day Amundsen's precise route is a matter of conjecture and debate. But by 30 January 1912 they are back aboard the *Fram*, and are heading for New Zealand, eagerly anticipating 'the unmixed delight of looking upon meadows and woods'.[60]

Scott will never know of this. On 16 January 1912, he stands sullenly by the tent which Amundsen had left at the Pole. He has lost the race by a month. The one trace Amundsen leaves shatters 'all the dreams predicated on the vacancy of this imaginary place'.[61] So the Pole could only ever be an intersection, a crossroads – never a place to rest, never a destination. Scott turns away from the nightmarish Norwegian flags, and begins his walk toward death, his coming apotheosis. On the passage down the Beardmore Glacier to the Barrier they halt, for a day, to collect geological specimens, 'Weight of sledge, so much. Increased by stones, 14 kilos.'[62] A few days later, one of the party, the seaman Edgar Evans, collapses. Perhaps a fall has caused a haemorrhage in his scurvy-weakened brain? Scott finds him 'on his knees with clothing disarranged, hands uncovered and frostbitten, and a wild look in his eyes'[63], and Evans dies that night in the tent as the rest look on. ('He screamed, "Stones! Stones!!"'[64])

Not an allegory at all, nor a discourse of nation and manhood. Instead a story of materiality – a story of surface. The word haunts Scott's final diary entries: 'Surface snow like desert sand' ... 'the surface awful beyond words' ... 'an impossible friction on the sledge-runners ... pulling for our lives we could scarcely advance' ... 'the surface remains awful, the cold intense' ... 'God help us, we can't keep up this pulling, that is certain. Amongst ourselves we are unendingly cheerful, but what each man feels in his heart I can only guess.'[65]

Introduction (part six)

What I do remember sharply about the Scott Polar Institute is the physical pleasure of the library archive. I remember the loom of the shelves above the narrow aisles and my supplicant crouch in those aisles. The books I consulted were mostly first editions from just before and after the First World War, large weighty volumes beautifully printed with still-sturdy bindings. I remember their gratifying heft in my hands and the sudden delicacy of the leaves through my fingers. Everything I read seemed charged with relevance. As Francis Spufford again acutely remarks, these tales produced 'reticent passion in the passionately reticent'.[66] *Amongst these books, like an anthropologist, I was transported to another world, of lithographs and facsimiles, quirks of expression and attitude, and sometimes, the crystal breath of coldness.*

This is what was memorable about Cambridge and the Institute: it was cold. From the pages before me there arose a chill which encircled me, settling numbly on the small of my back. It was not cold in the usual neutral sense: it was a culturally specific cold, one peculiar to the years between 1900 and 1913. It carried the frosted aroma of leather and tobacco, dogs and straw. A sentence would sometimes shiver across my shoulders. My hands froze around the books I held and carried from shelf to desk, I had to shake and flex them. I breathed in the painful air raggedly, feeling dizzy when I stood up. Perhaps this sounds fanciful, but it seemed a reality then, and it grips me now in recollection. I remember every lunchtime the library shut completely and I was obliged to while away an hour somewhere else. I carried my affective Edwardian Antarctic outside with me, where it mingled with the damper Fenland chill. Sometimes I went to a pub or café, but mostly, to save money, I sat eating my sandwiches in a bare park on the other side of the main road. The weather was always the same, flat and damply cold. The sky was a uniform pale grey, the sun a white polar disc. On the horizon of the park stood a row of angular, withered trees: in the smoky, frosted haze I imagined their denuded branches to be the masts and rigging of a wooden flotilla held fast in the pack ice.

29 March 1912

'I write the history of the South Pole,' Amundsen announces as the *Fram* reaches New Zealand,[67] but he couldn't be more wrong. Perhaps even as he pens these words, Scott is dying in his tent upon the ice, starving, with legs gangrenous from scurvy, cold and frozen to a point where any movement is a horror. But he has the insight to realise that nothing that happens to his body really matters now. He begins to project himself and his surroundings into a fitting, illuminated space; he begins, from the heart of the Antarctic and from the finality of his being as a polar creature, to irrevocably transform the landscape which has destroyed him. All that is needed for this narrative is someone to 'carry it northward to multiply unimaginably in the warmer world'.[68] 'Had we lived, I should have had a tale to tell of the hardihood, endurance and courage of my companions which would have stirred the heart of every Englishman.'[69]

12 November 1912

They find a tent and leave a grave. They take the diaries, the records, the specimens. They note that 'Scott seemed to have fought hard at the moment of death.'[70] They build a large cairn over the tent, mounted by a cross made from skis. It is a speck on a white plain, 'a grave that kings must envy'.[71] And this, perhaps, is the key moment of the entire expedition, the moment where they truly become the 'artistic christians'[72] of their aspirations. Standing before the scene they have created, perhaps they sense at last that they have moulded the appropriate frame within which their vision of Antarctica may be projected. The cairn and the cross alone have little sufficiency, but set amidst a vast bowl of undulating ice, encompassed by the western mountains, a recognisable and intelligible landscape is gathered together.

Yet no-one will ever see this scene again. Movements of the ice, horizontal and vertical, carry Scott and his companions first beneath the surface, then relentlessly back to the sea – and now it seems as if the story is hidden amidst an endless array of codas and recapitulations, as if the 'event' were but 'the slender twig upon which unforeseeable crystallisations will form',[73] as if those two original trajectories were simply the first lines of a chaotic etching obscuring the surface of their occurrence.

18 June 1928

The camera catches Amundsen as he shrugs on a flying-jacket. His eyes are invisible beneath his cap. He boards the plane, his ostensible mission the rescue of a former colleague now stranded on the Arctic ice, a colleague with whom he had quarrelled, bitterly, during the first flight over the North Pole. Of that journey Amundsen wrote, 'My function was now solely that of the geographer, watching the terrain far below ... we are all so pitifully small.'[74] He is, by all accounts, an unhappy, lonely man. The plane taxis, climbs, and heads north; Amundsen vanishing once more into smoothness, the ceaselessly shifting floes of the Arctic ice. This time he is never seen again.

Introduction (part seven)

My last visit to the Institute was in November 1999. By then much of this research was already drafted. It was my intention, as I remember saying to people at the time, to put a full stop on the whole thing. So I arrived to find the renovations at the Institute had been completed. An entire new library had been built, called the Shackleton Memorial Library, presumably out of a lingering sense of guilt at the way Scott's death had somewhat airbrushed his polar rival from history. The whole aspect of the building was completely transformed, and this caught me by surprise, although I had known that the building works were substantial. The Institute was gearing up for the official opening at the end of the week. Intense activity surrounded my desk, and at one point I was press-ganged into helping to mount a furled Union Jack over the new entrance doors.

Otherwise I spent quite a leisurely week browsing, reading tangential and ancillary works, and tying up loose ends. The new library was softly but warmly lit, and I relaxed in the metallic tincture of newly-installed central heating. A descendant of Shackleton's was to be guest at the opening on the Friday afternoon; I watched him being conducted through a rehearsal by the head archivist. As a member of the Institute (annual subscription: £5) I was also entitled to be present. But on the Friday lunchtime I collected my bags and left unnoticed. It was a bright lively day, the start of the weekend, and, crossing a border, I bought myself a chicken tikka sandwich and a cheap sci-fi novel on my way back to the train station.

4

Climates of Sight

Mistaken Visibilities, Mirages and 'Seeing Beyond' in Antarctica

Kathryn Yusoff

Immoral mapping

In 1842, the Antarctic explorer Charles Wilkes stood trial by court-martial on the charge of 'immoral mapping'. Wilkes faced an indictment of 'Scandalous Conduct Tending to the Destruction of Good Morals' for his designation of land on 19 January 1840, where there was none to be found. His claim was to have 'discovered a vast Antarctic continent … '. Charge VI, Specification I, read as follows: 'In this, that the said Lieutenant Charles Wilkes in his report, number 63, to the Secretary of the Navy, dated 11 March 1840, did utter a deliberate and wilful falsehood, in the following words, to wit: "On the morning of the 19th of January, we saw land to the southward and eastward with many indicators of being in its vicinity, such as penguins, seal and the discolouration of the water; but the impenetrable barrier of ice prevented our nearing our approach to it."'[1] The proceedings of the court-martial record that Wilkes had made a false entry as to the date on which he sighted 'Antarctic land'.[2] On 7 September 1842, the verdict was given: dropped as not proven. Although not charged, Wilkes' reputation and authority as a cartographer was ruined. Later defenders of Wilkes' reputation claimed that his 'immoral mapping' could be explained by recourse to the particular atmospheric phenomena of the Antarctic region. In the strange Antarctic light, Wilkes had seen a superior mirage.

Before Wilkes' 'designation of land', several officers had also reported seeing land, but Wilkes initially dismissed these sightings as cloud shapes, or atmospheric fictions. While he was cautious about the atmospheric conditions that were known to conjure land in the Polar Regions, Wilkes had the mindset of discovery: he was eager to transform the doubtful space of ice into a geography marked with his name. Tremendous financial, professional and personal urgency rested on these hitherto speculative geographies of the southern regions. As Daniel Henderson argues, 'His concentration on becoming the Antarctic Columbus, on finding the land Captain Cook had failed to sight, made him jumpy. … His diary entries during these weeks of searching fog and dodging icebergs indicate that he was a victim of what modern authorities term polar depression.'[3] In his diary Wilkes confessed his anxiety: 'The opportunity of seeing around us, though it is daylight, is of rare occurrence, and looking for land here is to be likened to a man groping in a dark room – with the liability of breaking his neck in search of what is not to be found except covered with snow.'[4]

On 15 January, in clear weather, Wilkes sketched an image in his personal journal of Antarctic land. The drawing was of the *Vincennes* held in the ice, with mountainous landscape in the background. In the following days Wilkes' account vacillated between fact and fiction: his own doubt and ambition literally making and unmaking the sight of land. He records, 'we ourselves anticipated no such discovery; the indications of it were received with doubt and hesitation; I myself did not venture to record in my private journal the certainty of land until after three days, after those best acquainted with its appearance in these high latitudes were assured of the fact; and finally to remove all possibility of doubt, and to prove that there was no deception in this case'. As the eye took up the sight of land, and pencil was put to paper, an image was created of a mountainous continent. As ambition and speculation gripped Wilkes, the image was where he realised his resolution. He was aware of particular polar conditions where condensed vapour looked like land which could beset polar explorers. This 'appearance' of land was so real, so alluring that it was recorded as a geographical fact. Only on the site of the fixed image could Wilkes counter these ambiguities of geographical 'knowledge' which was realised through uncertain sightings. Wilkes said,

> All doubt in relation to the reality of our discovery gradually wore away, and towards the close of the cruise of the Vincennes along the icy barrier, the mountains of the Antarctic Continent became familiar and of daily appearance, in so much that the logbook, which is guardedly silent as to the time and date of its being observed, now speaks throughout of land![5]

By 16 January 1840, the three ships of the expedition, *Vincennes*, *Peacock* and *Porpoise* together record a sight of land. Wilkes was later to write in his *Narrative of the U.S. Exploring Expedition*, 'On this date appearances believed at the time to be land were visible from all three vessels, and the comparison of the three observations, when taken into connection with the more positive proofs of existence afterwards obtained, has left no doubt that the appearance was not deceptive.'[6] On 19 January, Wilkes confirmed that what he saw was the *terra firma* of an Antarctic continent, possession was taken of Wilkes Land,[7] and a message was sent to the Secretary of the Navy to that effect.[8]

While the Antarctic landscape suggested slowness because of the 'lateness' of its discovery,[9] time was literally of an essence in the sighting and making of landfall. The

Figure 4.1 Detail of Antarctic Continent as drawn by Wilkes, in C. Wilkes, *Narrative of the U. S. Exploring Expeditions 1838–42*, Washington, 1840 (photograph by Kathryn Yusoff, New York Public Library, 2006).

French explorer, Jules Dumont d'Urville, had claimed discovery of the continent on the afternoon of 18 January. d'Urville claimed that he had made his discovery in advance of Wilkes by a few hours, but it afterwards transpired that he had forgotten the International Dateline, and had failed to add a day to his log when he crossed the 180th meridian. This made him later in the sighting of land by about ten hours. Upon his return home Wilkes was called on to answer that he falsified the records as to the date and facticity of his sighting. Jules Verne, champion of d'Urville, wrote in his account of the latter's voyage '…not until he reached Sydney did Wilkes, hearing that d'Urville had discovered land on the 19th January, pretend to have seen it on the same day'.[10] Attentive to the tenets of science fiction, Verne wrote an angry letter to Wilkes accusing him of conspiring to write fictional accounts.

Doubting Wilkes' claim, after being sent the details of the voyage, Captain Sir James Clark Ross set out in 1841 in the *Erebus* and *Terror* to Antarctic waters. Ross sailed over the assigned position of Wilkes Land and thus concluded that no such land existed. Ross' 1847 narrative[11] gives an account of the claims for and against Wilkes Land, claiming that Wilkes failed to follow standard cartographic practices and proclaimed land based on 'assumption of land' rather than on facticity. Ross comments that only what was 'really and truly seen' should be included and that which had the 'appearance of land' be marked so. He called Wilkes' discovery a 'pseudo-continent'.[12] Although Ross did not fully understand the climatic conditions that had created Wilkes' simulation of land, he named the discovery

Figure 4.2 Untitled (Kathryn Yusoff, Antarctica, 2004).

correctly. The climatic distancing device of landscape that Wilkes observed would highlight an unexpected condition of visual knowledges in the Polar Regions. As a landscape Antarctica is profoundly counter-intuitive for human inhabitation, but Antarctica is an extraordinary site from which to consider another kind of visibility that incorporates the fictions and breakdown of perception.[13]

Seeing beyond: superior mirages and the geographical 'gift'

While the Antarctic optic caused a number of cartographic failures, the mirage most strongly demonstrated the latent possibility of a 'geographical gift' to the normative European history of perception. Mirages are not optical illusions, they are real phenomena of atmospheric optics caused by rays bending in air layers with steep thermal gradients. Whereas light normally travels in a straight line, when light rays pass through air layers of different temperatures, they curve towards the cooler air. The rays then enter the eye at a lower angle than the angle at which the image lies, thus the image is displaced, and so a mirage is sighted. In this case the mirage is not, as commonly perceived, a false image but, more correctly, an image in the wrong place. Atmospheric refraction displaces almost everything we see from its geometric position – that is, rays of light are usually curved, and thus everything appears slightly displaced above its geometric or 'true' position. This displacement is known as terrestrial refraction. The image of the mirage is genuine, it is just an exaggerated displacement from a usual terrestrial location. A superior mirage means that there is an inverted image above an erect one, hence the image is lifted above the horizon. As Hobbs claimed, 'Less appreciated has been a fairly common phenomenon of looming – superior or polar mirage – which for considerable intervals of time brings land into view when it is very far below the horizon.'[14] The

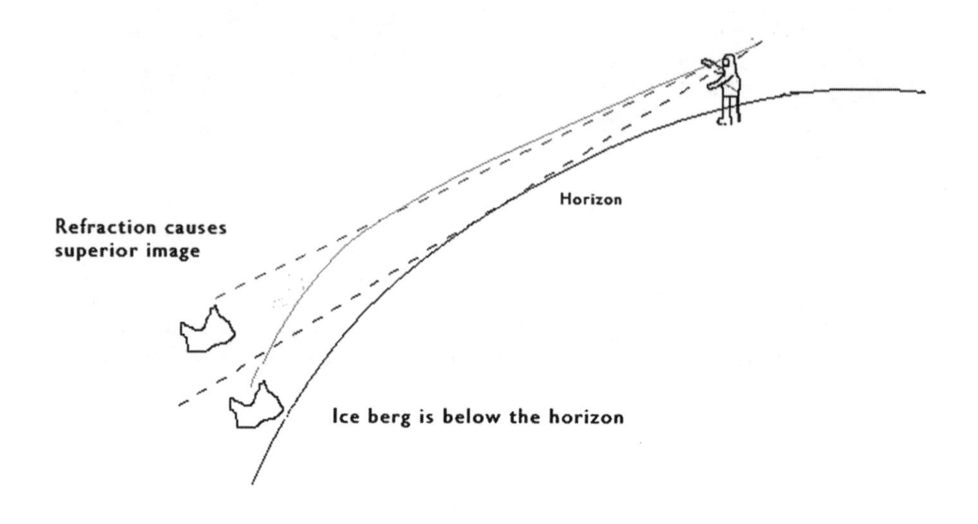

Figure 4.3 Diagram of a Superior Mirage (Kathryn Yusoff, 2006).

curvature of the earth normally restricts the distance that can be seen depending on the height of an object, where height is proportionate to distance perceived. A small iceberg would normally be seen at about 12 miles away from a ship, while a large mountain range could be seen from up to 70 miles. With the mirage, distant lands transcend the limited horizon of sight.

What the mirage amounts to is not just a tarnished reputation,[15] but the curious instance of lands that are seen when they are actually out of the line of sight below the horizon. So although the mirage holds false promise for the making of maps, as a tool of vision the mirage does offer a remarkable glimpse of what the earth's curvature has made invisible. Wilkes accurately mapped more than 1,500 miles of the Antarctic, with frequent landfalls that were made by estimating the distances from the ship, as the ice barrier prevented the physical confirmation of reaching land. The mirage allowed Wilkes to see a continent, to discover it in a position that he would have ordinarily been unable to see because of the earth's curvature. But that visibility came at a price, as things were really seen but incorrectly charted. What Wilkes sighted was a 'phantom displacement'; he saw an image of the landscape emitted through climatic constellations, a form of 'snow'[16] in the transmission of geographical information. This phantom displacement of the Antarctic would come to haunt many explorers that came after Wilkes, and the strange Antarctic light continues to confound many a visualising technology to the present day.[17] It is only in recognition of the historical frequency of the polar mirage that Wilkes Land remains a salient feature on Antarctic maps today.[18]

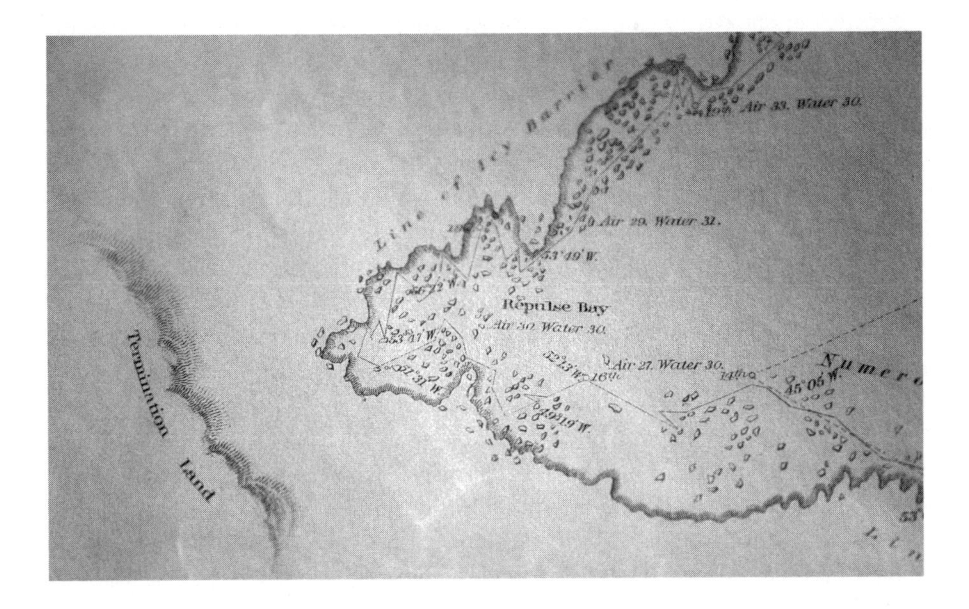

Figure 4.4 Detail of High Land Covered with Snow as drawn by Wilkes in C. Wilkes, *Narrative of the U. S. Exploring Expeditions 1838–42*, Washington, 1840 (photograph by Kathryn Yusoff, New York Public Library, 2006).

The geographical 'gift' of the mirage was to make the invisible visible to the eye of the explorer, i.e. to show lands that existed but were displaced and unavailable to view immediately, but this gift was also to show lands precisely where there were none to be found. Had the early explorers had a better understanding of these optical peculiarities, the mirage would have provided an invaluable aid for 'sighting' far distant land, land that lay physically beyond their horizons. Commenting on the phenomena of optical illusions, the artist Rachel Weiss suggests, 'In Antarctica, these illusions are of such scale and frequency that they deserve to share the appellation "real" with non-illusory events.'[19] The gift of these atmospheric sightlines may force us to consider what the artist Robert Smithson calls the 'climates of sight' that emerge from landscapes.

Climates of sight

The story of Wilkes' 'immoral mapping' through the mirage serves as a starting point to discuss the themes of this chapter, namely: the uncertain and shifting relation of the visual to establishing geographical 'truths', a consideration of how vision is geographically constituted, and the exposition of a hallucinatory and a normative vision. In short, Antarctica presents a visual disturbance in the production of geographic knowledge. Both Wilkes and his detractors attempted to come to grips with the flickering territory of this continent through discussions of fact and fiction, appearance and actuality, doubt and reality, the visible and the non-visible. These claims and counter-claims as to the fact and fiction of the geographical knowledge made by Wilkes, Ross and others set up powerful dialectic poles of the perceived knowledge in Enlightenment scientific practice. This has been noted in the work of Dorinda Outram (1999) and Sverker Sörlin (2005). Arguably it is the very indecipherability of the Antarctic landscape that directs us to rethink the role of the visual in Antarctic geographical knowledge and beyond. Antarctica suggests a topology of doubt that informs the formation of visual landscapes. This doubt emerges as much from the actual climate of a forbidding continent as from 'a climatology of the brain and eyes'.[20] In other words, Antarctica presents climates of sight that open into expanded visual geographies and expanded ways of considering a terrain that shifts and moves, like the weather.[21]

Given western languages' dependence on visual metaphors, it is hardly surprising that geography should have its own specific visual practices for establishing empirical truths.[22] The role of the visual in geography has had considerable attention, particularly the role of visualising technologies in the geographical practices of exploration and empire. Geography has been described as a visual mode of thinking and practice, a 'science of observation'[23] that produces a 'geographical gaze'.[24] In this work on visual geographies, analysis has tended to concentrate on the power of the visual in the formation of subjects and places, however there has been little consideration of the types of vision that do not realise their geographical object – vision that is contingent, conjuring, and often results in failure.[25] While existing studies have done important work in explaining the powerful relations within the visual medium, less attention has been given to the role of vision as a destabilising and radically disorienting sense within a specific locale,[26] where landscape *unsettles* such a fixed geographic gaze. This inversion of normative visual regimes, i.e. 'normal perception', allows for a generative expansion of the field of vision,[27] as supported by the instance of the superior mirage, that is both geographically contingent and regionally specific. Vision, in the polar regions, can be considered as a disturbance that offers glimpses of ecstasy and hallucination, as well as blindness and doubt.

As early as 1884 the polar regions were referred to as distinct 'zones', which as J.E. Nourse argued were more resistant to instrumentation than the moon.[28] In the Antarctic zone, the mirage suggests a distinct 'climate of sight' that is an essential attribute of this landscape. These climates of sight are not only particular to geographical regions, but they are also the conditions through which distinct and situated landscapes emerge. These landscape conditions include ice-blink, exposure, superior mirages, mock suns, phantom displacements, blindings, refractions, auroras and strange weather.[29] Antarctica demonstrates with acute clarity that geographical truth realised through vision is an instance of realisation amongst a whole number of appearances. The compression of distances and strange weather contribute to the difficulties of discerning 'form' in the Antarctic landscape, as the contemporary polar photographer Jean de Pomereu demonstrates. Antarctica is a continent of liquid boundaries – of flows, storms and imperceptible material that converts between liquid, airborne and solid states. 'Flying seas' was the name given to the blizzards blowing from the

Figure 4.5 *Absence*, by contemporary polar photographer, Jean de Pomereu, Antarctica, 2004 (courtesy of Jean de Pomereu).

South Pole. Mirages became a common aspect of Antarctic travel; the collapsing of depth often challenged perceptions of distance, as the proximity to the magnetic south foiled compasses. Thus, the Antarctic engaged early explorers in excessive problems of navigation and perception, disorienting their bodies, minds and instruments. This 'locational problem',[30] as Paul Simpson-Housley terms it, disrupted orders of visual knowledge. For example, in April 1915, the explorer Ernest Shackleton reported that he saw a sunset that appeared to set, reappear and then set again some time later. The sun repeated this for some time. Vision was no guarantor of apprehension. Ice in all its forms was, not surprisingly then, the main cartographic challenge of the Antarctic: ice storms, ice-blink, ice flows, ice barriers, ice tongues and white-outs all hindered Antarctica's 'mapping'. The site-specific nature of this sight both highlights the contingency of vision in the making of landscape and points to another space of consideration in the climatology of vision and thought. This climate of vision is both temporally and spatially contingent and thus offers a way of thinking about how we see place as continuously emergent.

Indeed, the climates of sight were such that Antarctica appeared and disappeared, and since no one could get near enough to the continent to physically apprehend it because of the icy barrier, vision (however troubling) was the only means of asserting its geography.[31] The difficulty of measuring distance was exacerbated by the fact that explorers could not get to the continental coast, nor could they actually ascertain where it actually was. This was due in no small part to the sea ice that formed a continuous covering over the continent to the various edges where it disintegrated. As William Herbert Hobbs states,

> In many cases of snow-covered lands there is not enough of individual character in the coastal features to permit of identification from different ship positions, and in such cases the newly discovered lands have of necessity been placed upon the maps on the basis of their direction and estimated distance, and as a consequences they are often as much as forty or fifty geographical miles too near when this is due to the atmospheric clarity alone, but as much as two hundred geographical miles when due to high superior mirage.[32]

Figure 4.6 *Vincennes* in front of the Icy barrier, January 30th, in C. Wilkes, *Narrative of the U.S. Exploring Expeditions 1838–42*, Washington, 1840 (photograph Kathryn Yusoff, New York Public Library, 2006).

Such was the nature of the Antarctic weather that the usually accurate practice of sightings was turned into speculation. While the empirical gaze of exploration was necessarily dispassionate, it is not hard to imagine how desire for a new continent might cloud such vision. Remembering Wilkes' comments on how seeing was likened to a blind man groping in the darkness we can begin to see the problems created by shadowy ice fields. Certain physical difficulties also become apparent when a gaze is strained to 'see' a continent. As Martin Jay comments, 'We cannot really freeze the movement of the eye for very long without incurring intolerable strain.'[33] Eyes have to be in almost constant motion, even when we sleep. When we fix a gaze our eyes start to cloud and we begin not to see. Staring and finding nothing is a form of optical paralysis. The human eye is limited by focal range. The over-reaching of the eye across vast distances in the Antarctic, because of the clarity of vision offered by unpolluted air and the unbifurcated horizon, results in strain to the organ of sight. Contemporaneously, in the Antarctic this strain is called 'bug eye', which refers to a stretching of the focal length beyond its normative range. In the Antarctic, vision can literally not realise the *longue durée* of gaze. This hyperopia creates what is called 'blindsight', where one sees but does not understand seeing.

The gaze belongs more certainly to a technological capacity than to the eye, extending and consolidating what the eye desires but cannot realise for itself.[34] Thus the technics of the sketch (in Wilkes case) is not only a consolidation of his speculative seeing, but a space of resolution for an impossible project of realisation (the icy barrier prevents landfall and the confirmation of touch). The sketch becomes a compensatory mechanism for realising desire and foregoing doubt. Here, in the practice of drawing, a material landscape is made that counters the shifting uncertainty of the materiality of Wilkes' sights.[35] However, the 'landscape' was barely detectable from the icy debris that was a feature of sky, sea and the far distant ice mountains. Urban Wråkberg argues that the icy barrier, along with the difficulties in detecting a coast or even recognising an outline or landmark made the traditional process of making colonial claims truly problematic.[36] [Fig. 4.6] The prime goal was 'to fulfil the first and foremost task of geographical research in the nineteenth century: the separation of land from sea by sighting, sketching and mapping the coast of the unknown. However, the very activity of defining an outline or coastal edge was obscured by the visibility of a clearly identifiable land/sea interface.'[37] If, as Primo Levi suggests, 'to comprehend is the same as forming an image',[38] the act of seeing is inseparable from the act of perception. The need to recognise form means seeing is about seeing 'something', and this is how in exploration the visual form was so necessary to the construction of a geographical object. Like Wilkes' sketch, the image gave form to a formless place – it is, what Roland Barthes calls 'an arrest of interpretation'.[39]

The sketch that Wilkes made is borne out of the blindness of a hallucinogenic field of vision and this quality is never fully left behind. The entanglement of these registers of blindness and seeing and what is real and what is imaginary alert us to the perpetual condition of vision in geographical possession. 'Discovery' enacts this contest between the desire for possessing the unknown and limited forms of apprehension. In Antarctica, knowing and making knowledge become further complicated by the presentation and withdrawal of those truths in the form of a mirage of a new continent. It is in the interplay between a desire for a clear visual encounter (to sight land) and the blindness of icy indeterminacy that the configurations of both are revealed. *Antarctica offers a double blinding* – the blinding of whiteout and the blinding of a rarefied atmosphere that condenses distance. This forgotten link between vision and blindness is discovery's burden. As the boundaries of vision and blindness break down, other expressions of knowledge emerge that exist in excess of the empirical and scientific, i.e. speculative narrative, in other words, ways of seeing beyond vision.

Speculative geographies

The problem of mapping the Antarctic continues to this day. Antarctica needs to be remapped more often than any other continent. On most maps the ice shelves are shown as permanent features, but how does one ascertain where the ice stops and starts when the Antarctic continent expands to double its continental size annually? The line of a map is always subject to a certain abstractness and redundancy, but in the case of the Antarctic this abstract quality is taken to the limits of the form, suggesting an exhausted cartographic logic. The extent and dynamism of glaciation in the Antarctic are unlike anywhere else on earth. Here, the usual modes of arresting landscape are woefully inadequate. As Admiral Richard

Byrd remarked in 1935, 'It's a curious ... fact that long after most astronomers [knew] there were no canals on Mars, no geographer ... could have told you whether Antarctica ... was one continent or two.' Not until the event of sensitive gravity meters, and later with seismic and radio echo soundings in the 1960s, did much of Antarctica's basic geographical character become understood.

Antarctica's dynamic ice processes are always working to erode the possibilities of a seemingly stable form of accounting for geographical space. Wråkberg argues, 'The slow pace of Antarctic exploration as a whole also indicated that there might be more to this than just adjusting field practices developed elsewhere to extreme polar conditions. The grand geographic project of the nineteenth-century Western culture seemed to have struck difficulties of a more profound nature in its encounter with the vast ice mass in the far south'.[40] What this Antarctic excess suggests is that there are entropic forces at work within the making of all maps. The hallucinatory capacity of landscape phenomena, such as the mirage, works to re-inscribe the very notions of geographical fact within these processes of accounting for spaces. As vision sagged under the weight of 'snow', this formlessness demanded a new order of knowing and observation, and a new order of knower that could contend with how the landscape was realised through speculation.[41]

For Wilkes, speculative vision is a troubling thing. His visions have the 'appearance' of land that cannot be taken as an assumption of fact. In this zone of troubling atmospheric phenomena, vision is a space of speculation. Yet it is also the place where mastery is realised through graphical inscription (map, image, sighting). Representational practice is the site of dialectic between cartography, narrative and image, and thus is a critical site of enunciation in the geography of place. Wilkes had been meticulous in controlling the production of narratives and objects from his expedition. In order to restrict counter-narratives, he reduced the number of scientists included in the expedition from twenty-five to seven, and he prevented them from examining their specimens below deck. All specimens had to be placed in his care. All members of the expedition were to keep journals as part of the performance of their duties, and to submit them to Wilkes for editorial approval at the end of the voyage. To counter the charges of 'immoral mapping' levied against him, Wilkes published his *Narrative* as an official account of the expedition. In the realm of the visual, the graphical practice of rendering an image of the continent may have brought phsychological resolution to Wilkes' speculative sighting, but once the location given by that sighting had been sailed over by Ross, doubt was cast on the production of all the geographical knowledge Wilkes had attempted to secure, and on Wilkes as a curator of that knowledge.[42] The forms of production to which his voyage had given expression were already circulating freely, and Wilkes' speculative vision had given rise to a number of other speculative geographies. The pictorial plates of Wilkes' *Narrative* formed the basis of Herman Melville's *Moby Dick* (1851).[43] Melville's novel, as well as Jeremiah N. Reynolds's *Mocha Dick* (1839),[44] Symmes' speculative 'Hollow Earth Theory',[45] James Fenimore Cooper's *Sea Lions* (1849), and Edgar Allen Poe's *Narrative of Arthur Gordon Pym of Nantucket* (1837), all enlarged upon and made fictitious use of the facts Wilkes had so scrupulously attempted to control.

In this chapter I have been interested in the optical effects that challenge a geographical 'art of describing' that is realised through vision. But, this graphical art of describing is as much about how sight is understood, managed and narrated as a form of perception, as it is about optics as such. As we have seen with Wilkes, the realisation of Wilkes Land was as embedded in the speculative nature of discovery as much as it is in the speculative nature of sight. In this sense, the realisation of vision as a form of geographical enquiry was apprehended through two representational practices, namely cartography and narration.[46] Through a discussion of the origins of the US Exploring Expedition and the speculative geographies it spurned, particularly in the example of Poe's *Narrative of Arthur Gordon Pym*, there is a dialectic of fact and fiction in geographies of exploration. The textual and imaginative space of geographical narrative is as much a site of speculation as encounters with the Antarctic landscape itself. That narrative is no less susceptible to the atmosphere of language than is vision.

The origins of Wilkes' US Exploring Expedition stemmed from John Symmes' petition for a US-led expedition to substantiate his Hollow Earth theory. Symmes' theory proposed that the earth was a semi-hollow sphere of concentric spheres that had their entrance at the poles. In his theory of this internal world, Symmes argued that the strange atmospheric refractions, luminous auroras and the variation of compasses indicated gases escaping from the 'hole at the pole'. Although Symmes' concentric concept had received extensive scientific criticism, no one had yet gone far enough to the poles to dispel his speculative theory empirically.[47] To support a bid for funds for a southern expedition, the Secretary of the Navy employed Jeremiah N. Reynolds to collect information from the public as to what areas of the globe were most in need of exploration.[48] Reynolds – although a keen supporter of Symmes' theory (and had lectured on the possibility of openings at the Pole) – made more subdued pleas for an expedition to the southern continent in favour of commerce (particularly of sealing and whaling). He collected information from captains' journals and logs from a number of coastal locations (including Nantucket) on what geographical territories had most validity for commercial exploration. Reynolds published his 'Address on the Subject of the Exploring Expedition, First Proposal' in *Harper's New Monthly Magazine* in April 1836. Even though the focus of this inquiry was on the commercial potential of the southern regions, the speculative quality of these geographies had a much stronger pull.

Indeed, one of Reynolds' lectures was attended by Henry Allan, the brother of Edgar Allan Poe. Poe was in turn inspired to write his only novel, *The Narrative of Arthur Gordon Pym of Nantucket*. It was in the context of Wilkes' departure for Antarctica in 1837/38 that Poe published his novel in serial form in the *Southern Literary Messenger*. The US public was focussed on Antarctic travel and the speculative geographies of Hollow Earth Theory that had initiated the expedition for 'discovery'.[49] Poe's *Narrative* presents the story of the explorer Pym, who ventured down to the southern polar latitudes. The account first appeared 'under the garb of fiction'. A year later Poe republished the work as a novel. When he did so, he added a preface claiming that the work was factual. Poe's fictional explorer, Pym, whose name was derived directly from Symmes, was on a similar quest: to find a hole at the pole and make fiction fact. Poe's narrative account formed a fictitious log, filling the days of his imaginary expedition to Antarctica with ever more speculative adventures – while simultaneously Wilkes recorded in his logs the days of a real expedition, which were subsequently held up as fiction. Poe's narrative ends with the hero's vessel plunging into a polar abyss, having fallen into Symmes' 'hole at the pole'. Wilkes' narrative ends with his court-martial and charge of 'immoral mapping'.

In these narratives one text of speculative geography was literally engulfed by another. In Poe's account the fantastical nature of the Polar Regions was used to convey its own form of fact, as the Antarctic was rendered a place stranger than fiction. Here it is useful to consider J.G. Ballard's repeated assertion that it is the environment that makes possible the unfolding logic of events.[50] Poe invites the reader to leap into the unknown with the explorer, and offers exciting new knowledge as the reward. It is a reward, however, which is swiftly withdrawn as Poe's literary structure circles from the end back to beginning, to demonstrate the circular logic of these self-reinforcing narratives. The structure is used to challenge the novel's fictions, and the conceit is rendered not as deceit but as a conceptual loophole in exploration's narrative formations. Poe's work performs what Smithson calls a 'mirror symmetry' to Wilkes' *Narrative*. His concerns are the black holes in perception, those rents in our language that highlight how our perception is orientated – visually and literally. Poe's novel is concerned with inversions; the pole becomes a hole and vortex, instead of an axis in which to plant a flag or claim a continent; real discoveries and scientific practices are incorporated into fictional accounts of imaginary expeditions; the validity of truths is questioned in order to make the account seem more factual. The novel begins with a 'fictional' Pym, writing a 'real' preface to the novel. He 'says' that because he distrusts his ability to write an account that will be accepted as the truth, he has allowed 'Mr. Poe' to print part of his story 'under the garb of fiction'. Pym says, 'I proceed in utter hopelessness of obtaining credence for all that I shall tell, yet confidently trusting in time and progressing science to verify some of the most important and most improbable of my statements.' Poe uses accepted notions of science to verify the truth of the tale. Underpinned by sound research into shipping, geography, methods and expeditionary accounts, Poe attempts to authenticate the tale through the precision of factual details to create an aura of science. This highlights how geographical description is the space of that dialectic between speculation and fact.

In the attempt to render fiction factual, Wilkes inadvertently instigated a set of knowledge to better describe an imaginary territory of a truer fiction. Is this ultimately the art of fiction: to explore the mirages of geographical knowledge? In Poe's literary fiction, and the geographical fiction of Wilkes, we witness the two ends of knowledge production – as geographical description attempts to close the distance between narrative and voyage and secure landscape in the traces (Wilkes), art opens it up (Poe, Melville). Poe's text served as a kind of speculation for Wilkes' narrative of exploration. His fiction takes the speculation in the text of geographical meaning to its truest narration, as the facts of Wilkes' geography are productive of a false narration. As the artist Robert Smithson comments, 'True fiction eradicates the false reality.'[51] Fiction implies the existence of fragile structures (or holes) around which our knowledge forms (as a fleeting testimony). Accepting the slippage of knowledge (its mirages), then calls into question the shadow of knowledge (its phantom displacement). Wilkes' geographical practices are his access to the unknown; Poe's fictional practices of unknowing are his access to knowledge. It is the mirage that brings to light, with a false light, the unexpected condition of this knowledge. We can see this 'unknowing' (or fiction) as a form of geographic speculation in relation to the unknown or – what later critics were to call Poe's *Narrative* – the first example of Science Fiction (SF).

SF was the most exaggerated form of scientific narrative that arose in direct relation to the forms of scientific narrative that were already imbued with such speculative fictions. In exploration, narrative was a form of aesthetic instrumentation that crafted the density of objects, more than it was a medium for the translation of things. And so, it had a transitional quality that acted as an aestheticising lens onto the unknown and peculiar. Arthur E. Shipley's narrative of the 'Zoology: on the abysmal fauna of the antarctic region' from the 1901 *Antarctic Manual* demonstrates exactly this conjuring force of such narratives.

> No light from the sun penetrates the deep sea. There is no day and night. In connection with this absence of light from without certain animals, notably the Fishes, Crustacea, some Echinoderms, and Worms, have developed phosphorescent organs, but the part they play in illuminating the depths can hardly be greater than that of the policemen's bull's-eye in lighting up London during a November fog. Corresponding with this darkness, lit up by an occasional phosphorescent flash, the animals of the depths have either lost, or are losing, their visual organs, or have developed enormous eyes ... If we could see the bottom of the deep sea, we should see, except in those few places where a current is active ... certain curious features occur over and over again in the deep-sea creatures for which there seems no obvious reason.[52]

The author goes on to describe how the creatures who have retained eyes, 'have, so to speak, followed an evolutionary path in the opposite direction, and instead of evolving immense eyes, have suppressed eyes altogether, their place has been taken by a great development of tactile organs'.[53] The concern with seeing that permeates the account is parallelled with the attempt to shed the light of knowledge onto such abysmal depths. To make visible is to make knowledge. Descriptive narrative is one of the fundamental tools in this process of visibility and perception. In a world structured into the explainable, the peculiar and the new, the 'abysmal fauna' introduced doubt only in so much as it questioned the order of things, but not necessarily the ordering strategies.

Narrative is clearly part of the scientific apparatus – the ability to tell a good yarn, to excite, stimulate (and embellish, where appropriate) was part of the expectation and construction of scientific accounts. As Michael Bravo and Sverker Sörlin comment, narratives 'are not only a means of describing material practices ... they are practices in their own right'.[54] These practices of narrative cartography provide a body of writing that was seemingly both poetic and objective in the measuring and observing of geographical formations. This dual process of the sensual and scientific descriptive registers of observation through narration and cartography gave geography its shape as a convincing form of knowledge production. The map provides the 'site' on which the narrative can take place. That Antarctica is often the site of inversions in understanding is not just a convenient literary trope of a far-away place, but is also based on the excessive cartographic and locational problems that the landscape posed to normative structures of both geographical thought and practice, which were the result of a radical difference to the temperate climes where these structures originated. Antarctica both maintained and subverted geographical knowledge: the fictions are perceptually true (such as the mirage) and the geographical facts possessed a fantastical quality that derived from the very strangeness of the geographical forms. It is not difficult to see how the scientific accounts of the Antarctic furnished and gave plausibility to other secondary narratives, such as the imaginative SF worlds of Poe, and later Jules Verne,[55] and contemporaneously Kim Stanley Robinson.[56]

Frederic Jameson sees SF as a crucial intervention in social thought, a cognitive space of critical imagining that offers a 'representational mediation on radical difference'.[57] The utopian potential of SF is its ability as a narrative form to imagine an outside to scientific knowledge, while maintaining a dialectic relation to it, thus making us aware of our logical imprisonments. Poe's Science Fiction, like the mirage, can be seen as a break in the circuit of dependent facts and practices that makes these relations visible. In Poe's terms, the outside can be seen as a stretching of the logic of scientific knowledge to suggest discovery is about the generation of questions not answers. For Melville, the whale is the manifestation of unknowing that challenges human perception to understand limits and the cost of exceeding those limits, through the drive of obsessive discovery. As James Kneale and Rob Kitchin argue, SF can be seen more as 'a gap: between science and fiction', an 'interest in the fragile fabrication of mimesis' that offers 'a privileged site for critical thought'.[58]

Stranger than fiction, utopic vision

Antarctica constitutes a privileged site for critical thinking about vision and its relationship to the establishment of geographical truths. Wilkes did not know how to map the mirage because his predisposition to novel forms of unknowing precluded that possibility. This did not make the mirage any less 'real,' but it did make the possibility of its understanding that much more distant. The mirage, while seemingly illusory, emerges from real conditions and real contradictions within vision. It is illusory only to the extent that it did not fit within the way Wilkes delineated and mapped territory, but it did open up new climates of sight that eventually expanded the visual knowledge of the Antarctic region. The mirage is dialectically linked to our perception of the real, to a geographical form from which we establish normalising strategies. This dialectic suggests that these phantom displacements are not opposed to perception, but an extended quality of the state of perception, of an altered perception specific to place. This suggests that investigating the conditions of unknowing holds potential for geographical thought. As Antarctica provided an awkward terminus to a trajectory of nineteenth-century geography, it also suggested most clearly 'openings' to other kinds of geographical knowledges that acknowledge the dialectic relationship of vision to blindness and unknowing. Ultimately, in this challenge to consider a porous and shifting vision resides a question of ethics, a question of cultural interaction with landscape. This ethics is borne out of an acknowledgement of limits and differences. Much like the recurrent 'zone' in SF, Antarctica offers a space of otherness and possible insight, where normative responses often become more of an encumbrance than an access to the unknown.

While the Antarctic visual disturbance had a dramatic effect on the nature and practices of Antarctic fieldwork, it did little to disrupt the tenets of geographical knowledge other than to present an anomaly, like the creatures from Shipley's Abysmal Zone. In practice, the Antarctic was too far away from Europe; it was peripheral in scientific terms during the nineteenth and twentieth centuries to disrupt the order of things. Yet, twenty-first-century contemporary representations of Antarctic place us most urgently into the gap between science and fiction, once so creatively occupied by Poe and Melville. If we transpose the metaphor of 'seeing beyond sight' to the speculative geographies of climate change predictions, which have been elicited from Antarctic ice cores, we see the generative gifts that contemporary Antarctic offers our perception. As ice core data forms the basis for climate prediction models that generate models of the future, we can see this prediction as a form of SF that has to contend with speculation and doubt to bring critical insight to future climate uncertainties. New conditions of instability in the ice challenge our ability to conceive of abrupt and shifting landscapes, and so it is through the critical lens of speculation that we proceed. In the Antarctic climatology of sight we are offered the gift of observing landscape change on a scale that requires a new paradigm of understanding, about both Antarctic and global visions. Once again we must take up the challenge of developing visual geographies that see 'beyond sight'; to be able to see that what appears as failure (the advent of climate change) is perhaps instead an opening into new, and even more accountable, 'climate of sight'.

5

Core Matters

Greenland, Denver and the GISP2 Ice Core

Heather Frazar

> On 1 July [1993], after five years of drilling, the Greenland Ice Sheet Project Two (GISP2) penetrated several metres of silty ice and reached bedrock at a depth of 3,053.44 metres ... producing the deepest ice core thus far recovered in the world.[1]

The Greenland Ice Sheet Project Two ice core (GISP2) is a 2-mile long, 5.2-inch-diameter cylinder of ice that was extracted at high latitude in central Greenland over the course of 5 summers between 1987 and 1993. I approach this 200,000-year-old scientific object[2] as a cultural geographer, with the basic assumption that *where* science happens matters. In what follows I trace various physical settings that are central to GISP2's existence as an object of scientific inquiry. My focus on GISP2's material life emerges from a more general, growing discussion in the social sciences which takes seriously the observation that the physical world plays a vital role in what and how people – in this case, scientists – do what they do.

Since at least the 1970s scholars have approached questions related to scientific fieldwork by directing significantly more attention to 'culturally'-generated doings of researchers than to the material circumstances with and within which those doings take place.[3] They have done so, no doubt, partly as a result of the scars environmental determinism left on the discipline of geography in the early to mid part of the twentieth century. More recent scholarship, however, works to recast the foundations upon which much of that literature stands. Some of these studies call upon feminist critiques of knowledge that query the assumption that '"knowledge" demarcates a coherent, surveyeable domain of inquiry.'[4] These critiques highlight ways of knowing that collapse traditional boundaries between knowledge about the material world and that world's participation in such knowledge. In tracing some of the kinetic aspects that support GISP2 research and the core's preservation, my broader aim is to advocate intra-active material settings. The prefix intra- is used throughout this chapter as an alternative to inter- so as to avoid the implicit connotation that the relevant aspects involved are discrete, bounded systems independent of their interaction.[5]

GISP2 and other science objects constitute syntheses of 'human' elements (knowledge-based and fabricated) and the so-called 'natural' ones that scientists locate in the field, extract, and transport back to the laboratory for investigation.[6] Integral to GISP2's scientific value, for instance, are the *c.*200,000 years it took Greenland's icy surface to form; they are why this core has been referred to as 'the Holy Grail of climate research'.[7] Such synthetic relationships – in this case, how past epochs intra-act with present economies of scientific value – exemplify the junctures of (GISP2) science that are central to this study. Other intra-actors to be considered are ice-sheet rheology (ice motion, or how ice flows), scientific coring and how GISP2 core segments are preserved and prepared for research. The discussion proceeds chronologically, beginning in Greenland – GISP2's place of origin – and ending in Denver, where most of the two miles of ice core is now stored.

Greenland's global ice sheet

> Scientists make science, but they do not do so entirely as they choose. Yet if scientific endeavour can yield true accounts about certain aspects of this world, it can only do so at particular times, in particular places, through particular procedures.[8]

The Greenland ice sheet presently covers some 81 per cent of the insular bedrock upon which it rests. The diverse glaciated architectures that comprise this and other massive bodies of ice are famous for being deceptively simple in concept and rife with complex dynamism *in situ*. If one were able to capture an accurate sense of what Greenland was like around 200,000 years ago – when the ice sheet's deepest layers were deposited – that is where this discussion would begin. Yet the best indicators of Greenland's climatic past are tiny samples of the atmosphere that originated as airspaces between snowflakes. When pressurised by the weight of accumulation, snow hardens into ice crystals and the interstices between snowflakes form air pockets.

> Those bubbles are the trapped leftovers of ancient atmospheres, not totally unmodified by time but largely so, enough to tell a great deal about the world's air thousands of years in the past – invaluable information for contemporary scientists struggling to fathom the vagaries of Earth's shifty climate. From deep cores taken at the polar extremes of Greenland and Antarctica, now the old air trapped in ice is revealing secrets of eons long gone.[9]

These tiny pressurised pockets contain some of the most valuable scientific materials the ice sheet holds: 'Air trapped in bubbles in polar ice cores constitutes an archive for the reconstruction of the global carbon cycle and the relation between greenhouse gases and climate in the past.'[10] When analysed molecularly, these ancient atmospheres betray particulate matter from literally all over the globe.[11] Earth's atmosphere is thick with particles that originate at different locations across its surface. Terrestrial molecules become airborne in countless different ways, circulate with other atmospheric stuffs and – due to climatic factors or gravity or both – settle back down to Earth in geographically non-discriminatory ways, forming uniquely configured dust-skins all over the globe. These skins may be comprised of geographically diverse particulate matter, such as methane gas from the tropics, volcanic ash from the Pacific Northwest and continental dust from the Saharan desert. A large percentage of terrestrial methogenesis occurs, for instance, in the tropics, yet high-latitiude ice cores are very good methane gas indicators. From a geographic perspective, this is particularly interesting in light of the fact that the poles and the tropics are conventionally – imaginatively and actually – 'polarised' places.[12] Their material coalescence in the ice sheet illustrates the fact that, while Greenland's ice sheet may accumulate locally, it is an ice mass of global composition.

Furthermore, when rarefied terrestrial particles are considered in light of their atmospheric circulation and material provenance, the categorical assertion that GISP2 is 'a piece of Greenland' begins to unravel. What promotes this unraveling, specifically, is the way polar ice collects. Most terrestrial sites receive, churn up, and exhale what cyclically becomes atmospheric fallout. Because annual snow deposition keeps polar atmospheric fallout sequentially ordered and prevents it from becoming airborne again, the poles entomb most of what they receive. (It must be said that sublimation is an exception in that it is a form of polar release; however, the majority of particulate substances remain entombed.) As such the poles are unique archives of myriad 'places'. Because most airborne materials are recycled and recyclable, particles that land on Greenland may have had many previous places of origin, and in this light are already (in and of themselves) instantiations of layered 'places'. Central to this polar accumulation of places is the fact that depositional strata are laid down over time. Yet it is somewhat unconventional to assert that time is a factor in distinguishing, for instance, 'this' geographic location from 'that', because latitudinal and longitudinal designations are generally understood to be fixed, a-temporal points on the globe.[13] That GPS designations, for instance, are understood to pinpoint the same geographic locations repeatedly, implies that there are also persistent and useful notions of geographic locations as fixed. Such 'place' designations become relative (unfixed and unfixable), however, when shifting continental plates and geomorphic aspects such as eustasy and isostasy are considered. These two terms indicate terrestrial elevation changes due to massive load variations, most often related to glacial accumulation, sublimation and/or retreat. Bearing these terrestrial processes in mind, even measurements as apparently straightforward as sea-level changes become relative. In sum, because terrestrial earth shifts over time, even specific GPS 'locations' are fundamentally mobile.

Polar sites in particular, however, subvert static notions of 'location' and 'place' owing to the fact that ice flows. Unlike non-icy terrestrial places, frozen landscapes in high places are mobile – they flow over and into (or onto) contiguous locations in relatively short periods of time (flow rates vary, depending on local aspects such as slope, rates of snow deposition, accumulation, sublimation and temperature). Moreover, as the ice sheet slowly creeps across

Greenland's bedrock, it not only gravitates over different places, it also hardens (under increasing pressure from accumulating snow) around air pockets younger than its own depositional age:

> We report the methane data on a modified GISP2 gas age time scale, which accounts for the fact that gases are trapped between 80 and 100 m below the surface of the ice sheet and are therefore younger than the surrounding ice.[14]

As such, any given portion of ice sheet is composed of materially and temporally disparate substances. It could be argued that such subterraneous aspects – like polar-ice plasticity, and dust entombment – provoke geographic concerns particular to the fact that latitudinal/longitudinal designations are not typically regarded as having depth and that by (literally and figuratively) mining the nodal point 72° 36' N, 38° 30' W (the GISP2 extraction site location), this discussion simply engages different sets of physical or conceptual conditions than do surficial, geometrically-cast geographic designations. Yet it is useful to consider the proposition that terrestrial locations are generally thought to embody extensions somewhere in between the extremes of their abstract surface designations and their material, concrete depths. What determines where these two join – or, in other words, how far down, conceptually, a 'place' extends – is intimately linked to issues of value and the physical environment. For instance, the potential value of materials underneath particular locations, as evidenced by archaeologically-sensitive sites or sites where drilling or mining for resources is at issue, demonstrates that places extend to various depths, depending on what their depths physically contain. The ice sheet's subterraneous qualities render it a scientifically valuable location – all the way down, so to speak. In the following section I consider how the icy properties I have discussed harbour material potentials that are both engaged and abbreviated in the production of the GISP2 ice core.

Naming, locating and producing 'GISP2'

> The Summit region has proven to be an ideal site from which to recover deep ice cores. The mean annual C air temperature at Summit and minimal occurrence of melt layers throughout the record assure the *in situ* preservation of a broad range of gaseous, soluble and insoluble measures of the paleoenvironment. The C ice temperature measured at the base of the two cores assures that the ice sheet in this region is frozen to its bed. This, in combination with only gently sloping local bedrock topography and surface siting close to the current ice divide, minimises the possibility, throughout most of the thickness of the ice sheet in this region, of any ice flow deformation ... that would disrupt the original depositional order of the record.[15]

Long before GISP2 technicians began to drill the 'deepest ice core thus far recovered in the world', teams of researchers and scientists were calculating where the extraction site might best – scientifically speaking – be located. Data sets were mined, cross-referenced and synthesised, to determine exactly which conceptual 5.2-inch vertical column of Greenland's ice sheet would be named 'GISP2' and drilled into a physically discrete entity. Discovering (locating and naming) the extraction site introduced novel conceptual boundaries and physical torsions to what, for hundreds of thousands of years, had been one massive, morphic body of ice. To invoke a well-known scientific lament: as soon as something is measured it has been altered, and in this case, numerical calculations conceptually converted a massive ice sheet into potential discrete fragments of itself. Prior to GISP2's extraction, then, Greenland's ice sheet had already been altered: 72° 36' N, 38° 30' W was now a discrete place – a unique and distinguishable site where multitudes of goods, people, and tools were to arrive, make camp, and bore into the ice. Interestingly, through the physical torsion of coring, an imagined sense of this site as 'historically locatable' emerges: bringing long-buried ice to the surface incites queries about what was going on 'there', for instance, 200,000 years ago. Geographically speaking, however, there was no 'there' there then; GISP2 ice formed over various locations, having flowed into that specific spot in temporally staggered succession. In short, the ice sheet forms as one enormous, internally mobile entity.

To further consider the ice sheet's plasticity, I suggest a geographic thought experiment that traces trails (or flow-routes) of GISP2 ice crystals and other particulate substances. If such complex configurations could be mapped, the sheet's molecular architecture would be revealed as an ornate set of overlapping, patterned movements, which point to the fact that the ice's 'place' of origin is truly manifold. By 'place of origin' I mean to specify that different ice strata originally landed over various geographic coordinates on the Greenlandic bedrock; not, as discussed above, that particles in the ice originated from different geographic locations around the globe. Vertical cross-sections of the ice sheet would show that the ice's stratified flow architecture is staggered: because the whole ice-body receives snow and flows seaward (down and out), its structure along any given vertical plane will evidence ice that has moved through other vertical planes. Deeper (older) ice is more geographically saturated in this respect – it has moved over more of Greenland's bedrock (note that individual annual layers do not move independently; their crawl seaward is viscous, cumulative, and regional in nature). In light of such depositional flow, GISP2's vertical, 5.2-inch columnar shape emerges as a structure that works against some of the ice sheet's compositional features. Joseph Rouse's view of 'authoritatively binding natural modalities' is germane to the observation that vertical coring efforts are not always congruent with internal ice sheet complexities.

> One might say in retrospect that human beings have always been natural beings causally subject to the opportunities and constraints of belonging to nature. Naturalism, however, is a commitment to the intelligibility and thereby the *authority* of whatever necessities and possibilities nature affords. Scientific practices are where such natural modalities must show themselves as authoritatively binding.[16]

I am particularly interested in Rouse's notion of nature's 'intelligibility'. I suggest that readable (or intelligible) aspects of ice cores are 'the authoritatively binding' ways of knowing, which result in material disruptions and intrusions of other ice-sheet attributes, like horizontal mobility and flow patterns. The latter clearly exemplify ice-sheet attributes

Figure 5.1 The large geodesic dome that housed GISP2's twenty-metre-long drill (video still from *Core Matters, or GISP2 Chronologies*, courtesy of Heather Frazar, 2005).

that are hypothetically intelligible but are not intra-active in the coring process (in other words, there are many intelligible things about ice – some of them are intra-active in the coring process and some of them are not). Which is not to say that the sheet's mobility is therefore unintelligible or even partially ignored by scientists – it isn't – but that that the horizontal motion of ice is not one of the ice-sheet architectures that shape GISP2 as an object of scientific practice.

Obviously there are many scientifically significant ways in which the ice sheet's structure is congruent with the core's architecture. As the quotation that opens this section indicates, the sheet's summit, its highest place, holds the 'best' ice for the enterprise of coring:

> only gently sloping local bedrock topography and surface siting close to the current ice divide, minimises the possibility, throughout most of the thickness of the ice sheet in this region, of any ice flow deformation ... that would disrupt the original depositional order of the record.[17]

Indeed, central to the core's value is the fact that strata in the upper 2,790 metres have remained true to their original depositional order.

> [There] is compelling evidence that the stratigraphy of the ice is reliable and unaffected by extensive folding, intrusion, or hiatuses from the surface to 2,790m (110,000 years ago).[18]

Each layer is internally consistent, meaning that particles deposited during specific annual cycles are understood to be absent in other strata. At the time of its extraction, GISP2 provided the best continuous sequence of annual layers scientists had ever seen.[19] Another vertically congruent aspect is top-to-bottom temperature variations. The ice sheet's coldest point is approximately a mile beneath the surface and a mile above bedrock, which means that mid-ice-sheet is the coldest portion. Warmer temperatures at the surface, and geothermal heat from the bedrock keep ice in the top and bottom layers of the ice sheet warmer than the midsection. Surface-to-bedrock temperature gradations therefore parallel the core.[20] These and other icy material aspects intelligible in the context of a 5.2-inch-diameter core, are what bolstered the impressive scientific endeavour of turning a specific vertical cylinder of Greenland's ice sheet into two miles of core.

Once 72° 36' N, 38° 30' W was conceptually and physically reached, GISP2 took some time to core:

> The GISP2 core was drilled over five summers, during which about 50 scientists, drillers, and camp staff have lived atop the flat, white expanse of the ice sheet, extracting and processing lengths of core.[21]

GISP2's drill tower significantly exceeded the ceiling height of the large geodesic dome that housed its twenty-metre-long drill [Fig. 5.1]. This drill consisted of a specialised drill head, a core barrel, chip catcher, motor, instrument package, and anti-torque knives – all suspended from 4,000 metres of cable. The drill was lowered to the bottom of the borehole where two to six metre sections of core were drilled, broken off at the base, and winched to the surface. Core sections were retrieved from great depths and pressures that were relayed (along with other information such as temperature, the drill's angle and power consumption) to technicians at the surface. This information was vital to the core's scientific viability. Before being handled, core segments required time to 'relax' – this was necessary owing to surface-to-bedrock pressure differentials. Deep in the ice sheet, air bubbles are highly pressurised; when brought to the surface, 'un-relaxed' air could potentially burst the ice if segments were not handled with care.

Under ice: GISP2 in the science trench

After relaxing, core sections were delivered to the 'science trench' – a large room cut into the snow where processing and analysis takes place. [Figs 5.2, 5.3 and 5.4]

> One of the difficulties of GISP2 was figuring out how to analyse the ice ... it was decided to build a lab in the ice sheet, and do the work there. This was not nearly as easy as it sounds. ... The entire processing line was placed in a trench that had been

Figure 5.2 Under Greenland's ice sheet: stairs leading down to the 'science trench', a large room cut into the snow for processing and analysis (video still from *Core Matters, or GISP2 Chronologies*, courtesy of Heather Frazar, 2005).

> cut twenty feet into the snow using a giant snow-blower, and then roofed with beams and boards. ... The roof of the trench was slowly squashed toward the floor by the weight of snow piling up, but the design served admirably throughout the project and remained accessible for a few years afterward.[22]

Core sections were then passed through a core processing line: a series of stations where core is sampled, packaged and labelled for shipment. One of the biggest concerns at the extraction site and in the trench was keeping the core segments clean. Because compound concentrations can be extremely low, samples could easily become contaminated; researchers thus wore 'clean suits' in the trench, to lessen the likelihood of introducing potential contaminants to the storage environment. Throughout this process, it was critical to preserve cores' proper surface-to-bedrock orientation. Thick black arrows – written directly on the first layer of clear-plastic packaging – indicate directionality [Fig. 5.5]. If an arrow-direction is missing, determining which end is up is impossible. Because this plastic is sometimes removed for sampling purposes, keeping track of the core's orientation was another central concern during sampling and packaging procedures.

In situ, the Greenland ice sheet has been its own unfailing curatorial custodian for the past 200,000 years; removed from their places of origin, however, ice cores are utterly fragile objects. The segments' physical vulnerabilities – from unstable air pockets to contamination

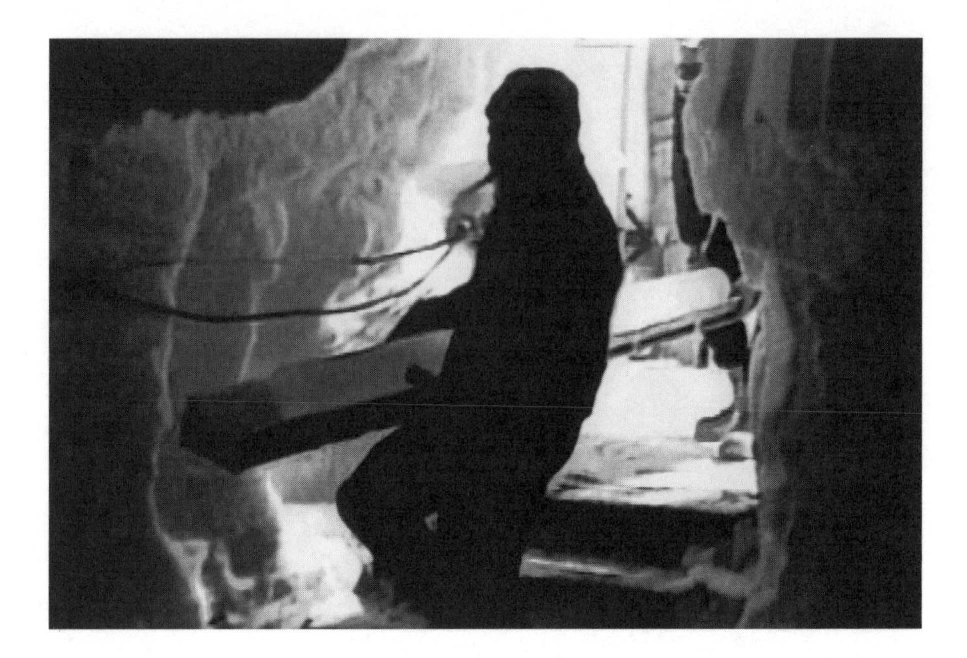

Figure 5.3 In the science trench, an ice core is moved by hand to the next station in the core processing line (a series of stations where the core is sampled, packaged and labelled for shipment) (video still from *Core Matters, or GISP2 Chronologies*, courtesy of Heather Frazar, 2005).

and possible labelling errors – demonstrate that the coring effort was a raw material intervention. The once-solid ice sheet had been drilled into exposed, delicate cylinders. Interestingly, these dual characteristics of ice (stability and vulnerability) functioned symbiotically in the GISP2 science trench, where Greenlandic ice functioned both as the protector and as that which was being protected. This emphasises that what researchers brought to the GISP2 extraction site both transformed and was transformed by the ice sheet's own structural and chemical complexities. Once fully processed (labelled, sampled and packaged) in the trench, core segments were ready to begin the long journey from Greenland to the National Ice Core Laboratory (NICL) in Denver, Colorado.[23]

Denver: GISP2 at the NICL

> The NICL is a physical plant for storing, curating and studying cores of ice taken from polar and other glaciers around the world. These cores represent a long-term, unbroken record of material deposited by the earth's atmosphere. The Lab provides scientists with the capability to conduct examinations of ice cores without having to

Figure 5.4 Ice cores (at rear of image) are lowered into the science trench for sampling, packaging and storage until they are shipped to the NICL (video still from *Core Matters, or GISP2 Chronologies*, courtesy of Heather Frazar, 2005).

> travel to field sites. ... The facility houses the world's most comprehensive ice-core collection available to the scientific community. NICL is a joint program funded by the US Geological Survey (USGS) and the National Science Foundation (NSF).[24]

GISP2 is presently stored inside the Denver Federal Center complex at the NICL, where it is archived amidst (literally) tons of other ice cores. Measuring 8,000 square feet, this facility stores over 16,000 metres of ice, extracted from 86 different global boreholes. Walking down the aisles of the NICL's main ice-core storage room is not unlike walking down the aisles of a large university library. Most libraries of course do not maintain a constant temperature of –35 °C, and unlike the NICL's collection, a certain percentage of circulating university library books are replaceable. By contrast, none of the NICL's holdings can be replaced; ice cores are singular, and if they melt they are, so to speak, history. In this sense the NICL's archive is more akin to a museum than to a library. Yet the NICL is first and foremost an active scientific research facility, which means that the materials it houses are regularly cut open and portioned out for research. In other words, protecting ice cores does not necessarily mean preserving them intact forever. Unlike facilities where material investigations are performed mainly to aid in the preservation and restoration of those materials (such as natural history, art and archaeology museums), the material analyses that go on at the NICL

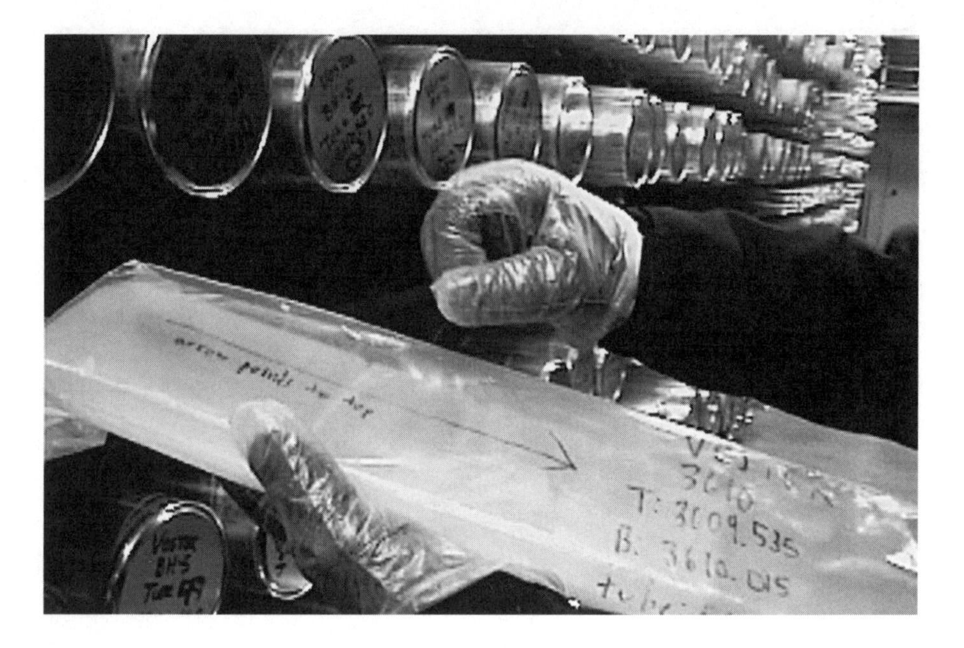

Figure 5.5 A NICL ice core segment, packaged in plastic and inscribed with orientation and depth indicators (video still from *Core Matters, or GISP2 Chronologies*, courtesy of Heather Frazar, 2005).

sometimes involve the intentional dissolution of the very materials it exists to protect. Thus, for all the significant aesthetic and organisational likenesses the NICL bears to other archival/archiving institutions, it has unique material concerns that must be dealt with in scientifically viable ways.

The second part of this chapter focuses on the curatorial processes that core segments undergo upon arrival at the NICL, the ways in which segments are archived and accessed by researchers, and how data are extracted and recorded. Following these observations is an examination of the logistical aspects involved in shipping GISP2 core segments from the NICL to other national and international research laboratories, which highlights the geographically provocative elements of these multi-sited, ice-core deployments. Focussing on the practical aspects involved in transporting, protecting, and analysing the core calls attention to how core- and lab-based materials function intra-actively to shape GISP2-related scientific practices and knowledge.

The NICL's freezing archive: GISP2 accession and stepping into the cold

Upon arrival at the NICL, ice-core shipments have often been in transit (by way of land, sea and air) for months. Shipments from Antarctica, for instance, may take three or more months to reach the NICL. When loads of ice arrive in the US (either at airports or shipyards) the last leg of the journey is usually completed by semi-trailer. Standard NICL procedure requires that extra (empty) air-controlled vehicles accompany all loaded trucks in case unexpected mechanical issues threaten a shipment's successful, i.e. unmelted, transfer. Once the icy cargo boxes have arrived at the NICL's loading dock, the curators' central concerns revolve around keeping the ice cores cold and locatable. These concerns are first addressed by transferring the shipments out of the trailers (temperature controlled to –20 °C), directly into the –35 °C storage freezer. Once unloaded, the processes of ice-core 'accession' begin: accession refers to all steps involved in receiving and properly archiving ice cores once they have arrived at the NICL. Before being shipped from the extraction site, every container and all container contents will have been tagged with 'transit coordinate numbers' (TCNs), which are entered directly into the NICL database upon arrival. There are no intermediary steps in this data-entry procedure; when shipments are unloaded into the freezer, technicians with electronic clipboards check the contents of each shipment against a TCN checklist that travels with the shipment, and has been updated at every transfer juncture along the route. The next step is to record each cargo container's 'temperature logger', a device that continuously monitors containers' internal temperatures for the shipment's duration. The need for high levels of accession accuracy becomes clear when one imagines successfully receiving nearly two miles of GISP2 ice (keeping each three-foot section in proper alignment) in staggered succession, over a period of five years.

Once they are safely deposited into the freezer, and entered into the database, core segments are lifted by hand out of their containers and placed on NICL storage shelves. Shipments can weigh up to 20 tons, and transferring the segments by hand is still the only way cores are moved inside the NICL; apparently this remains the most reliable mode of handling the metallic-silver cylindrical containers in which the core segments are packaged. A recent (not yet fully implemented) addition to the NICL's accession checklist is a high-resolution digital imaging system that will potentially scan every inch of ice that enters the NICL. This imaging process will significantly increase the handling hours dedicated to processing new core shipments before they are deemed 'fully' archived (see page 77 for the discussion of this process). After all processing tasks have been completed, core segments are delivered to their newly assigned shelf designations, each sample in-between lengths of core that at one time preceded and followed them in vertical depth.

At first sight the main storage freezer appears like an archivist's dream. Towering rows upon rows of silver cylinders – brightly lit, perfectly spaced, and labelled with tiny black digits – sit uniformly in an otherwise profoundly stark environment [Figs 5.6, 5.7 and 5.8]. There are no visual signs of the Greenlandic ice sheet.[25] Upon entering the freezer, an

Figure 5.6 GISP2 ice core segments – packaged, labeled, archived, and awaiting researchers in the -35 °c main freezer at the NICL (video still from *Core Matters, or GISP2 Chronologies*, courtesy of Heather Frazar, 2005).

aesthetic austerity greets you no less harshly than does the wall of –35 °C air into which you have just stepped. Exhale is immediately white, eyelashes (or any exposed hair) begin to collect frost, and one's cheeks and inhalation burn slightly. Because cold suits are required attire in the freezer, one does not feel the cold bodily until ten or so minutes in, when face and limbs begin to stiffen. Contrary to popular belief, cold is not pumped into freezers; heat is taken out. I was informed of this fact by the refrigeration system's head technician with whom I had conducted an interview previous to entering the freezer. So rather than my experience in the freezer being cold *per se*, I was aware, instead, of an immense lack of heat. As this unwavering environment begins to relieve visitors of their heat, they are reminded of the brute fact that this environment was developed for ice and not for human beings. If the ice–human hierarchy is not already clear (especially as one's lungs begin to sting with cold), the warehouse-sized room also presents visitors with visual denial at every turn – you cannot see a single square inch of the miles of ice around you.

This massive freezer is a storage space; no research is, or can be, carried out there because it is simply too cold. For example, electrical wires (wires in general) freeze stiff in this environment. Also, for obvious reasons, no NICL staff or visitors are (legally) allowed in

Figure 5.7 Rows and rows of GISP2 cylinders stored in the profoundly stark environment of the NICL's warehouse-sized freezer (video still from *Core Matters, or GISP2 Chronologies*, courtesy of Heather Frazar, 2005).

the freezer alone. There are two 'warmer' rooms in which scientists and NICL curators perform imaging procedures and ice-core research (described below); these rooms are kept at a cool –25 °C. All three rooms atmospherically assert that the physical properties of ice not only dictate environmentally binding terms, but the NICL's very existence. The ice's temperature requirements are strictures that necessitate the NICL's existence and shape a large majority of the technical and resource-consuming processes that go on there. As discussed in the next section these and other icy strictures inform how researchers approach GISP2 at the NICL.

High-resolution core: imaging and analysis at the NICL

> Why should we be concerned with the nitty-gritty of laboratory practices? Because the architecture, social structure, and cultural siting of laboratories matters; it matters to the character of the science produced, it matters to the shifting definition of what counts as experimentation and who counts as an experimenter.[26]

Figure 5.8 The NICL's freezing archive is often likened to a museum or a library (video still from *Core Matters, or GISP2 Chronologies*, courtesy of Heather Frazar, 2005).

The implementation of a digital imaging system has been a top priority at the NICL because, owing to extensive research on specific strata, portions of the core are dwindling in size. And as more core is requested for research, even small fragments of certain sections will one day no longer exist. High-resolution images[27] will then be scientists' sole access to certain sections of GISP2. Interestingly, when an image becomes the best version of a core segment available, the NICL becomes an archival institution in the more traditional sense described earlier; one responsible for the 'timeless' preservation of a digital archive. To produce this digital image archive, each core segment must be stripped of its packaging and sent through a precision table-saw: a vertical (length-wise) centimetre is removed, creating a clear 'window' through which annual strata can be clearly scanned. The windowed core segment is then placed in a fitted tray that lights the core from above and below, and is driven at controlled speeds underneath a mounted digital camera. This camera is connected to a computer monitor and software program that processes and stores incoming visual data. The core is then re-packaged and deemed fully archived under the new NICL (image-archive) guidelines.

As mentioned above, this image-archiving process demands considerably more physical effort at the input end of an ice core's life in the NICL archive. I emphasise this increase in the NICL curators' archival (non-research-based) interactions with core segments particularly because it can mean the inverse for researchers' ice-core interactions later on.

Digitally imaging the core will in some cases allow scientists to derive data from a two-dimensional version of the core rather than physically examining it. A core's visual stratigraphy, for instance, can be investigated using high-resolution images of annual strata. And two-dimensional images – whether they appear on monitors or in print – are obviously very different scientific items than are physical portions of the Greenlandic ice sheet. Such information can be accessed online. This option significantly lightens certain responsibilities for the NICL in that researchers who would otherwise request portions of the core to be sent to their labs, or who would travel to the NICL directly, are now able to do some forms of their research online.[28] Temperately-environed computer screens and sheets of photo paper upon which GISP2's image can be examined, demand vastly different research environments than do physical core segments which, at the very least, necessitate researchers' physical presences in freezing laboratories.

Given potential perspectival problems with single-angle views of the core, it is generally agreed (for visual stratigraphy as well as other research) that viewing the 'real thing' is always a researcher's best option. Sometimes, however, even the core itself provides questionable material views of certain strata, necessitating that researchers seek out correlative strata in the other Greenlandic ice cores for comparison.[29] This investigative progression – from illegible details in an image of GISP2, to 'truthing' (in the sense of ground-truthing) the imaged details against the actual core, to the final option of comparing two physical cores – speaks to larger issues associated with the layers of investigative removal researchers find between themselves and the Greenlandic ice sheet. I trace the layers of removal back to the ice sheet itself because it is the entirety to which all (the relatively tiny) core samples metonymically refer. When researchers mention 'strata' they are actually referring to a layer of snow and atmospheric fallout the size of the Greenlandic ice sheet. The core shape itself is a massive reduction (in more ways than one) of the body it samples. This is why it is better understood when compared with other Greenlandic cores, and is also why researchers viewing images of GISP2 represent several tiers of investigative removal. Rouse states that, 'We are accountable to what is at stake in our belonging (causally and normatively) to the material-discursive world,'[30] and in order to be accountable as such he asserts that, 'scientific laboratories, and other experimental, observational or even theoretical equipment should be recognised as aspects of prosthetically embodied agency.'[31] These statements suggest that scientists must be accountable for where, and by what physical means, they carry out their research.

One might argue that most procedures carried out at the NICL depend on visual aspects of two-dimensional data just as much as researchers in front of computer screens in temperate environments. And there is, no doubt, a heavy reliance on visual aspects in carrying out matter-based scientific procedures (like drilling, taking vertical cross-sections or obtaining melt-water for particle analyses, etcetera). In such cases, however, vision is not the central data-extraction tool. Cored ice must be cut in ways that maintain its structural and scientific integrity, and vision is but one of the tools required to successfully manipulate core segments to desired ends. In these situations vision is a sense-tool that aids in ice-core dissection while also monitoring and responding to its materiality. In sum, vision is one of many 'embodied agencies' that function in tandem to extract ice-core data from physical ice cores. And as is true in a wide array of scientific circumstances, vision can be a restrictive variable as well. What looks like two or three individual strata might in fact be one year's deposition with anomalously dark banding owing to smoke released by a massive forest fire. This anomaly can be detected through electrical conductivity tests that are sensitive to the presence of seasonally regular acid-level variations in the core. As discussed further on, research tools that aid researchers' capacities in one arena typically afford sets of constraints in others.

Other physical aspects affecting researcher agency are related to the ways in which scientists are bodily and environmentally restricted during ice-core analyses. When entering the exam room or freezer for any sustained period of time, researchers and NICL curators 'suit up'. This normally entails covering one's body in a full-length thermal jumpsuit, warm boots, thick gloves, a hat and some form of face covering. In short, one's body is cloaked from head to toe in thick, warm materials. Even ergonomically-designed protective gear is physically restrictive.[32] For example, warm hands are often traded for dexterity, as gloves are temporarily removed for detailed tasks. So while their protection from the cold affords scientists the freedom to examine ice for longer periods of time, it also contributes to unique sets of practical challenges.

The two spaces most frequented by researchers at the NICL are the 'clean room' and a free-standing 'dark room' where black curtains are draped around an ice-core viewing unit. Both spaces are intentionally small for practical, environmental reasons. Inside the clean room air is continuously filtered to reduce ambient contaminants. This room is kept at –25 °C and is used for analysing environmentally-sensitive samples such as the chemistry of ice-core air bubbles. In this environment, researchers wear 'clean suits' and thin plastic gloves over their warm layers to prevent samples from being contaminated. Notably, as ice samples become more exposed during research, the scientists investigating them must take strict measures to ensure they are less exposed. The less exposure a sample has to other materials, the better a research context it is; the clean room is thus physically diminutive most simply because it is easier to maintain contamination-free levels in smaller areas. An even more compact research area is known as the dark room: a black-curtained space in which an ice-core viewing unit is located, with just enough room for two people to stand directly in front of a well-illumined ice core. In this light-controlled environment specific wavelengths of light (ultraviolet or red, for example) are cast through core segments to reveal molecular aspects of their annual strata.

In sum, the NICL's materially responsive environments reveal that ice-core research is informed as much by researchers' actions and abilities as by their obligations to ice-core composition. Such obligations cannot be separated from practising productive forms of ice-core research. This mutual dependency between researchers and the ice they investigate reveals GISP2 research as a series of methodologically intra-active endeavours.

The NICL *as 'lending library':* GISP2 *in circulation and 'party ice'*

There are two reasons why accessed – or, archived – ice core segments leave the NICL. The most common reason is that researchers request specific portions for analyses at their home research institutions. Part of the NICL's purpose is to make cores available to outside institutions, and it is also their responsibility to ensure that the ice is safely returned. Some ice, however, leaves the facility permanently. Small pieces of individual segments can be researched in ways that compromise their scientific value, which means of course that those portions are not returnable. This is usually understood given the context of the research, and is made clear before segments leave the NICL. Yet evidently not enough ice leaves the NICL permanently: an increasing burden is that the NICL's main storage freezer is, 'about one-hundred-and-three per cent full'. This statement was made by John Rhoades, the NICL's Assistant Curator, who, during an interview in 2003, explained that curators are dealing with over-capacity in two ways: one is to install high-density shelving units that will allow more core segments to be stored per cubic foot in the freezer, and the other is simply to get rid of some of the ice. The latter results in what is called 'de-accessed' ice. Ice thus leaves the NICL for two very different reasons: either because it is currently valuable for research, or because it has become so devalued that the NICL cannot afford to keep it on the shelf.

In both cases, however, ice cores continue to circulate. From a geographical perspective, the transported and transportable material aspects of NICL ice cores are complex. The thousands of carefully packaged and marked containers at the NICL hold material representations of places as globally polarised as Greenland, Siberia, Africa, and Antarctica. It is difficult to grasp the geographical array one steps into when entering the NICL's main freezer. This is compounded by the fact that, as discussed above, the ice cores themselves contain myriad matter-based geographies. Inside each columnar tube rests a core that, in and of itself, may hold atmospherically transported Saharan dust, tropical methane, and pollen spores from different geographic locations. That this geographically complex collection of ice also regularly circulates to other national and international research institutions with the goal of producing information (stories) about historic atmospheres adds further layers to GISP2's mobile geographies. Yet do these geographically complex layers indicate deeper levels of geographic obfuscation? Or do such interwoven sets of geographic movements and matters reveal a scientific and archival system that is entirely in keeping with ice cores' inherently (structural, scientific, geographical) global reaches? I argue the latter.

By circulating the cores themselves to diverse national and international ice-core research sites, the detailed undertaking of sorting through cycles of atmospherically-circulated global stuffs is itself geographically diversified. This means that GISP2 research comes out of different physical sites of production. It is beyond the aim of this study to outline how other scientific practices specifically diverge from those at the NICL, but my general point about the diversification of GISP2 research is meant to point to the potentially productive aspects of such ice-core dispersal. If, as I suggest above, ice cores themselves have particular sets of constraints and possibilities that researchers and research institutions must meet, they will be met in fundamentally different ways in different places. I am not suggesting that location-specific potentials are always productive; a contaminated 'ancient atmosphere' sample is a lost set of valuable data, and without a sufficiently clean 'clean room', attempting to extract atmospheric ice core data will simply result in wasted core. Yet if scientists research ice cores via standardised actions confined to laboratories with the same lay-outs, temperature regulations, clean rooms, and tool-capacities, those points of scientific juncture with the ice would also remain standardised, and this would result in a significantly less dynamic arena of global ice-core research. That ice-core research varies from place to place is a well-understood fact amidst those who practices it. The fact that cores are dealt with in different ways in different places is the topic of many scientific discussions that centre on archival and research-related laboratory procedures. The following excerpt appeared in an 'InterICE' conference summary written by the NICL's Technical Director, Todd Hinkley:

> Representatives of twelve countries gathered in Milan, Italy, for InterICE, a first meeting of 'international ice core establishments', to compare and discuss ideas about best practices for acquisition, storage, curation, and distribution of the ice cores that have been drilled from the polar and temperate glaciers of the world.[33]

Two NICL conference attendees reported that the initial aim of InterICE was to produce a list of 'best procedures' for the curation of ice cores; yet they found that a 'best procedures' model was not nearly as productive or informative as was simply taking notes on each country's standard ice-core procedures. Given the fact that ice-core storage facilities vary so greatly (in some locations in India and Pakistan, for instance, cores are stored in large restaurant freezers), this latter alternative seems an obvious one. However, it took assembling international ice-core technicians, curators and scientists to recognise that certain procedures are 'best' depending on where you are, and what means you have to conduct curation and research there.

David Livingstone asserts, 'Cultivating a geography of science will disclose how scientific knowledge bears the imprint of its location.'[34] I agree, but would emphasise the addition of a third important aspect to Livingstone's two-fold equation between scientific knowledge and place: that is the object of scientific inquiry itself. As I have discussed specifically in the case of ice, the object of inquiry can be both an imprinting and imprinted element in this three-fold scientific equation. It makes material demands on, and shapes how scientists are able or unable to access its holdings. Thus as long as GISP2 is scientifically valuable enough to be requested for research outside the NICL, GISP2 research will continue to have equally dynamic, site-specific potentials.

At the other end of the NICL value spectrum is ice that is permanently removed from the facility. Ice is determined 'de-accessible' by the collective opinion of several research bodies who fund the NICL, namely the U.S. Geological Survey (USGS), the National Science Foundation (NSF) and the University of New Hampshire. Once the cores are deemed no longer part of the NICL archive, next there exists the problem of what to do with the devalued ice. A joke around the facility is that previously archived cores suddenly, at the wave of certain authoritative hands, become 'party ice'. This so-called party ice is brought out for visitor demonstrations and visits from broadcast institutions like the BBC, who want a 'good show' in the exam rooms. De-accessed ice is also advertised on ice core research websites as available for educational purposes. When asked if ice is ever simply left to melt under the Colorado sun in the NICL parking lot, no one could give me a straight answer. I am left with the assumption that de-accessed ice is either used for impressive display at the NICL or re-cycled into other information-bearing institutions, where it circulates amidst diverse economies of scientific value.

Conclusion – 'participatory' core matters

This study proposes that scientific outcomes are produced by collective, non-hierarchical intra-actions of researchers, their laboratories, their methods of research and the objects they study. This proposition reinforces the belief that scientific knowledge about the physical world should not be dissociated from the material conditions leading to that knowledge. While tracing how atmospheric fallout is captured in icy strata over the Greenlandic bedrock and then re-captured by researchers who analyse it in controlled scientific environments highlights productive aspects of GISP2 research, it does not provide any definitive answers to questions social scientists raise about intra-active production(s) of scientific knowledge. Yet obtaining answers is not my aim; the goal, rather, has been to reconnect the core's data-based stories[35] with their material underpinnings.

Furthermore, rather than aiming to dissect the scientific practices that make ice core research possible – so as to expose them as vulnerable or debilitatingly subjective – connective materialities between researchers and GISP2 ice have been exhibited. In doing so, this study has brought certain geographic and 'postepistemological' concerns into dialogue with actual GISP2 research. Some would argue that it is not the job of those who study science to 'do science' themselves. Yet the work of social scientists can, and should, be scientifically participatory without attempting to be scientifically productive in the conventional sense. In sum, being participatory (rather than retrospective and reactionary) means being situated in tandem with scientific work, rather than taking contrary positions amidst its fields of activity and production.

High Altitudes

6

Mountains: Between Pure Reason and Embodied Experience

Philippe Buache and Alexander von Humboldt

Bernard Debarbieux

On 15 November 1752, Philippe Buache, a qualified mathematician and architect, and deputy geographer to the Académie Royale des Sciences since 1730,[1] presented a paper to the academy entitled: 'Essai de géographie physique, où l'on propose des vues générales sur l'espèce de Charpente du Globe, composée des Chaînes de Montagnes qui traversent les Mers comme les Terres, avec quelques considérations particulières sur les différents Bassins de la Mer, et sur sa configuration intérieure' ('Essay in physical geography proposing general perspectives on the structure of the globe, which is made up of mountain ranges crossing the oceans and lands, with some particular considerations regarding the different sea basins and the internal configuration of the sea').[2] The title is grandiose, as was the paper's ambition: to propose a new theory regarding the position of all oceans, mountains, islands and rivers on a world scale. Buache's theory was as follows: the Earth is marked by chains of mountains which join together from one end of the continents to the other. These mountain ranges divide immense 'river basins', which then open into three large 'seas'; which he calls the Ocean (the Atlantic), the Sea of the Indies (the Indian Ocean) and the Great Sea (the Pacific Ocean). Each of these large seas is divided into maritime basins – always three per ocean – which are separated from each other by 'marine' mountain ranges. These marine mountain ranges are consistently the underwater

Figure 6.1 'Carte physique de l'Océan', in Buache, *Cartes et tables de la géographie physique ou naturelle, présentées au roi le 15 mai 1757*, quay de l'Horloge, Paris, 1754 (courtesy of Bibliothèque Nationale de France, Département de la reproduction, Paris).

extensions of the terrestrial mountain ranges, invisible to the observer except where they graze or rise above the surface of the seas in the form of 'islands, reefs or shoals' [Fig. 6.1].

When applied to South America, this ordering principle assumes the existence of several major mountain ranges: those for which Buache already possessed several descriptions, such as the Andes; and those which were deduced from his theory and according to him lay between the Orinoco, the Amazon and the River Plate basins, and between Brazil and Guinea toward the Fernando de Noronha islands [Fig. 6.2]. In truth Buache didn't invent the range which separates the Orinoco and Amazon basins; it had already been suggested on several previous maps, notably by Hondius (1606 and 1630) and Fritz (1690). However, the accounts of the American Indians brought back by seventeenth- and eighteenth-century explorers and cartographers, such as Sanson (1656) and, later, La Cruz (1776) led some to believe that such a mountain range did not exist; the two basins were being said to communicate via one or several watercourses used by the local people and their small crafts. But Buache

Figure 6.2 'Carte physique de l'Ocean' (detail), in Buache, *Cartes et tables de la géographie physique ou naturelle, présentées au roi le 15 mai 1757*, quay de l'Horloge, Paris, 1754 (courtesy of Bibliothèque de Genève, J-M Meylan, Genève).

didn't take these accounts seriously, arguing that the natives were accustomed to carrying their light canoes over short distances to pass from one watercourse to another.

Moreover, in his planispheres, just as in his maps of Guiana commissioned by the colony's Governor, Philippe Buache shows a mountain range between Orinoco and Rio Negro as great as the watercourses it separates. In a note attached to this map, he writes that 'the communication which is supposed to exist between the Orinoco and the Amazon is a geographical monstrosity which la Cruz's map has groundlessly propagated and in order to correct this matter one need only recognise the direction of the great range which divides the waters.'[3]

On 20 May 1800, Alexander von Humboldt and Aimé Bonpland feigned to take up Buache's invitation. They had left Corunna several months earlier for the four-year expedition that would take them across the north of South America.[4] They arrived on the continent at the port of Cumana on the Caribbean coast. From there, they organised their first expedition of nine months covering the eastern part of Nueva Granada. In mid-May 1800, they spent ten days following the Cassiquiare, a tributary of the Rio Negro, and, without setting foot on land, arrived at the Orinoco, which empties most of its waters into the Caribbean. They proved in this way that the Orinoco and Amazon basins do communicate via this curious watercourse, an imposing bifurcation in the river from one basin to the other. In truth, Humboldt had been sure of this tributary's existence even before leaving Cumana; his own research and his local informants had convinced him that this communication did in fact exist:

> For half a century, no one has doubted the communication which exists between these two great river systems. The main objective of our navigation was therefore only to establish by way of the stars the point where it enters the Rio Negro and its junction with the Orinoco'.[5]

However, he was well aware that he was dealing with a curious geographical phenomenon worthy of being confirmed and observed: 'a phenomenon which seems so bizarre that I went on location to check for myself (and which) calls for special attention.[6]

The coordinates taken from his observation ('3° 10' north latitude and 68° 37' west of the Paris meridian line longitude') served as proof and facilitated verification at a later date. As for Humboldt's actual observations, which were recorded in abundant notes and cited in several later publications, these were instrumental to a general school of thought on the locations of mountains and the best method to adopt in order to determine their location. Humboldt makes an ironic reference to Philippe Buache's theory: 'I was fairly pleased to recognise this mountain range (guessed at by Buache) once on location. During the night I passed through the part of the Orinoco in my dugout where Mr. Buache hypothesised that the river bed was broken by a cordillera'.[7] He continues to mock the theories of geographers from the middle of the previous century, 'This bifurcation, which so long mystified geographers when they were making their maps of the Americas'[8] gave him the opportunity to denounce more simplistic lines of thought – 'mountain ranges (in the New World) do not stand up like walls on horizontal planes'[9] – and their Europe-focused visions.

> Accustomed to considering the rivers of Europe only in those parts where their course was enclosed by two crest lines, … we have a great trouble in conceiving of the simultaneous existence of these winding courses, these bifurcations, these river communications of the New World.[10]

He also took the opportunity to criticise an era of geography which had been excessively theoretical and for which field observation had been of little interest. In May 1800, Bonpland and Humboldt definitively concluded a controversy that had raged for over a century.

The Cassiquiare controversy could be treated as merely an anecdote about the confrontation of two opinions and two attitudes concerning an imaginary mountain range. It could also be taken as a symbolic example of a scientific controversy between one person who formulates a theory and another who shakes this theory's very foundation by making a contradictory observation. So be it. Here, however, I want to suggest much more: a confrontation between two ways of conceiving mountains as objects of knowledge and, more particularly, two ways of perceiving natural objects, first as an element in a planetary structure, second as a form born from a particular lay-out of the Earth's materials. When analysed in this way, it is certain that the Cassiquiare controversy opposes two states of knowledge and two different methods for constructing scientific knowledge, but also, and more particularly, two theories of knowledge which each accord quite a different status to mountains, especially with regard to their material nature.

Thoughts and names for mountains in the eighteenth century

In order to establish the gravity of this controversy, one must remember that it uses a term, 'mountain', whose accepted meanings varied greatly at the time when Buache published his *Essai de Géographie Physique*. In the *Encyclopédie* edited by Diderot and d'Alembert, the article on mountains written by d'Holbach gives this definition: 'great masses or inequalities of the Earth which make its surface rough'.[11] But, throughout the volumes and the pages of this encyclopaedia, the term is used to designate not only the 'the Andes cordillera', but also the seven hills upon and around which Rome was built, 'Table Mountain' near Cape Town, as well as the original site of the town of Angoulême, situated on a limestone acropolis between Bordeaux and Poitiers. The volumes from the Académie Royale des Sciences accept a similar diversity of definitions: a *mémoire* published in 1755 was entitled 'Discovery of a Petrified Tree Stump Found in a Mountain in the Étampes Area'.[12] Today we would describe this hillside at best as the rim of a plateau located about thirty kilometres south of Paris. Besides, common usage has appointed the toponym 'Montagne Sainte-Geneviève' to a feature which rises modestly a few metres higher than Notre-Dame de Paris. In a similar vein, French explorers baptised a hill with an altitude of around 200 metres just outside Montreal as a 'mountain', sometimes known as 'Mont Royal'.[13]

When they came to the Alps and the Pyrenees, the travellers of the century were very hesitant as to the terms they should use to describe such an environment. Some speak of mountains to designate the slopes which frame the deepest valleys.[14] Others speak of 'mountains piled one on top of another, in such a way that once you arrive at the summit of one, you find a plain where the foot of another mountain begins.'[15] Lastly, there are those who were fooled by the meaning given to the words 'mount' and 'mountain' by the Alpine residents, which in fact designated high pastures and passes, and who were therefore disappointed upon arrival at Mont Saint Gothard, conceived by Buffon and Buache as the culminating point of the Alps, to find only prairies and summits of secondary altitude.[16]

In Buache and Humboldt's time, the word 'mountain' therefore had several very different significations and, more importantly, it designated realities based on very different environmental practices and conceptions. In everyday speech, it referred to a point of

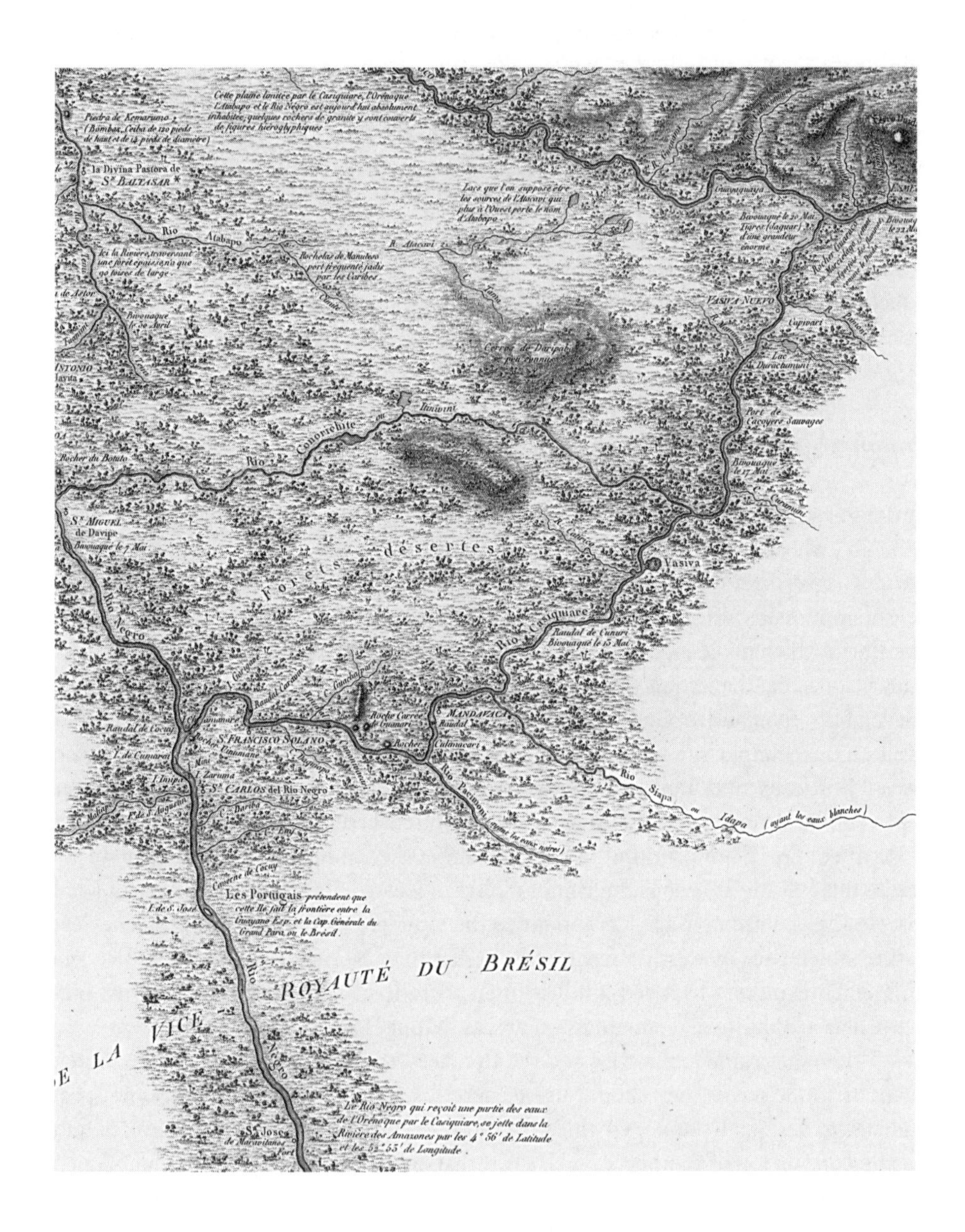

Figure 6.3 'Carte itinéraire du cours de l'Orénoque, de l'Atabapo, du Casiquiare et du Rio Negro … dressée sur les lieux en 1800…' in Humboldt, *Atlas Géographique et Physique des régions équinoxiales du nouveau continent*, Schoell, Paris, 1814 (courtesy of B. Debarbieux).

passage on an itinerary (Saint-Gothard), as well as a place for the cultivation of pastures (the mountains of the Savoie shepherds), and even a modest hill standing out on the horizon (Sainte-Geneviève). In the technical vocabulary, the term designated both forms that were very modest in altitude and gradient (la Montagne d'Étampes), as well as very large series of peaks. It was not until the beginning of the nineteenth century that scientific terminology decided on a relatively homogenous set of meanings and expressions ('mountain massif', 'mountain range') which were relatively stable and shared in common among specialists in different disciplines.[17]

Bearing these conditions in mind, the analysis of the Cassiquiare controversy involves more than questions of disagreements over the facts – is there, or isn't there, a mountain range between the Orinoco and Amazon basins? – one must discover the exact meaning and scientific status of the concept of mountains[18] for both of the authors implicated.

The mountain according to Buache: an element in a system of objects

In the middle of the eighteenth century, a number of Buache's contemporaries recorded their research into the complexity of the configuration of terrestrial forms. In 1749, the Count de Buffon presented his own *Théorie de la Terre* and reported an apparent lack of order: 'this immense globe displays on its surface heights and depths, plains, seas, marshes, rivers, caves, chasms, volcanoes, and upon our first inspection we can see no regularity, no order to it.'[19] Buache's 'Essai de géographie physique' must also be understood as the expression of his desire to find order in this apparent disorder, and to identify some principles by virtue of which natural objects may hold together. The theory of the continuity of mountain ranges rests upon these assumptions. It treated mountains analogically as 'a kind of framework, which [he] envisages as the support for different parts of the terrestrial globe and which is formed of high ranges encompassing and crossing it'.[20] With the continuity of mountain ranges postulated in this way, river basins can be understood as mere surfaces enclosed by the pieces of the framework. As these basins were better identified than mountains in the eighteenth century, Buache's theory allows him to define mountains by way of understanding rivers.

> I thought that ... I had to use the clues left by the rivers. We can't deny that the origins of rivers and streams naturally indicate the height of the terrains where they source their water to nourish and fertilise the lands they cross as they descend from the high places, whether it be by steeper or shallower slopes, until they empty themselves into the sea. Neither can we doubt the liaison and the relationship that mountains have with rivers.[21]

By the same reasoning, maritime 'basins', understood as the extension of river basins, correspond to the areas circumscribed by the underwater mountain ranges, themselves the extension of the terrestrial ranges. Buache's system is therefore first and foremost logical ordering of natural objects in space, objects which are organised into reasonably simple and complementary categories.

The triumph of cartographic order and the disdain for experience

Buache's system thus accords great scientific importance to absolute space. Natural objects explain each other through their respective location on the surface of the Earth. However, if terrestrial space constitutes the system's reference point, it is through the space on the map that Buache construes and expresses the system's intelligibility. Buache was a prolific cartographer, and a specialist who made the map a tool for understanding and reasoning. It was a tool for communication in the sense that Buache expected maps to give an immediate account of the layout of terrestrial forms. In a 1756 planisphere,[22] he adopted a projection centered on the North Pole, something quite rare for his time, which allowed a view of the continents of the northern hemisphere as they close in on one another, their promontories and the ranges that cross them almost touching. In another planisphere, which he made for the Dauphin to whom he taught geography,[23] Buache was one of the first to place America to the east of the Old World so as to reveal more clearly the imagined continuation of mountains between Alaska and Siberia.[24]

The map was also a tool of reasoning in the sense that Buache expected it to show not only the formations that had already been observed by explorers, but also those objects whose existence could be deductively surmised. For this reason, his maps demonstrate not so much the state of knowledge established by the explorers of his time as the product of his own logical reasoning. That reasoning was based on the idea that the proximity of natural objects to each other comes from their mutual determination. The cartographic proximities between mountains and water courses are evidence of the cause and effect relationship which he imagined existed between them: 'It is good to see the liaison between them [mountains and basins] and their mutual dependence. This is what this system shows at the very first glance.'[25] In this attitude Buache was unquestionably a geographer, if we regard eighteenth-century geography, like today's, as a discourse which explains phenomena according to their respective locations.[26]

According to Buache then, maps were an essential mode of expression and reasoning, to the point that their authority exceeded on-site validation of theories and direct experience of natural formations. He himself did not travel; we only know of a few trips linked to his work on the northern half of France. He did of course invite those who lived or worked in the areas about which he spoke to recount their observations, particularly the sailors from whom he claimed to collect observations of shoals.[27] He certainly compiled travel and exploration notes, but these were not collected in a systematic fashion and he was known to reject facts brought back to him if they contradicted his theory. This was the case for the Cassiquiare, as the reliability of the field information was deemed uncertain.

Buache expressed no more interest in questions of mountain geology. His observations only ever concerned topography, never the nature of the rocks revealed at the surface. Neither did he attach great importance to measurement. There were, however, many specialists from the previous century who attempted to measure the gradients and altitudes of mountains, but their estimations were not systematic and varied greatly between specialists. Yet from the middle of the eighteenth century, the methods of measuring things improved radically and the Academy of Sciences' records reveal a growing number of observations and technical refinements. Buache accords them barely any importance at all in his own works. Nonetheless, he himself had occasion to resort to some systematic measurement when it proved essential to his analysis: he carried out depth soundings in the English Channel from which he deduced a map of isobaths.[28] This method allowed him to prove the existence of an underwater 'mountain range' under the Straits of Dover. But although he suggested that such a mapping procedure be adopted for measuring and representing contour lines, he does not seem to have pursued this. In truth, he preferred to deduce altitudes from the slope of rivers.

> I thought one could refer to the knowledge given us by the slopes of several rivers according to several observations of erosion or experiments on their speed, etc. This can lead us to determine the difference between the height of their source and their mouth; as it seems that if one knows the slope of the river courses, one can determine the elevation of the places where they source their water.[29]

However, this proposition does not seem to have been followed up.

The hierarchy of mountains

This attitude does not belie an indifference towards establishing a hierarchy of mountains and their ranges; quite the opposite, such an idea was essential to his system. But his hierarchy is a structural one and is not concerned with mass, volume or altitude. In Buache's system, terrestrial mountain ranges and watercourses are graded into three types according to their position in the ensemble: the 'great mountain ranges' that correspond to the continental back bones. The 'lateral mountains' are primary branches from these and circumscribe the basins and main watercourses, which he proposes to call '*fleuves*'. 'Coastal mountains', themselves branches of the 'lateral mountains', fall into the sea, marking the separation of the 'coastal' river basins.[30] He calls a 'plateau' the area where the major ranges join together at their highest point.

> Terrestrial ranges seem for the most part to extend like rays from certain places which may be the highest on the Earth, and a sort of plateau, formed by mountains as if grouped together and piled one atop the other … I observe that of these plateaus, the most remarkable are approximately in the middle of Asia [Fig. 6.4] and of each of the two parts of America, also that there is at least one very large one in Africa, and two lesser ones in Europe.[31]

In other words, the importance he accorded to watercourses and to mountains had nothing to do with intrinsic features of height or matter, but everything to do with their position in the system. And for this purpose, the map counts for far more than field observation. Therefore, the absence of a high-altitude mountain range in the place where his theory supposed it to be does not constitute a major problem in Buache's eyes; a range, even modest in verticality, remains major within the structure if it separates river basins orientated towards different large seas.

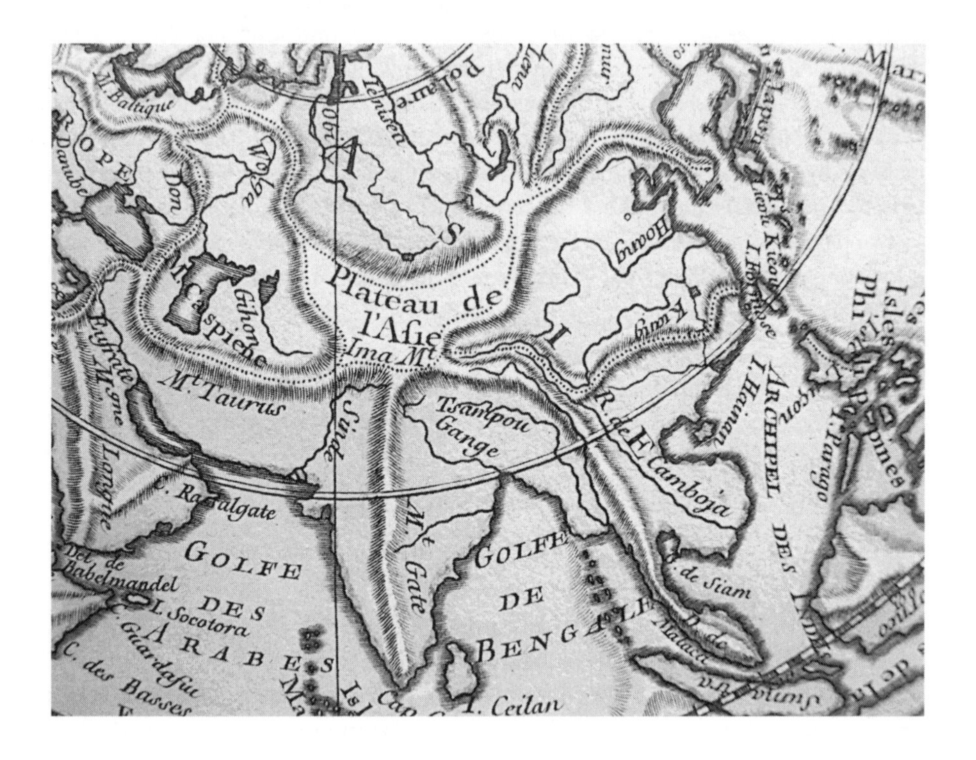

Figure 6.4 'Carte physique de la Mer des Indes' (detail), in Buache, *Cartes et tables de la géographie physique ou naturelle, présentées au roi le 15 mai 1757*, quay de l'Horloge, Paris, 1754 (courtesy of Bibliothèque de Genève, J-M Meylan, Genève).

Reasoning that was modern but whose science is disputable

We could consider Buache and his reasoning pre-modern and link both to theories in vogue throughout previous centuries, such as tenth-century Arab geography[32] and the 'theories of the Earth' from the sixteenth and seventeenth centuries, which, like Buache's, credited empirical observation less than deductively constructed global systems. However, Buache's theory was eminently modern on several levels. Contrary to his predecessors and to some of his contemporaries, Buache imputed absolutely no authority to medieval or ancient knowledge and eliminated any metaphysical or religious speculation: the system he described had no Creator[33] or historical teleology. Buache's method was also modern in his absolute confidence in deductive reasoning: for example, although knowledge of the Antarctic was still extremely tenuous at the time, he formulated a theory on the configuration of this continent from observations of the size of blocks of drifting ice (not yet called icebergs) reported by sailors.[34] Isabelle Laboulais-Lesage has suggested that this way of working, writing and mapping reflects Buache's concern with manipulating the institutional rhetorics of science within the Académie Royale des Sciences, in which geography did not enjoy unanimous recognition.[35]

On the other hand, his system was echoed widely across French and German geography into the nineteenth century, as well as in political philosophy and economics, which advocated the adoption of 'natural borders' to determine the territorial limits of states within Europe and America.[36] This application took little account of mountain geology or the material advantages, minimal as they may have been, of determining limits by way of watersheds. The main advantage of fixing borders along watersheds, according to those who supported the idea, is that it follows the 'order of nature' and has the convenience of easy cartographic representation, being perceptible 'at first glance'; whence it is deduced that borders are difficult to agree indisputably by any other criteria.[37]

Yet, the modernity of Buache's theory was no guarantee of its scientific status. The lack of importance Buache gave to having his theories empirically validated and the scant regard he paid to observations contradicting his system quickly discredited his propositions within scientific circles. Direct experience of those objects for which he had devised a system was not considered a criterion for validating them, an attitude which quickly proved to be at odds with the scientific method dominant during his lifetime. Consequently, even though one can find traces of his influence in a great number of major eighteenth-century scientific documents, he was increasingly the subject of veiled criticisms by naturalists well before Humboldt began to publish. However, it wasn't until Humboldt entered the scene that the break was complete and definitive.

Throughout the second half of the eighteenth century, physical geography texts that first criticised Buache's theory didn't wholly distance themselves from it. The same can be said for the *Encyclopédie*, which nonetheless cites Buache only once.[38] In the entry devoted to 'physical geography', Nicolas Desmarets radically shifted the field and methods of this branch of geography by thoroughly criticising '*géographie de cabinet*' (armchair geography). He advocated a type of geography which was closer to physics and the study of causalities between physical phenomena:

> Nearly all phenomena … are only useful in the relationship they have with other phenomena … The true Philosophy lies in discovering those relationships hidden to near-sightedness and carelessness … We shall gradually rise to more general views, through which we shall grasp several objects at once: we will understand the natural order of facts; we will link phenomena; & we will cover at a single glance a series of analogous observations, which will build effortlessly on one another.[39]

It was also necessary to give precedence to the patient observation of the facts *in situ* for all explanations.

> We are now fairly convinced of the inconveniences associated with this idle presumption which leads us to guess at nature without consulting it … Therefore we want facts & observers appropriate for grasping and successfully gathering them … the observer must guard against any preconception, any bias which is static and dependent on a system which has already been devised.

As for the observation of nature *in situ*, he mistrusted fast or superficial observations – 'A general & rapid casting of the eye teaches us nothing but what is vague' – and advocated that particular attention be paid to the physical attributes of natural objects. As analysed by an historian of eighteenth-century geography,

> An intelligent observer will not restrict himself so much in his technical discussions to the external forms or structure of an object, without also taking an exact knowledge of the matter itself which in its diverse amalgams contributed to producing it; he will even exactly link one idea with the other. This matter, he will say, affects this form; he will conclude one from the other, & vice versa. The physical geography advocated by Desmarets is therefore light years away from Buache's geography and close to the natural history project which was then taking shape, and which the former would get even closer at the end of the century.[40]

However, he borrowed the hypotheses of continuity, including submarine continuities, and the hierarchy of mountain ranges, from the river basin theory:

> All mountains form different principal ranges which are linked, united with each other, & which touch the surface of the continents with their main trunks and with their collateral ramifications. Mountains, which are truly the primary stems, represent very great masses in both height and volume; they ordinarily occupy and cross the center of the continents: those of a lesser height are born from these principal ranges; they gradually decrease in size as they move away from their main stem, & expire either on the coasts of the sea or in the plains.[41]

Other authors tried their best to juxtapose these two geographical approaches to mountains within two different branches of the discipline: Robert de Vaugondy proposed that

> we still distinguish geography into 1) natural; in regards to the divisions that nature has put on the surface of the globe by the seas, mountains, rivers, isthmuses, etc. and in relation to the colors of the different peoples, to their natural languages, etc. 2) historical ... 3) civil or political ... 4) holy ... 5) ecclesiastical ... 6) and lastly physical geography; this last branch considers the globe of the Earth, not so much from the point of view of what forms its surface as from what makes up its substance.[42]

Even if his method was criticised from early on, Buache's publications lastingly influenced scientific circles through his conception of a privileged object of their interest: the continuity of mountain ranges.

Mountains according to Humboldt: form, matter and experience

Thus, in disputing the course of the Cassiquiare, Humboldt was not the first to oppose Buache's system, but he was one of the first, along with Conrad Malte-Brun, to renounce it completely. The location and linking of mountain ranges greatly interested Humboldt, but he never addressed these subjects with the help of Buache's theory. He did sometimes use Buache's vocabulary, although often in order to distance himself from it.[43] In order to formulate his own idea of the ordering of relief on the Earth's surface, he made observations in Europe, in America and most notably in Central Asia in 1829 through an expedition sponsored by the tsar. He also collected eye-witness accounts and proceeded to draw a marked distinction between local informants familiar with a given region and those who worked from presupposition, termed by Humboldt as 'dogmatic and careless'.[44]

But above all, his study of the 'direction of the different mountain systems' was motivated by his desire to understand the structure of the globe, believing that the design of mountain systems 'offers one of the characterising traits of the internal make-up of our planet'.[45] In his research into this make-up, he moved progressively further and further away from the Neptunist conceptions of his tutor in geology, Abraham Gottlob Werner, and favoured 'the action that the interior of a planet works on its outer crust', which he called both 'volcanism'[46] and 'volcanity'.[47] Early nineteenth-century thinking on the formation of mountain ranges was in flux and Humboldt wanted to contribute to it through his understanding of mountain systems. His curiosity about the 'internal make-up of our planet' directed his attention to the material composition of mountains, to the physics of the Earth in the sense that Desmarets spoke of: 'physics, as its name implies, restricts itself to explaining the phenomena of the natural world through the properties of matter'.[48] The way Humboldt drew the landforms of Andean volcanoes proves his attention to the matter [Fig. 6.5].

It was in the name of this primacy of matter in the physical study of mountains that Humboldt was able to refer back to Buache's theory and propose an alternative:

> It is ... by a false application of the principles of hydrography, that from the safety of their office desks, geographers have tried to determine the direction of mountain ranges in countries whose river courses they believed they understood precisely. They imagined that two large water basins could only be separated by large elevations, or that a large river could only change direction because a group of mountains blocked its course. They forgot that very often, either because of the nature of the rocks, or because of the incline of the strata, the highest plateaus don't give rise to any water course, and the sources of the greatest rivers are far from high mountain ranges. Also, up to this point, attempts to draw physical maps according to theoretical thought have not been entirely felicitous.[49]

Mountains put to the test of direct experience and scientific instruments

Strong in his materialist convictions and in his mistrust for any claim lacking empirical validation, Humboldt accorded the greatest importance to the *in situ* observation of the objects he spoke about. His accounts of his expedition in South America demonstrated how carefully he had examined surface exposures of rock, whilst Bonpland examined, categorized and took samples of the flora they encountered. During his trip along the Cassiquiare, Humboldt increasingly observed the rocks and their juxtaposition, drawing from Werner's geology training. This concern for detailed observation can also be seen in the importance that he and Bonpland gave to very heterogeneous phenomena: the Chiriva palm-trees, the

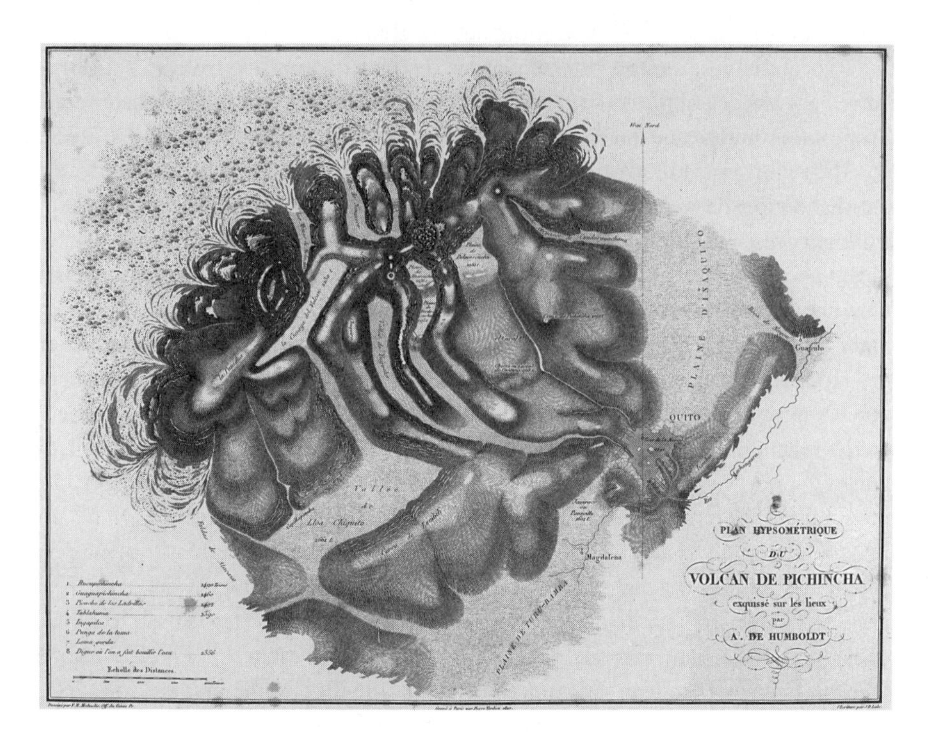

Figure 6.5 'Plan hypsométrique du volcan de Pichincha tel qu'observé sur les lieux', in Humboldt, *Atlas Géographique et Physique des régions équinoxiales du nouveau continent*, Schoell, Paris, 1814 (courtesy of Bibliothèque de Genève, J-M Meylan, Genève).

black-and-white veins which streaked the granite on the river banks, the mosquito attacks, the temperature of the water, the air vapours which prevented them from seeing the beauty of the night sky.[50] Later, during his expedition to Central Asia, he declared an even greater faith in direct field observation. At the end of *Asie Centrale*, he added an historical note which gave a clear account of his travelling conditions and demonstrated his concern for familiarising the reader with what he really did and saw. In the same breath, he criticized Marco Polo for having treated equally what he had seen and what he had been told.

Humboldt's observations relied very much on sight, but he also made great use of scientific instruments. He devoted a large part of his activities in America to measuring such phenomena as the geometrical position of places, summit altitudes, the times of sunrise and sunset, atmospheric pressure, temperature, intensity of the blue of the sky, etc. Everything the instruments of his time could measure, he measured. He travelled with a collection of instruments – sextants, theodolites, barometers, thermometers, chronometers, quadrants, compasses, eudiometers, electrometers, hygrometers, etc. – gathered before his departure[51] and which he learned to use in Germany. The direct experience of mountains, which he considered to be so decisive, thus combined unmediated sense observation, measurement by scientific instruments and causal and classificatory reasoning. Wishing to be truly in touch with nature, he structured his report by alternating between his observations, with or without instruments, and the interpretation of his findings. One of his favourite measurements was altitude as determined by barometer, measuring the decrease in atmospheric pressure with elevation, not because it was the most original of measurements, but because it provided a point of reference for the ensemble of his observations and comparisons. In this way, Humboldt measured several hundred summits,[52] constructed numerous 'height tables' and slope cross-sections juxtaposing measured altitudes and on-location surveys. Last but not least, he invented diverse modes of graphical representation which allowed him to compare the altitude of similar phenomena in several mountain ranges. So Humboldt's version of the mountain, in contrast to Buache's, had dimensions (the height of the summits, the average height of each range, the surface of the massifs, etc.) which he tried to relate to the material constitution of mountains.

Mountains put to the test of the body

One of the most original and least-noted aspects of Humboldt's method lies in his observations of the reactions of his own and his travelling companions' bodies to the influences of the environment. Generally speaking, in accordance with his holistic view of nature, he attributed a power to excite the senses and to develop one's sensitivity to immersion in the natural world.

> In the forests of the Amazon, as on the slopes of the Andes, I felt that the surface of the Earth was alive everywhere with the same spirit, the life even which is in the rocks, the plants and the animals, as in the heart of humanity from one pole to the other. Everywhere I went I realised just how much the relationships I formed in Jena [where I conducted part of my academic training] were having a profound influence on me, and how much, inspired by Goethe's perspectives on Nature, I had gained new organs of perception.[53]

He also spoke of scientific instruments as 'new organs'.[54] The body, whether assisted by instruments or not, and the mind are the faculties which allow humans to enter into a relationship with nature.

Moreover, in the name of the physical method he adopted, Humboldt endeavoured to identify his body's responses when exposed to the elements. Before even immersing himself in the tropical world, he used his body in order to observe reactions to exogenous stimulation.[55] At the summit of the great Tenerife peak, Humboldt observed the effect of the extreme temperatures on his skin;[56] in the Amazon, he recorded Bonpland's illnesses, as his colleague was more sensitive than he to humidity and mosquito bites. However, it is in his report on his ascent of Chimborazo that this feature of his research is most apparent. His ascent of the Andean volcano, then considered the highest summit on Earth, proved to be a defining moment in his journey.[57] In his scientific writings he constantly played down the heroic aspects and scientific value of this venture, but his correspondence and the booklet he published much later[58] show that he was very attentive to his physical responses to this climb, for example the pain in the hands caused by contact with the rock: 'We had to use hands and feet in places where the ridge turned into a sort of isolated and very sheer shelf... As the rock was at very acute angles we were wounded quite badly, especially in the hands.'[59] He related this back to similar experiences during his trips in the Alps and his climb up Tenerife. He explained the different pains experienced in the different contexts by the different nature of the rocks encountered. He also reported pain in his foot 'caused by the accumulation of *niguas* (*pulex penetrans*)',[60] under the skin that the altitude and the cold had apparently awakened. He reported his own and his companions' sicknesses, his 'need to vomit' and his difficulty in breathing, bleeding from the face and, as often as possible, he analysed these inconveniences the way he had done so many other manifestations of the effects of altitude observed in other contexts.

> Our gums and lips bled. The layer of conjunctivitis over our eyes, for all of us without exception, was filled with blood. These externalisations of blood in our eyes and bleeding from the gums and lips did not worry us at all as we knew about them from a great number of previous examples. In Europe, Mr. Zumstein showed blood at a much lesser height on Mont-Rosa.[61]

Lastly, by way of synthesis, he writes,

> All these phenomena vary greatly, depending on age, constitution, skin sensitivity and previous physical exertion; however, for each individual they are a sort of measurement of the rarefaction of air and the altitude reached. According to my observations in the Andes they occur, in white men, when the barometer rests between 14 inches and 15 inches 10 lines. We know that ordinarily the heights to which aeronauts claim to have risen deserve little faith, and if Mr. Gay-Lussac, a sure and extremely exact observer, did not show blood on 16 September 1804 at the prodigious height of 21,600 feet, and therefore between Chimborazo and Illimani, it should perhaps be attributed to a total absence of muscular movement.[62]

Mountains put to the test of the emotions

Lastly, whilst Humboldt believed in the analytical virtues of experiencing high places directly, including through the immediate reactions of his own body, he also believed in the more all-encompassing virtues of experiencing the entire landscape. Many authors have noted the new importance that Humboldt gave to landscape and the highly conceptual value it took on for him. In his writings, landscape is the ordering of natural formations in space, an order which is perceptible 'at first glance'. Although he does not deny the capacity recognised by Buache of maps and charts to summarise information,[63] the capacity of vision to react to the environment *in situ* counts for much more. This capacity of his objectified landscape to account for the ordering of natural objects was optimal in mountains: equatorial mountains were

> the part of our planet's surface where even in the smallest expanse, the variety of Nature's impressions is as large as possible ... In the colossal mountains of Cundinamarca, Quito and Peru, scored by deep valleys, man may look upon all the families of plants and all the stars of the firmament all at once ... It is here that the bowels of the

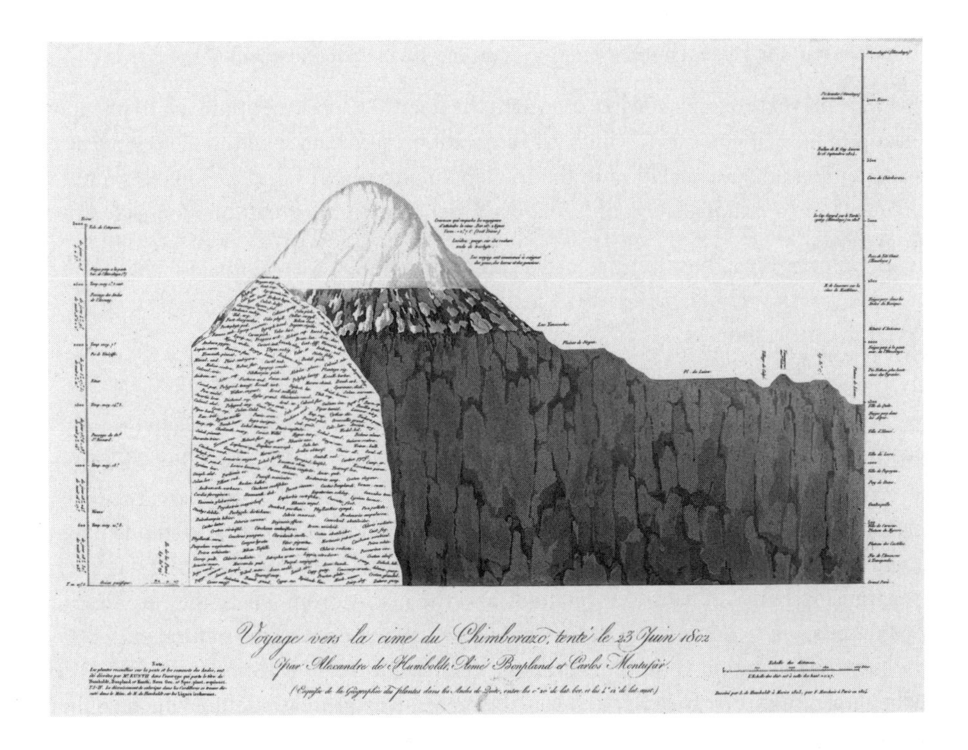

Figure 6.6 'Voyage vers la cime du Chimborazo tenté le 23 juin 1802 par Alexandre de Humbolt, Aimé Bonpland et Carlos Montufar', Humboldt, *Atlas Géographique et Physique des régions équinoxiales du nouveau continent*, Schoell, Paris, 1814 (courtesy of Bibliothèque de Genève, J-M Meylan, Genève).

> Earth and the two hemispheres of the sky lay out all the richness of their forms and the variety of their phenomena; it is here that the climates and the vegetation zones they determine are superimposed as if in layers, and that the laws of fall in temperature, easy to grasp to the intelligent observer, are written in indelible ink on the rock walls of the rapid slope of the Cordillera.[64]

Furthermore, for Humboldt the virtues of objectifying landscape formations with the eye were inseparable from their effects on the emotions of those who looked upon them. He wrote ecstatic pages on tropical landscapes and the emotions they had provoked in him.[65] But in so doing, he sought less to embellish his writings with subjective impressions than to open his field of research to the participation of human emotions in the general harmony of nature. This Goethian ideal of total knowledge, rich with the combined virtues of art and science, and whose scientific dimension included not only knowledge of the natural facts but also human experience of them, was best implemented in mountain landscapes.

> The aspect of the mountains contributes no less than the forms, size and groupings of the plants, no less than the different species of animals, the shades of the canopy of

> heaven and the intensity of reflected light in determining the character of a landscape and the general impression that man receives of different zones of the Earth.[66]

In this way, his method of knowledge opened the door to a 'positive approach to phenomena in relation to human emotions',[67] in that Humboldt, in accordance with the *Naturphilosophen*, 'considers phenomena in relation to the human emotions and mind as consubstantial with nature itself and a manifestation of humanity's inclusion in the great interconnected totality of the universe'.[68]

Conclusions

The Cassiquiare controversy, with which we opened this discussion and which brought into opposition, by several decades and several thousand kilometres, Philippe Buache and Alexander von Humboldt, represents much more than a simple disagreement between two specialists as to the existence or non-existence of a mountain range. It demonstrates two different conceptions of scientific knowledge, two ways of considering (or not considering) the relationship between natural formations and the matter from which they are made, and two quite opposite evaluations of the benefit of field experience in the natural environment. Consequently, the notion of mountains about which both speak so abundantly did not designate the same thing. For Buache, they were elements in a natural structure which could only be understood with the distance provided by relating categories of natural objects cartographically. The form of mountains, and a fortiori their materiality and altitude, counted for very little in terms of their position in an architecture of the globe itself, of which he believed them to be constitutive. For Humboldt, mountains were volumes from the history of the Earth's crust and a source of diversity and complexity in the distribution of life on Earth; they were to be approached methodically and with particular attention to the evident relationships between substance, appearance and observable effects. In such circumstances, the notion of mountains employed by two such dissimilar projects had little chance of generating compatible statements in either form or content. The Cassiquiare project exposed this fundamental incompatibility. We can therefore view it as a decisive moment in the history of geography: the triumph of one concept of physical geography over another. But even though it was a triumph it was fleeting, as one of the deepest foundations of Humboldt's research – the belief in a fundamental harmony in the ordering of the forms and forces of nature and humanity – did not outlive him.

7

Domesticating High Places

Mount Athos: Botanical 'Garden of the Virgin'

Veronica della Dora

Nothing seems further from the image of a majestic peak reaching towards the heavens, than the self-enclosed space of an island, or a garden. The former, transcendent, awe-inspiring, sublime; the latter Edenic, tranquil, serene. Yet, it has been argued, mountains are 'nothing but islands on the land' – even 'gardened' islands.[1] Mountains can resemble islands and botanical gardens, as 'vertical microcosms' characterised by microhabitats at different altitudes. They have long constituted privileged observatories for natural scientists. Pliny reports those who, in order to pursue research on plants, scoured '*culmina quoque montium invia et solitudines abditas omnesque terrae fibras*'.[2] Josias Simler of Zurich (1574) regarded mountains as 'unequalled [fields] for the observation of the processes of nature',[3] whereas Johann Reinhold Forster (1729–98), the German naturalist on Cook's second voyage, was struck by Table Mountain at the Cape of Good Hope, because of its insular resemblance, 'in the sense of being a circumscribed physiographic form upon which processes could be observed operating'.[4]

This chapter focuses on Mount Athos, a fifty-kilometre mountain-peninsula in the north Aegean that has had an impact on Western natural scientists' imagination and practice as few other peaks in the Mediterranean have. With twenty monasteries and a population of 1,800 Christian Orthodox monks, Mount Athos has been a continuously self-ruled monastic community for over 1,000 years. Culminating in a 2,033-metre-high peak, the 'Holy Mountain of Orthodoxy' is one of the most dramatic landmarks of the Aegean and one of the most quoted mountains in Classical antiquity.

Figure 7.1 South-western view of Mount Athos, Russian sacred print, 1902 (courtesy of Agioritikē Chartothēkē).

According to local tradition, Mount Athos is the site the Virgin personally chose as 'her garden', on her way to Cyprus [Fig. 7.1]. She had good reasons to do so. The varied geomorphologic structure of the peninsula, radically different from its 'flatter' (and typically Mediterranean surroundings) reflects its climate, vegetation and fauna, making Athos a unique microcosm. A succession of microclimates follow one another from the sea level up to the peak: from Mediterranean climate along the coast, to a temperate type in the interior across the central mountain chain, and Alpine towards the summit.[5]

Like the Virgin herself, natural scientists have long been charmed by Athos' unique botanical variety. They have also been captivated by the preservation of ancient species of flora and the appearance of 37 endemics, favoured by the geographic isolation of the peninsula and a monastic way of life that has had minimum impact on the surrounding environment and has banned grazing animals for over a millennium. With cultivated land occupying only five to ten per cent of its surface, Athos is the most forested part of Greece. Its 1,453 taxa and 350 species of mushrooms form a botanical mosaic rare in such a small area as the peninsula's 336 square kilometres.[6] One could say that Mount Athos is 'a microcosm which summarises the entire world' – the 'botanical totality of Eden'.[7] Its inhabitants continue to call the peninsula 'the Garden of the Virgin'.

Besides acting as 'landscapers of the Garden', as their cultivated terraces and ancient walled gardens show, the monks consider themselves the guardians of a long Byzantine herbalist tradition rooted in ancient Greece.[8] Saint Athanasius, the founder of the oldest monastery on the peninsula (AD 963), is himself said to have used herbal remedies to cure a fellow monk.[9] If this local scientific tradition has exploited Athos' plants mainly for 'practical' purposes, for at least five centuries Western botanists have conceived of 'the Garden of the Virgin' as a true botanical garden. How did it become such?

This chapter investigates the complex interaction between the territorial imaginations produced by different scientific traditions and the physical geography of Mount Athos. In particular, it explores the ways in which this wild and sacred high place turned into a space for the production of science, how a 'natural botanical garden' has been made through its 'domestication' by diverse gazes and fieldwork practices. These include pre-modern natural philosophy, Linnaean 'antiquarian taxonomy', Humboldtian vertical zonation, and modern ecological theories. The appellation of garden is more than metaphorical: in the West gardening has long represented a trope for the domestication of new worlds, both in the physical and metaphorical sense, and we know that 'fixing a boundary between the wild and the cultivated is the primary act of gardening.'[10]

David Livingstone among others has emphasised the importance of geography in the construction of scientific knowledge. Particular physical places, he argues, have proved central in shaping scientific theories.[11] Mount Athos' lure for different scientific communities rests in its specific physical configuration no less than its internal natural variety. It presents the scientist with a 'given', rather than negotiable, boundary – that of its coastline. As Jeremy Paxel notes, 'Living on an island gives you a defined border; lines on maps are arbitrary, beaches and cliffs are not.'[12] It is by its quasi-insular 'natural' boundary that Athos' innumerable species are contained, and thus rendered manageable by science. Athos' readability to the Western eye is further enhanced by the 'panoptical arrangement' of the peninsula, topped by its majestic summit. In other words, beside being an extraordinary geographical object rising on the horizon, the Athonite peninsula is an ideal space for mapping, a place inspiring 'cognitive order', or rather facilitating the imposition of order upon nature: a European Chimborazo.

The cosmographic garden

Athos enjoyed the reputation of being an extraordinary place at least since Classical antiquity. Its summit, 'higher than the place from which the rains fall' was populated, according to Pliny, by legendary long-lived snake-eaters who could witness the sunrise three hours before those on the seashore.[13] In the Middle Ages, serpent-eaters were displaced by no less peculiar creatures: natural philosophers. In his *Voiage and Travayle* (1356), Sir John Mandeville described Athos' summit as a site accessible only to 'wise men' conducting astronomic observations, holding a wet sponge on their nose to obtain oxygen at that altitude, and inscribing on the ground mysterious letters unwashed by rains or winds [Fig. 7.2].[14]

Figure 7.2 J. Mandeville, *Wise men on the summit of Mount Athos*, *c*.1410–20 (courtesy of the British Library).

The mountain's mythical aura was extended to its venerable visitors. By the very act of climbing its peak, these 'wise men' separated themselves from the world, from human society – a necessary pre-condition for science to take place.[15] Mount Athos therefore became an island 'outside of this world' not only for the monks and the hermits dwelling on its slopes, but also for scientists. On Mount Athos each searched to attain the invisible, the transcendent, Truth.

But Mount Athos had more to offer wise men than its exceptional height. During a diplomatic mission to Constantinople in 1546, Pierre Belon du Mans, the apothecary of Cardinal de Touron and pioneer in taxonomy and comparative anatomy, paid a visit to the peninsula. He penetrated its deepest recesses, walked through the monasteries' cultivated enclosures, plunged himself into the thick forest, mingling with the scents of flowers and the music of the nightingales. He marvelled at every detail, from trees never seen in his own country to tiny creatures mentioned by the ancients, and even commented on the monks' diet. 'The multitude of springs and streams, the variety of herbage and evergreens, the woods and pleasant shoar,' he concluded, 'do all render Mount Athos one of the most charming places in the world.' Athos was a true '*paradis de délices*', for the monk as much as for the botanist.[16] It was a complex metaphorical space; one inscribed with ancient myths and Edenic visions; a space for the realisation of scientific knowledge, but also one where the Renaissance 'cosmographic dream' could be realised: where the greater cosmos appeared as a cabinet-of-curiosities within a garden-island that could be surveyed at a glance.

The dream could be visually fulfilled by ascending the mountain: abandoning for a while the botanical *délices* of the forest and the monastic precincts, to struggle with hard rock; forgoing the mild Mediterranean breeze to face freezing, high-altitude winds. In the Renaissance, the figure of the cosmographer was allegorically identified with that of the 'insulist' climbing 'to the top of the highest eminence [and seeing] the coast developed symmetrically around him, inscribed on the sprawling sea as if on the rectitude of a map'.[17] The island topped by a high mountain peak allowed him to shift scale between the topographic and the cosmographic; to dominate his own (micro)cosmos with an Apollonean gaze.[18] Such a perspective represented order over against the 'chaos' of nature. On the top of Athos, Belon's eye was embedded within a body struggling 'to endure the persistent cold', and yet not deprived of the 'pleasures of rationality'. The coast of the Athonite peninsula marked out a line between the rational and the irrational, the known and the unknown, like the boundary of a large botanical garden, or *hortus conclusus*.[19]

Long associated with moral discourse, gardened islands offered an emblematic language for negotiating the new spaces of Renaissance oceanic exploration.[20] 'Textual cabinets of curiosities', grouping unsystematised historical notes, geographical descriptions, and accounts of local costumes, or exotic natural objects, cosmographies inevitably privileged the insular.[21] Like other early Renaissance travellers such as Cristoforo Buondelmonti and André Thévet, Belon was fascinated by islands.[22] Crete, Lemnos, Thasos, Mytiline, Samos, Rhodes, and indeed Athos: each island (or quasi-island) corresponded to a stop in his journey through the Aegean and a chapter of his account. Each island embodied a specific micro-cosmos as a bounded cartographic space not dissimilar to Francois I's *cabinet de singularitez*, to which Belon was a frequent visitor.

The 'gardened island' maintained its centrality in early western environmentalism. Both physically and textually, it was, first of all, a metaphor of the mind. The island garden enabled newness and complexity to be dealt with 'within familiar bounds but simultaneously allowed and stimulated an experiencing of the empirical in circumscribed terms'. Stirring Western geographical imagination as earthly paradises, tropical islands and their 'acclimatisation gardens' became privileged sites for taxonomic observation and experimentation from the seventeenth century.[23] As a precursor of this tradition, Belon found on Athos his own Garden of Eden. 'Baptising' herbs, trees and animals, he became a 'new Adam' producing a pre-Linnaean taxonomy. However, the French scholar was merely the precursor of a long series of Western naturalists who ventured to Athos and conceptualised it as a 'naturally' bounded taxonomical space.

The Linnaean garden

> Clearing the island [of Lemnos] ... we were not far distant from the south point, when the sun with a glowing tint sunk behind Athos, forming a grand conical figure with an insular appearance.[24]

The vision of Mount Athos from the sea on a September evening was not new to John Sibthorp. The Oxford Sherrardian Professor of Botany had landed on the peninsula for the first time in 1787. For him, as for Belon, Athos represented only one (but perhaps the most exciting) stop in an extensive journey to the Levant. Yet, unlike the French naturalist's, Sibthorp's journey was planned years ahead as a modern scientific expedition. Surrounded by drying papers and phials, the scholar was not alone on his floating laboratory. With him were not the ambassadors and diplomats who had accompanied Belon, but a true scientific team: his friend John Hawkins, a wealthy Cornish gentleman interested in geology, Ninian Imrie, Scottish captain of the Royals at Gibraltar and a mineralogist, and Ferdinand Bauer, an especially hired German draftsman who would later join Matthew Flinders' voyage to Australia.

The expedition's goals were ambitious: to collect different organic and mineral specimens, and above all, to compile a comprehensive Linnaean classification of the Greek flora and fauna. Sibthorp's enterprise resonated within the broader globalising project of Enlightenment natural history, which aimed at the representation, classification and ordering of the world.[25] While closer to the recent great Pacific voyages and their scientific teams than to the gentlemanly English Grand Tour, Sibthorp's expeditions to the Levant, however, did inherit the broader philological project linked to the former tradition. The Oxford botanist was particularly interested in identifying plants mentioned in Classical texts. It was the Classicist's opinion that scientific fieldwork in the Levant would 'furnish some valuable illustrations of various passages in the works of Aristotle, Theophrastus, Dioscorides, Aelian, and

Pliny', and 'the botany of the ancients ... would be more easily explained if the names used by the modern Greeks were known.' Systematic research had so far been prevented by the 'barbarousness [infecting] with its violence the morals of men over the whole area, [making] investigation of its natural products a very difficult and dangerous task for foreign travellers'.[26] It was only thanks to Sibthorp's 'adventurous mind' and scientific expertise that ancient plants, lost in remote 'barbarised' lands, but also in the 'chaotic plentitude of nature', could be discovered like archeological remains and, once identified, 'put back to their place' in Linnaeus' taxonomic system.

Fusing practical realities with imaginative constructions, Mount Athos suited both the naturalistic and the antiquarian spirit of the expedition. On the frontispieces of two volumes of the *Flora Graeca Sibthorpiana* (1806 and 1840), a ponderous ten-volume work illustrated with Bauer's 966 hand-coloured illustrations, the mountain figures in its 'garden' and 'island' variants respectively: in Volume II as a Romantic green idyll full of 'natural productions' waiting to be labelled [Fig. 7.3], and in Volume VIII as a dramatic cone rising out of the stormy waters of the Aegean, the storm-lashed rock witnessed with wonder by the Argonauts, and which cost the Persians their fleet.[27] [Fig. 7.4]

If Belon had visited Athos with Dioscorides in his mind, rejoicing and wondering at unexpected encounters with ancient plants, Sibthorp and his team disembarked on the peninsula with Dioscorides' in their hands, resolved to label and collect the 'natural productions' of ancient Greece from within a unique 'assemblage of natural beauty'.[28] The boundary of this enchanted garden had been negotiated even before landing.

> A pebbly shore rising into a steep rock of primitive marbles, on which appeared a variety of curious plants, made me impatient to land. I could discover from our vessel *Erica multiflora* in full flower empurpling spots of the rock. On landing, I found near the beach the beautiful sea-lily, *Pancratium maritimum*. The *Arbustus Andrachne* grew on the hanging cliffs on which I gathered from low procumbent shrubs specimens of *Globularia alypum*, and under its shade, entwined by the rough *smilax*, the sweet-scented *coronilla*.[29]

Mount Athos' taxonomic beauty was overwhelming and no less picturesque than the ancient ruins charted and measured by contemporary travellers. It was a beauty to be domesticated through identification, translation and appropriation. During his stay, Bauer, the draftsman, restlessly sketched Mount Athos' floral productions, noting colours on a numeric scale that allowed him to complete his pencil sketches at home in his workshop. For Sibthorp, Hawkins and Imrie, domestication implied the 'rationalisation' and dissemination of visual information, as well as of natural materials, such as mineral and floral specimens, bulbs, and seeds. Domestication transcended the physical boundaries of Athos to enter those of new, artificial microcosms: Hawkins' mineral cabinet, Sibthorp's herbarium and 'plantations sacred to Greece' in the Oxford Physic Garden, and the Royal Gardens at Kew, one of the greatest botanical 'centres of calculation' of Europe.[30]

However, domestication implied order as a primary characteristic. This was achieved on the peninsula through the naturalists' combination of discursive and physical practices –

Figure 7.3 View of Mount Athos on the frontispiece of Sibthorp's *Flora Graeca*, Volume II, 1813 (courtesy of the Gennadeion Library, Athens).

Figure 7.4 View of Mount Athos on the frontispiece of Sibthorp's *Flora Graeca*, Volume VIII, 1833 (courtesy of the Gennadeion Library, Athens).

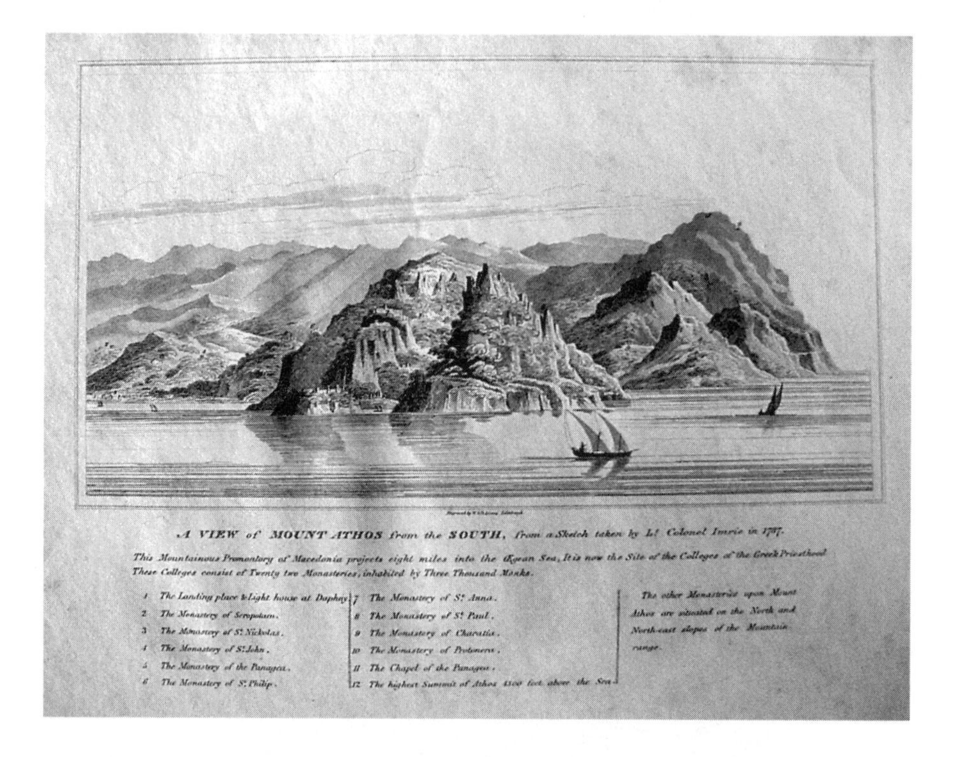

Figure 7.5 View of Mount Athos from the sea in Imrie's *Catalogue of Specimens*, 1817 (courtesy of the Gennadeion Library, Athens).

through their gaze, but also through their actions and movements. Like Belon, the party ascended Mount Athos' peak. For the masculine Enlightenment scientist, the act of 'scaling the highest mountains, climbing the most rugged rocks' was in itself a way to domesticate nature, even before achieving the 'insulist's' Cartesian view from above.[31] As the four men climbed higher, 'trees became scarce; and the higher regions of the mountain rose naked above [them]'. Sensuality gave place to transcendence.[32] Sibthorp was rewarded by the richness of *plantae sylvaticae*, by a number of trees observed in different parts of Greece, but above all by endemics 'not seen anywhere else'.[33] Imrie, the captain mineralogist, also collected a true trophy worthy to be displayed beside the specimens he stole from the Bath of Pithia and the temple of Theseus: a piece of primitive marble 'taken from the highest summit of Mount Athos'.[34] On Mount Athos, 'rarity' was to be found at the highest places after a physically demanding climb, the same one undertaken by Orthodox pilgrims searching for a closer contact with the divine on the Holy Mountain.

From his first journey, Sibthorp compiled a list of 450 plants, and during his second visit he gathered seeds of no less than 1,500 species.[35] Beside being a unique site for collecting, however, Mount Athos was also a remarkable 'site to collect'. Within his

Catalogue of Specimens (1817), Imrie added plates of Mount Helicon, Parnassus and Mount Athos: the most noteworthy peaks conquered during the party's journeys to the Levant. Mount Athos was captured from the ship [Fig. 7.5]. Emerging from the flat sea surface, its image was of self-contained, almost domesticated sublimity. The peninsula was a 'natural' place for self-display. It incarnated the Enlightenment notion of 'the world as exhibition'.[36] As in a museum, a gallery or one of the newly invented panoramas, on their ship the naturalists passed by and admired Mount Athos' monasteries and 'romantic ravines'. They accurately labelled and catalogued them, after having reduced Mount Athos' majestic summit to hill and the peninsula to an ensemble of Edenic islands. But this 'sea approach' would soon be challenged.

The Humboldtian garden

In 1839 Mount Athos was visited by one of von Humboldt's most eminent pupils: the German botanist August Grisebach. Unlike Sibthorp, Grisebach did not approach the peninsula from the sea, but from the land, having crossed the remotest Balkan mountain regions. This represented more than a logistical difference. It reflected two distinct inquisitive traditions dominating nineteenth-century botany: the 'floristic' and the 'morphological'. The former emerged with Linnaeus and was concerned mainly with taxonomical classification. The latter originated with Alexander von Humboldt and studied the geographical distribution of vegetation in relation to environmental parameters. Both rested on scientific exploration: Linnaean floristic taxonomy reached its climax with Cook's great oceanic voyages, morphological plant geography with von Humboldt's continental penetration.[37]

A Prussian, a mining official rather than a naval officer, von Humboldt spent five years exploring the interior of South and Central America. His voyage was self-consciously different from his British colleagues'. It served territorial unity, rather than insular knowledge, giving privilege to synthesis over isolated facts, and measurement over collection. A 'true', holistic history of nature was to overcome the Linnaean 'artificial' descriptions: 'A physical portrait took precedence over the more familiar florilegia and hydrographic charts.'[38] Searching for natural unity in diversity, von Humboldt envisaged in vegetative communities both a manifestation of the cosmos' transcendental coordinating principle and a field of geographical inquiry.[39] He criticised Linnaean botanists for exhausting their energies with 'details', ignoring 'the big picture', occupied as they were with the discovery of new species and their classification. He stated that he 'would much rather know the exact and elevational limits of an already known species than discover fifteen new ones.'[40] Grisebach self-consciously continued von Humboldt's programme for a plant geography, of which he came to be regarded as one of the leading exponents.[41]

Sibthorp and Grisebach's scientific expeditions to the Levant re-enacted on a small scale the great 'epic journeys' marking their respective scientific traditions. Sibthorp's Aegean island-hopping parallelled Cook and Finley's scientific journeys through the Pacific islands; Grisebach's land route through the Balkans consciously mimicked von Humboldt's

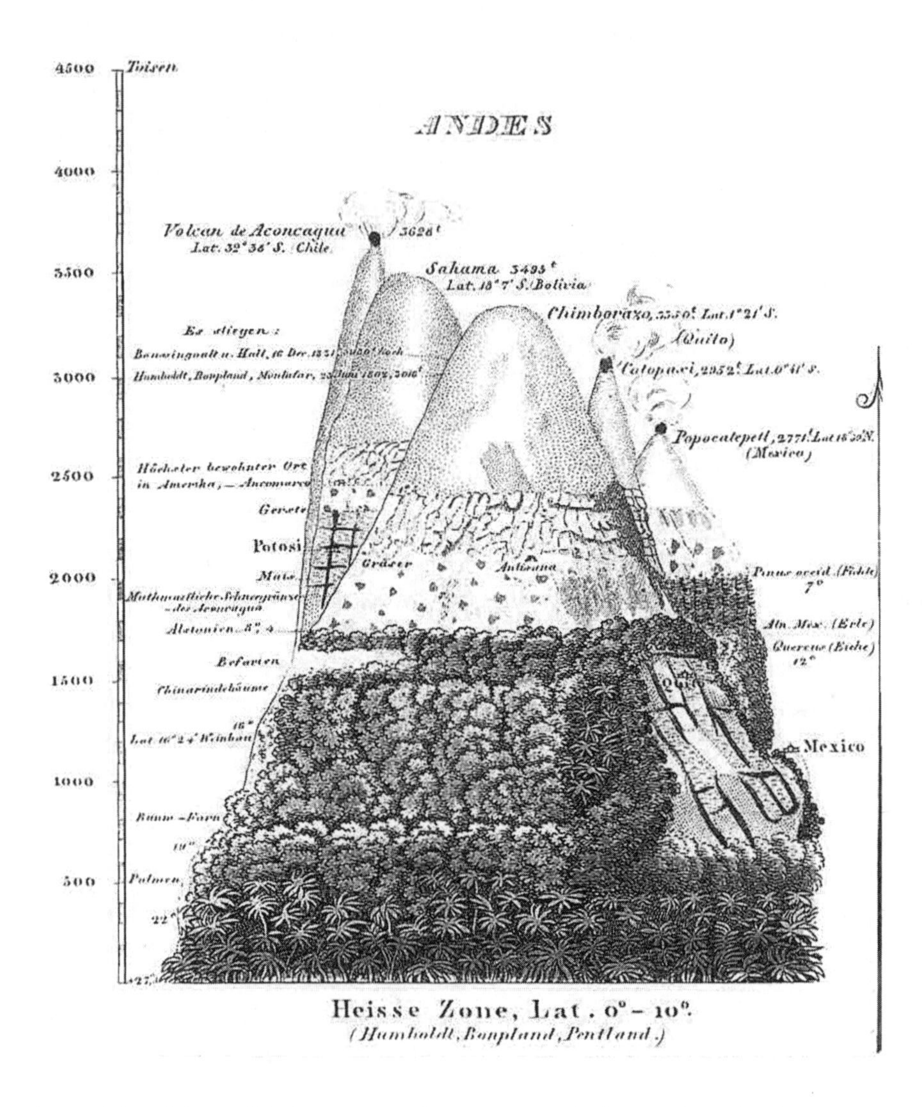

Figure 7.6 Mount Chimborazo and other prominent Andean peaks in Berghaus' *Physikalischer Schul-Atlas zum Kosmos von Alexander von Humboldt*, 1850 (courtesy of Archiv Verlag Braunschweig).

march into the interior of the South American continent. His exploration of Thrace, Macedonia, Albania and Bithynia (1839) proved revelatory, and beneficial to his career to the same extent as von Humboldt's Andean journey. In his *Cosmos* (1858), the latter justified his 'continental choice' as the most suitable to his unitarian vision. Unlike his British colleagues, he boasted to have seen

> not only the littoral districts, such as are alone visited by the majority of those who take part in voyages of circumnavigation, but also those portions of the interior of two vast continents which present the most striking contrasts manifested in the Alpine tropical landscapes of South America, and the dreary wastes of the steppes in Northern Asia.[42]

Grisebach, who had read von Humboldt's South American account, regarded his own enterprise as no less important: famous Royal Navy surveyors and historical topographers such as William Martin Leake, he noted, had limited themselves to the coasts of Greece and Asia Minor. Few researchers had ventured to the interior, and none had ever described it in the form of a logbook. While bordering directly on his homeland, these lands remained 'very much under-examined, as a large extent of Asia or America'.[43]

As the vivid tropical pictures in Humboldt's South American account inflamed Grisebach's geographical imagination, empirical data and measurements were zealously recorded in his logbook, following his master's model. What von Humboldt claimed to have experienced on the Andes, Grisebach sought in the mountains of Rumelia. If during the previous century oceanic explorers had transposed the geography of Classical Greece to Pacific atolls and tropical islands,[44] Grisebach made the poetic spaces of Classical antiquity 'tropical'. In this inverse process of 'spatial poeticisation', Mount Athos became Grisebach's own Chimborazo.[45] The Ecuadorean peak had been employed by Humboldt in his famous 'Physical portrait of the tropics' (1807) to exemplify his geographical vision. Reappearing later in Berghaus' *Physikalischer Schul-Atlas zum Kosmos von Alexander von Humboldt* (1850), the mountain embedded 'all the phenomena that the surface of our planet and the surrounding atmosphere present to the observer ... the general results of five years in the tropics' [Fig. 7.6]. The majestic mountain, then believed to be the highest in the world, condensed huge expanses of territory into a single vertical ascent. In a perpendicular rise of 4,800 metres, 'the various climates succeed one another, layered one on top of the next like strata.'[46] To Grisebach, Mount Athos, to which he dedicated 125 of the 360 pages of his account, looked just as extraordinary. Nowhere in Europe, the German botanist enthusiastically claimed, had he seen such a luxuriant vegetation: this could only be compared to 'the vivid representations through which the travellers have transmitted us the incomparable organic nature of the Tropics'.[47]

Mount Athos was fascinating not just because of its dramatic differences from its surroundings, but because, like Humboldt's Chimborazo, 'the geological image of vegetation, time and space, history and geography, [were] subjected to the naturalist's gaze'. On Mount Athos, as in the Tropics, global order was made visible locally.[48] Grisebach believed in the Humboldtian notion that plants and organic forces were distributed over the globe according to mathematically determinable limits, and were thus mappable like heat or magnetism. Demonstrating that the changes in plant distribution by altitude match the ones by latitude, von Humboldt implicitly exalted the micro-cosmic nature of mountains.

> Among the colossal mountains of Cundinamarca, of Quito, and of Peru, furrowed by deep ravines, man is enabled to contemplate alike all the families of plants ... There, at

Figure 7.7 Athos' peak with its 'hat', as seen from the promontory (photograph by Monk Apollò, Docheiariou Monastery, 2005).

> a single glance the eye surveys majestic palms, humid forests of *Bambusa*, and the varied species of *Musaceae*, while above these forms of tropical vegetation appear oaks, medlars, the sweet-brier, and umbelliferous plants, as in Europeans homes. ... There the different climates are ranged the one above the other, stage by stage, like the vegetable zones, whose succession they limit; and there the observer may readily trace the laws that regulate the diminution of heat, as they stand indelibly inscribed on the rocky walls and abrupt declivities of the Cordilleras.[49]

This scheme was reflected not only in Grisebach's scientific conceptualisation of Mount Athos, but also on his physical experience and narrative of the place. His journey began from what he re-baptised 'Holy Forest' and, like his predecessors', it culminated on Athos' peak. Moving on mule-back through the luxuriant woods and the successive crests of the promontory, like 'the naturalist entering the primeval forests of South America', Grisebach took the reader through different 'belts'.[50] He domesticated Mount Athos by slicing it into layers by altitude. The mountain, he argued, could be 'naturally' divided into three main regions: the evergreen (0–405 metre elevation), the wooded (405–1,884 metres), and the Alpine (1,884–2,339 metres). The wooded region could be in turn divided into a spruce forest zone, *laricio* forest zone, and deciduous-tree forest zone (*Laubwalde*), and the Alpine into a fir forest and a herb vegetation zone.[51]

Grisebach's understanding of Mount Athos, however, was not purely scientific. Like von Humboldt's Andean journey, Grisebach's ascent constituted an overwhelmingly sensual aesthetic and emotional experience. Echoing Schiller's notion that 'freedom is in the mountains', on the top of the Chimborazo and other majestic Andean peaks, von Humboldt was pervaded by a sense of inner calm. '... These vapours, circulating around the rocky ridge, soften its ... outline, temper the effects of light, and give the landscape that aspect of calmness and repose, which arises from the harmony of forms and colours.'[52] On Athos' peak Grisebach experienced a similar sensation:

> As much as the panoramic view over a surface of sea, islands and shores, the half radius of which is 25 miles, might captivate the eye, as much as this panoramic view should move even the most impoverished fantasy, to be able to unite in a single line of vision so many famous mountains and islands of antiquity in a most comfortable manner: yet the tableau of the foreground, the view of the depth, is much richer, livelier and more stimulating. Great shapes, dazzling colours speak directly to the feeling mind. The deep abysses, the high marble rocks, the manifold green, the indigo and lapis blue: all of this has a very similar effect on the eye as when the ear is stimulated by powerful and harmonious sounds, which the receptive organ [the eye] instantly knows how to mediate with the mood of the soul. The sense of landscape, like the musical ear, is an innate quality, and partially can be formed by beautiful impression. But if contrasts which are abrupt and at the same time in a certain sense reconciled have their greatest effect in this sphere, it is here particularly the vicinity of the sea to the wildest [rocky] formations of the fortress, which lends a calming character to the grandiose nature.[53]

Inner calm derived from visually mastering the surrounding natural elements and conceptualising them as parts of a harmonious whole. But the whole envisioned by Grisebach was the transposition of what von Humboldt experienced on the rock of Manimimi, above the Great Cataract of the Orinoco River. Arriving at the summit of the rock, von Humboldt's eye, like Griesebach's, was immediately captured by the insistent 'thing-ness' of great geomorphic objects – 'Enormous masses of stone, black as iron, issue from its ... bosom. Some are paps grouped in pairs, like basaltic hills; others resemble towers, strong castles, and ruined buildings.' The naturalist was charmed mostly by the contrasting effects produced by colours and vegetation. The gloomy tints of rocks caused the same contrast 'with the silvery splendour of the foam', as that of the steep Athonite ravines with the blue surface of the Aegean.[54]

For von Humboldt, sensual interfusion with the mountain environment and its elements helped the scientist achieve a more intimate, spiritual contact and thus penetrate the mysteries of the cosmos:

> When the human mind first attempts to subject to its control the world of physical phenomena, and strives by meditative contemplation to penetrate the rich luxuriance of living nature, and the mingled web of free and restricted natural forces, man feels

> himself raised to a height from whence, as he embraces the vast horizon, individual things blend together in varied groups, and appear as if shrouded in a vapoury veil.[55]

Grisebach's spiritual fulfilment ultimately derived from a similar panoptical mastery of *Cosmos*' visible and invisible forces: it derived from 'the consciousness of finding [himself] at the centre of the great theatre of nature',[56] a theatre to be experienced through von Humboldt's two-fold approach: a preliminary sensual abandonment to the grandeur of nature, followed by the careful observation of landscape physiognomy and the 'rational' investigation of physical laws.[57] On the peak of Mount Athos, which Grisebach envisaged as the junction of earth, heaven and soul, lyrical abandonment to nature soon gave way to scientific observation:

> The air was completely quiet. At 9:00 the thermometer showed a temperature of 10°, 5R. After a quarter of an hour the fog suddenly opened up from north to northeast. The landscape from Thasos to Thessalonica, as well as the Holy Forest were spread out before us: a map-like view, but with colour and shape. I began to examine the peninsula, which was closest and best known; I saw the Holy Forest, like a flat, green bulging hill gently extending down at the center of the strip of land to the Gulf of Stellaria in a softly rounded form ... [on the promontory below the peak] I saw only a few forest islands. These were lost under the rocky mass. Then I ... distinguished very clearly, based on the shade of green, the line which separates coastal bushes from the forest region.[58]

Grisebach's attempts to identify Mount Athos' vegetational zones and master the surrounding landmarks with gaze and compass were abruptly interrupted by some mist: 'The curtain of this spectacle of nature play is suddenly lowered,' he noted in his diary.[59] But the natural scientist did not give up his hopes: at 10:15 his thermometer had steadily risen to 13 °.

> During one hour the cloud remained temperamental, providing me with an opening now here, now there. Thus, as through the window of a tower, the largest part of this extensive panorama, probably more than 2,000-square-miles wide would spread before me piecemeal in complete clarity, because, except from the summit cloud, the sky was completely clear ... Probably ten times had I set up my magnetic needle: just as the needle found its position, the cloud gathered again, like a floating demon.[60]

At 11:00 the curtain lowered completely and Grisebach had eventually to be content with a 'problematic [horizon] line' and a puzzle to solve.

> In the meantime, I remained until 11:45 on the summit, and still at 11:30 I measured a temperature of 16.3 degrees, an increase of nearly 6 degrees in three and a half hours. This phenomenon is very mysterious to me. How is it possible that in the calmest air and in a steady increase in temperature here at the isolated and only place of the horizon a cloud forms spontaneously, partially disappears, but on the whole gradually increases in size and finally completely envelops the summit at more than 2,000 [metres]?[61]

Grisebach's gaze was not limited to Athos' vegetational and climatic phenomena. Like von Humboldt's, it penetrated the remotest geological recesses of the mountain-peninsula. If

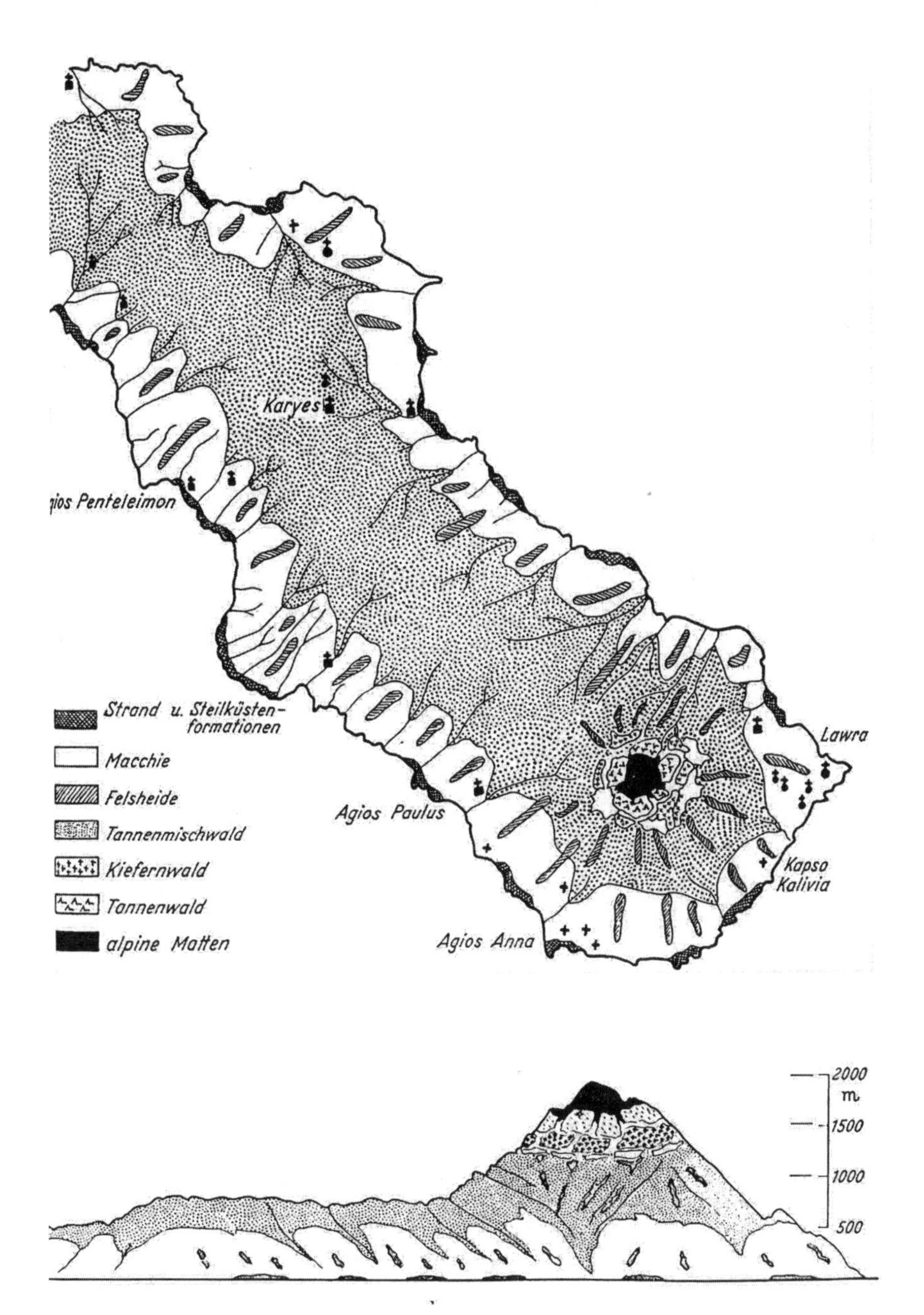

Figure 7.8 Rauh's map and profile of Mount Athos flora's altitudinal zonation, in W. Rauh, *Klimatologie und Vegetationsverhältnisse der Athos-Halbinsel und der ostägäischen Inseln Lemnos, Evstratios, Mytilene und Chios*. Heidelberg: Springer-Verlag, 1949, p. 565 (courtesy of Springer-Verlag).

Imrie was content with gathering rare specimens from different areas of Mount Athos, Grisebach aimed at exploring the dynamic volcanic forces that gave the peninsula its form and life.[62] While the Scottish Royal Navy officer was satisfied with Mount Athos' 'exterior' sea view, the German naturalist's scientific vision pierced well beyond surface: it turned Mount Athos into an object of metaphysical enquiry. Grisebach's vegetational belts rested on seven subterraneaous geological zones 'visible' only to the scientist's mind's eye.[63]

Grisebach's Humboldtian approach to Mount Athos – as an integrated, multi-layered, botanical and geological laboratory and observatory for climatic phenomena – remained deeply influential in the scientific conceptualisation of the Holy Mountain. New data, more accurate observations and more sophisticated technologies kept building on Grisebach's Humboldtian model. One century after the publication of Grisebach's account, the botanist Werner Rauh gave visual expression to the altitudinal zonation of Athonite vegetation through observations and photographs taken in each different 'belt'. These were brought together through a profile similar to the one Grisebach must have repeatedly envisioned in his mind [Fig. 7.8].[64]

From Grisebach's time, Mount Athos continued to prove a powerful magnet for German-speaking natural scientists. Until the end of the Second World War (and after), scientific scholarship on the Holy Mountain remained overwhelmingly German.[65] Perhaps Grisebach's Athonite experience ended up touching also his master. In order to imagine the highest spot of the Earth, von Humboldt 'piled' Mount Athos on the top of his favourite mountain.

> If we were even to picture to ourselves Mount Pilatus placed on Schreckhorn, or the Schneekoppe of Silesia on Mont Blanc, we should not have attained to the height of that great Colossus of the Andes, the Chimborazo, whose height is twice that of Mount Aetna; *and we must pile the Righi, or Mount Athos, on the summit of Chimborazo, in order to form a just estimate of the elevation of the Dhawalagiri, the highest point of the Himalaya.*[66]

The ecological garden

The paling, or garden border, suggests protection from wild, 'corrupting' or threatening forces beyond. The garden and island metaphors thus carry a sense of fragility and uniqueness: like an oasis, or the image of the Earth floating in the darkness of space.[67] In the early twentieth century, Mount Athos, a quasi-island already 'gardened' by different botanical traditions, was regarded as one of the last remnants of a great Mediterranean coniferous forest which supposedly once covered the higher parts of the entire Macedonian region, but which had disappeared under 'the combined attacks of man and his flocks and the action of erosion'.[68] It was a widespread idea that the whole Mediterranean region had suffered the same fate. As Grove and Rackham have recently demonstrated, the 'ruined landscape theory' first emerged from the comparison of the idyllic green settings used by European Renaissance and Baroque painters, who had not ventured farther than Rome, with the site experience of the first travellers to eighteenth-century desolated Greece. The catastrophic effects caused by Europeans and their imported grazing animals on newly discovered remote Oceanic islands like St. Helena provided further 'empirical' evidence: 'it was easy to suppose that Mediterranean coasts and islands had suffered a similar fate in the distant past to that of these fragile, oceanic islands in the recent past'.[69]

The same theory drove Sir Arthur Hill, director of Kew Gardens, and W.B. Turrill, keeper of Kew's Herbarium and Library, to Athos in spring 1934. The two botanists envisioned the peninsula as a perfect counter-example to St. Helena: a true oasis that had escaped degeneration thanks to the thousand-year-old monastic ban on grazing animals – in scientific terms, a 'permanent area of exclosure'.[70] Despite its typically Mediterranean gardens, olive groves and meadow-land surrounding the monastic complexes, most of the peninsula was covered with 'primitive' natural vegetation, resembling, according to the botanists, much of pre-glacial Europe's plant-covering.[71]

The idea of 'primitiveness' was a powerful one in the first decades of the twentieth century. Constructed in Western geographical imagination as 'the home to "wild" and "primitive" cultures and natures', the Balkans appealed to an increasing number of ecologists.[72] While regarding himself a 'professional plant taxonomist', Turrill could be included in this category, as by the late 1930s he had carried out a certain amount of research in the newly emerged field.[73] Introduced for the first time in 1935 by Alfred George Tansley, the word 'ecosystem' referred to a 'holistic and integrative ecological concept that combined living organisms and physical environment into a system'.[74] This idea had a tremendous impact on natural scientific studies. In 1951 Turrill became the first taxonomist president of the British Ecological Society, founded by Tansley in 1913, and Tansley himself prefaced Turrill's famous work on Balkan plant geography.[75] Exploiting Tansley's ecological ideas, Turrill sought a dynamic approach to modern taxonomy. Mapping the range and distribution of taxa within a group through field observation and statistical analysis could throw light on the place of origin, the migration and the history of range changes of the group as a whole and of the taxa within it. As anthropologists were busy charting the 'cradle of civilisation', Turrill, resting on the assumption that each taxon has its own 'place and time of origin', speculated on Balkan plant migrations and their possible 'cradle'.[76]

Blurring the boundaries between anthropology and ecology, Turrill, Tansley and many other ecologists of their time, regarded the Balkans as a unique phyto-geographical link between Europe and Asia, characterised by no less than 141 'cosmopolitan' species. 'Seat of great Classical cultures', Europe's powder keg was also a 'centre of species making and dispersal'.[77] In order to illustrate such processes, Turrill divided the Balkan region into smaller floristic areas. Mount Athos, with its sixteen endemics, constituted one of these territorial units. The peninsula was in turn divided into altitudinal zones. Unlike Grisebach's 'physiognomic belts', Turrill's zones were 'ecologically' delimited as complex microhabitats communicating through two-way vertical migrations: Athos was a 'primitive' microcosm, and yet one in continuous motion.[78]

Its ancient endemics were for Turrill unique treasures within the Mediterranean's 'thousands of square miles of deforested hill slopes over-grazed by sheep and goats in periodic transhumance'.[79] If ecological virtue was to be envisioned in stability rather than change, in 'tolerant' rather than 'aggressive' species, then Athos represented an ideal site for 'benign ecology'.[80] By a strange kind of metempsychosis, monastic ideals and virtues imbued its plants, and vice versa. Hill defined the peninsula 'a plant sanctuary, a unique botanical paradise where the works of God in Nature may also be fully appreciated and studied'.[81] In the field, religious and aesthetic sensibility mingled with scientific practice. As Turrill collected samples of soil 'as likely to show extreme pH ranges dried and tested colorimetrically on return to Kew', Hill enjoyed the 'many floral treasures' revealed to him while 'climbing up the steep hillsides along the rocky paths'.[82] Among relics of saints and of the Holy Cross, the two botanists were shown by the monks 'a piece of burning bush' and the 'old vine of Saint Simon' at Hiliandar. Besides wonderfully illuminated manuscripts, ancient icons and the many precious treasures preserved in the monasteries, in the field they could appreciate precious botanical rarities, such as 'a fine, pale-yellow mullein, branched like a candelabrum'.[83]

Hill and Turrill returned from their expedition to Mount Athos with a collection of 500 specimens. These were brought to the Kew Herbarium for identification. Duly mounted and processed with a mixture of mercuric chloride and carbolic acid, the new specimens were sorted and inserted in their proper covers in the permanent collection. Hill and Turrill's 'floristic booty' complemented the historical collections of the great Athos botanical explorers of the past, starting with Sibthorp. From garden, the peninsula had become a rich 'field archive' connected with that of the Kew Herbarium. Since the days of Sibthorp's first expedition, a two-way stream of botanical samples and names flowed from Athos to London, and vice versa. On the one hand, through plant naming – *Ebenus sibthorpii, Sedum grisebachii*, etc. – the 'great botanical pioneers' attached their 'eternal' memory to Athonite ground. On the other, as dried specimens of *Centaurea sanctae-annae, Astragalus monachorum* or *Armeria sancta* took their way to London, monasteries, monks and Athos itself 'exited' the peninsula, bringing a touch of sacredness into the Herbarium's drawers. Not only did endemics' denominations communicate to botanists their place of origin, but acted also as effective reminders of their 'sacred Edenic' nature.[84]

Conclusions

Bruno Latour has argued that, 'an invisible world of belief is mistakenly built beyond the world of science, whereas it is almost the opposite: science gives access to a form of invisibility and religion to a form of visibility.'[85] Both science and Orthodox Christianity rest upon 'icons' as 'mediators' to the metaphysical. If for the Orthodox faithful sacred icons are well-recognised 'doors' to the divine, for the scientist 'representation' has been traditionally discarded in favour of two extremes: 'the representing Mind and the represented World'.[86] Through the analysis of different scientific renderings of Mount Athos, emblematically the

Holy Mountain of Orthodox Christianity and home to hundreds of ancient sacred icons, this chapter has re-evaluated the intrinsic legacy of science and representation, and the central role played by the specific material nature of place in the mutual exchange between the two.

Within different scientific traditions, the most varied imageries have been superimposed on Mount Athos: from medieval legendary site accessible only to 'wise men' to biblical earthly paradise with its new species to be named by Western pre-Linnaean taxonomists, from antiquarian taxonomists' cradle of Classical species to ecologists' cradle of primeval Mediterranean vegetation, or from Linnaean quasi-island to Humboldtian tropical peak. From the times of Belon to those of Turrill and Hill, Mount Athos' vertical circumscription, its 'self-contained sublimity' provided botanists and ecologists with a 'naturally' coherent framework and a reassuring sense of 'finitude'. An ensemble of potentially uncharted species (or dynamics), and yet at the same time a space which could be dominated with a single gaze from its summit, Athos came to embody poles as distant as sublime 'wilderness' and what Yi-Fu Tuan has named 'the hearth', 'a world in miniature ... [of] beauty, comfort, goodness'.[87] An ideal space for 'gardening' (and 'mapping'), a domesticated high place, Mount Athos supports Gaston Bachelard's claim that 'the cleverer I am at miniaturizing the world, the better I possess it', and so, 'the better I narrate and circulate it'.[88]

8

Astronomers at Altitude

Mountain Geography and the Cultivation of Scientific Legitimacy

K. Maria D. Lane

In August 1909, American astronomer William Wallace Campbell, Director of the Lick Observatory, left his home near the summit of Mount Hamilton in California's Diablo Mountains and travelled with a small expedition party to Mount Whitney in the Sierra Nevada Range. His purpose was to observe the planet Mars with spectroscopic instruments, that would allow him to settle a simmering debate over whether the Martian atmosphere contained any measurable amount of water vapour and, thus, whether the red planet might be habitable.[1] To achieve his goal, Campbell had determined that measurements were needed from 'the highest point of land in the United States', where the density of Earth's own atmosphere would be lowest and therefore least disruptive to the very sensitive processes required to assess the composition of the red planet's atmosphere.[2]

Starting from the village of Lone Pine, Campbell and his group travelled by carriage and horseback up the slopes of Mount Whitney to a base camp at 10,300 feet. After two days spent adjusting to the effects of altitude, they continued their ascent on pack animals, despite the fact that 'the weather for two days past had been threatening' and that they suffered snowstorms above 12,000 feet.[3] After a difficult final ascent, they reached the 14,000-foot summit, where a shelter had been constructed specifically for the expedition's purposes. According to Campbell, their arrival at the mountain's peak could hardly have been more dramatic, for just as 'Director Abbot opened the door to receive us there were two violent discharges of lightning, near enough to be felt by most members of the party.'[4]

After setting up a temporary observatory and adjusting instruments in continuing bad weather, the astronomers welcomed a clearing of the skies that provided atmospheric conditions that were 'as perfect for our purposes as could be wished' for the next two nights. On his third and final day of astronomical observations at the summit, Campbell reported

> the sky was absolutely clear; the wind was from the fair-weather quarter; the humidity was low; and the sky was remarkably blue. On occulting the Sun behind the roof of the shelter one could look up to the very edge of the Sun with no recognisable decrease in blueness. I had never seen so pure a sky before.[5]

Campbell exposed numerous spectrographic plates of the moon and Mars, capturing what he considered conclusive proof that the Martian atmosphere was virtually dry.[6] He published his findings in a widely circulated *Lick Observatory Bulletin*.

Within the American astronomical community, the Mount Whitney expedition was considered a success. In reporting that the Martian atmosphere contained less water vapour than could be perceived by modern instruments, Campbell had contributed pivotal data to a larger debate over the possibility of advanced life existing on Mars.[7] Campbell felt that his expedition had settled the issue by taking unimpeachable data from a much higher altitude than 'at all the observatories where the Martian spectrum had previously been investigated'.[8] Although Campbell's opponents at the Lowell Observatory in Flagstaff, Arizona continued to insist on the existence of both water and life on Mars, the Mount Whitney expedition was widely considered the final word on the subject. Most professional astronomers cited Campbell's work as reason to forgo further Mars investigations, and advocates of Martian life never regained their stature, or credibility, within the discipline of astronomy. Although a popular mania for intelligent Martians – which had begun in the 1890s and reached fever pitch by 1907 – continued for several decades, its intensity waned noticeably after 1909.

As this episode indicates, the high-altitude and mountain location of astronomical work became a locus of legitimacy for American astronomers around the turn of the twentieth century. Campbell's description of the alternating sublimities and difficulties of his Mount Whitney expedition displays two themes that emerged in astronomical writing as the first mountaintop observatories were built in the American West in the late 1800s. First, astronomers began to gain prestige among their peers and in the public eye by emphasising the isolation and purity of the remote mountains in which they worked. Thus Campbell's emphasis on the 'perfect', 'remarkable' and 'pure' atmospheric conditions he achieved by virtue of ascending America's highest peak. Second, astronomers strategically emphasised the rugged and challenging characteristics of their mountain locations in order to distinguish themselves from established metropolitan observatories and to cultivate credibility for their claims. Thus Campbell's report details the 'great difficulty' of planning and executing the Mount Whitney expedition in pursuit of scientific knowledge.

These representational manoeuvres will be traced here primarily by examining episodes of research into the planet Mars. Over the two decades that the possibility of advanced Martian life was taken seriously in American astronomy (roughly 1890–1910), a number of prominent astronomers and observatories participated in the discussion. As the timing of the Mars debates generally coincided with a critical period in astronomy's history, which was marked by the building of new observatories, the professionalisation of observatory staff, the emergence of expert specialisations and the transition from planetary to stellar topics, representations of place played a critical role in the establishment of modern American astronomy. In an era of prominent scientific mountaineering, polar exploration and field expeditions, American astronomers' strategic association with mountain geography was not merely a means to gathering new data, but also a means of cultivating legitimacy.

Geographies of science

Recent studies of the 'geography of science' have come to the forefront of scholarship concerned with knowledge production. The classic works in science studies, which focussed on the contingent and situated nature of scientific knowledge, essentially begged a spatial question without addressing it directly.[9] More recently, Livingstone's push for an explicitly geographical approach to the study of science has inspired a substantial body of scholarship.[10] The places in which scientists conduct their work, the pathways and networks along which scientific claims travel and the unique locations in which audiences engage with scientific knowledge have all been shown to have important influences not only on the substance of scientists' work, but also on scientists' ability to gain credibility.[11] The spatial settings in which scientific work is undertaken are no longer viewed 'as passive backdrops, but as vital links in the chain of production, validation and dissemination'.[12] This scholarship helpfully nudges us beyond the problematic constructivist-versus-realist debate over the 'true' nature of 'science' by acknowledging the plural and varied natures of science, scientists, scientific investigation and claims to scientific knowledge, in their many spatial variations.[13]

Livingstone's repeated calls for attention to science's geography have focussed on three major themes: site, region, and circulation.[14] The sites in which scientists work are now acknowledged to have a fundamental impact on the way knowledge claims are constructed and prepared for dissemination. Important recent work on this theme has shown that scientific knowledge is produced in a multiplicity of sites, including not only the controlled laboratory, but also the field, museum, hospital, pub, coffee house, bazaar, ship, body, etc.[15] The micro-geographies affecting each site of science are 'central to the veracity of the knowledge produced', despite the common perception of science as a 'placeless' activity that does not vary by location.[16] On a broader scale, regional geographies influence not only how scientists will approach their work, but also how that work will be received. The role of local scientific societies, for instance, has important regionally-specific effects on the legitimisation of scientific work.[17] Finally, geographies of circulation between sites, regions and audiences are now seen as important determinants of scientific knowledge and its credibility. Because scientific practices are typically separated from witnesses or audiences by some spatial distance, the establishment of trust (and, therefore, legitimacy) usually requires a circulation of knowledge claims. The spatial- and socio-geographic dimensions of this circulation influence the nature of the claims themselves, as well as their reception.[18]

These dimensions have been brought to bear on one of the most complex spatial divisions in the scientific world: the distinction between field and laboratory. Laboratory science is often considered *placeless*, with location said to have no impact on universally replicable findings. Field science, on the other hand, is considered site-specific, in that results cannot be replicated from one place to another, given that local variation itself is typically the topic of study. In legitimacy contests, bench scientists will savagely criticise results that can be produced in only a single site, whereas field scientists will reject investigations that do not show a sophisticated understanding of the uniqueness of the field site in question. Science is practised differently in these two spaces, and legitimacy is therefore cultivated differently.[19] Traditionally, field scientists emphasise 'the heroic quest of the naturalist-explorer', while bench scientists prioritise 'mastery over Nature through the steady, distanced gaze of the scientist'.[20] This fundamental distinction between objective distance and active contact as means of accessing natural reality certainly complicates our understanding of the geography of 'science'. Field scientists and bench scientists must invariably interact, communicate, collaborate and mediate the intricacies of their two worlds.[21]

What of the main concern here, the astronomical observatory? Is an astronomical observatory a field site or a laboratory? An observatory is essentially a controlled space, like a lab, but its scientists pursue observational work rather than experiment. Results and findings are theoretically supposed to be replicable, as in a lab, but the physical location of various observing sites has a significant impact on what types of observations can actually be made successfully. In essence, then, the astronomical observatory is a unique scientific site, in which the elements of field and lab co-mingle with no buffer or border zone between them.[22]

This dual identity can be read most clearly in astronomers' representations of their observatory locations. During the establishment of the first observatories in the American West, astronomers were especially effective in gaining legitimacy by representing their practices as both controlled and heroic, which was possible only by association with the new, high-altitude and mountain observatory sites. It is important to note, however, that although these observatories were located in mountain sites, that fact did not automatically produce this legitimacy. Astronomers, writers and audiences had to engage actively with the representation of astronomy's mountain geography to create the effect of legitimacy. Representations in science have been shown to influence what claims to knowledge can be made, what social networks can be activated, what alliances can be cultivated, what legitimacy can be established and how audiences can be manipulated.[23] In the case of the new American observatories at the end of the nineteenth century, this representational power was mobilised to portray astronomy as a mountain science. Like natural science, geology or even meteorology, American astronomy's reputation at this time became connected to popular enthusiasm for travel, fieldwork and adventuring in remote mountains and at high altitudes.[24]

Astronomy and the American West

Several new observatories were built in the American West at the end of the nineteenth century. They were hailed as great advances for the discipline and for American science, partly because of their large telescopes, professional staffs and commitment to new areas of stellar research. But the profile and status of these observatories were also highly dependent on their physical locations. Those that were in non-urban or mountain locations were automatically taken seriously, even with smaller telescopes and less experienced astronomers. Those closer to metropolitan areas or at lower altitudes, on the other hand, struggled to establish legitimacy, despite having large telescopes and highly trained staff astronomers.

The University of California's Lick Observatory, established in 1888, was the first 'big-science' institution in the United States. Endowed by California businessman, James Lick, the observatory was envisioned from the beginning as a world-class institution that would outshine all other observatories in two regards: first, it would have the most powerful telescope in the world and, second, it would be sited on a mountaintop with excellent conditions.[25] Lick's predilection for a mountain site was influenced by recent enthusiasm among astronomers for the benefits of improved atmospheric steadiness at high altitude, which supposedly 'would amply repay the inconvenience' of transporting materials and asking astronomers to live in difficult and isolated conditions.[26]

Lick himself was involved in the site selection and apparently gave his blessing to the remote peak of Mount Hamilton in the Diablo range, partly because he was enchanted by the fact that he could see its summit from his own home near the south end of San Francisco Bay.[27] At 4,200 feet high, the mountain exceeded Lick's minimum elevation criterion of 4,000 feet. This height and California's reputation for clear skies created the powerful assumption that the site would be ideal for astronomy. No formal evaluation of Mount Hamilton's atmospheric characteristics had been performed, in fact, before the site was officially selected and the County of Santa Clara induced to build an expensive 26-mile road to the mountaintop site.[28] Given the size of Lick's investment and the height of the astronomical community's hopes for its new centrepiece observatory, it was perhaps fortunate that when the site was eventually tested, the atmospheric characteristics were deemed to be very good! Before this determination, however, Mount Hamilton had already received favour, not because of the particulars of its scientific advantages but more because it fit a romanticised notion of the mountain as a proper location for astronomy. As the editor of an astronomical journal remarked: 'One year on the summit of the California mountains affords the opportunities which twelve years of observations in the changeable climates of other states do not furnish.'[29]

Lick's second ambition – to have the world's most powerful telescope at his observatory – was also fulfilled, but this quality was rarely remarked without simultaneous reference to the observatory's mountain location. The Lick Observatory's own director, Edward Holden, issued a widely circulated pamphlet, which through illustrations emphasised the site of the observatory, rather than the observatory's famous telescope.[30] Likewise, the very first volume of the new journal, *Publications of the Astronomical Society of the Pacific*, included this telling quote in its 'news briefs' section,

> Telescopes ... 'cannot be formed so as to take away that confusion of rays which arises from the tremors of the atmosphere. The only remedy is a most serene and quiet air, such as may perhaps be found on the tops of the highest mountains above the grosser clouds'. Sir Isaac Newton, in his *Opticks*, AD 1730.[31]

Mobilising the undisputed (and 250-year-old) authority of Newton in support of mountain-based astronomy, the new observatory and new society showed the extent to which geographical location mattered to the new astronomical science. The mountain location of the Lick Observatory was a major component of its status and credibility, quite separate from the observatory's actual work and contributions to research in stellar astronomy.

The second large-scale American observatory, the University of Chicago's Yerkes Observatory, provides another example of the role geography played in establishing credibility for astronomical institutions. Like the Lick Observatory, Yerkes was funded by a philanthropist who wanted his observatory to boast the largest telescope in the world. Much of the drama surrounding the new observatory's planning and construction in the 1890s, in fact, focussed on its attempt to 'lick the Lick' by installing a telescope with a 40-inch lens, which would famously exceed the 36-inch lens of Mount Hamilton's celebrated instrument.[32] The Yerkes Observatory was conceived as a centrepiece of the University of Chicago and of the city of Chicago, both then emerging on the national and international stages.[33]

There was only one problem with the Yerkes Observatory: its location. Given the University of Chicago's desire to maintain a close association with one of its showcase units, a site was selected for the observatory in Lake Geneva, Wisconsin, which was 'then just at the limit of leisurely commuting distance by train' from Chicago.[34] It was also, coincidentally, a 'resort for the choicest people of Chicago', whom the University of Chicago president wanted to lure as donors.[35] Although the site selectors were confident that the Lake Geneva location was fine for astronomical purposes, the observatory's spatial association with the city and the easy life proved to be a constant hindrance.

Observatory director, George Hale, found himself constantly defending the site selection, thus revealing deep concerns about the site's influence on the legitimacy of the observatory. He repeatedly provided technical explanations of the site's atmospheric advantages but also regularly emphasised his observatory's remoteness as a way of perceptually distancing it from urban Chicago.[36] At the dedication of the observatory in 1897, for instance, he thanked attendees for travelling to a site so far 'removed from the neighbourhood of great cities, and from the more populous regions of the United States', though in fact most of them had taken only a short train ride from Chicago.[37]

In these representations, Hale was forced to acknowledge the favouritism usually shown to mountain sites, particularly that of the Lick Observatory. He tried to rebuff this favouritism by arguing that mountain locations were not necessarily a guarantee of good astronomical research and by suggesting that his Lake Geneva institution was every bit as

Figure 8.1a First of the two plates which opened Lowell's first astronomical book *Mars* (Boston: Houghton, Mifflin & Company, 1895) shows the San Francisco Mountains, which could be seen from the Lowell Observatory.

credible as the Lick.[38] Despite these efforts, however, Yerkes was persistently dogged by accusations of 'bad seeing'. Even several of Yerkes' own astronomers admitted their site's inferiority to the Mount Hamilton as a matter of fact, and Hale himself soon grew tired of the difficulties of observing at Yerkes.[39] He left Chicago in 1903 to establish a new solar observatory outside Pasadena on Mount Wilson, elevation 5,700 feet. Despite the Yerkes Observatory's massive telescope, its generous funding, its meticulous organisation and its soaring expectations, it never managed to rise above concerns about its location. Yerkes was considered an excellent site by Eastern or Midwestern standards, but could not truly challenge the western mountain sites for prestige.

By contrast, the Lowell Observatory – more meagrely equipped, funded and staffed than either the Lick or Yerkes Observatories – managed to achieve considerable acclaim by promoting the excellent conditions of its site above Flagstaff, Arizona, elevation 7,000 feet. This small-scale observatory was founded in 1894 by a wealthy amateur astronomer, Percival Lowell, who intended a research programme focussed on visual observations of the planets, specifically Mars. In an era of increasing spectral and stellar work, an observatory

The Hermitage

Figure 8.1b Second of the two plates which opened Lowell's first astronomical book *Mars* (Boston: Houghton, Mifflin & Company, 1895) depicts one of the observatory residences almost as a frontier outpost. Together, these images created a strong visual connection between the Lowell Observatory and western high-mountain landscapes.

dedicated to the visual investigation of a single planet seemed an anachronism. With this singular interest, Lowell could hardly have expected to earn much esteem among professional astronomers and major observatories. He did not help his case by publishing his observations alongside speculative interpretations of the Martian surface as an inhabited landscape (described in more detail in the next section). Lowell's propensity for taking quasi-scientific arguments directly to popular audiences through magazines and lectures seemed to go against every promising trend in American astronomy. In thus antagonising leading American astronomers, Lowell inspired numerous assaults against his own and his observatory's legitimacy.

Lowell, however, managed to establish and maintain significant credibility, especially in the public eye. One of the most important things he did in this regard was to emphasise the remoteness of his observatory's location, the superiority of its altitude, and the excellence of its climate. In his publications, he regularly emphasised that he had investigated climatic conditions in numerous western sites before selecting high-altitude Flagstaff 'for the purpose of getting as good air as practicable'.[40] He relied on this fact heavily in asserting that his observatory was much more credible than any on the East Coast or in urban areas, lamenting that 'at the present time most observatories are situated where man is greatly handicapped in his own efforts toward the stars' by city smoke, electric lights and other pollutants of atmospheric visibility.[41] He even went so far as to argue that his observatory was on equal footing with the world-class Lick Observatory by virtue of his advantageous location, despite the great difference between their telescope powers and staff experience.[42]

Popular writers and audiences responded enthusiastically to this strategy, regularly commenting on the advantages of Lowell Observatory's high-altitude location when discussing the Mars debates. Although professional astronomers generally did not express any enthusiasm for Lowell's theory-driven methods, his speculative hypothesis and his targeting of popular publications, they often found themselves forced to admit the quality of his location. Simon Newcomb, who never accepted Lowell's theory about the inhabitants of Mars, nonetheless wrote of the Flagstaff observatory, 'Its situation is believed to be one of the best as regards atmospheric conditions.'[43] Such comments indicate the extent to which geographical location had achieved parity with other factors which also defined an astronomer's credibility, such as one's professional rank and the power of one's instrument.

It should be noted that Lowell Observatory is not in the mountains. Rather, it is located on a high mesa. This fact apparently escaped many of Lowell's readers and audiences at the time, however. The observatory was just assumed to be in the mountains by virtue of its reported remoteness, altitude, climate, and general location in 'the West'. A well-known astronomer, for example, referred in a publication to the excellent climate of the 'Arizona Mountains' and lauded Lowell's site on 'Flagstaff Mountain', which does not exist.[44] Lowell and his associates did nothing to correct this frequent mistake. On the contrary, they actively cultivated such a close association with mountains. One of Lowell's small staff described the observatory's location thus: 'It is a trifle short of 7,000 feet above the sea and is ten miles south of the San Francisco Peaks whose highest point is 12,800 feet in elevation.'[45] The San Francisco Peaks so prominently noted in this quote had nothing whatsoever to do with the observatory, but they (and their height) were regularly mentioned in connection with the observatory. Lowell's first book, *Mars*, actually included photographs of the San Francisco Peaks alongside photographs of the observatory buildings, implying that the observatory was in fact in the mountains. [Figs 8.1a and 8.1b] Both Lowell and his most experienced astronomer, William Pickering, were members of the Appalachian Mountain Club and were known for their climbing enthusiasm, which deepened the observatory's connection to mountain landscapes.[46] These mountain representations created by the Lowell Observatory relied on an already-established and widely accepted notion of high mountains as ideal sites for astronomical science. By tapping into this association, Lowell managed to generate significant credibility for himself and his work.

The movement of observatories away from the urban centres of the East Coast was seen as part of the inevitable professionalisation and industrialisation of astronomy, processes that were taking place across the sciences in America as a whole.[47] Amateurs, who had been fully integrated into the discipline in the middle of the nineteenth century, quickly lost their footing in this transitional era.[48] The notable exception of gentleman-amateur Percival Lowell and the success of his Lowell Observatory show the power that representation of place carried within the processes of scientific legitimisation. The new mountain locations for western observatories were clearly important to the topical and methodological transitions underway in turn-of-the-century American astronomy. However, it was the representation of these mountain locations that proved fundamental to establishing the credibility of observatories and astronomers. This can be seen quite clearly in debates that raged over the planet Mars and its geography.

A sublime view of the red planet

Over the decade and a half spanning the turn of the twentieth century, an extraordinary popular mania developed in the United States around the idea that Mars was inhabited by intelligent beings. Starting in the late 1870s, some European astronomers had reported seeing geometrical patterns on the Martian surface. Despite disagreement among professional American astronomers as to the visibility, existence or meaning of these patterns, popular audiences responded enthusiastically to Percival Lowell's bold interpretation that the lines were most likely a network of irrigation canals. Backed by an impressive map of the so-called 'canals', Lowell asserted that the lines proved the existence of an advanced race of Martian canal-digging engineers.[49] To the chagrin of disciplinary leaders intent on advancing the rational status of astronomy, Lowell's sensational claims were reported widely in newspapers, discussed frequently in general interest magazines, and presented regularly to popular audiences on both sides of the Atlantic.[50] As a result, the term 'canal' became the standard designation for linear features on Mars, though the existence of water was always much in debate. Despite their general lack of interest in planetary astronomy, scientists such as Newcomb of the Nautical Almanac, Hale of Yerkes Observatory, and Campbell and Holden of Lick Observatory responded to Lowell's growing fame by conducting their own Mars research and trying to discredit him. In the process, they hoped to protect the scientific reputation of their discipline by exposing Lowell as an amateur whose claims were unsound, unscientific and based on little more than optical illusion.[51] In the ensuing credibility contest, mountain representations played an important role because much of the manoeuvring over personal, professional and institutional legitimacy centred on the locations of the various observers. Each observer usually insisted on the superiority of his own position while denigrating his opponents' locations. In this rhetoric, high-altitude, remote, isolated, mountain observatories maintained the upper hand, using two primary themes to assert their credibility.

The first theme focussed on the sublime nature of mountains. In one sense, the sublimity was technical. With increasing altitude, air becomes less dense and contains fewer particles, meaning there are fewer opportunities for air molecules to impede or refract the path of light as it passes through Earth's atmosphere. All other things being equal, distant celestial objects thus appear brighter from high altitude positions than they would from sea level.

Furthermore, high altitude sites provide the opportunity to rise above dense cloud-cover and escape the visual distortion caused by water vapour molecules. Distance from urban areas also reduces the effects of pollution and heat, both of which impede clear views of the heavens. So the higher and more remote the observatory, the more sublime its conditions for scientific work. Lick Observatory, the first American observatory to see the Martian 'canals', emphasised this theme in its 1892 reports confirming earlier European findings. Though Mars was very low in the northern sky in 1892, Holden reported that the pure atmosphere and large telescope at Lick allowed for numerous observations and sketches of Mars at a time when most other American observatories reported a dismal failure in their attempts to get good views of the red planet.[52] The perfection of Lick's mountain location again became a theme in 1894, when Lick astronomer Campbell tackled the conventional wisdom about water vapour on Mars. In publishing controversial findings that showed little or no water vapour on the red planet, Campbell referred to the 'extremely unfavourable' conditions under which past observations had been made. He then lauded the high altitude of Lick Observatory, 'which eliminates from the problem the absorptive effect of the lower 4,200 feet of the Earth's atmosphere, with all its impurities. Most of the old observations were made from near sea-level.'[53] He thus used representations of the pure and sublime characteristics of the Lick Observatory site to validate his controversial position regarding the science of Mars.

In addition to boasts about the technical perfections of high and dry air, western astronomers also cultivated legitimacy with colourful descriptions of the sublime vistas their observatories offered of surrounding terrestrial landscapes. From a mountaintop or mesa cliff, the astronomer's view of his home planet was said to be spectacular. A *Scientific American* feature article on the new Lick Observatory typically emphasised the new facility's view of California:

> In speaking of the outlook from Observatory Peak, which is 4,802 feet in height, Professor Holden says: 'It would be difficult to find in the whole world a more magnificent view than can be had from the summit just before sunrise, on one of our August mornings. The eastern sky is saffron and gold, with just a few thin horizontal bars of purple and rosy clouds ... The instant the sunbeams touch the horizon the whole panorama of the Sierra Nevada flashes out, 180 miles distant ... The Bay of San Francisco looks like a piece of a child's dissecting map, and is lost in the fogs near the city. The buildings of the city seem strangely placed in the midst of all the quiet beauty and the wild strength of the mountains. Then you catch a glimpse of the Pacific in the southwest and of countless minor ranges of mountains and hills that are scattered toward every point of the compass, while, if the atmosphere is especially clear, you can plainly see to the north Mount Shasta, 175 miles distant.'[54]

Not only did this detailed representation garner interest from popular audiences, but it also conferred authority on all claims to clear vision coming from the Lick Observatory. If Holden could see with such clarity beyond the fogs of San Francisco, all the way to majestic Mount Shasta, then Lick Observatory's claims for seeing the surface of Mars could also be trusted.

Percival Lowell used and extended the effectiveness of these themes in his own early publications, when he was trying to establish his new observatory as a legitimate site of scientific knowledge making. He opened nearly every publication with a discussion of the clarity of high-altitude air in Arizona, thus predisposing readers to accept his later claims about having discovering numerous Martian canals.[55] He also successfully repelled attacks by Hale, Newcomb and a number of British skeptics by turning attention away from the content of their critiques and toward the location of their urban observatories.[56] In Lowell's rhetoric, an inability to see the Martian canals was linked to impure or polluted observing sites. His own remarkable ability to see increasing numbers of canals, on the other hand, could be attributed to the purity and sublimity of his own site.

Lowell also deftly emphasised a moral purity associated with sublime mountain locations. Removed from civilisation, he claimed, high-altitude astronomers were free from corrupting influences that would otherwise denigrate the purity of their investigations, observations and intentions. In repetitive yet persuasively eloquent arguments, he contended that proper investigations of Mars could be done only in high, remote places.

> [The astronomer] must abandon cities and forego plains. Only in places raised above and aloof from men can he profitably pursue his search, places where nature never meant him to dwell and admonishes him of the fact by sundry hints of a more or less distressing character ... Withdrawn from contact with his kind, he is by that much raised above human prejudice and limitation.[57]

In representations of this type, Lowell effectively tapped into a national enthusiasm for wilderness that was just then emerging in the United States.[58] This enthusiasm was strongly associated with the American West, allowing Lowell to make sweeping generalisations about the inferiority of the East for astronomy: 'Not till we pass beyond the Missouri do the stars shine out as they shone before the white man came.'[59] His skillful responsiveness to popular sentiment allowed Lowell to cultivate large audiences even though professional astronomers rejected many of his arguments about Martian canals and inhabitants. The romantic representation of his scientific exploits in the sublime air of the American High West carried great authority with general audiences.

Heroic explorations of Mars

A second theme that promoted and maintained the legitimacy of high-altitude and mountain observatories represented the ruggedness and physical challenge associated with working in the mountains. Textual descriptions and graphical depictions of snow, ice, bad weather and dangerous terrain reinforced the concept that the best investigations of Mars were being done in wilderness settings. In such representations, the astronomer was painted as a 'heroic and manly figure', confronting mountain wilderness and rising to its challenges in the name of science.

The heroic-astronomer theme had long been tied to mountain observatories in general, not just those that undertook observations of the planet Mars. Director of the Lick Observatory Holden published a monograph in 1896 on 'the conditions of good vision at

Figure 8.2 Holden's *Mountain Observatories* (Washington, DC: Smithsonian, 1896) featured numerous images that emphasised the climatic challenges and isolation of the world's mountain observatories, including this image of Holden's own Lick Observatory after a snowstorm. Most of Holden's images also appeared as plates in *Publications of the Astronomical Society of the Pacific* between 1893 and 1896 (courtesy of Smithsonian).

mountain stations all over the globe', in which he lauded the world's high-altitude observatories. Perhaps most striking about this volume was that it was illustrated with numerous vivid graphics depicting astronomers and observatory buildings on remote mountaintops [Fig. 8.2].[60] In these images, which Holden had collected from various publications and observatories, astronomers were shown to be every bit as hardy as the seasoned polar and glacial explorers then making headlines throughout Europe and North America. In the most extreme examples of this visual trope, astronomers were depicted as miniscule figures in ominous, vertical landscapes, often in the act of trekking through deep snow or crossing threatening crevasses. Their supposed destinations – summit observatories – were always excluded from the visual frame to accentuate the wildness of the setting [Figs 8.3, 8.4a and 8.4b]. Needless to say, Holden's volume contained not one image of a passive astronomer seated at a telescope. The astronomer-as-heroic-adventurer trope required that astronomers be represented as mountaineers, not as observers. In Holden's book, these dramatic images were accompanied by a textual narrative that recounted the difficulties astronomers had reported while living and working at various high-altitude facilities: violent weather, forest

Figure 8.3 The astronomers' 'Mountain Camp' depicted in this image is dwarfed by Mount Whitney, site of Campbell's 1909 expedition to photograph the spectrum of Mars. From Holden's *Mountain Observatories* (Washington, DC: Smithsonian, 1896) (courtesy of Smithsonian).

Figure 8.4a The first of two images titled 'On the Way to the Mont Blanc Observatory' in Holden's *Mountain Observatories* (Washington, DC: Smithsonian, 1896). Here astronomers are depicted as fearless mountaineers in an ominous landscape (courtesy of Smithsonian).

fires, snow-blindness and mountain-sickness, as well as isolation, discomfort and monotony, to name a few. Holden cast these potential negative features in a decidedly positive light that embraced the heroic-astronomer persona: 'Devoted men can always be found to undergo necessary hardships in the pursuit of scientific truth.'[61]

The debates over Mars, its canals and its inhabitants trafficked heavily in this type of representation. Most often, the portrait of the heroic-astronomer was evoked implicitly through counter-portraits of urban or sea-level astronomers as unmanly and untrustworthy in terms of their Mars claims. Lowell, for instance, often rhetorically challenged his critics to visit the Lowell Observatory, noting that everyone who had observed from Flagstaff had seen canals on the Martian surface. In such challenges, Lowell implied that only those astronomers who were hardy enough to undertake a westward journey were capable of good scientific vision. No wonder the eastern astronomers had never seen canals, he suggested – they were not man enough. To discredit his critics at the Lick Observatory, against whom he clearly could not level the same charge, Lowell suggested instead that the men working on Mount Hamilton were not capable of using their powerful telescopes properly in their excellent setting.[62] Lowell's principal attacks on his opponents thus focussed either on their failure to obtain a sublime location or on their failure to meet the challenges of the scientific endeavour in a sublime location. Campbell, at the Lick Observatory, responded in kind, levelling similar criticism of Lowell's own staff. In explaining differences between his spec-

Figure 8.4b The second of two images titled 'On the Way to the Mont Blanc Observatory' in Holden's *Mountain Observatories* (Washington, DC: Smithsonian, 1896). Here astronomers cross a threatening crevasse with seemingly casual ease (courtesy of Smithsonian).

troscopic results (which found no water vapour on Mars) and those performed at the Lowell Observatory (which indicated plenty of life-supporting water on Mars), for instance, Campbell argued that the Arizona astronomers probably did not understand fundamental issues related to mountain geography and that their data therefore could not be trusted.[63] Scientific manliness – the ability to confront and ably conquer wilderness challenges in pursuit of knowledge – was thus powerfully mobilised as a means of legitimising various claims regarding the nature of Mars.[64]

Expeditions in search of the red planet

The two dominant, mountain-related, representational tropes in the Mars debates – mountains as sublime scientific sites and mountain astronomy as a difficult, heroic, manly endeavour – found a powerful fusion in the representation of astronomical expeditions. Around the turn of the century, the quest for definitive Mars observations inspired several expeditions: challenging treks through rugged and difficult wilderness conditions in search of perfect, remote, sublime sites of

Figure 8.5 Representations of Harvard College Observatory's astronomical outpost near Arequipa, Peru invariably referred to the formidable Andean mountains surrounding it, as shown in this image. Frontispiece for *Astronomy and Astro-Physics*, New Series 5, No. 105 (May 1892).

science. Though astronomical expeditions were fairly common in the nineteenth century, they were generally aimed at seeing a celestial object or event that would be geometrically invisible from the home location. A solar eclipse that would be visible only in certain areas of the globe, for example, might require an expedition to northern Africa, or East Asia, or India.[65] The new expeditions to observe Mars – though similar in style (and levels of publicity) to these solar eclipse expeditions – were oriented instead around getting a better view, not a unique view.

The first major expedition by an American observatory in this vein was Harvard's investigation of mountain sites in South America during the 1880s. At the same time the vaunted Lick Observatory was being planned and constructed in California, Harvard College Observatory's director, Edward Pickering, obtained funding for a high-altitude, satellite observatory. A much-reported expedition to the Andes Mountains resulted in establishment of a research station near Arequipa, Peru, elevation 8,000 feet.[66] This station, which was originally intended to undertake a programme of photographic mapping of the southern skies, quickly became known for its studies of the Martian surface. The first director, Pickering's brother William (who later moved to the Lowell Observatory), claimed that the perfect atmospheric conditions at Arequipa enticed him to study Mars and its enigmatic markings during the red planet's close approach in 1892. He felt he would otherwise be wasting a glorious opportunity to contribute to knowledge about Mars, given the 'splendid atmosphere' above the Andes at his 'remote and isolated position'.[67]

In reporting his findings about Mars, Pickering regularly mentioned the rugged yet sublime location from which he had made his observations. Photographs of the observatory always showed stunning snow-covered peaks in the background [Fig. 8.5], and the elevations of surrounding peaks were mentioned in nearly every dispatch from the expeditionary station. Pickering himself, an avid mountaineer and member of the Appalachian Mountain Club, undertook multiple ascents of the nearby El Misti volcano, and his successor, Solon Bailey, eventually established a meteorological station on its peak at 19,200 feet. Bailey wrote dramatically of his conquest of the volcano, revealing a powerful entanglement of scientific interest and the romantic pursuit of the heroic. 'El Misti stands alone. At first a sort of awe kept me from considering as possible the establishment of a station on its summit; but always, as I looked upon it, the impulse became stronger and stronger, and finally it could not be resisted.'[68] He wrote excitedly about the 'skill and stamina' required for climbing such a high mountain, reporting, 'the difficulties of the ascents were increased, at heights of 10,000 feet or more, by attacks of *soroche*, a mountain sickness that caused dizziness, faintings, nausea, and sometimes loss of consciousness'.[69] The story of this expedition-within-an-expedition became famously associated with the southern observatory, emphasising the heroism and dangers of astronomical expeditions.

It was not only the eastern observatories that sent expeditions to high altitude. Even the western and mountain-based American astronomers went on expeditions strategically designed to improve their credibility in the Mars debates. In the face of increasing criticism of his colourful hypothesis, Lowell conceived a South American expedition of his own in 1907. Appointing well-known eclipse expeditioner David Todd of Amherst as director, Lowell sent a small party from Flagstaff to the Andes Mountains to observe and photograph the surface of Mars. His stated intent was to capture definitive photographic evidence of the Martian canals, thus proving the optical illusion theory incorrect. At the same time, however, Lowell clearly relished the opportunity to create a popular sensation that reflected favourably on the legitimacy of his observatory and its scientists. He cabled the press at every opportunity with news from the expedition and enjoyed the development of a bidding war between several magazines seeking first publication rights to the expedition's findings.[70] Much of the intrigue of the expedition lay in the merger of the two tropes identified above – a heroic search for a sublime site of science.[71]

In answer to the popular furore over Martian canals that Lowell stoked with his 1907 expedition, Campbell plotted his 1909 expedition to Mount Whitney. Just like Lowell's expedition, Campbell's was a carefully planned endeavour meant to settle the life-on-Mars debate by cultivating unimpeachable legitimacy for his scientific claims. Assuming the heroic-astronomer persona quite effectively, Campbell described in his official report a very difficult ascent of the mountain and a painstaking setup of his scientific instruments, made especially arduous by harsh weather. The conditions at the top, however, were said to be sublime, as captured in Campbell's rapturous claim cited above that he 'had never seen so pure a sky before'.[72] These powerful representations of the expedition were critical to the legitimacy of its results, which might otherwise have been seen as extremely limited and inconclusive, given that Campbell observed Mars with the spectroscope on only two nights and reported stormy weather both before and after. The presence of humid air or some other anomaly could have easily tainted results gathered by extremely sensitive equipment over such a short period of time. But Campbell's 1909 results – gathered at the summit of the highest mountain in the continental United States – were received as conclusive and final within the professional ranks. The heroic efforts he had made, the sublime conditions he had attained, and the powerful representations he then created to communicate with his professional colleagues and the wider public ensured a very powerful legitimacy for his scientific claims.

Conclusions

Astronomical expeditions to high mountains became focal points in the turn-of-the-century legitimacy wars over Mars, with popular opinion swinging back and forth in response to expeditionary findings. Astronomers' aggressive and strategic representations of their mountain experiences combined two extremely powerful tropes in support of their claims and reputations. On one level, astronomers succeeded in aligning themselves with popular heroic endeavours like mountaineering and polar exploration. At the same time, however, they relied on a popular reverence for sublime mountains as the foundation for their claims. These expeditions thus merged the instrumental authority of the mobile observatory-laboratory and the personal authority of 'manliness' with the critical geographical authority of high-altitude landscapes.

This acknowledgement, celebration and even embellishment of the site of science raises interesting questions about the nature of the legitimacy Mars astronomers constructed for themselves. By emphasising individual experience and the uniqueness of individual observing locations, mountain-based astronomers actually undermined their profession's claims to universal truth. This paradox perhaps explains some of the lingering difficulty in separating amateurs from professionals before the second decade of the twentieth century, a difficulty that allowed Percival Lowell to establish a powerful credibility for himself and his claims that Mars was inhabited. Only when American astronomy had largely abandoned its sea-level and urban sites later in the twentieth century, fully relocating to the mountains, did the geographical uniqueness of individual sites begin to lose relevance. Only then could instrumental superiority and professional standing re-emerge as primary variables in the legitimacy equation. In the era of Mars debates and the popular canal craze, however, a metropolitan-versus-mountain dichotomy provided the critical means of differentiating among the credibility of observatories, astronomers and hypotheses. The higher, the more remote, the more rugged and the more sublime, the better.

Part 2

Local Knowledge and Science in High Places

9

Stewards of the Mountains

The Poetics and Politics of Local Knowledge in the Valaisan Alps

Gilles Rudaz

In the conclusion to *Mountains of the World: A Global Priority*, the geographers, Bruno Messerli and Jack Ives, and anthropologist Robert Rhoades set an 'Agenda for Sustainable Mountain Development'. In it, they specify 'seven prerequisites for a twenty-first-century mountain agenda'. In its broader sense the first prerequisite, called the 'Mountain Perspective', means taking into account the specificity of mountains. In its narrower, and here more privileged sense, this can be defined as the way mountain people see the world. The argument for the mountain perspective is that, 'Most of what has been written about mountains, or performed upon them in the guise of aid and development, has been undertaken from the outside: by flatlanders and mainstream institutions, whether government or private, business or academic, conservationist or political. Very often a mountain perspective has been absent'.[1]

While traditionally considered as socially and economically closed, historians and ethnologists have shown that Alpine communities have been open societies since as early as the Middle Ages. This is what Pier Paolo Viazzo calls the 'Alpine Paradox'.[2] Their openness has been clearly reinforced in modern times with the development of transport and communication systems. The most important thing to realise here is that it is not possible to do an analysis of mountain perspective in isolation, but we rather need to consider also the interplay between the representations developed by mountain dwellers and those of outsiders. The main argument here is that there are competing representations of mountains, and that local populations, in order to stay in the game when it comes to defining the various modes of mountain management, make special claims to consubstantiality between themselves and the mountains.

Two conceptual problems face any discussion of the mountain perspective. The first is the difficulty of defining mountains, and the second is the fact that local societies traditionally do not define themselves as 'mountain people'.

Defining 'mountains' and identifying communities as 'mountain people'

The recurrent problem 'mountain researchers'[3] face is the difficulty of defining their object of study: what is a mountain? In 1933, in the preface of Jules Blache's book focussing on relationships between humans and mountains on a world scale, Raoul Blanchard, leader of the group of Grenoble geographers who gave a major impetus to Alpine geography, noted: 'Even a definition of mountains which would be clear and comprehensive is in itself almost impossible to provide.'[4] About sixty years later, despite mountain areas and their populations having acquired an increased recognition on the international political scene, in *Mountains of the World* the geographers Jack Ives and Bruno Messerli and the cartographer Ernst Spiess underline that 'the inability of mountain scholars to produce a rigorous definition, which has universal application and acceptance, has often led to time-consuming debate with no satisfactory result.'[5] In the context of the globalisation of mountain issues, geographers' reflections on the definition of mountains gather new momentum.[6]

Mainly viewed as a category of relief, mountains are above all considered as an object of the natural world, as a geosystem independent from society. So, the majority of attempts at formal definitions of mountains resort to physical criteria: usually altitude, slope and landscape forms. These criteria are based on the 'effect' of the relief, which can be best summarised as 'the climatic degradation caused by altitudinal fact, altitudinal belting of landscapes, resulting milieus and human activities, amplification of phenomena and natural hazards due to slope effect.'[7]

We are indebted to the geographer Isabelle Sacareau for a definition of mountains which establishes a link between material reality and representation of space: 'a category of space bearing multiple "territorialities" of which the altitude and slope systems constitute a topographic and/or climatic discontinuity distinct enough from the surrounding spaces as to be perceived as different from them, both by the populations that inhabit it and those that don't'.[8] Such a statement raises the need for social consensus in order for the 'mountain' object to exist. However, in our perspective, the fact of being recognised by both 'insiders' and 'outsiders' is not a necessary condition to the validation of an entity called a 'mountain'. More important is the fact: everyone has his own conception of mountains! Also, Enlightenment scientists or Romantic writers did not seek the approval of the local populations to create a 'mountain' object. The point here is that, while scientists produce formal 'geographical objects', in everyday life without formality societies do so as they apprehend the world.

In a paper entitled 'Réalité et perceptions comparées des Andes au Pérou et en Colombie', Olivier Dollfus shows how 'the perception and significance of the Andes are not the same in the two largest Andean countries'.[9] In Peru the mountains are regarded as a 'poor and underdeveloped' periphery, 'a back-country with problems': whereas, 'the Andes do not exist in Colombia.'[10] A common geographical entity, the Andes, exists materially in two territories; in one it is perceived as a relevant unit, but not in the other. Without denying their material existence, the focus here is on mountains 'as objects institutionalised by societies'.[11] In other words, the varied social interpretations of a material reality become of interest.

Designation becomes central as construction.

> To designate means to extract an individuality, that is to say an entity recognisable according to some of its attributes, from an undifferentiated phenomenal universe, i.e. from an environment of undetermined complexity. The designative act, thus, is to confer an order since it selects a set of properties, compacts them into a name and imposes them as determinative to a feature of the terrestrial surface.[12]

This process corresponds to the creation of entities of meaning, based on a partition and selection within the terrestrial unity. Thus, the designation of a spatial object has referential implications by introducing a 'here' and a 'there'.[13] The geographical object exists necessarily in relation to other geographical objects, and positions itself according to them. The pertinence of a geographical object is determined by the position it occupies within a whole system of objects and not by a pertinence inherent within itself. As Isabelle Sacareau points out: 'Mountains cannot be studied independently of either their relationship with other categories of space, or of the elements which structure and mesh these territories according to different spatial scales.'[14]

The construction of a category 'mountain' is thus social, i.e. the product of collective imaginations,[15] scientific[16] or political[17]. It also has implications in terms of identity politics. As researches have shown, local societies in high places do not traditionally define themselves as 'mountain people'.[18] Usually, mountains define an outside world, and mountain people are defined as such by those who do not dwell there. Despite these elements, a process of re-appropriation sometimes occurs where communities themselves embrace the identity of mountain people. Here, I give special focus to the processes whereby such societies affirm and manifest their identity as mountain people.

The specific case is a famous mountain region in the Swiss Alps, the Valais, also known by its tourist moniker of 'Matterhorn State'. This is one of the twenty-six states[19] of the Swiss Confederation comprising the higher valley of the Rhône River and the contiguous side valleys. It is the mountain region described in Josias Simler's book of 1574, *Vallesiae descriptio*. It was also the setting for Jean-Jacques Rousseau's *La Nouvelle Héloïse* (1761), which marked a turning point in Western awareness of mountains. A quantitative analysis of published travel books reveals clearly that at the beginning of the nineteenth century Valais stole the limelight from Bernese Oberland to attain the archetypal status of the Swiss Alps.[20] Having the highest density of summits 4,000 metres or higher, Valais emerged definitively as a Mecca of the Alps, with the advent of mountain climbing in the second half of the nineteenth century.

From agro-ecological altitudinal belt to political structure

Traditional mountain societies are commonly organised according to a mode of exploitation based on the complementarities of altitudinal biogeographic belts. These societies are mainly oriented towards the practice of animal breeding. Given the characteristics of slope, climate and soil, breeding allows the exploitation of otherwise unutilised and non-cultivatable surfaces. The presence of a series of dwellings spreading from the villages to the high pastures attests to a strategy of maximising the use of vegetation belts and, more specifically, the fundamental resource of grass. Management is based on an annual cycle. The community spends winter in the village. The herds are moved at the end of spring towards an intermediate level, called '*mayens*', before being brought to the high mountain pastures at the summer solstice to remain there until the autumn equinox. Then, the cattle are brought down again to the *mayens*, before returning to the village for winter. With new prospects of speculative opportunities around the economy of breeding, the development of technical installations and a specific social organisation occurred.[21] This operating system, characterised by the migration of both cattle and men and by specific constructions (temporary dwelling, cowshed, barn), appeared towards the second part of the High Middle Ages. In 1906 the geographers Jean Brunhes and Paul Girardin, provided an example of this organisation in their case study of a side valley of Valais considered archetypal, the Val d'Anniviers.[22] The diagram [Fig. 9.1] was inspired by their work. The axis indicates the altitude in metres and the ordinate represents the months. The dotted lines represent the people's movements and the continuous line traces the animals' movements.

This vertical organisation of human activities is found in the farms but also in the communities' political structures: municipal boundaries extending from the valley bottoms to the top of high mountain pastures. The communities thus hold properties on the various belts of vegetation. The report presented to the State of Valais, in April 1903, concerning the dividing of the 'Greater Municipality of Lens' into four municipalities illustrates the need for communities to have diversified resources on their territory. The different cultivations correspond to the vegetational belts.

> The obligation we held to partition this territory in a normal way, in so far as possible in light of natural restrictions, and in one piece, did not always allow us to make proportional allotments of the various cultivations, pastures, forests, meadows, vineyards ... [23]

The idea is both to have access to diverse resources and to have access to the grass resource at different temporal scales. There is a migration of the activities based on the vegetal cycle of the grass. Every belt has its importance and the land-use system is based on a coordinated use of the various levels. This mode of exploitation is also found in the parcelling of farmland.

In traditional Alpine societies, the terms 'alp' and 'mountain' refer to high pastures which are used for the summering of cattle, the term 'mount' indicating a pass. The moun-

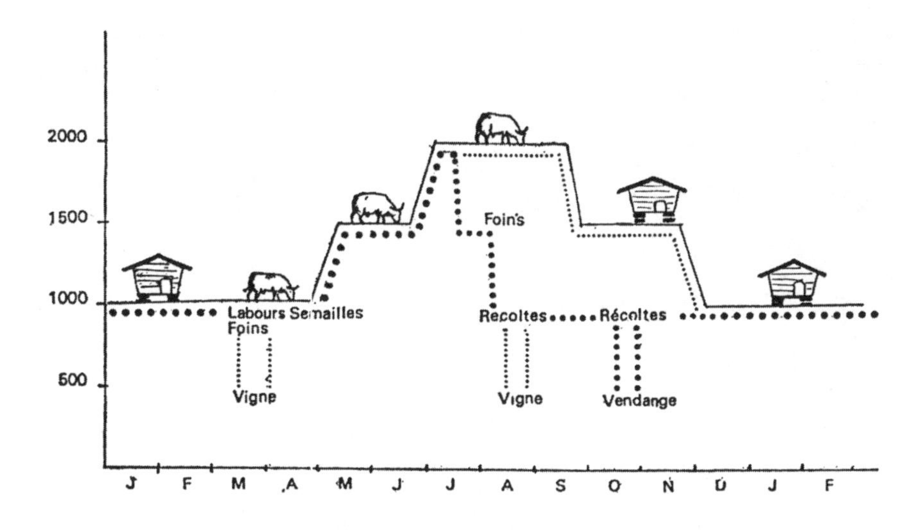

Figure 9.1 The traditional land-use system, in P. Claval, *Eléments de géographie humaine*, Génin, Paris, 1974. Sketch based on the work of J. Brunhes (courtesy of LexisNexis, Paris).

tains are designated because they are considered a useful space. So, this term is limited to the pastures used for summering the cattle, whereas the zone of glaciers and rocks is treated as a marginal space lacking resources and thus not requiring designation. Defining the 'mountain' as a space temporarily exploitable to economic ends, the local populations do not necessarily recognise themselves as 'mountain people'. The appellation, mountain people, does occur, but to name the herders who take care of the cattle in the high-altitude pastures during the summer season.

Life comes from above

Many cosmogonies from very varied cultural contexts believe the origins of the world or humans to lie in high places.[24] Because of their role as water sources providing the essential element of life, mountain spaces are often perceived as the geographical source of life itself. In the Bible, the resting place of Noah's Ark on Mount Ararat after the Great Flood figures the mountain as a place of origin and renewal. A long-standing legend in the Valais is that of 'Lake Valais', a body of water which now no longer exists. Some villages located at an altitude of 1,300 metres are said to have been harbours in the past, and places are found at these altitudes with names such as 'Stone of the Boatmen'.

Figure 9.2 S.W. King (1821–1868), *Breithorn and Petit Cervin from the St-Theodule Pass – Val Tournanche*, 1858, Collection Helm&Helm, Lindach am Neckar (courtesy of Polygraphicum).

In Valaisan popular tradition, there is a consistent belief that the process of settlement originated in the uplands and moved to lower areas. The founders of the villages are believed to have come from initial settlements, situated at higher altitudes that have since disappeared. Toponyms refer to regions once cultivated or inhabited that have since been deserted. These migrations from upland to lower areas are linked to unfavourable climate change. This change corresponds to the Little Ice Age extending from the middle of the sixteenth century to the middle of the nineteenth, and is marked also by an increase in rainfall. The resulting spate of natural disasters and the growth of glaciers is conventionally explained by local people by the poor behaviour of the community or some of its members. The climatic evolution and its consequences are certainly the origin of the myth of the Alpine populations' lost 'Golden Age'. Numerous tales speak of a time when pastures were more luxuriant and cows provided milk in abundance, before the villages and pastures disappeared under snow, ice and even rocks, as a consequence of some villager's misdeed, the most serious of which being a refusal of hospitality to somebody in need, most often a vagrant.

According to local tradition, at the foot of the St-Theodule Pass [Fig. 9.2], between the Monte-Rosa and the Matterhorn, was a populous town. A man, to whom hospitality was declined, cursed the town, predicting its end under snow and ice.

> And everything happened as he said. Immediately after he left, the climate became harsher. That same fall, snow fell abundantly and was followed by an extraordinary cold. It is said that one old blind man, sitting near his stove, asked if this snow mass was white, or still reddish, like it had always been before. When he was told that it was white, he shook his head and sadly said: 'Let us leave. It is time to leave the mountains for a better sheltered land, the snow will never disappear again.' And just as he predicted, the snow did not melt, but soon formed a vast glacier which year after year extended by three miles, and which still gains ground today.[25]

This specificity of local environmental perspectives remains apparent today. In 2003, ProClim, the Forum for Climate Change and Global Change, a platform of the Swiss Academy of Sciences, claimed that the persons in charge of winter-sports tourism did not recognise the danger global warming represented for their activities.[26] Those managers come mainly from local populations. Whereas climatic change is largely perceived as a threat by the whole of Swiss society, local mountain populations do not seem particularly worried, even though their lives would be more affected than those of the populations of other areas of the country. Being largely dependent on winter tourism, they worry mainly about the impacts of global warming on the snowline and the duration of the winter season, as well as resulting natural hazards, such as the melting of the permafrost, which would threaten their living space. However, they put the experts' predictions into perspective and consider the issue with a certain serenity: 'We are used to seeing it (the glacier) go up and down over the centuries.'[27] Indeed, in the collective memory, there are still memories of trade with the neighbouring valleys, e.g. Valley of Aosta (Italy), via passes which have long since been iced over or blocked with snow and become unusable.

'Poor' mountain communities

In early nineteenth-century descriptions of the Valais, a distinction between the plain (of the Rhône) and mountains is the favoured way of explaining Valaisan geographical realities. Thus, the French delegate in Valais, Joseph Eschasseriaux, wrote in 1806:

> In Valais there are two sorts of populations and two different climates; the first of these populations, dwelling in the mountains and breathing a purer air, is generally healthier and more vigorous, but a little wild; the second, dwelling in the valley, is generally speaking the most degraded and most disgraced type of nature, and will soon die, if it doesn't regenerate itself by alliances with foreigners and with the men of the higher areas.[28]

The core of these descriptions of Valais depends upon a determinism traceable to Montesquieu, in which the environment impresses a certain number of characteristics on the populations which live there. According to this perspective, nature favours the inhabitants of higher altitudes who are considered 'stronger' and 'more spiritual' than the inhabitants of the plain. Their economic condition is also regarded as better. In local tradition one also finds this vision of a greater ease in the high places.

According to the argument that mountains cannot be understood independently of their relationship to other categories of space, the Rhône plain faced such drastic modifications since the 1860s that the category 'mountain' itself could not remain unscathed. In the middle of the nineteenth century, two major events fundamentally modified the already-existing relationship between plain and mountain – first, the transformation of the Rhône plain from a marsh into the 'orchard' of the country after the regulation of the river, and second, the arrival of the railway which reinforced the Rhône's role as an economic axis. The 'plain' emerged as a new space of development.

At the end of the nineteenth century, whilst the ideology of 'progress' reigned unchallenged, a negative image of mountain people emerged.[29] The ambition was 'to open the mountain', to break down the supposed isolation of the mountain dwellers. It was not only a question of bringing them closer geographically, but also morally to the canton of Valais as a whole: a normalising process. Interventions were preached: the building of roads particularly fitted this vision. According to Kilani, the narrative took a particular turn 'in its constant reference to nature and the techno-economic factors to describe and explain the social and cultural condition of the mountain dweller'.[30] In this context, a new image of mountain people emerged. They appear as destitute beings, fighting for their survival in a hostile environment. The mountain communities are now depicted as isolated and poor.

This poverty was regarded as inherent to the condition of the mountain dweller. 'To make nature responsible for poverty is to reinforce the image of total misery which one wants to give of mountains; it is also to justify the external intervention – that of the reforming action of the Valaisan State, or that of industrial progress – on mountains.'[31] As pointed out by the historian, François Walter, two conditions were necessary for the new integration and the valorisation of the mountain areas. On the one hand, the situation of marginalisation of mountain areas had to appear intolerable. On the other, potentialities had to be detected in order to be exploited.[32]

Thus, mountains began to attract a general interest as reserves of energy. The first hydro-electric concession in Valais was granted in 1890. In 1916, the federal law on the use of water power for electricity generation was voted in. Dams were constructed in the inter-war years: '… glaciers start to look like gold mines to those who up until then had hardly been concerned with them and the question arises of determining whether in fact the municipalities or the State are the legitimate owners.'[33] This new perspective on mountains was reflected within the Valaisan Parliament where one saw two opposing camps. On the one hand, State Minister Lorétan considered that the 'unproductive grounds', the 'places without master', were properties of the State.[34] The 'unproductive lands' were designated by tradition as spaces which did not have resources, that is to say, they lay beyond pastures and forests as spaces of ice and rock. On the other hand, the local deputies believed that these lands belonged to the municipalities. Even if the first debates were directed towards precise objects, namely the renting of an ice cave of the Rhône glacier for tourist purpose or the construction of a mountain lodge in the area of Saas-Fee, people were definitely anticipating when it came to the hydro-electric stakes. The question was whether these grounds were uncultivated, in a narrow sense, or productive, in a broader sense. On 17 November 1930 the Valaisan Parliament concluded: 'municipalities have the right to negotiate grounds, snows and water, which belong to them without question.'[35] The category 'mountain', initially designating high-altitude pastures, was being extended towards new spaces.

Valais as the archetype of the Swiss mountain region

As mountain planning started, a paradoxical valorisation of the images of mountains could be observed.[36] Mountain people were figured as guardians of certain basic values within Swiss society and, a few decades later, within Valaisan society. The discussion of Swiss identity is old and received a boost with the evolution of the country's economic and social conditions from the middle of the nineteenth century.[37] Whereas Switzerland experienced strong industrial and urban development, a discourse about identity grounded in pastoral reference was elaborated in opposition. The Swiss national exposition of 1896, which specifically honoured Alpine populations, illustrates this tendency.[38] This deep national attachment to mountain societies is a valorisation of a past and it constitutes a response to the insecurities of an emerging industrial and urban society. In the inter-war climate of uncertainty, the anti-urban tendency of Swiss nationalism became accentuated. National moral values were supposed to be preserved in rural areas, particularly in the mountains, with the figure of the mountain peasant, simple and hard-working, being held up as a paradigm. In a society in full transformation, a society which was becoming increasingly urban, mountains were a place where traditions and moral values could be preserved. High places acquired the status of cultural conservatory. Valais, by virtue of its relative isolation,

> appears as a uniquely privileged place to play the role of conservatory of traditional values in a world of change. Valais and Valaisans offer the image of what Switzerland of the heroic times was, virgin landscape and Alpine populations, hard working, sober, taciturn, proud, instinctive and religious to the point of superstition. To stay in Valais, is to immerse oneself in this pure Alpine beauty and to thence to morally replenish oneself amongst the guardians of true Swiss values.[39]

In this way, Valais was often referred to as the 'Old Country'.

Local societies do not define themselves traditionally as 'mountain people'. In 1866, the Swiss Alpine Club celebrated its birthday at the summit of Bella Tola Mountain in the Anniviers Valley. Most probably its members went there more to see 'mountains' than 'mountain people'. However, the inhabitants of the St-Luc village, situated under the summit, decorated their village and indicated at the entry to the village '*Bienvenue chez nous les montagnards*' ('Welcome to the home of the mountain people'). The sociologist, Bernard Crettaz, who relates this anecdote, interprets the act as 'a sign of new accultured identity'.[40] Whereas the use of the term mountain people was uncommon, knowing that aspects of mountain life had become validated, the inhabitants began to perform according to these expectations carried by exogenous stakeholders.

Figure 9.3 B. Roten-Calpini (1873–1962), *Saviésanne au blé*, n.d., oil on canvas, 64 x 82 cm, Musées des Beaux-arts, Sion (courtesy of Musées cantonaux, H. Preisig, Sion).

Art historian, Marie-Claude Morand, has discussed the role played by foreign painters in the construction of the Valaisan cultural identity.[41] At the beginning of the twentieth century under the authority of Ernest Bieler, the 'Savièse School' of painting was founded. The school focussed on Valaisan traditional mountain societies as symbols of permanence in a changing world. The subject matter of these artists included scenes of everyday life depicting the traditional practices of a rural society in the mountains. Mountain women, recognised as key actors in the preservation of the tradition, were central figures in these paintings [Fig. 9.3]. The Savièse School, which would have an influence well beyond the state of Valais, largely contributed to the valorisation of a traditional society and introduced a change in perspective. 'Contrarily to previous decades, it is no longer the exaltation of grandiose and iced solitudes but mountains which are cultivated, domesticated and dwelled in by mountain people.'[42] It is the mountain as a living space that is essential. Valais corresponds, according to these outside visions, to the archetype of a traditional mountain society.

Within three decades one can see a process of self-appropriation of this perception by the Valaisan population itself, a process highlighted by Marie-Claude Morand who speaks about the transformation of 'an exotic thematic repertory of outside use' into an 'identity image of local use'.[43] In the 1920s, there was a consensus in Valais about the development opportunities of the region by means of tourism. If it experienced a tourist development from the end of the nineteenth to the beginning of the twentieth century, this was slowed down by the First World War. The succeeding economic crisis pushed the Valaisans towards a national, rather than international, clientele. The mountain scenes, which were the fame of the Savièse School, appeared on state tourist promotion posters. Little by little, the Valaisan population conformed to expectations of the broader Swiss population. One can see a multiplication of companies specialising in local costume and clothing styles. This appropriation of a cultural identity that originated outside, an identity centred on a traditional mountain society, results from the impetus of tourism, whereas this same industry was depicted at the time as a threat to the moral integrity of the local populations.

Mountains as a political category

The concerns of the Swiss political world for mountain populations are long-standing. In the already mentioned context of the urbanisation of Switzerland at the turn of the twentieth century, authorities worried about the depopulation of the rural and mountain areas. The assistance bases for mountain populations were set up in the mid 1920s with the vote by the Swiss Parliament of the Baumberger motion focussing on the depopulation of mountain areas. It obtained the support of press and political opinion and found unanimity among all political parties in Parliament; there was a consensus in favour of intervention on behalf mountain populations.

The Baumberger resolution and the succeeding political initiatives granted new status to mountains in two respects: first as population reservoir and second as a determining 'piece of the puzzle' of the socio-political profile of Switzerland. During the Second World War, the mountain rose up the symbolic scale. In the climate of crisis and uncertainty produced by the European war, strong speeches of national cohesion were elaborated with a focus on the mountains. To support the mountain populations seemed essential, a moral duty meriting the efforts of the entire country. During this period, the mountains and more particularly the Alps, gained an additional importance because of their role as natural defences and the space they offered to protect the nation. The mountains played a crucial role on behalf of the nation as a whole. Political action was aimed overwhelmingly at maintaining mountain populations and supporting farming communities facing economic difficulties.

In the context of policies addressed specifically to mountains emerges the need to establish a uniform, administrative definition of mountains. This task was carried out between 1944 and 1949 and would lead to the elaboration of the cadastre of agricultural production, which defined a mountain zone based on 'the most important factors of production': length of the vegetation period, atmospheric precipitation regime, exposure to the sun, access possibilities and land.[44] 'Obtaining a political status for a geographical object depends on the social implications of the singularity that is recognised for it.'[45] The fact of identifying a mountain object and of granting it a political status reflects the societal considerations that the object implies; one regarded worthy of benefiting from a specific treatment.

At the same time, one can also see the creation of associations of support for mountain populations and the constitution of groups in defence of their interests, such as the 'Swiss Group of Mountain Peasants' founded in 1943. This group was later renamed 'Swiss Group for the Mountain Populations' (1973) and is now entitled 'Swiss Group for Mountain Regions', and is the umbrella organisation for mountain people interest groups in Switzerland. In Valais itself, the Group of the Mountain Populations of French-speaking Valais (GPMVR) was founded in 1945.

The post-war period is characterised by unprecedented economic expansion. The wealth gap between the mountain areas and the rest of the country widened markedly. Federalist Switzerland was unwilling to tolerate such gaps. With increased inequality, the mountains became areas to save. Policies in favour of mountains were reinforced and the mountain lobbies gained in strength.

The abandonment of mountains

In the second half of the twentieth century, mountain societies faced profound changes, especially with the development of resources in mountain areas. The 1950s marked the growth of hydro-electric dams and tourism. These changes affected the basic activity of agriculture whose consistent decline characterised the post-war economy with growing salary differentials between farming and industrial labour. Valais was characterised by *pluriactivité*, individuals having two or more professional businesses. There was a moral dimension to the development of such activity: industrial worker-farmers kept a bond to the land. 'Which bond would still retain the population in our villages if no cultivation of the ground were carried out there?'[46]

With the abandonment of the mountains, lands went fallow and some returned to a wild state. Since the 1950s this has become a principal concern of the mountain community lobbies. In 1963, Joseph Moulin, one of the leaders of the GPMVR claimed: 'I personally feel a twinge in my heart when I see a field fall fallow.'[47] Primarily, there arose a sense of what one might describe as non-accomplished work. Thus, in its 1960 annual report, the GPMVR refers to 'land that had previously been gained from the forests or wild lands now lying fallow'.[48] Joseph Moulin was disturbed by the people's apparent disinterest in farming activities, for 'this land that our parents worked'.[49] It was thus more the non-exploitation which was taken into account, because even if it was recognised that certain grounds no longer corresponded to the criteria of productivity or profitability, it was felt to be impossible to let these lands go wild. 'It is necessary to admit the abandonment of grounds too remote, badly located, which will never be profitable. Still, one should not simply let them turn fallow but transform them into pastures or into forest plantings.'[50]

Mountains were designated by their populations. However, these people's own characteristics became vague. While turning their back on agriculture, they lost one of the elements, indeed the main element, of their specification. The reduction in the agricultural activity threatened the status of mountain communities as cultural custodians and especially of moral guardians of the nation's values. The abandonment of the land meant the loss of cultural reference marks.

If the abandonment of the mountains had a clear moral dimension in the 1960s, it gained an environmental dimension in the 1970s. The work of the mountain farmers appeared essential to the maintenance of landscape, of biodiversity and for security reasons, such as practices preventing avalanches. Mountain lobbies recall that 'the mountain people are the true managers of the territory and fight against the extension of fallow lands.'[51] Mountain farmers had to respond to new missions. The agricultural policies supported these activities, often qualifying them as 'gardening'.

In January 2000, in an official publication of the Swiss Federal Office of Environment, Forest and Landscape, ideas about landscape dynamics were developed, considering the return of wilderness in some valleys. The worries of the mountain lobbies peaked at the idea of the mountain as exclusively natural space. For instance, the GPMVR condemned that the environmental approach, as the lobby conceives it, does not take into account the "environed", i.e. the local communities.[52] In other words, the mountain people were no longer a necessary component of the mountains.

Consubstantiality between the mountains and the mountain people

Many opinions expressed by various stakeholders concern the mountains. Much has been projected onto the Swiss mountains. Local populations and particularly those mountain people lobbies wished to maintain the mountains as a living space and thus of their own development.

> Mountains have important assets to put forward and must, absolutely, rely on their inhabitants. These days they are subject to much greed, as much from doctrinaire environment protectionists as from big financiers from large metropolises. It is more imperative than ever that mountain people take things into their own hands, ally themselves and counterweight this foreign expansionism. We do not want these people who supposedly want to ensure the happiness of Alpine people in spite of those people themselves. We wish to decide our destiny ourselves.[53]

The basic legitimisation discourse is to deny the legitimacy to exogenous stakeholders to have a voice because they do not live in the place. Mountain people present themselves as pressed between promoter-speculators, who come from large metropolises and who are only interested in profit, and 'environment protectionists who are very often doctrinaire and ignorant of realities of mountain life'.[54] By reducing the groups of stakeholders with sights on the mountains to three, the two extremes are easily disqualified. The mountain people thus assume the middle ground, taking on the role of safeguard, being the only ones capable of keeping the right balance concerning the management of the mountain areas.

In the context of links between materiality and cognition, we might place the concept of 'stewardship' at centre of this argument. The claim to the role of mountain steward is justified by the knowledge that mountain people have of their environment. They accumulate a practical know-how and, even if they are no longer peasants and earn their living on the plain, they argue that they maintain a superior knowledge of the mountains. Within the collective imagination they continue to be people from the high pastures. The Group of the Mountain Populations of French-speaking Valais uses the word 'ignorance' of mountain regions when speaking about the promoters of the new Swiss regional policy and about the sympathisers of the return of the wolves in the Alps, to both of which the mountain lobby is opposed.

By presenting himself as the best manager, the mountain dweller can develop two principal forms of power.[55] On the one hand, he can mobilise a legitimisation strategy. Bearer of knowledge of the mountain environment, he can position himself as its best manager. A certain consubstantiality between mountain dweller and mountain is thus evoked. In the 1960s therefore, to designate a politician involved in the defence of the interests of mountain people, the term of 'child of the mountain' was sometimes used. But, as we have already seen, it is working the land that links people to the mountains. On the other hand, the mountain dweller can mobilise a pressure strategy. If such people desert the mountains, deep changes will occur with disadvantages for the whole of the society: degraded landscape, loss of biodiversity, increase of natural disasters, and so on.

In opposition to the main outside trend which considers mountains above all as a natural space, mountain people point to mountains as areas which have been inhabited and cultivated for centuries.

> From time immemorial, the Alpine arc has been inhabited, been used as nourishing earth favourable to various human activities. By their familiar presence, human beings have shaped the landscape, threatened by abandonment and exposed to the advance of wastelands. A pleasant lifestyle centered around picturesque villages has been developed by mountain people through time.[56]

The historical dimension of the relationship between mountain people and mountains is often mentioned. In expressing its concern about the Swiss national plan for the reintroduction of lynx, the Agriculture Service of the State of Valais underlines its refusal 'to accept the principle of the slow exclusion of Alpine people and their animals from the territory that Providence and History gave to them in management'.[57]

This means that to avoid disqualification necessitates an affirmation of consubstantiality between 'mountain people' and 'mountains' and thus to postulate a very particular legitimacy defining the modes of management of such areas. The use of the term *montagnard* – 'mountain dweller' – falls under such a logic. It is a strategy which, in relation to the claims of other stakeholders, makes it possible to conform to certain expectations by showing that one is the most capable of offering solutions. Between the lines of this discourse is the claim that the 'mountain people' are the best managers of the mountains.

During the European Conference on Territorial Cooperation between European Mountains, the vice-president of the Italian Union of Mountain Communes and Communities, Riccardo Maderloni, highlighted the point: 'When men abandon mountains, mountains follow men.'[58] This quotation underlines that mountain landscapes, which have been validated until now by the whole of the society, are the product of an interaction with man and traceable over centuries. It is a question of making mountains and mountain people inseparable, so that it becomes impossible to think of one without the other. This is what has been indicated by *consubstantiality*. Thus the arguments of stewardship and consubstantiality lie at the core of a strategy aimed at maintaining the right of local self-determination. These discursive constructions reaffirm the mountain as a living space above all, a place where specific communities live and are shaped.

10

Sea Ice Mapping

Ontology, Mechanics and Human Rights at the Ice Floe Edge

Michael T. Bravo

In December 2005, the Inuit Circumpolar Council (ICC) signalled a dramatic new way of thinking about the ontological status of Arctic sea ice.[1] Its chair (2002–6), Sheila Watt-Cloutier, presented the Inter-American Commission on Human Rights with a petition which argued that the United States, by failing to sign up to the Kyoto Agreement, was infringing Inuit human rights. The argument was presented in a straightforward manner in plain English, stating that the impacts of emissions 'have proven particularly damaging for the Inuit and other people of the Arctic. It is not an exaggeration to say that the impacts are of such a magnitude that they ultimately could destroy the ancient Inuit culture.'[2] Inuit well-being depends on their hunters' access to populations of marine mammals, which in turn depends on keeping the sea ice in a stable state by not interfering with seasonal patterns for formation and melting. There is an increased threat to marine mammals like seals and the sea ice environment in which they live and are hunted. Sea ice knowledge and use are at the core of traditional Inuit coastal culture.

As evidence, the ICC could point to the fact that the overall average concentration of sea ice in the Arctic Basin has shown a steady linear decline for three decades. This was supported by publicly available satellite data from the National Snow and Ice Data Center in Boulder, Colorado. The timing of the petition followed soon after the public release of the Arctic Climate Impact Assessment (2004–5), the most detailed climate impact study yet undertaken, with the sanction of the Arctic Council and the International Arctic Science

Committee (IASC).[3] Watt-Cloutier's petition has by the originality and novelty of its moral claim – that climate change is a human rights issue – captured the imagination of new audiences, sensitised by a growing consensus about the reality of warming induced by human activity. (There is also the possibility that extreme weather events like Hurricane Katrina that inflicted large-scale damage on the city of New Orleans in 2005 may be linked to climate change.) The argument about the violation of Inuit human rights appeals to the 1947 Declaration on the Rights and Duties of Man; and secondly, that the United States, by not signing up to the Kyoto Agreement, was a cause of these human rights violations. Consequently the petitioners were seeking 'relief from human rights violations resulting from the impacts of global warming and climate change caused by acts and omissions of the USA'.[4]

The petitioners went on to ask the Commission to make an 'on-site visit' to the Arctic 'to investigate and confirm the harms suffered by the named individuals whose rights have been violated and other affected Inuit, and to hold a hearing to investigate the claims made in the petition'. Moreover the petitioners asked the Commission to issue a report recommending that the United States: 1.) adopt mandatory measures to cut greenhouse gas emissions and co-operate on other international efforts, 2.) take into account the impacts of greenhouse emissions on the Arctic and affected Inuit before approving all major government actions; and 3.) implement a plan to protect Inuit culture and resources including, *inter alia*, the land water, snow, ice, and plant and animal species used or occupied by the petitioners.[5]

One striking feature of the petition of relevance to the essays in this book, and specifically to the grasp of indigenous politics, is that the IACHR can make on-site visits in order to 'engage in more in-depth analysis of the general situation and/or to investigate a specific situation'.[6] The petitioners' invitation to visit the Arctic in turn recognises that seeing the Inuit way of life at the ice-floe edge is central to understanding its importance as a home, part of the Inuit living environment, or, in other words, that context and a sense of place are of the essence in understanding the argument about the cultural importance of ice. Whether this sense of place would enable the Commission to witness human rights violations associated with the loss of sea ice deserves closer examination of the mechanisms by which the rights are being infringed. Certainly the commissioners would have an opportunity to see, first hand, aspects of the hunting culture.

The request for a visit deserves at the very least a sympathetic response, because the notion of ice as a productive territory and homeland runs counter to most other cultural traditions which associate ice with barrenness and aesthetic monotony,[7] with Romantic sites of mystery and inner discovery,[8] or with a hermetically sealed record of past climatic events.[9] None of these, however, even remotely helps one to understand the subtleties of how sea ice functions on a practical level for hunters of marine mammals, nor do they tell us why ice is rapidly becoming politicised – the historical, cultural and philosophical contexts of sea ice are essentially new territory for political philosophers, yet serve as an important point of departure for understanding contemporary Inuit world-views. There is a risk that commissioners may, for a lack of detailed knowledge of the Inuit language and way of life, tend to romanticise the relationship between sea ice and Inuit culture. It would be understandable if they mistakenly supposed that Inuit enjoy a seamless and intuitive relationship with ice – as though they were 'at one with the ice', somehow feeling their way through it simply by virtue of great sensitivity. Inuit knowledge of sea ice is, however, highly rational and is based on a body of precise knowledge, detailed linguistic terms and rule-bound practices, which, like any form of expert knowledge, becomes to a certain extent embodied and intuitive.

Human ecology is the chief explanatory framework used in studies of the impact of sea ice loss, notably in the *Arctic Climate Impact Assessment*. Human ecology can explain relationships between human and marine mammal populations in the food chain of Arctic marine ecosystems, but none of these is a substitute for understanding the rules and traditions according to which Inuit live in a sea ice environment. Offering only a few examples of the words Inuit elders use to describe what it is to live on the edge of the ice floe should show those who have not visited the Arctic how a landscape in which stability and movement go hand and hand and in which hunters cope with danger by learning the many different codes of wind, currents and tides that largely determine sea ice movements, lies at the heart of the Inuit traditional way of life. This will also invite readers to think more deeply about what human presence as part of a landscape of ice means in practice.

The politics of the request for a Commission hearing to involve a visit to the Arctic calls to mind the Mackenzie Valley Pipeline Enquiry commissioned by the Canadian government in 1974. It broke new ground by travelling the length of the Mackenzie River and receiving firsthand the testimony of Dene, Inuit and Metis peoples' views about the possible impacts of a pipeline running the length of the Mackenzie Valley on their ways of life.[11] The Berger Commission's report brought about a moratorium on pipeline development to enable native peoples to settle their land claims before taking a position on oil, gas and mineral extraction. The parallel between the Inter-American Commission on Human Rights and the Berger Commission, though not perfect, is sufficient that the petition can be seen as attempting to give voice to the concerns of Inuit through a non-binding advisory commission gathering evidence through *in situ* hearings. However, the Inter-American Commission on Human Rights has not yet been persuaded to take up the petition. The Commission informed Watt-Cloutier in December 2006 that it 'will not be able to process your petition at present ... the information provided does not enable us to determine whether the alleged facts would tend to characterise a violation of rights protected by the American Declaration.'[12] With the recent sudden rise in political interest in climate change, perhaps augmented by Watt-Cloutier's nomination for the Nobel Peace Prize, the IACHR indicated its desire to improve its understanding about the general issues surrounding climate change and human rights, and invited Watt-Cloutier to Washington, DC, to make a presentation and to speak to some of the Commission's concerns.[13]

What significance should be attributed to this attempt to put the United States in the dock for an infringement of Inuit human rights? Should it be understood as an advance in human rights theory or a media-savvy attempt to make sensational headlines? The story behind the human rights argument is that it was tabled at the United Nations Conference on Climate Change in Montreal in December 2005. This meeting came in the wake of the failure of the Kyoto talks, at a time when international environmental negotiations on carbon emissions were making little progress. According to Paul Crowley, lead counsel for the team who prepared the legal case for the petition, it received an enthusiastic response from other participants who recognised the Inuit claim as a fresh and just way of framing states' duties and responsibilities to indigenous peoples. What emerged from this meeting was confirmation that the 'global discourse on climate change had been expanded from a technical and economic discussion to include human impacts and human rights.'[14] This catalysed the ongoing conversation between the Inuit Circumpolar Conference (ICC), the Center for International Environmental Law (CIEL) and Earthjustice, an environmental law NGO, which had begun as early as 2002.[15]

The ICC petition should be seen as articulating the many day-to-day events that mark the Inuit relationship with sea ice. The petition's legitimacy derived partly from the fact that it brought together a coalition of 63 individual Inuit petitioners in addition to the ICC's international political mandate to represent Inuit across the United States, Canada, Denmark and Russia. For such a petition to work, evidence about ice needs to be meaningfully linked at multiple levels: local ice geographies, national and international political bodies and transnational scientific audiences. The simplest way to do this is to draw a line between science and culture, by treating sea ice loss as a real scientific fact with a causal relationship to a complex, affected culture. Adopting this pragmatic, realist position is sensible, since sceptics might be tempted to argue that the notion that Inuit have a profound relationship to ice is a romantic construction. The sceptic might also claim that a culture that markets itself as exotic will inevitably exaggerate the unique spiritual qualities of ice specific to that culture, characteristics that cannot be independently verified. In philosophical terms, this position is accurately described as scepticism in the sense that it argues that true knowledge about Inuit traditional relationships to ice simply is not possible. If that is true, the Inter-American Commission on Human Rights could conclude that the proposition, that ice is a human rights issue, is an article of faith or belief rather than a truth claim that could be verified.

In less polemical terms, readers may fairly ask the question, what facts about Inuit use of sea ice can be established and what kinds of judgements do Inuit make about ice that directly affect their well-being? One must explore Inuit beliefs about the ontology of ice, and how its 'conditions of existence' are changing. The public audience that follows climate change stories largely recognise that Inuit use sea ice for hunting. The ICC's petition and the documents they cite carefully document the importance of ice for Inuit, drawing on both Inuit voices and scientific evidence. Using a similar approach in relation to specific philosophical questions about the way Inuit interact with sea ice these questions arise: do Inuit gives names to sea ice like they and other cultures give place-names, for example, to bodies of water, human settlements, or routes through mountain passes? Do they classify different kinds of sea ice? Are they able to apply rational rules to sea ice? The material value of sea ice in Inuit traditional culture remains poorly understood outside those whose families have actually lived at the ice floe, and the work of several anthropologists.[16] The sea ice is an environment in which categorical distinctions, constant observation and rule-based judgement – about sea ice – constitute stable ways of knowing and anticipating its behaviour. This knowledge is part of the skilled practice for the harvesting of marine mammals. Furthermore, these judgements about the behaviour of ice are central both for success in hunting and for personal survival.

Towards the end of the essay, having gained some rudimentary understanding about Inuit knowledge of sea ice, the political character of mapping sea ice is revisited. At first glance, the quest to map local formations and movements of sea ice appears quixotic; and yet even moving sea ice is to some extent predictable in its response to the seasons, as well as winds, currents and tides.[17] Yet if it is rationally embedded in daily Inuit marine mammal hunting activities, one might suppose that it has simply evaded cartographic representation until now for technical reasons. As navigation in Arctic waters acquires increased international coverage, the old stereotypical images of monotonous ice-covered seas are being replaced by detailed maps and ice forecasts serving a range of state and commercial interests.

The rest of the world is coming to realise what Inuit have known for centuries: that ice is in principle sustainable, and therefore should enjoy the kinds of legal protection and state regulation afforded to other resource sectors. When the process of settling northern land claims began about 30 years ago, the legal status of ice was left largely ignored, although its importance for Inuit culture was well known.[18] Today the Canadian government is preoccupied with the question of sovereignty over her still-icy Arctic waters; for other nations the idea of a navigable North West Passage protected by the Law of the Sea is extremely appealing; for the United States an inaccessible ice-filled Canadian Arctic is perceived to hold advantages for national security; and for environmental organisations the protection of ice offers new regulatory territory to fight threats from contaminants to the fauna and flora. For northern peoples themselves, the ice continues to be part of their economic and cultural way of life. With a certain irony, Sheila Watt-Cloutier argues that 'our way of life is based on the cold, with lots of ice and snow; we are, in essence, defending our right to be cold.'[19] Yet Inuit find themselves in a situation where other stakeholders value ice not so much as a place to live, but as a football in a geopolitical game of energy and security played by the developed nations.

The loss of sea ice language

Although the vocabulary of the landscape is still alive and very much in use amongst some Inuit today, the complexity of the vocabulary and the precise subtleties of meaning are being lost. Inuit researchers readily admit that the vocabulary of elders 20 years ago was substantially greater and more sophisticated than it is today, and that the loss is intergenerational. It is some consolation that over the last twenty years, ethno-linguistic studies of Inuit culture have resulted in important published works that preserve, explain and codify some of the Inuit vocabulary. Some of these studies have taken place in the settlement of Igloolik, which hosts a research centre where Igloolik residents Maurice Arnatsiaq, Paul Irngaut, John MacDonald, Leah Otak, George Qulaut, and Louis Tapardjuk (amongst others) have played an instrumental role in supporting language-based research projects by building collaborations and lending their own considerable expertise. Chief amongst their joint successes has been a collaboration with the Igloolik Elders Society (the Inullariit). In their capacity as organisers and researchers, they have formed their own collaborations as well as partnerships with visiting, university-based researchers in order to record traditional Inuit knowledge across a range of topics. The research centre, or 'the Lab' as it is locally known, has a rich archive of elders' interviews and life stories. Although far from exhaustive in its coverage of subjects, it has since its inception in 1986 documented important accounts of the experience and knowledge of the last generation of Inuit elders to have lived a traditional life before the creation of settlements in the 1960s; most of those elders have since passed away. This historical legacy involves much more work than recording recollections. Many Inuktitut words have specific or technical meanings that, without careful analysis and translation, will be lost, even though they may be recorded.

University-trained researchers have reaped the rewards afforded by the oral history project to enhance the quality of their own investigations on subjects of Inuit traditional knowledge in as diverse areas as zoology, navigation, cartography, climate change and law.[20]

Comparing approaches to naming and classifying ice are important for illuminating different cultural perspectives and understanding how knowledge can be shared.[21] Several researchers have begun to compare Inuit knowledge of sea ice with scientific traditions.[22] These studies represent a major step forward in understanding Inuit perspectives on sea ice, but the job of comparing Inuit knowledge with science is still at an early stage. Just as oral historical research with elders has been the key in the Inuit context, any comparison with scientific naming and classification practices must be equally informed by research in history of science and historical geography. The treatment of sea ice in the history of science is fragmented by different approaches and contexts: natural historical research of whalers,[23] scientific instruments in chemistry and natural philosophy,[24] science and romanticism,[25] and controversies over the transport of glacial erratic boulders. Some classification systems have undergone radical changes over time. Natural history classification systems have been built on a range of very different assumptions ranging from pragmatic factors like convenience of observation and usefulness to assumptions about the hidden structures of nature's order. To make matters more complex still, many aspects of scientific classification have been recognised as artificial in the hope that truly natural systems would eventually emerge. So there are pitfalls in comparing and contrasting Inuit knowledge of sea ice to that of scientists, even restricting oneself to present-day science, because the language is informed by a mixture of traditions as diverse as shipboard navigation, mineralogy, physics, and microwave communications. It is clear that there is always a danger of misrepresenting science in the intellectual pursuit of demonstrating the sophisticated knowledge of ice in other cultures.

In news reports informed by research in the environmental sciences, the behaviour of sea ice is normally presented in terms of standardised, quantified measures such as concentration, total volume, and variability (e.g. ACIA 2005) and using standardised vocabulary (WMO). The preference for numerical descriptions in part reflects the credibility granted to quantitative analysis as an index of objectivity in the sciences, a phenomenon analysed by the historian of science Theodore Porter in his classic study *Trust in Numbers*.[26] Numeracy is of course much more than a preference: it is built into the powerful digital software developed by climate change computational modellers and institutionalised in the organisation and funding of science.[27] We should not overlook the mundane fact that at present satellites cannot indicate with any precision the complex movements of local winds, currents and tides that move sea ice in a myriad of complex patterns. It is true that scientists working on icebreakers can either make transects of sea ice or study sea ice processes up close, but their mobility and coverage is highly restricted, so that meteorologists cannot make detailed predictions of the local patterns of movement of ice. General predictions from modellers about the impact of sea ice loss on Inuit culture are at best crude over the short and medium terms, but this is not to dismiss or underestimate the accomplishments of scientists who study ice. In fact, some Inuit hunters in Northern Canada consult the government's regular satellite regional sea ice forecasts before setting off hunting. If local sea ice movements cannot be adequately forecast by scientists for local navigation in the Arctic, how do Inuit respond rationally to sea ice? The answers lie in the skill base of the Inuit themselves.

Inuit hunters have traditionally studied the sea ice while travelling and hunting. Their reliance on sea ice for hunting seals and walruses persists in the face of rapid social and cultural change. Terms like 'experience' and 'awareness' conjure up a close relationship to the environment, but on their own their significance within Inuit culture is not adequately conveyed. This was brought home early in the Oral History Project, in an interview in which a member of the research staff at the Igloolik Lab, Paul Irngaut, who agreed to act as interpreter to interview a monolingual local expert on sea ice, Aipilik Inuksuk.[28] The conversation about sea ice knowledge started with a much more personal and purposeful tone because of the link between them. Paul, a young man in his twenties, had explicitly asked Aipilik to make use of advanced Inuit technical terminology rather than holding back for fear that he would not understand. This prompted Aipilik in turn to advise how young people should learn about sea ice *in situ*. As everyone interested in Inuit knowledge of the natural world discovers, communication, observation and practice on the land is the traditional classroom of Inuit knowledge.

There are of course plain cartographic facts that an inexperienced outsider can understand quickly from reading an atlas and an introductory geography text.[30] Igloolik is a small island situated about 10 kilometres north of the continental mainland and that ice formation is crucial for getting off the island to hunt in any of the half dozen principal directions of travel. It is situated at the southeast entrance to Fury and Hecla Strait, and to the northwest of Foxe Basin. These two continuous bodies of water separate Baffin Island from the mainland. The marine currents in these waters are the key ingredient responsible for sustaining the rich marine ecosystem in the area and for Igloolik's appeal as a site with good access to seals, walruses, arctic char, beluga whales and polar bears. In the autumn, sea ice is formed in these waters or it is brought in by swift currents driven by the winds.

Inuit place-names reveal detailed geographical classification and terminology for land and sea, although one would have been hard pressed to find these names on any map until very recently. For example, Inuit call the large body of water separating the mainland from Baffin Island, *Ikiq*, an Inuktitut word meaning 'strait'. The place-name *Ikiq* has no precisely equivalent name in English. Place-names in Inuktitut can refer to the same area, but with different boundaries, or to different kinds of features, often much more specific locations in Inuktitut than terms like 'point, inlet, or bay' in English.[31] *Ikiq*, for example, overlaps with the Foxe Basin to the south and east (named after Luke Foxe, a seventeenth-century explorer) and Fury and Hecla Strait to the north and west (the ships' names of William Edward Parry, an early nineteenth-century British explorer).

Sea ice also has a toponymy. The same waters when frozen over in winter carry new names. The sea ice has hundreds of features, of which only a few have widely recognised toponyms.[32] For example, journeys to hunt caribou at well-known locations like Siuraajuq on Baffin Island to the north, during the summer require a day's journey by boat crossing Ikiq. This is relatively straightforward navigation with islands acting as landmarks along the way and the wind when blowing from the prevailing direction, northwest, serves as a compass. In the winter, hunters crossing the sea ice use a more complex system of landmarks, including ice features and snowdrifts (*uqalurait*) aligned with the prevailing wind.[33] Travellers need to keep an eye out for weak ice, the signs of which are often subtle or even concealed. Moving ice, snow covered ice, cracks in the ice, poorly formed ice are all potentially life-threatening formations. Fast-running currents drive the moving ice, which keep the waters in the main channel of *Ikiq* open as late as December, while shaping the fixed positions, patterns and construction of the different kinds of sea ice.

Certain features are formed annually; they are semi-permanent features of the icescape. Shown in Figure 10.1 are several named ice features in the vicinity of Igloolik (island). The most conspicuous ice ridge is called *Agiuppiniq*, situated about 10 kilometres to the north-east, and running in a north-west/south-east axis.[34] While hunters sometimes find it a difficult obstacle to traverse on their way up to *Siuraajuq* (marked with an arrow in Figure 10.1), it is also a critical navigation landmark for navigating across *Ikiq*, locating other places, and on a long return journey a sign that home is near.[35]

Taxonomy and toponymy in geography are cultural tools for organising space and giving meaning to landscapes. George Quviq Qulaut, an Igloolik hunter, who was for many years operations manager at the Igloolik Resource Center, explained that the name *Agiuppiniq* means 'filing' because the ice ridge is formed by a current carrying moving ice through deep water past land-fast ice grounded in shallow water.[36] Louis Utak, an Igloolik elder, offers a similar explanation: 'the ridge is caused by the current bringing a field or large area of moving ice into contact with and rubbing against the land-fast ice. This causes pieces of ice to detach themselves from the moving ice and form the ridges.'[37] The moving ice collides as it passes the land-fast ice, pieces break off and pile up, creating the ridge. Qulaut's account of its name testifies to a mechanical, hydraulic, causal explanation – the action of currents over the submarine topography. For the Inuit of Igloolik this special ice ridge is a designated feature of the landscape in its own right, as real as the currents and topography that define its annual, seasonal presence. As a landmark, it is also important spatially for fixing the location of other places. For example, Anthony Qunnut uses it to describe the location of a particularly favourable location for seal hunting, *Mauliq* (a name that refers to the method of seal hunting by breathing holes). *Mauliq* is a narrow stretch of ice just to the side of a place called *Pikiuliarjjuk* in such a position that the ice ridge *Agiuppiniq* is still visible,

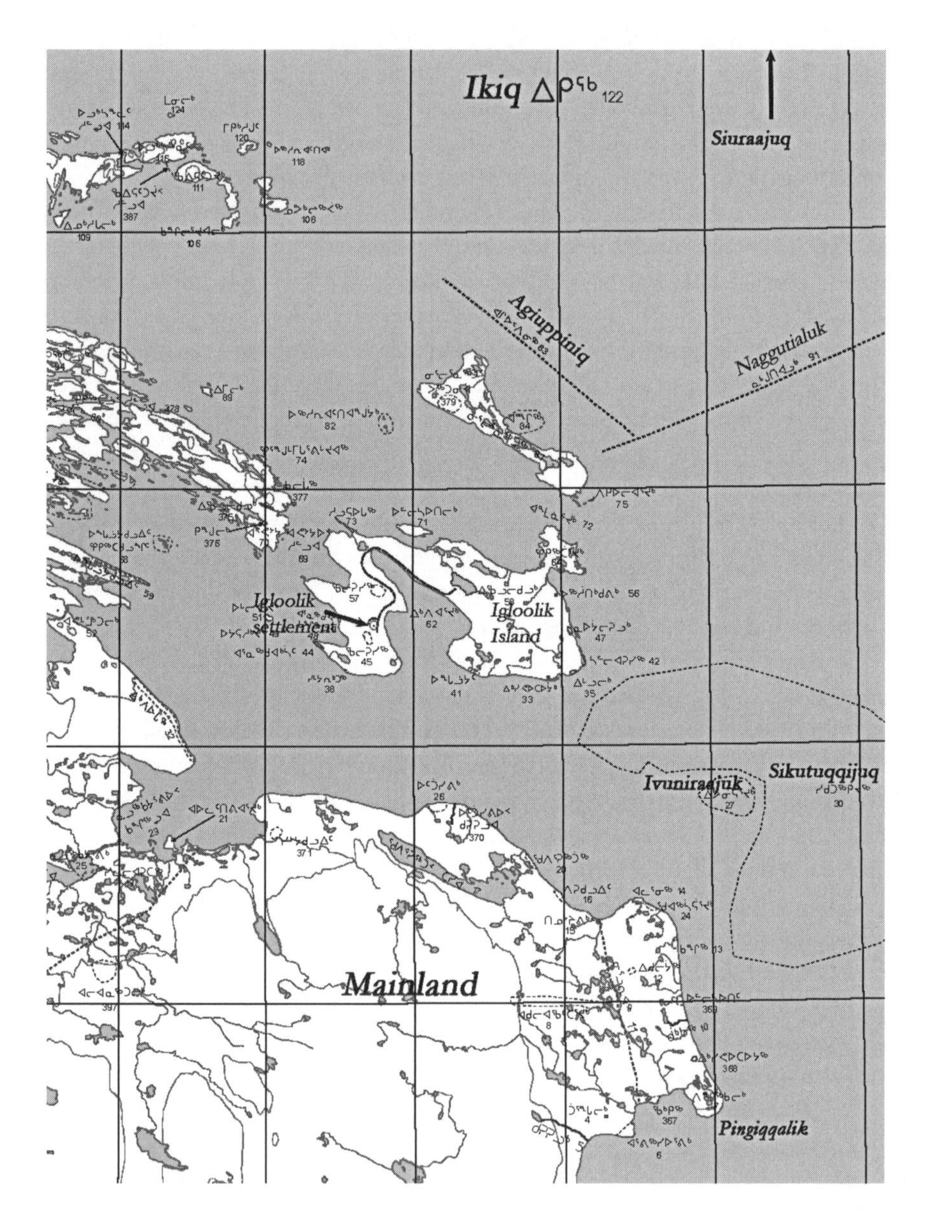

Figure 10.1 Map of Igloolik area with place-names. Principal place-names in this article are shown in Latin characters. All other place-names are drawn in the syllabic alphabet. The adjacent numbers refer to a legend in which the names are spelled in transliteration, accompanied by brief explanations or translations of their meanings into English (Source: Inuit Heritage Trust Inc., Draft Map Iglulik 47D, Cartography and Research by Claudio Aporta; produced under license from HMRC, with permission of Natural Resources Canada).

but at a distance.[38] According to Louis Utak,[39] *Agiuppiniq* is known locally by another name – some people call it *Minuirnniq*.

Using the example of *Agiuppiniq*, we can make four philosophical observations about the Inuit practice of giving place-names to ice: 1.) it is realist in that the place-names correspond to the material substance of the ice itself; 2.) it is causal in making reference to the mechanical law-like behaviour of the current and floating ice that creates the ridge; 3.) it is nominalist only to a limited extent because the names are in some cases also descriptors; and 4.) it is relational in that the names are part of a web of spatially interconnected positions. Whether these characteristics are true for most or all ice toponymy is a question for further research and debate that may be answered by a new project called SIKU, taking place during International Polar Year, dedicated to mapping sea ice.[40]

The names of three ice features that were common knowledge to the Igloolik Inuit are shown on the map in Figure 10.1: *Agiuppiniq* (an ice ridge), *Sikutuqqijuq* (ice formed at the floe edge which separates, breaks into pans, freezes, and collides with other pieces, forming thick, rough ice) and *Ivuniraajuk* (an area of ice build up). That these features are becoming much more widely known is thanks in part to the collaborative work of Claudio Aporta, who has been working with Inuit hunters using simple but effective Global Positioning Satellite (GPS) technology to lay down their trails and routes on standard 1:250,000 topographical maps. Lynn Peplinski, the Toponymist at Inuit Heritage Inc., has been able to draw on this research to include ice place-names in the next generation of topographical maps using Inuit place-names exclusively (from which Figure 10.1 is derived). They will undoubtedly be well received by Inuit who, as well as appreciating their own language, enjoy discussing place-names because of the richness of their associations and the close links between oral histories and places.

Emerging from the research about ice carried out for the Igloolik Oral History Project has been an interactive educational module called *Anijaarniq* (2006), developed by a team comprising Igloolik-based educators, illustrators, language experts, translators and researchers led by Aporta. By looking at the map of Igloolik, students can click on the place-name '*Agiuppinq*', which then enables them to listen to recordings of the voices of Aipilik Innuksuk[41] – who has since passed away – and Louis Alianakuluk[42] recounting how their families used to set up winter camp there by the ice-floe edge.[43]

Although sea ice is a critical habitat for Inuit, little has been written about its ontological status – what makes ice a living environment? Although the elders' testimony tells us that the ice is dynamic, it is clearly not alive *per se*. If one acknowledges that Inuit culture is shamanistic, or what used to be called 'animistic', one might suppose that Inuit imagine that the ice is animated by spirits – but ice is not normally credited as living in its own right. Very exceptionally one hears accounts of animals being chased across the ice, and in order to avoid giving themselves up to hunters, the animals disguise themselves by taking on the appearance of a feature of the ice, or even a block of ice.[44]

It is equally true that many Inuit feel a kind of reverence for many aspects of their environment particularly the *sila*, which is often translated as the weather, but which points to something greater and commands enormous respect. According to Alex Spalding, it is simultaneously 'an indicator of environment, an indicator of locality and an indicator of intelligence or spirit'.[45]

This reverence is an acknowledgement of the shared relationships that sustain human and animal life, which is made possible in part by the *sila* and the *siku* (sea ice). Though the ice is inanimate, it is a necessary condition for the reciprocal relationships between people and animals. Part of that reciprocity, as anthropologists often emphasise, is that animals are said to give themselves up to the hunters, who must treat the animals with care and respect. But these relationships do not exist in a vacuum. The sea-ice environment enables Inuit and marine mammals a place in which they have mobility and find sustenance.

Mobility is very important because there is more to making a home than building a house or an igloo. The great importance of mobility to the hunters and the animals is closely linked to the multiple dynamic states of ice, ranging from the very stable to the rapidly dissolving or transformative states. Sea ice is anything but inert, and even stable ice can change unpredictably, forming and reforming in a seemingly infinite variety of patterns. Even where there is multi-year, land-fast sea ice, its surface changes with wind and precipitation. The boundary between the land-fast ice and the moving sea ice – the floe edge – defines the Inuit habitat in winter because it is here that seals or walruses congregate within relatively easy reach of hunters. These animals meet the basic traditional nutritional and clothing needs of the people, and they have very many other uses besides. As such, the sea ice is an essential component in the Inuit life-sustaining environment.

The Inuit knowledge of sea ice, of which these examples offer only a glimpse, is predictive both spatially (ice behaviour at another location) and temporally (forecasting). This requires possessing a proper weather and ice vocabulary, knowing how to apply weather rules, practice in their application and sustained experience in observing conditions, for example, the ice conditions at the ice floe near *Pingiqqalik*, which is a small peninsula on the mainland and a traditional camp for hunting walruses. The shape of the peninsula is such that it juts out in a southerly direction from the mainland which itself curves around from nearly an east–west axis to a north–south axis [Fig. 10.1]. Hunters at *Pingiqqalik* could rely on the walruses being reasonably plentiful out by the ice floe edge. (Indeed, they have become more plentiful in recent years.[46]) Before Inuit set up new camps, they generally planned their moves, assessing the timing based on different factors. The time of season, thickness of the ice and visibility were naturally important, but there were also more subtle factors. Wind direction and intensity were important for predicting what conditions could be expected out at the ice floe and how those conditions might change. George Kappianaq, an elder who knew those conditions well, explained this by first pointing out on a map where he would normally have his land camp, just to the north of *Pingiqqalik* adjacent to a lake. If the wind was *akinnaq*, an offshore south-west wind perpendicular to the prevailing north-west wind, it 'was said to keep the floe-edge ice free', blowing the moving ice away from the land, and posing 'a threat to those that were hunting on the land-fast ice'.[47] If the wind veered around to the north-north-west or to the prevailing north-west (*uangnaq*), hunters would anticipate the moving ice (*aulajuq*) being driven into contact with the land-fast ice (*tuvaq*). The *aulajuq* would give the hunters access to the walrus' feeding areas where they come up to breathe in open water or newly formed ice between the pans.[48] No less importantly, the correct wind reduced the risk of being blown out to sea on moving ice. As the wind came into line with the axis of the lake next to their camp, that was the sign so that the men to 'get ready to move on to the moving ice that morning.' This meant that the wind was blowing the moving ice into 'contact with to the land-fast ice' on the west side of *Pingiqqalik*, while the bight on the east side of the peninsula would be blown ice-free.[49] This shifting of the moving ice at *Pingiqqalik* is said to *sanimuak*, that is to the right or the east out to sea.[50] If the south-east (*nigiq*) wind, which often carries precipitation, was blowing, hunters tended to steer clear of the floe edge. The start of a snowfall in a *nigiq* wind was a sign that the wind would soon shift to the opposite direction and that returning to safe ground was a matter of urgency, or even cause for worry (*nangiattuq*).[51]

Getting stuck on the moving ice could not be ruled out when hunting at the floe edge – not all secrets of the ice are revealed even to the most seasoned observer. Noah Piugaattuk[52] said, 'The wind is a real liar,' referring to its capacity to deceive hunters, particularly the fickle south-easterly *nigiq*; the same is sometimes said for currents and sea ice. Each is capable of behaving capriciously and threatening life in very real ways. Felix Alaralak warns of the dangers posed when surface frost forms in the late winter or early spring on the 'lee side of newly frozen open water'. This is 'caused by the sun and the cold temperature', and gives the surface the appearance that it is thick. 'Some of it may be very thin but you cannot tell the difference especially at this time of the year, even when the snow has not fallen (which would further conceal the thin ice).'[53]

The danger of being taken away on the moving ice, when you suppose yourself to be still on land-fast ice, illustrates why the practical landscape of inhabiting the ice floe can be accompanied by strong emotions because of the possibility of danger and suffering. Felix Alaralak captures this succinctly: 'When you are caught out on the moving ice you cannot help but feel a sense of despair'. There is a great feeling of uncertainty because 'you cannot tell whether you are going to be stranded for a long time or whether this is going to be a short [one].' One must therefore 'take supplies for emergencies … hunger is not comfortable … but it is nothing compared to thirst … You cannot go without water for three days therefore you must always carry fresh water ice with you at all times even if you are not going to use it.' It is sometimes possible to find lifesaving fresh water while on the ice in the form of old *qinu*, powder-like soft ice formed by the crushing of two ice masses.[54]

Keeping your nerve on the sea ice under pressure is a mental challenge. In Alaralak's own words: 'You are constantly busy; you now must have common sense in order for you to survive; and there is now the danger of you falling into the water and other unpleasantness'.[55] Some moving ice fields are more dangerous than others, and knowing the different kinds of behaviour is crucial. In some areas, the moving ice gives a warning by travelling down along the floe edge, hugging it, before setting out to sea; whereas close to Igloolik the moving ice 'just goes in and out … and it can be dangerous.'[56]

When caught out on moving ice, how do experienced hunters go about finding their way back on to land-fast ice? There are many rules of thumb that can be applied to particular situations, but none of them applies universally. A conversation between two experienced hunters can illustrate some of the more subtle judgements involved in living on the sea ice. Maurice Arnatsiaq, still an active hunter (and a retired research centre technician at the

Igloolik Lab) asked his late friend, Felix Alaralak, 'if you are on the moving ice and coming back to the land-fast ice ... but darkness befalls you so that you would feel that there is no way of getting on to the land-fast ice in the darkness, is it wiser for you to return to the thicker moving ice?' Felix's response was slightly unexpected. His priority would be 'to keep your clothing as dry as possible'; this means going to places where there are ice ridges 'because the surface is usually frozen, [whereas] when you are on the flat ice the surface does not freeze up because the water is right beneath it'. The conversation illustrates how these hunters require tactical expert knowledge to ensure their survival when leaving behind the relative security of the fixed ice for the moving ice. Ice is never simply dismissed or romanticised as an unknown or beautiful wilderness: it is too important and dangerous – above all, too close and intimate a landscape – to give it that kind of aesthetic distance. Above all else, counselled Felix, 'one should not make any attempts to get on to land-fast ice out of desperation, otherwise you can have accidents which might be devastating.'[57]

Mapping the sea ice

The floe edge is an unusual feature in western cartographic traditions, but it is by no means unknown. In the narratives of naval explorers, delineations of the ice were significant in demonstrating the likely existence (or not) of navigable channels and passage, and by extension the accessibility of resources and therefore the value of territorial claims. When William Edward Parry sailed into the Foxe Basin in search of a North West Passage in 1821, he went to great pains to show that he had examined the ice during the three seasons he explored the region. The general outline of the ice was drawn by his surveyor, a midshipman named James Bushnan. Also published in his official narrative were three Inuit-drawn maps drawn at Winter Island, showing Parry *Ikiq* and the neighbouring channels he would have to explore, that he subsequently named Fury and Hecla Strait. One of the charts drawn by Iligjaq (spelled Iligliuk by Parry) shows the compass rose based on the Inuit wind directions together, as well as the floe edge along the mainland coast, labelled as 'Line of Ice along which the Esquimaux travel in the Spring'.[58] As well as being a testimony to the quality of Parry's ethnography (which is still consulted by Inuit researchers), it is evidence that the territorial significance of sea ice for Inuit hunting and travelling, was clearly appreciated by scientifically trained, senior naval officers of the British state.

I went to live in Igloolik in 1988 to work on two projects, one of which was to learn more about Inuit navigation skills and to compare them with those of the naval explorers, as well as those that I myself had learned growing up sailing on inland rivers and lakes. When I had the opportunity to meet Aipilik Innuksuk, I was keen to show him James Bushnan's chart of Fury and Hecla Strait drawn in the summer months of 1822. I remember Aipilik casting an authoritative eye over the chart, visualising what he was reading off the map, and breathing new life into the ice contour by giving me some idea as to its changing position, 'Right now the floe-edge goes through here close to the land. Most of these [contours] marked on the map would be close to the land if it were to be made today. Right now this part here [near Igloolik] is similar to the current conditions but [on Parry's chart] it goes way up there towards Baffin Island'.[59] This remark that sea ice contours are now much closer to the land than two centuries ago is interesting in its own right: it is one piece of evidence about the changing sea ice that can be weighed up alongside others in understanding climate change. Innuksuk, like most people in 1988, was not discussing climate change. What his remarks actually show is that his command of sea ice knowledge and conditions operated across a range of scales, at the regional (Igloolik and environs) as well as the local or place-specific level. There is further evidence that he was adept at making temporal and spatial comparisons of ice-forming processes. For example, he went on to explain that 'this part [near Igloolik] "freezes to stability" much more rapidly ... [whereas] I would imagine that this place [north near Baffin Island] at the moment is just starting to become stabilised. [In the vicinity of Igloolik], once the temperatures are cold enough to form ice, it tends to stabilise very quickly.'[60]

Given his subtle knowledge of the movement of the sea ice formation across *Ikiq*, the question arises whether Aipilik Innuksuk or other elders had generated techniques for mapping the movements and locations of the sea ice. 'When they [Inuit] want to show someone that does not know ... they will draw a map, but only if that person does not know. Otherwise they know the floe-edge because they hunt on it. All they have to do is go towards the edge and they will find out where it is located.'[61]

Times have changed since Aipilik Innuksuk saw James Bushnan's chart and now Inuit are very much taken by sea ice maps. Why should they be so interested in adopting these in their arsenal of new technology? They provide a new set of tools for anticipating the spatial and temporal behaviour of the sea ice, and can therefore make their life at the edge of the floe that much safer. Aporta and Higgs[62] have recently argued that the rapid acquisition of handheld GPS devices by Inuit over the last ten years, offers a valuable new companion to traditional land skills, but equally poses new dangers, especially when used alone without the traditional knowledge. The insights of the elders make it plain that to have knowledge of locations and directions at one's disposal without knowing the routes and reading the weather signs is asking for trouble.[63] So, too, the recent arrival of handheld GPS technology and broadband internet services to Inuit communities presents new opportunities as well as dangers. Some hunters who can afford the broadband service now consult Environment Canada's daily satellite regional ice forecast when planning their trips.[64] As well as learning traditional knowledge of hunting from their parents, students will soon acquire the rudiments of wayfinding at school using their PCs to explore the *Anijaarniq* CD-ROM (now being piloted in Nunavut schools), alongside the ice forecasts.

To understand better the growing investments in mapping the shifting territory of sea ice, one can reflect on the circumstances that led to the large-scale mapping of Inuit land use some thirty years ago. In 1973 two events of seismic proportions sent shockwaves through the Canadian state. The first was the quadrupling of oil and gas prices by OPEC in 1973, which forced all nations to focus on energy security, and in the case of the United States and Canada, to explore for new reserves in the Arctic Ocean. The second quite different challenge to traditional notions of national security was the Supreme Court of

Canada's decision in Calder *versus* Attorney-General of British Columbia (1973), which recognised the non-extinguishment of aboriginal title since being recognised by the British Crown in the Royal Proclamation of 1763.[65] The decision's effect was to say that in all cases where native title to lands had not been formally extinguished by treaty or sale, aboriginal title continues to exist, even though the precise meaning of that title remains undefined in Canadian law. In the wake of these events, the government of Canada announced its intention to start negotiating comprehensive land claims treaties with native groups, so that ownership could be settled, to clear the way for northern development. Following this decision, the Inuit undertook a mapping exercise in every Inuit settlement in which all hunters were invited to record the traditional hunting routes and locations of their families and ancestors. This project produced hundreds of detailed maps showing the location of traditional Inuit habitats and routes for subsequent use in negotiating land claims. The results of the study were published as the *Inuit Land Use and Occupancy Study* in 1976.[66]

When the Nunavut Land Claim Agreement was signed in 1993, the Inuit of the Eastern Arctic were negotiating a territorial claim on the understanding that it would legally protect their territorial right to continue subsistence activities at the floe edge, but they were not then thinking about the stability of the floe edge itself. The loss of the sea ice and the threat to the land-fast ice is a political predicament for both Inuit and the Canadian government with international implications. The Canadian government may be keen to bank on Inuit occupancy and use of their territory to strengthen national sovereignty claims. Until now, the Inuit could rightly argue that this represents a major contribution to the nation which deserves greater recognition. The IACHR petition proposes a different kind of argument, one that is relatively independent from traditional concepts of nationhood and sovereignty. Examining how Inuit culture is actually lived at the ice-floe edge draws attention to what it means in terms of the everyday reality of sovereignty – what it means for Inuit to be stewards of the ice they inhabit. Franklyn Griffiths has recently argued that 'stewardship is the enactment of sovereignty.' Inuit are the 'keepers who secure, watch over and look after their Arctic lands, waters and fellow nationals in an era of unprecedented climate and geopolitical change.'[67]

For centuries sea ice has been treated by political philosophers, navies, trading companies and even theologians as a barrier to what has long been supposed as 'natural prosperity' associated with the commerce and free navigation of the high seas. Philip Steinberg in his study, *The Social Construction of the Oceans*, argues that the oceans today are predominantly imagined as a series of cost-free abstract spaces, connecting international nodes with access to markets, in which the oceans themselves, their biotic and human inhabitants are largely invisible. In legal terms, this vision is supported by the United Nations Convention on the Law of the Sea (UNCLOS).[68] This legal framework in recognising the sovereignty of states, does little to recognise the responsibilities of stewardship for the oceans or the welfare of oceanic peoples. If the moving sea ice is replaced by open waters in the Arctic, *Agiuppiniq* may eventually become a thing of the past, a place erased from the seasonal map of everyday Inuit navigation. Then the nuanced metaphor of the *file* may be replaced by the more overt friction associated with two conceptions of freedom associated with ocean-spaces: on the one hand a market-driven model which is based on the freedom of navigation on the high seas, and on the other hand the freedom of a people to act as stewards for the seasonally changing sea ice that is necessitated by their needs for shelter and sustenance. That the Inuit have traditionally subsisted at the interface between land-fast and moving ice is beyond a shadow of doubt. If propelled by climate change into a future landscape without sea ice, the Inuit would be forced to give up the traditional way of life entailed in being stewards of the ice-floe edge. Further critical analysis will determine the conditions under which stewardship of a changing landscape constitutes a human right. What is clear in the meantime is that states which fund scientists to map and track the formation and destruction of habitats like sea ice are increasingly being forced to recognise that they have legal and moral duties to consider the implications of policies and actions that affect the sea ice. The petition to the IACHR is an invitation to consider how states wield their considerable political and economic power to the benefit or detriment of the human rights of indigenous peoples. That imaginative leadership in debating these issues is still largely driven by individuals and non-state actors like Sheila Watt-Cloutier and by institutions like Earthjustice and the Center for International Environmental Law is the firmest indication of the challenges to those who want to secure legal protection for the stewardship of the environments of maritime cultures.

11

Canada Day in Resolute

Performance, Ritual, and the Nation in an Inuit Community

Richard C. Powell

The Arctic regions have often been conceptualised in the Western imagination as antagonistic spaces where pathological natures are to be overcome. The unrelenting physicality of both passage through and dwelling in this environment, combined with spatial isolation, contribute to the ideological resources required to construct meanings for such landscapes. Indeed, it is the valorisation of the ability to meet this corporeal challenge that has historically encouraged visitation from non-indigenous peoples. Moreover, polar sublimity continues to circulate across global spaces. Recent debates over climatic changes and impacts upon charismatic mega fauna such as polar bears, for example, have resulted in focussing international attention on the Circumpolar Arctic.

But for all its universal attraction, the Arctic is also home to the Inuit. The Arctic is Nuna Vut – Our Land. In Canada, the political recognition of this is evident in the settlement of the land claim between the federal government and the Inuit, resulting in the creation of the Territory of Nunavut on 1 April 1999. With this redrawing of political cartography, the implicitly colonial depiction of the Arctic as an uninhabited wasteland has been recast as an episode consigned to histories of empire. As such, the region has begun to provide an exemplar case for studies of post-colonial resistance and indigenous self-determination. Through force of will and organisation, the long process of reparation and rehabilitation between western states and indigenous peoples has, at least, commenced.

As might be expected, the territorial instantiation of Nunavut notwithstanding, the relationship between Inuit and Canada remains volatile. The many 'colonial presents' in the contemporary world have variegated geographies.[1] In the Canadian Arctic, histories of colonial dispossession and state intervention have been retold through indigenous self-determination. This chapter shows how cartographic refashioning can have remarkable consequences for those peoples achieving control over their own lives. As newly enfranchised members of the precarious Canadian nation, Inuit have begun not only to discard, but also to embrace, elements of the wider national culture.

What is most important is that Arctic lands are spaces of encounter. The Arctic has witnessed histories of encounter between different groups: explorers and missionaries with Inuit, scientists with indigenous peoples and even, more recently, between scientists and adventure tourists. What holds these variegated encounters between Inuit and Qallunaat[2] together around a common thread is that all have been skewered by conflict and all revolve around power relations. Feminist anthropologist Sherry Ortner has shown, in work on the history of interactions between Sherpas and Western mountaineers in the Himalayas, how encounter is fundamental to social histories of *both* communities. As Ortner argues, in contexts of encounter 'what is at issue are the ways in which power and meaning are deployed and negotiated, expressed and transformed, as people confront one another within the frameworks of differing agendas'.[3]

This chapter uses the notion of encounter as a point of departure to think more seriously about the Arctic-as-homeland. Whilst processes of domesticity and colonialism are persistently enacted, the Arctic can also be thought of as a social space. That the power relationships underpinning these interactions have historically involved racism and epistemic violence should not distract us from examining cross-cultural encounters in the ethnographic present. Different human actors interact in the Arctic and, as they do so, they perform important social practices. In other words, Arctic spaces can be conceptualised as involving social formations that must be analysed not as inherently pathological but as, in many ways, commonplace.

Despite this apparent need for understanding the social Arctic, it was not until the 1970s that anthropological attempts were made to document contemporary spaces of encounter in Canada's north. Research by Hugh Brody and Robert Paine uncovered the sociology of settler communities in northern Canada [Fig. 11.1]. As well as power relations positioning Inuit in subordinate roles, Paine uncovered the malign impacts upon both communities of the consistent expectation of tutelage relationships between whites and indigenous peoples.[4] In an elegant ethnography of Iqaluit, Brody was able to demonstrate more starkly the destructive tensions evident between settlers and Inuit.[5]

In more recent decades, the Canadian Arctic has become an arena of contestation in the debates over global climatic changes. Encounters between settlers and Inuit have thus begun to be supplemented by those between Inuit and environmental scientists. Such interactions result in social positionings and thus produce apprehension within both communities.

The notions of ritual and carnival help explore how Inuit relieve community tensions and negotiate identity in these spaces of encounter. Drawing on theories of ritual developed by anthropologist Victor Turner, this chapter pursues the enactment and alleviation of social tension. This is accomplished by drawing from a single ethnographic interlude – the performance of Canada Day in the settlement of Resolute in 2002.[6] Resolute is the site of a federal

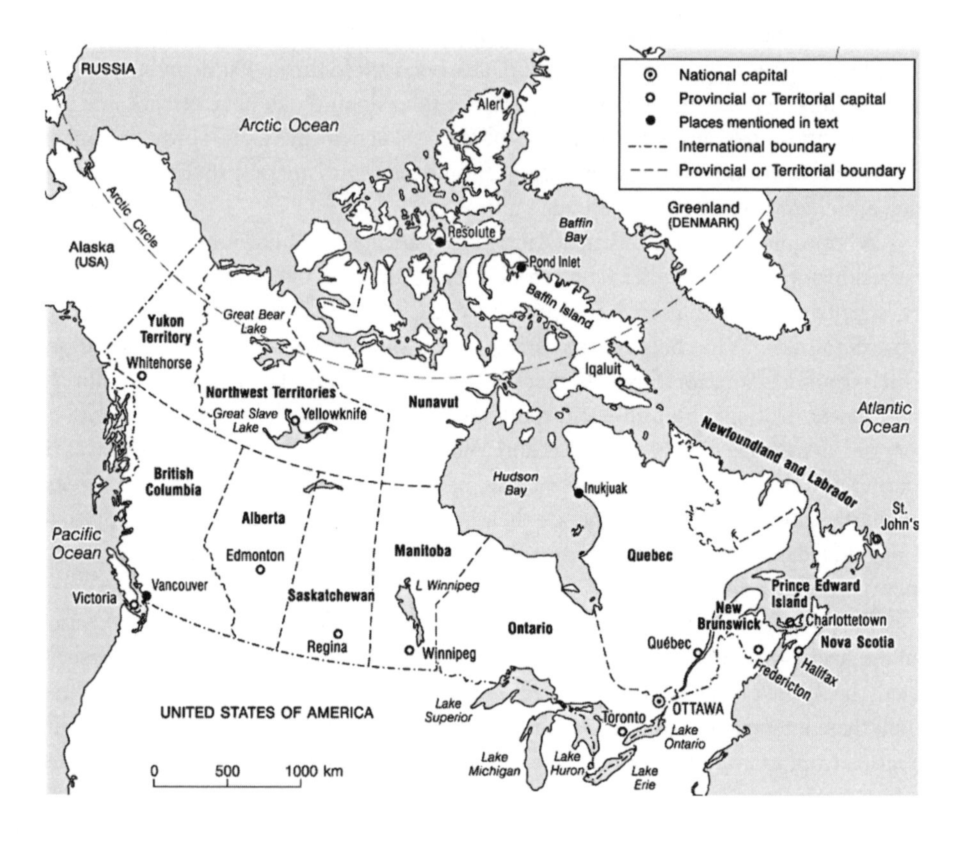

Figure 11.1 Location map of Canada.

government scientific field station operated by the Polar Continental Shelf Project as well as the second most northerly community in Canada, and it possesses a controversial history of encounter between Inuit and Qallunaat.

It should be noted at the outset that this chapter is not depicting an ethnography of Inuit at Resolute. Rather, it deploys an ethnographic account of encounters between scientists and Inuit during one particularly significant moment during field research. However, before discussing these events, it is necessary to expand upon Turner's understanding of ritual.

Theories of ritual, carnival and social dramas

Victor Turner construed societies as constantly enacting social dramas. Influenced by the Manchester School of Social Anthropology associated with Max Gluckman,[7] Turner saw such dramas as performing '"classificatory" oppositions' among communities.[8] Social dramas allow communities to identify conflicting groups and for individual members to distribute associations accordingly. These dramas are both episodic and pervasive across human activities. As Turner puts it, 'social life, then, even its apparently quietest moments, is characteristically "pregnant" with social dramas.'[9] For Turner, this theorisation was exemplified through the example of the Rio carnival. The carnival, as the apogee of consumptive excess and through the inversion of standard social roles, enables the *relieving of the pressure of existing social conflicts.*[10]

The theory of the carnival, of course, owes much to Mikhail Bakhtin's study of Rabelais.[11] For Bakhtin, carnivalesque moments enact the inversion of quotidian social hierarchies: in short, they form instances of the everyday world being 'turned upside down'. As Stallybrass and White point out, the convergence of Bakhtin's notions of carnival with parallel trends in symbolic anthropology was particularly significant.[12] Across both the social sciences and literary studies, scholars became interested in the subversive potential latent within instances of quotidian life. Anthropologists, such as Sherry Ortner, interrogated societal rituals in order to reveal wider cultural processes.[13] More recent work by geographers has included investigations of gender performance at the Rio carnival and the politics of the annual Caribana festival for the Afro-Caribbean community in Toronto.[14]

Rather than a discussion of Turner, this is an attempt to decipher some sort of social structure from such dramas,[15] to examine the notion that communities enact episodic rituals as a way of relieving social tensions. The participation in such carnivalesque moments allows the inversion of power relations within both everyday life and within the broader Canadian state.

The performance of the Canada Day celebrations in Resolute performs just such a sociological function. This claim is demonstrated by discussing the Canada Day ritual as a drama of social actors. To situate the discussion, however, it is necessary to outline the historical geography of Resolute. In doing so, it should become apparent as to why the performance of Canada Day at this site is of such ethnographic note.

A history of Resolute: communications hub of the Canadian Arctic

The hamlet of Resolute, Nunavut, is located on the southern edge of Cornwallis Island [Fig. 11.2].[16] Archaeological traces of Thule encampments dating from over 300 years ago have been found on Cornwallis and neighbouring islands. However, the location of both the Inuit hamlet and a scientific research station at Resolute was fortuitous. Indeed, there was never any formal intention to develop any modern presence at Resolute at all.[17]

Although Cornwallis Island was first visited by Edward Parry during his search for the North West Passage in 1819, the hamlet of Resolute Bay was named after *HMS Resolute*, a ship abandoned by the British expedition under H.T. Austin during 1854.[18] It was not until the Second World War, however, that extensive human activity was evident in these High Arctic regions of Canada.

Geopolitical considerations after 1945 had led to discussions between the Canadian and US militaries over the need to establish meteorological bases and maintain a presence in

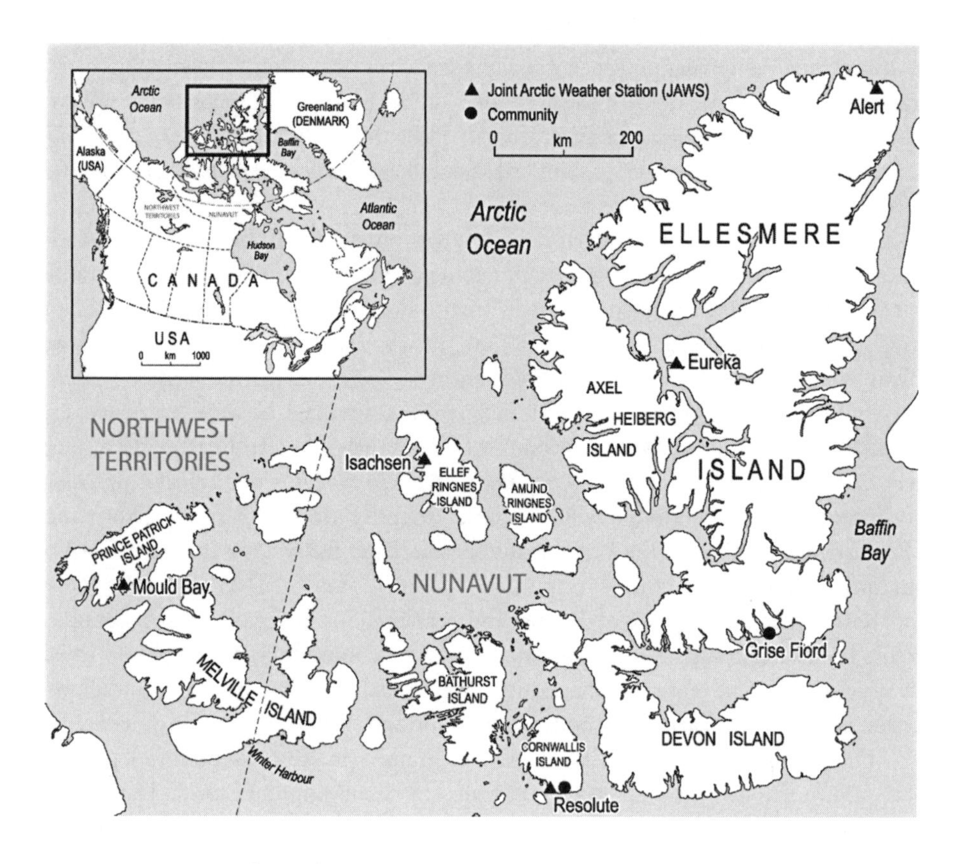

Figure 11.2 Map of Canadian High Arctic.

the High Arctic. In February 1947, an agreement was reached to establish five Joint Arctic Weather Stations (JAWS) in the region. These bases were to be constructed at Mould Bay, Eureka, Alert and Isachsen with a central station at Winter Harbour on Melville Island. However, in summer 1947, during the sea mission to construct the supply station at Winter Harbour, the propellers of the icebreaker *USS Edisto* were damaged in heavy sea ice. This resulted in the remedial choice of an alternative site on nearby Cornwallis Island.[19]

Given this hasty adoption of Resolute Bay, a number of unanticipated issues were to emerge with the harbour as a landing site for sea traffic. The harbour was ice-free for a season of only seven weeks and possessed shallow landing beaches. There were also further complications resulting from drifting sea ice. Such problems notwithstanding, given the difficulties establishing any such station from the outset, the Royal Canadian Air Force constructed an airstrip at Resolute in 1949, thereby consolidating its status as the communications hub of the High Arctic. In the following decades, the airport acted as a central coordination site for scientific and military activities by the Canadian Government. During the massive expansion of natural resource exploration over the 1960s, Resolute served as a logistical centre and saw the growth of various commercial operations. The Canadian military maintained control of Resolute airport until 1964 when management was transferred to Transport Canada. When the US withdrew support for the JAWS in 1970, the meteorological station at Resolute was maintained as a High Arctic Weather Station (HAWS) by Environment Canada.

As this discussion suggests, the connection between Canadian political sovereignty and the location of Resolute has remained since its earliest emplacement. These military and scientific presences were to be increased by resettlements of Inuit to Resolute.

A history of Resolute: a relocated Inuit community

In the summer of 1953, three Inuit families from Inukjuak (Port Harrison), Quebec, together with a family from Pond Inlet, were resettled at Resolute Bay, following the recommendation of the Federal Department of Northern Affairs and National Resources. At the time, the stated reasoning for relocation was the alleviation of pressure from hunting on the ecosystems of northern Quebec. By the early 1950s, the area inland from the east coast of Hudson Bay had supposedly suffered a serious decline in game, particularly impacting on caribou herds.[20] It was thought that the Inuit would be able to provide a seasonal labour force for the airport and central bases at Resolute. A small Royal Canadian Mounted Police (RCMP) detachment was also deployed in Resolute to administer the relocated families.

In total, twenty-two Inuit were transported to a region beyond their imagined, and practical, geographical landscapes. As perhaps might be expected, major economic hardship was encountered by the Inuit families at Resolute Bay. Meteorological records since the 1940s indicate that Resolute consistently has colder temperatures, more precipitation (as snow), and lower visibility than almost anywhere else in the Canadian Arctic. The environment and winters were considerably harsher than those encountered in northern Quebec, resulting in problems of inappropriate clothing and nutrition. This was further complicated by the complete diurnal darkness encountered at Resolute for over five months every year. Inuit came to know their new home as *Qausuittuq*, or the 'place where dawn never comes'. Moreover, by being relocated outside normal hunting areas, the families were often unable to use their own traditional skills and practices. Many Inuit had simply to rely on scavenging for food from refuse left on the base complex.[21]

A number of social problems emerged from the relocations. Inuit women were effectively confined to the community, because the RCMP disapproved of possible relationships developing with military and civilian personnel stationed at the base. The RCMP effectively facilitated a social-spatial separation of the hamlet from the base. In instances where cross-cultural encounter did occur, these often revolved around the airport bar. Difficulties with alcohol and suicide were to become common within the community.[22]

Through the 1960s, further Inuit migration into the community resulted in the town site expanding directly under the airstrip approach. The community was therefore transferred in 1975 to its present location eight kilometres from the base complex and airport. Connected only by a single-track road, this has reinforced the separation of the two populations.

Figure 11.3 Resolute Hamlet, August 2001 (photograph by R.C. Powell).

The major reason for the relocations appears to have been part of an attempt to demonstrate Canadian sovereignty over the High Arctic. It was believed that Inuit, being indigenous to northern Canada, helped sustain political claims by the government of Canada to the region given perceived threats consequent to increased military presence by both the US and USSR during the early Cold War. This was obviously problematic from its very inception, given that the Quebec Inuit did not possess traditions adapted to the environments of the High Arctic. However, the institutional mindset of the 1950s was predisposed to this sort of welfare colonialism, believing that Inuit were being relieved from suffering caused by lack of success on hunting grounds around Inukjuak. It should also be noted that members of the administering Department of Northern Affairs and National Resources have continued to state that the Inuit families were fully accepting of the relocations.[23]

In the late 1970s, some Inuit returned to Inukjuak at their own expense. This led the Makivik Corporation, a group established by the Inuit of northern Quebec (or Nunavik), to seek compensation and an apology from the federal government in 1982.[24] Following the establishment of the Royal Commission on Aboriginal Peoples (in 1991), the survivors of the original resettlement from Quebec were awarded CDN$10 million compensation in 1996 after the publication of the report.

Resolute currently hosts a population of around 215 of which 79 percent were reported as of 'aboriginal identity' in the 2001 Census of Canada.[25] This population is mainly composed of Inuit, a detachment of RCMP officers and a few other Federal and Territorial employees (such as teachers), and periodic visitors [Fig. 11.3].

This brief history of Resolute is important, as it indicates that the relationship between the Canadian state and the Inuit of the hamlet is fraught and contested. The question remains as to what the consequences might be for Inuit identity in Resolute.

Reformulating Inuit identities and the creation of Nunavut

Attempts to create a pan-continental national identity in Canada have existed since, at least, Confederation in 1867. The tense history between the two founding nations of French and English Canada need not be relayed here, but debates around Canadian national identity have been reinvigorated in recent years by notions of multiculturalism.[26] The traditional issues of bilingualism and asymmetric federalism have come into contest with those of indigenous self-determination and immigration.

What is important for our purposes is that in much of this discourse around nationhood, Inuit have come to occupy the apex of a refashioned Canadian identity.[27] For political commentator, John Ralston Saul, First Nations peoples form a critical strut of a tripartite Canada, together with Anglophones and Francophones.[28] But Inuit, because of the importance of northern environments in this imagined geography, form the core of the 'positive nationalism' required for Saul's Canada. As Saul concludes his extensive essay on nationhood and Canada's place in a globalising world,

> The Inuit quality of *isuma* summarises that essential context. It has as much to do with positive nationalism as with the public good. *Isuma* – intelligence that consists of the knowledge of our responsibilities towards society. It is a characteristic which grows with time. If you choose to look, you can find it at the core of events through the long line of Canada experience. It is an intelligence, the Inuit say, which grows because it is nurtured.[29]

Inuit traditional knowledge and practices have thus come to be seen as fundamental characteristics of the Canadian nation. This remarkable reversal of fortune needs to be seen in the context of the creation of the new Canadian territory of Nunavut in 1999. Inuit activist, John Amagoalik, remarks that it was not so long ago that journalists travelling north 'almost never failed to refer to the Arctic as a "wasteland where nobody lives"'.[30]

Following the resolution of the land claim between the Inuit and the government of Canada, the Nunavut Land Claims Agreement was signed in May 1993. This agreement provided for the creation of Nunavut and the establishment of a public government for the governance of this new territory. Although Inuit would form the majority of the population, around 85 percent, it was not an indigenous political structure.[31]

The government of Nunavut therefore allows for a degree of indigenous self-determination within the existing structures of the Canadian state. As might be expected, Nunavut has had complicated impacts on Inuit conceptualisations of identity. For some, the rehabilitative political processes involved in the creation of Nunavut will not be complete until Inuit Qaujimajatuqangit (IQ) – traditional knowledges, skills and ways of thinking – have been completely incorporated into the government structures. Nunavut might mean 'our land', but the bureaucratic structures of the fledging territorial state are very much those of Qallunaat.

Like all identities, the Inuit sense of self is complicated. An Inuk informant from Pangnirtung, 'Rex', had a Qallunaat father and Inuk mother. During conversations, Rex revealed that he had suffered racism, as he put it, 'from both sides' during his childhood, but especially from other Inuit. His mother had kept him away from her Inuit family because of social problems endured by the community through the 1970s and 1980s. Yet Rex feels firmly that he is Inuk. Furthermore, Rex believes it is sad that, 'in Resolute and Grise, Inuit commonly speak English not Inuktitut'. This is different from the situation in other settlements, such as Igloolik and Pangnirtung, where Inuktitut is commonly spoken across the community. In short, there is a geography of the performing of Inuit identity within the new territory of Nunavut and, in Resolute, being Inuk is particularly complicated.

Traces of the state: federal presences in Resolute

Across Nunavut, apprehension remains for Inuit at any manifestation of the federal state. These stresses are exacerbated by both the permanent and the seasonal presences in Resolute. The current federal contingent in Resolute includes a two-person RCMP detachment, a minimal Environment Canada staff at the weather station, a small Transport Canada staff at the airport and the large seasonal population of the Polar Continental Shelf Project.

One evident tension is the manifest hostility expressed by Inuit towards the RCMP. An adolescent informant from the hamlet told me that he did 'not like the police, because of what they did in the old days'. These stories had been passed on to him, like traditional hunting and navigation skills, as part of his process of becoming Inuk in Resolute.[32] However, the RCMP detachment is situated within the community. It is the scientific research of the Polar Continental Shelf Project (PCSP), based at the airport, that provides the major influx of people into Resolute during the summer months.

The PCSP facilitates research by scientists from all over Canada and the world. These scientists include those from Canadian universities, various research branches of the government of Canada and non-Canadian researchers from countries such as Denmark (Greenland), the US, Japan and the UK. Each year, the PCSP supports over 120 field parties. These groups vary in size from two to three scientists to large parties of ten to twelve researchers. The continual arrival and departure of scientists thus involves around 300–400 individuals over the duration of each field season.

This presence has an important impact on the long-term sustainability of the Inuit community, not least by making viable two arrivals/departures by jet aircraft from Ottawa every week during the summer. However, as Ralph Alexander of the Resolute Hamlet Council puts it, there has been an evolving relationship between the scientific base at the airport and the local community.

> It has changed an awful lot. Back in the '70s, you had the base and you had the village. And there was a bar, so everybody, sort of, knew everybody else. And the bar closed in '81, which may have been a good thing in one way – a little less drinking. But then in another way, it meant that people didn't meet each other anymore. And, by this point in time there are people at the base that nobody here even knows about. But, at the same time, twenty years ago the base did what they were gonna do and you did what you were going to do. Now ... there's more regulation of what happens. So you have a better idea, at least, of some of the management area, the higher levels. So you know more or less what's being done by Polar Shelf, what field parties are going out where. To ensure that they're not going to cause any problems for people who actually still hunt.[33]

It would appear, then, that attempts to manage research through new licensing arrangements operated by the Nunavut Research Institute in Iqaluit, have allowed Inuit, or at least their political representatives in local government, more knowledge of activity on their territories. This means that the ostensible view of the PCSP within Resolute is relatively indifferent. There is suspicion of the activities of scientists, but issues of potential interference with wildlife or hunting grounds are decreasingly sites of serious dispute. As Alexander argues, the current view of PCSP by the inhabitants of Resolute is generally dispassionate.

> It's kind of neutral. I mean there's always going to be somebody saying, 'well, they're going up, and they're just surveying the animals, and that's not good for us'. And there's like the other thing, 'well, they're coming up, and what they're doing isn't bothering anything, but like, we don't get anything out of it'. And, you're kind of saying, 'well, look, there are people being employed out of it, so there is some benefit'. I think you're going to see that anywhere you go. I think the biggest thing is, when you don't know, you think that maybe what they're doing is hurting your hunting or causing problems with the animals. And, once you see what they're doing, it's usually of very little interest. ... Because they're not hurting the wildlife. You've got two people sitting in a tent on Ellesmere Island for a week taking water samples. ... The only ones that really concern anybody here is if they are doing helicopter surveys. Is it going to go into wildlife areas?[34]

This indifference notwithstanding, there are still major dependencies between the base and hamlet communities. A principal interaction between the base population and the hamlet is through employment. Indeed, the potential provision of seasonal labour by Inuit was an initial justification for the indigenous relocations to the region. However, many base jobs are performed by migrant labour from Newfoundland. As Alexander argues though, in many ways the lack of reliance on seasonal labour opportunities with PCSP is actually an indication of the relatively high levels of employment in Resolute.

> I think it has always been a fairly high level of employment here. In a lot of the communities you had very high levels of unemployment. Here, you don't. Now, a lot of the jobs here are in the Co-op or the Hamlet. And there's two hotels in the community, so there's employment there. And there's a third hotel up at the airport. Polar Shelf has never employed a lot of people from the village. But they do employ one or two every year. In fact, they employ them through the Hamlet. It saves them paperwork.[35]

Nevertheless, although most of the PCSP staff are from southern Canada, this Inuit labour is crucial to the functioning of the organisation. Rachel and Emma, part-time cleaners at the PCSP base, and Alistair, who drives the water truck and does some manual labour on an 'odd-job' basis for PCSP, are all from the hamlet of Resolute. One of the base cooks, Sarah, is from Inuvik in the western Arctic (i.e. she is Inuvialuit). Every Sunday afternoon, Emma and other Inuit women from the village, and sometimes their children, visit PCSP to talk to Rachel and Sarah in the dining room at the base. Topics for discussion would include issues such as regional and dialect differences among Inuit.

Another major interaction between the base and the community is through the employment by field parties of Inuit guides as security against threats from polar bears. Strict regulations on the size and composition of field parties supported by PCSP mean that research teams will often hire a hunter to join the party for a period in the field. The stark seasonality of this Inuit labour with PCSP means that it is combined with other wage employment and subsistence activities. As Alexander states, during July 2002, various individuals helped in scientific activities in the field without any formal recording of their presence.

> However, right now, they have three people from the village working. There's somebody who works with them every year, and then there's a couple of people that they hire on a need basis. ... But the other people that they have working for them right now are working in town. And that's people we... One person is paid through the Hamlet, one person is a direct employee. However, we're not really an employment agency. Somebody may call me up. In fact, they do call up, and say 'well we're going out somewhere, can you give me some, a couple of, names of people that might be interested'. And we'll give 'em two names, and we'll give them 'phone numbers. And it's up to them. And we don't even know if they go out or not.[36]

Other everyday interactions between scientists and base staff at PCSP and the local community remain limited. Such encounters involve occasional economic transfers at the local Co-op store. Scientists and base staff will make trips to buy soft drinks and sundries from the store whilst on base.

Despite the general low-profile of cross-cultural engagements in Resolute, it should be noted that colonial views of Inuit still persist. Such traces of the colonial present are often covert rather than ostensible. This is evident in the pervasive use of the term 'locals', rather than Inuit, by the PCSP base staff and the majority of older scientists. However, contemporary colonial ideologies are deployed in the starkest terms by wealthy, transient traffic through Resolute airport. Adventure tourists often manifest strongly racist attitudes towards the people of Resolute. Consider, for example, the following passage from an account of journeying to Ellesmere Island by Canadian explorer and travel writer Jerry Kobalenko:

> My partners in crime likewise commented on how they felt like 'stray cats' or 'bag ladies' in Resolute. Sometimes we [visitors] came prepared to spend substantial amounts of money and still felt like second-class citizens. Resolute's icy heart had seen too much. Too many foreign polar bear hunters willing to drop $20,000 in four days, leaving thousand-dollar tips in their wake. Too many North Pole expeditions with

> half-million dollar budgets. Too many planeloads of doctors and stockbrokers. Too many cruise ships disgorging ladies in furs (mink, not caribou) and men with glaring, corporate eyes who plunk down two thousand dollars for a narwhal tusk during their one hour on shore. Resolute is like Las Vegas: impossible to impress, no matter how much money you throw away. ... But, at worst, Resolute could be so disheartening and humiliating that I would return home never wanting to go north again. Yet, like cold, fatigue, soft snow, high winds, and partners from hell, I soon forgot Resolute and remembered only Ellesmere.[37]

Resolute, for Kobalenko, precisely because it is a social space, is disheartening. It acts only as logistical fulcrum necessary to facilitate passage to the imaginary, and uninhabited, landscapes of northern Ellesmere Island.

Notwithstanding some important interactions, then, it would appear that the historic socio-spatial segregation of the scientific base and the local community and associated ideologies persist, or are even reinforced, in contemporary Resolute. However, this lack of interaction is completely subverted on a specific day each summer.

Enacting the ritual of Canada Day

Each year, on 1 July, Canada Day is celebrated throughout Canada. There are obviously geographical variations in the sincerity with which these festivities are held across the country. Significant pageants are generally associated with certain parts of Canada, such as Ontario, Manitoba and British Columbia. Similar to many civic festivals in Western nations, however, there is often reluctance to take such projects seriously. In Vancouver, for example, the marking of Canada Day is often treated with an embarrassed disdain. National celebrations do not fit well with the imagined Canadian sense of self. However, in Resolute, Canada Day is one of the very few occasions when the scientific base community and the local, Inuit community interact. What is most interesting about the mainly Inuit hamlet of Resolute is the degree to which the community participates in symbolic acts of Canadian national identification.

Resolute hosts an annual Canada Day parade. This is followed by a series of celebratory events encompassing a large bonfire, a communal barbecue and a series of competitive river-crossing races. The Canada Day festival is organised by the Hamlet Council. As well as local dignitaries, such as the Mayor of Resolute, the participants in these events include almost every member of the community. In these circumstances, it needs to be remembered that the PCSP scientists signify the federal presence in Resolute. In short, the scientists embody the Canadian state. These Canada Day events can be seen as part of a carnivalesque ritual that involves relief of community tensions.

Canada Day commences with a lunchtime parade in which the fire truck, festooned with local children, leads a convoy of all of the vehicles in the village up to the airport complex [Fig. 11.4]. The fire truck is driven by Alistair, the Inuk who is employed to drive the water truck for PCSP. At the airport, more vehicles join the convoy, before all participants travel a couple of kilometres across the tundra to a nearby riverbank for the other festivities.

Figure 11.4 Vehicle parade on Canada Day passing the Polar Continental Shelf Project base complex, July 2002 (photograph by R.C. Powell).

In July 2002, a group of scientists wanted to join the parade. All were Canadian, coming from regions across the country, except for myself, a British ethnographer.[38] The request to participate was important because PCSP scientists perform a crucial role in the relieving of tensions by becoming figures of ridicule during the carnivalesque festivities. As this narrative of events should suggest, from the very first instance, the scientists are unwitting actors in an unfolding local comedy.

The scientists believed that the parade was to start in the centre of the hamlet at 13h00. Mainly because they had, perhaps purposefully, been misinformed of the parade's starting time, as they travelled over to the hamlet to join the convoy, the scientists met the fire truck and other vehicles coming in the opposite direction up the single-track road towards the airport. The vehicles had apparently left the community at 12h30. The scientists therefore had to reverse their vehicle, in front of the entire parade, for over six kilometres, until a wider embankment allowed space for the truck and other vehicles to pass. This involved the complete convoy of vehicles travelling past and waving to the scientists, whilst also tooting their car horns and mocking them, before the scientists' vehicle was able to join the rear of the parade. The parade then continued towards the airport and base complex, where all the vehicles paused for about five minutes. Once at the base complex, most of the eager scientists, except for James, a biologist who felt that he was too old for such activity, climbed onto the roof of the fire truck together with the Inuit children.

Figure 11.5 Community celebrations on Canada Day, near Resolute, July 2002 (photograph by R.C. Powell).

It is important to note that, except for Alistair in the truck cab, the only adults travelling on the fire truck were scientists. While we were on top of the truck, a female graduate student asked an Inuk child if he would get cold without a hat. Astutely, he replied, 'No, we won't, but you might!', causing all twenty or so children to laugh hysterically. The scientists were thus also mocked by the children. However, their exotic status as outsiders within this local celebration of national identity meant that the scientists tended to play up their role at these cross-cultural moments. On the roof of the fire truck, scientists sought to entertain the children by showing them their expensive digital video cameras. Other valuable personal goods acted as significant novelties in these spaces. Indeed, it could even be argued that new technological artefacts helped to stabilise the contact ritual.

When the convoy reached the river, a large bonfire constructed the previous day was set alight [Fig. 11.5]. Most of the scientists then spent their time pruning sticks with penknives, thereby creating toasting forks for the children to roast marshmallows on the bonfire. Again, little attempt was made to speak or interact with adult Inuit.

Whilst food for the community was prepared on a large barbecue, a series of races was organised from one bank of the river to the other. These races involved young children, older children and adolescents, and adult men and women. Many of the younger scientists participated fully in these activities. In doing so, these participants realised that, like local powerholders such as the Mayor and RCMP officers, they should be seen to take part but not to be

Figure 11.6 Community river-crossing races, near Resolute, July 2002 (photograph by R.C. Powell).

victorious. For example, a number of scientists theatrically fell into the river while leading the race. This further enabled socially acceptable mockery of the federal state embodiments, thereby facilitating the carnivalesque dissolution of usual hostilities.

There were also signs of social tensions within the village being dissipated. This was especially evident when the river race for women came down to a very close finish between the Inuk wife of the (non-Inuk) Mayor, and Emma, a former Co-op worker and PCSP employee [Fig. 11.6]. It was obvious that the community wanted, what was perceived to be, an 'Inuk' victory. The connection to employment by the Canadian state therefore appeared to be less divisive than that of being married to a non-Inuk. After Emma's victory, the majority of attendees at the barbeque made a point of congratulating her individually.

Despite interacting with children in a paternalistic way, and participating through the inversion of power-roles in the river-crossing races, scientists also attempted to initiate conversations with some of the Qallunaat inhabitants of Resolute. Both scientists and these local people would bemoan military activities in the area. Often perceived as leaving polluting traces in the landscape, neither scientists nor other local non-Inuit were happy with the supposedly unsupervised activities of the Canadian forces in the Arctic. There was a more powerful form of federal presence on Cornwallis Island against which both groups could unite in their antagonism.

The lack of conversational interaction between scientists and adult Inuit notwithstanding, the general atmosphere of the Canada Day performances was ostensibly very friendly. However, James, the biologist, was obviously uncomfortable and left the festivities early. It was evident that he was not enjoying watching the activities and, as a man of around 45 years of age, he apparently did not feel able to participate in the races. James had experience of environmental science projects on the territories of other indigenous groups in southern Canada. Despite his discomfort, he commented that 'the atmosphere is not as unfriendly as an Indian Reserve.'

Inuit nationalism in Resolute

There was a general sense that the Inuit of Resolute wanted to convey, at least ostensibly, pride in some sort of Canadian identity. The Canadian flag was prominently displayed from the fire truck during the entire duration of the parade and other festivities [Fig. 11.7]. Every child had little Canadian flags painted on both cheeks. In many ways, there was much more celebration of symbolic Canadianness than I ever observed during two Canada Day events that I participated in whilst living in Vancouver.

Moreover, the question continually pressed onto scientists by Inuit on Canada Day was: 'Are you Canadian?' If the scientists answered in the affirmative, they were encouraged to join in with the festivities or to share in the food. The implication was very much that, on this particular day, both Inuit and Qallunaat should remember their commonalities rather than their differences.

The carnivalesque moment of Canada Day allows Inuit to stress Canadian aspects of their identity. In doing so, such practices problematise facile binaries between agents of the imperial state and indigenous subjects in the colonial present. Furthermore, apparent nationalistic celebrations by Inuit help undermine, perhaps ironically, simplistic understandings of patriotism in multicultural states.

The performance of Canada Day in Resolute similarly raises important questions about Canadian nationalism and its connection to Arctic science. The supposed need to defend Canadian sovereignty is often still deployed in arguments for increases in federal research funding by northern scientists.[39] The ethnographic evidence indicates that, notwithstanding their Inuit identity, in Resolute people still wish to celebrate their Canadianness. As the then Director of the Nunavut Research Institute (NRI), Bruce Rigby, put it, 'I think you'll find in the north, northerners in general are probably much more nationalistic than anyone in southern Canada.'[40] In response to this question of nationalism, current executive director of NRI, Mary Ellen Thomas, states,

> This debate came up recently when there were claims of who owns the North Pole. And that the Russians had made some claim to the ownership of the Pole, and the Danes had made some claims to the ownership of the Pole, and the Americans had made some claims. And the question was, 'well, why isn't Canada out there, claiming

Figure 11.7 Canadian flag displayed during Canada Day celebrations, July 2002 (photograph by R.C. Powell).

> the North Pole?' And my answer to that was, 'because we don't need to'. Because the reality is we're already here, we have a presence here and an identity here. And this whole question of sovereignty to me is just a joke. I mean, it serves someone else's interests. But for the people who live here, the Inuit people, this is their land.[41]

Given the creation of Nunavut, Inuit become able to celebrate all forms of identity, including that of 'Canadian', in whichever way they see fit. As Rigby puts it,

> And I think you'd find an awful lot of people who are just a little bit uncomfortable with someone else's nationalist road. It doesn't make them any less Canadian. Or any less nationalistic. But it just means that people aren't willing to allow themselves to play into somebody else's agenda. And I think that's one thing that I've learned over the years here. People are very strong up here.[42]

That the demonstrations of such Canadian identity allow the relieving of both external and internal social tensions is to be expected of any such carnivalesque event.

Conclusion

Ethnographic investigation of the performance of Canada Day in Resolute allows us to think more seriously about the notion of the Arctic as Inuit homeland and the implications for debates about national identities. Resolute is not a wasteland of nobodies. It is home to peoples that have suffered both interference and indifference from the Canadian state. These peoples have continued to maintain culturally meaningful lives in the face of such dominating institutions.

Like Bakhtin's carnival, the celebrations of Canada Day outlined here are not to be understood as simply a loyalist reinvigoration of the state. Rather, Canada Day involves the 'temporary suspension, both ideal and real, of hierarchical rank' in Resolute.[43] In doing so, the celebrations facilitate a 'special type of communication impossible in everyday life' between scientists and inhabitants of the community.[44] Moreover, Inuit relations with the Canadian state are characterised by ambivalence, an ambivalence made manifest in the rituals enacted on the first day of July.

Social life in the Arctic involves the use of moments such as Canada Day to deal with the continual embodied presence of the Federal state. Inuit lives are constructed through events that allow the alleviation of tensions internal to this construction of the social order. The account outlined thus supports Jean Briggs's classic ethnography of the methods Inuit use to resolve conflict.[45]

Moreover, such events constantly enact the colonial present. Recent research in critical Inuit studies has stressed the complicated relationships between aboriginality and Canadian identities in northern Canada.[46] For Inuit in Resolute, the birth of Nunavut has not placed them outside the Canadian state but has instead allowed the reformulation, during carnival and ritual, of cultural relationships within it. The creation of Nunavut appears to have resulted in complicated refractions through Inuit identities and these require more attention from students of nationalism.

Resolute is an itinerant home to the scientists, mechanics, pilots and other maintenance staff who enact scientific practices in the Arctic. It is through such agents that Inuit experience an otherwise distant Canadian state. As this chapter has tried to indicate, the interactions between these groups, historically involving dispossession and racism, have important ramifications in the present. Only when the Arctic is envisaged as a social space, encompassing places wherein different humans interact, resist and celebrate, will a full understanding of such regions be facilitated. It is through ethnographic observation of such practices that the assumptions of many theories of the nation and the colonial encounter are revealed. Inuit self-determination has unleashed the potential for the reformulation of national spaces through the enactment of everyday life.

Although always structured by power, the complexity of these human interactions needs to be understood for the future subsistence of these high-latitude places. As the Arctic regions become ever more crucial to global environmental futures, it is imperative that these interdependent histories of encounter be remembered and that their diverse voices are documented. In outlining some of this history, this chapter suggests that the social geographies of the Canadian Arctic have very important consequences as spaces for encounter. It is less that indigenous resistance reverses colonial axes of power than that self-determination reveals the complex intertwining of cross-cultural understandings.[47]

12

Paektudaegan

Science and Colonialism, Memory and Mapping in Korean High Places

Jong-Heon Jin

In 1990, two professional climbers in South Korea, Nam Nan-hee and Kwon Kyung-up, hiked the full length of the Paektudaegan following the ridge line of the peninsula from its southern extremity – Chirisan, adjacent to the southern sea – to the northern point of Paektusan (Mount Paektu) on the Chinese border region, long considered the symbolically most important mountain in Korea and the originating point of Paektudaegan. Paektudaegan denotes a continuous mountain chain stretching between these two peaks. This line of high places has historically been considered the backbone of Korea: a sacred spine suggesting territorial unity within the country. The type of mountaineering the two climbers undertook along the ridge line is known as *jongju* and is increasingly popular in modern Korea.[1] They travelled intermittently, doing a week of actual walking per month, between September 1990 and September 1991. The total length of the range they travelled was approximately 700 kilometres, all within South Korea. The expedition was supported by the climbers' journal, *People and Mountain* (*Saram kwa San*), which serialised their travelogue during the year. Nam wrote the narrative, Kwon, a poet and climber, wrote numerous poems about the journey. These climbers were not the first to travel the length of Paektudaegan. Beginning in the late 1980s, mountaineers were known to walk the length of Paektudaegan, but none of their journeys was publicly recorded. Thus, stories concerning Paektudaegan were not widespread. In this sense, the serialising of the travelogue played an important role in making the Paektudaegan issue popular.

Eight decades earlier, between 1900 to 1902, the Japanese geologist and geographer Koto Bunjiro (1856–1935) also travelled in these mountains, accompanied by a retinue of six men and four ponies. He made two winter journeys in Korea for the purposes of surveying the peninsula over 266 days, totalling 6,300 kilometres.[2] After the survey, he returned to Tokyo and wrote a paper for a Tokyo University journal. His fieldwork was the first modern geomorphologic survey of the peninsula.[3] His goal was to reveal how internal geological structure is manifested in the external topography.

It is interesting to juxtapose these two expeditions and reflect on what has happened in the representation of Korea's high places, especially Paektudaegan, during the past century. Put simply, contemporary climbers Nam and Kwon attempted to reclaim an indigenous knowledge of Paektudaegan they claimed had been lost and forgotten since Koto Bunjiro's colonial exploration. Koto's challenging project of subordinating landform to geological analysis established a new geography of Korea's mountain ranges, intended to replace the traditional representation of mountain systems focussed on Paektudaegan. Whereas the traditional representation of mountains was based on the topographical features on the surface of the substantial landscape and its symbolic rendering as the unified Paektudaegan, Koto's science was a geological restructuring of mountains. Accordingly, Paektudaegan was deconstructed and divided into several individual mountain ranges based on their inner geological structure.[4] As a 'modern' and scientific way of representing Korean mountains Koto's system endured through the twentieth century. Thus, in postwar South Korea, the T'aebaeck range rather than Paektudaegan was considered the backbone mountain: geology served to confirm political geography in making a severance between mountain ranges in the north and those in the south. The meaning of 'backbone range' attributed to T'aebaeck was minimised within the explanatory frame that described the topography of South Korean territory, depriving it of its symbolic power. The status of Paektudaegan as the territorial origin of Korea was disrupted and Paektudaegan was banished from the realm of public discourse.

In the late 1980s, Paektudaegan was being revived through an increasing public interest in traditional geographical knowledge, ignored since the introduction of modern geography in the early twentieth century. The rediscovery of Paektudaegan over the last two decades was made possible by virtue of the pioneering work of climbers and independent cartographers. It eventually became an embodied landscape through which the collective desires and imagination of national unity is being created, implicitly mediated through the discourse of a North/South Korea reunification.

The story of Paektudaegan's emergence as a national territorial symbol reveals how natural landscape is continually reconstructed as a form of social identity and is explained scientifically by references to culture and society; it shows the way in which a particular territorial society is constituted and imagined through the discourse and practice of nature and science, considering especially the reassertion of indigenous knowledge in the context of what can also be considered a post-colonial society. The contested representations of the whole national territory is a symbolic landscape, where the discourse of geography as scientific knowledge is verified and historicised by reworking pre-modern, indigenous, geographical epistemology.

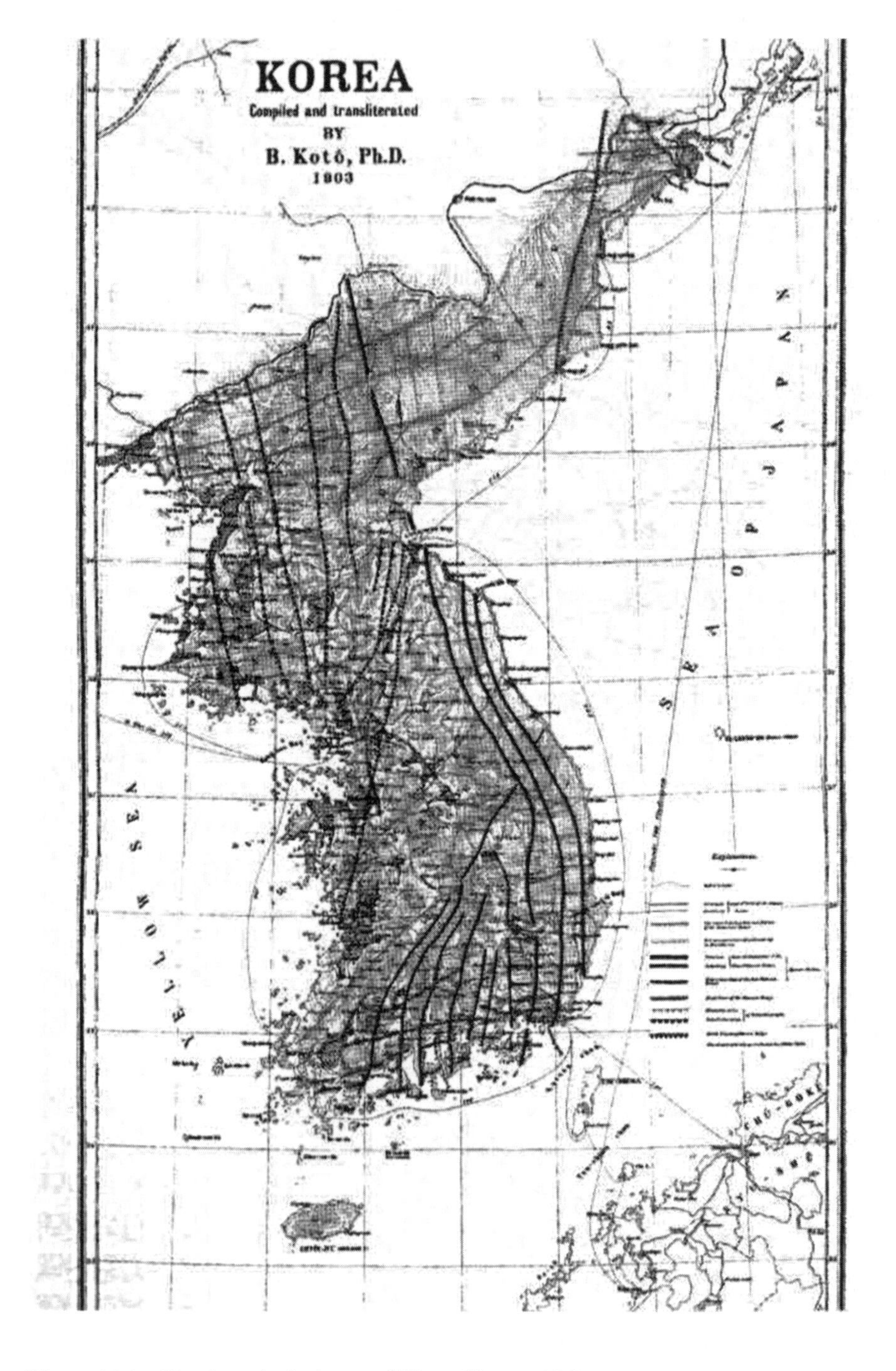

Figure 12.1 Koto's geological map of Korea (Koto, 1903).

Situating scientific knowledge

Koto's research on Korea's mountain system can be situated in the context of Japanese colonial encroachment that involved geological and mineralogical surveys of Korea implemented in the 1880s. Even though Korea was officially annexed to Japan only in 1910, it had become vulnerable to Japanese economic invasion and political intervention since the Kanghwa treaty between the two countries in 1876.[5] In this respect, the survey is easily reconfigured within the discourse of power/knowledge, using scientific practice in the implementation of the Japanese colonial project.

To avoid an instrumentalist view of scientific knowledge as the straightforward 'social construction of nature', the argument of Bruce Braun persuasively explains the way in which scientific knowledge and practice played a key role as an integral part of colonial governmentality in Canada during the late nineteenth century.[6] Braun argues that 'science is constitutive of political rationality rather than merely its instrument.'[7] Braun's exploration of 'geological landscape' effectively concretises Bruno Latour's argument that the discourse of politics and society, broadly social science, has never been separated from scientific discourse and reasoning in modern society, which Latour refers to as an 'entire modern paradox'.[8] Braun's 'geological landscape' is not just an alternative way of seeing nature to that of a distanced world witnessed and understood through objective vision.[9] It is formulated from the utterly opposite end of Latour's 'great divide'. Whereas environmental historians use the landscape to bring nature back into social theory, Braun's 'geological landscape' focuses on how society comes into being through the engagement with nature via abstract scientific/economic calculation. While the the environmental historian explores the strata of meanings accumulated above the surface, Braun examines the hidden vertical structure of territory below the surface. Therefore, geological landscape eventually collapses the surface to make transparent where the memory and culture are embedded.

This approach supersedes the instrumentalist view of colonial science in which the coloniser takes advantage of modern knowledge of nature to consolidate power structure and domination, a still common assumption in Korean nationalist historiography. The role of the 'geological (or geomorphologic) vision' introduced by Koto should be seen in a theoretical context similar to Dawson's vision in Canada as outlined by Braun. Koto not only introduced scientific knowledge to a 'new' territory, but also established a political and social vision of that territory itself. However, Koto's research and his geological vision have subsequently been rendered as either neutral, innocent and objective scientific knowledge or a sign of colonial encroachment undertaken with malicious intent. Latour's and Braun's argument on society and scientific knowledge provide ample conceptual equipment for deconstructing such a dualistic confrontation. Thus, much more needs to be explained to elucidate how Koto's scientific practice is situated in the historically contingent configuration of scientific knowledge and the shaping of Korea as colonial territory. Thus Koto's arguments must be examined in detail.

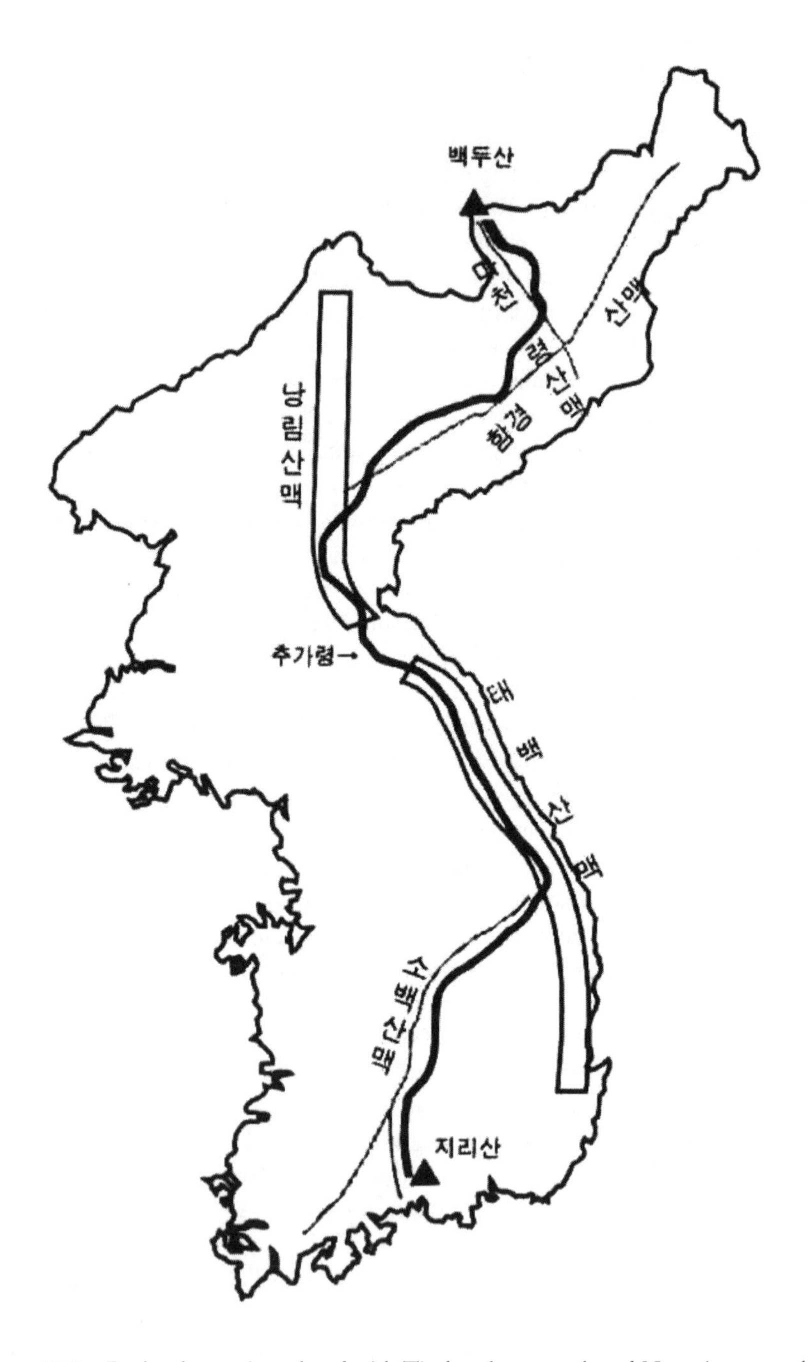

Figure 12.2 Paektudaegan is replaced with T'aebaecksanmaeck and Nangrimsanmack. The two newly defined mountain ranges are separated in the south and the north (S. Cho, 1997, p. 137).

Colonising traditional geography through a 'New Science'

The application of a Western-influenced 'geological vision' fundamentally disrupted the framework of traditional Korean geographical knowledge. Koto's project can be used to trace how scientific knowledge, which was introduced by Japanese scholars, deconstructed the colonised territoriality and reconstructed from it the image of modern landscape.

First, with the introduction of German geomorphology, the territory of the peninsula was incorporated into a global scientific discourse and practice. Koto drew upon European geological terminology and theory to classify the high places of the Korea peninsula into three categories in terms of the direction of the geological axis: the Sinian (Chinese) range, the Korean range and the Liau-tung range. According to his geological examination, a group of mountain ranges in China has a similar direction to the Sinian range, reflecting a shared geological axis. When Koto, basing his analysis on von Richthofen's classification, referred to some mountain ranges as the 'axis folds of the Sinian system', any Korean cultural and historical meanings inscribed in the mountains were erased. Layers of cultural inheritance were replaced by the accumulation of geological strata. In Koto's graphic representation of Korea, the national boundary is designated merely to delimit the spatial scope of the research.

Second, traditional knowledge of topography was detached from its inherited conceptual framework and reconfigured by an imposed geological vision. In his geotectonic map of Korea [Fig. 12.1], the internal geological structure is superimposed on the delineated topography of the peninsula, reducing the geographical exterior and its details to an underlying geological truthfulness. Geological lines drawn across the topography stir a tactile sensation analogous to a scar on a face, while at the same time alluding to the possibilities for resource extraction and provisionary change into a progressive modern space.

Third, ultimately and most importantly in Koto's geomorphology, as noted above, Paektudaegan was no longer a backbone mountain range for the peninsula; the T'aebaeck range assumes pre-eminence on the basis of geological features. He abandoned the Paektudaegan concept, and broke the unity of the mountain chain [Fig. 12.2]. The T'aebaeck range was now drawn from the middle of the peninsula to its southern tip. By reconfiguring this mountain range, Koto effectively disrupted traditional geographical understanding, signalling in geology the end of the territorialised Korean body politic, a prelude to the birth of 'new' and scientific Korean geography.

The displacement of Paektudaegan was implemented by a two-sided, modernising spatial discourse comprising both homogenisation and fragmentation. The geomorphologic vision transformed the hierarchical, pre-modern spatial structure into modern homogenous space. The division and fragmentation of the geological representation seen in the map effectively sundered the unity of a hierarchically integrated pre-modern space. Such re-ordering of space was made possible by the elimination of the symbolic power in both Seoul, the political centre, and Paektudaegan (Paektusan), the spiritual backbone. The desacralisation of these two locations was accompanied by the homogenisation of the whole territorial space. The projection of a new spatial vision invalidated the mystical, inherited relationship

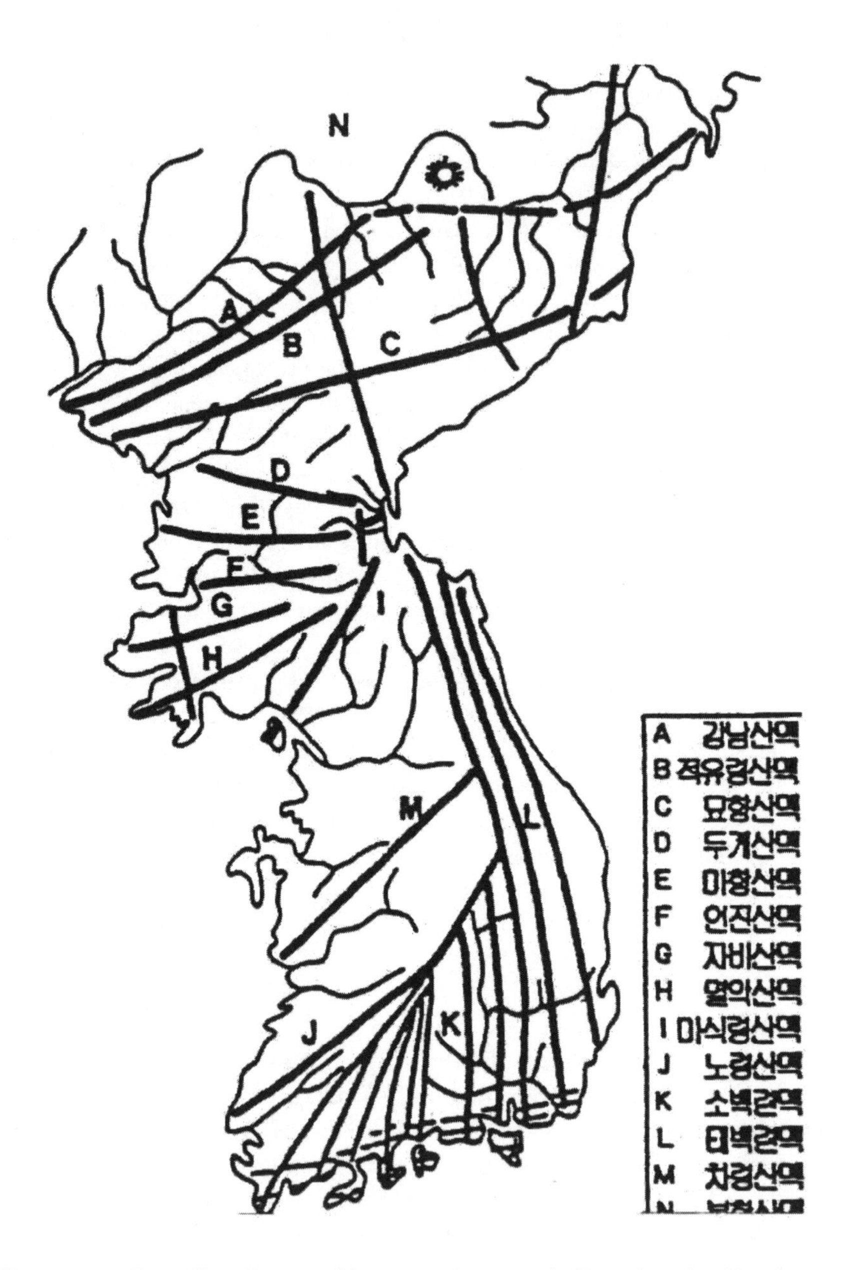

Figure 12.3 Yasu Shouei's map of the mountain system in Korea based on Koto's geological map. This can be considered an archetype of the current official understanding of the Korean mountain system. T'aebaecksanmaeck (L) (M. Park, 1996).

between culture (politics) and nature, once authorised by cosmological engagement with the sacredness of Korea's mountains. Nature was detached from history and culture, and in its disenchantment ceased to play the role of naturalising a pre-modern power.

The overlap between topography and geology represented in Koto's work not only represents a colonisation of the territory by Western scientific discourse and Japanese power as an agent of modernisation, but also shows the internal tension within the Western sciences, geology and geography, at a particular historical phase. According to Bruno Latour,[10] immutable mobiles such as maps make it possible to accumulate and transfer knowledge of the colonised within a colonising society. Conversely, they are also an effective medium through which the configuration and evolution of knowledge in colonising societies themselves are revealed. In other words, Koto's investigation on Korean territory is a situated process of a particular form of colonial science coming into being within the colonising society.

Such an unstable disciplinary evolution is explicitly represented in Koto's geographical paper. In it, the scientific method of geological survey is supported by a geographical engagement with the culture and history of Korea. By using historical references, Koto shows that he did not wholly ignore the holistic geographical vision, enabling him to represent the entire territory as an integrated land surface. He suggests six reasons, most of them geographical, for dividing North and South Korea: 1) historical development, 2) geological structure, 3) climatic difference, 4) topographic difference, 5) difference in vegetation and 6) the differing personalities of the two people.[11]

The two visions, geographic and geological, are juxtaposed rather than interwoven, causing a fundamental instability in his method. For example, when Koto divided the peninsula into north and south, in terms of topographical features reflecting internal geological lines at the beginning of his argument, he also pointed to the historical and cultural differences between the north and the south, further attempting to naturalise the division based on non-geological reasoning. The presumed divide was important because it became the basis of severing Paektudaegan.

> *I venture to call the former North and the latter South Korea*. This dividing line is not only convenient for *descriptive purpose*, but is almost a natural boundary. Firstly, because it is the boundary of historical development ... the north is the old Cho-sŏn, while the south was little known during these early periods ... It was only later times that the whole peninsula was united under the one government of Koryo or Korea (918–1392), which was replaced by the present I-family,[12] the last Chosun.[13]

Koto's confusing oscillation between geography and geology cannot be ascribed solely to his own methodological inability. Rather, it is also due to 'historically contingent configuration' of the evolving global scientific discourse. The term 'geomorphology' became more popular at the time when the British geographer, H.J. Mackinder, referred to it in his lecture on 'the half artistic, half genetic consideration of the form of the lithosphere',[14] suggesting that the advent of geomorphology, seen as a creative way of 'picturing the world', was not free from the contemporary geopolitical instability of the *fin-de-siècle*. Another clue toward verifying this assumption is provided in this remark by Koto.

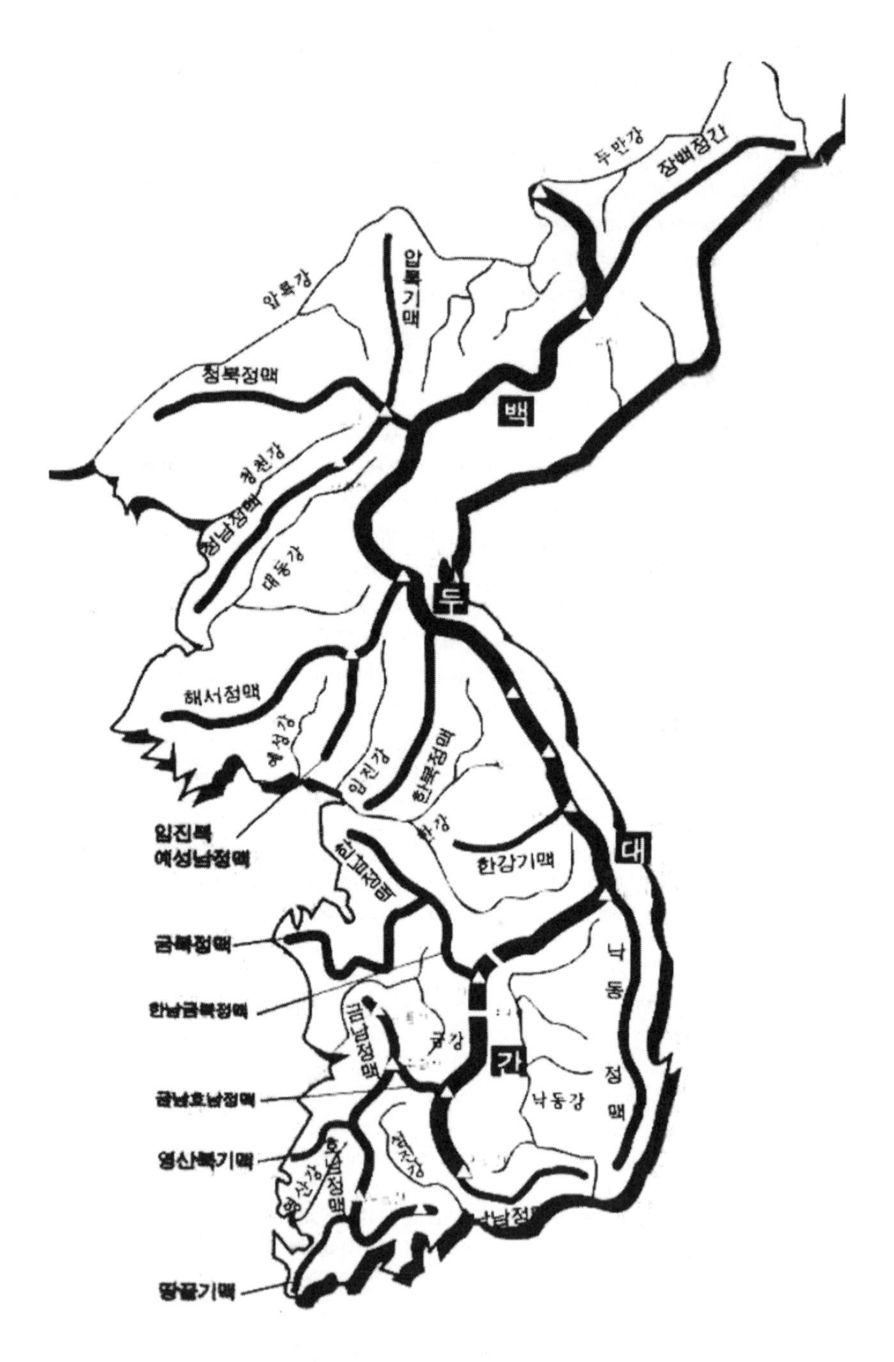

Figure 12.4 Representation of the restored traditional mountain system based on an interpretation of the ancient literature, Sankyongpyo. Paektudaegan ranges from Paektusan to Chirisan (S. Cho, 1997, p. 271).

> The peninsula of Korea presents most interesting problems in the arrangement of its mountains and in its underground structure. Professors F.V. Richthofen and C. Gottsche have made an attempt at their solution ... The peninsula seems to have interested our two masters almost as deeply as it has the political leaders [i.e. Japanese] of our times.[15]

The analogy of the scientist and the politician inadvertently reveals the way in which a particular spatial trajectory of knowledge may depend on, or further facilitate, the implementation of the political colonial project. For Koto, the role of geomorphology in its evolving stage was to provide a political landscape with scientific verification on a distant land surface.

Koto's interpretation of the mountain system was modified by the Japanese geographer, Yasu Shoei, in his textbook *Korean Geography* (*Hankuk Chiri*), published in 1904. Yasu's text had an enormous influence upon the establishment of an official mountain system on national maps and in geographical education during the succeeding colonial period.[16] Two maps, Figure 12.1 and Figure 12.3, show the similarities of the two geographers' representation of mountain ranges, both of which contrast with traditional understanding of mountains seen in Figure 12.4. The geologically ingrained mountain system was only to be repeated and consolidated by modern geographical literatures, including school textbooks during the colonial period, but remained as the scientific understanding of the formation of landforms, an unquestionable representation of mountain ranges, until the late 1980s when it was challenged by nationalist claims for the restoration of the traditional land view.

The reason why such a colonialist framing of the territory has been so widely accepted is that it was considered an unmediated and incontestable, modern, scientific statement rather than a partial, and unstable, colonialist construction of knowledge. It did bring Korean geology in line with a global scientific discourse, which is difficult to establish with the more traditional, culturally specific perspective. It rendered traditional epistemology out-of-date and disposable, as is always the case in the confrontation between the universalistic, yet dualistic, view of western science in opposing indigenous knowledge. The examination of Koto's geology within the narrative of colonial discourse serves to re-historicise geographic knowledge and to deconstruct the dichotomy of neutral and objective western science and of traditional geographical knowledge as cultural heritage. Accepting that Koto's scientific method is situated and historical, we also need to explore the other side of its claim to objectivity; the supposed homogeneity of traditional knowledge as non-science.

Korean traditional geography as heterogeneous knowledge

One of the widespread assumptions in colonial studies is that indigenous knowledge in pre-colonial society is monolithic and homogenous. This was not the case in pre-modern Korea. Andre Schmid argues that 'geographical knowledge during the Chosŏn dynasty was hardly unitary'.[17] According to him there were two geographic traditions in pre-colonial Korea:

administrative discourses and geomantic principles. However, *p'ungsu*,[18] the mode of thinking that underlies the concept of Paektudaegan, almost disappeared from the realm of geography with the introduction of Western geographic knowledge in the late nineteenth and early twentieth century, when social reformists and 'Enlightenment' thinkers criticised it as a corrupted and superstitious custom.[19]

The two traditions are not easily separated in their evolution. Administrative discourse includes diverse maps and geographical literatures complied by the government, and it was long based on the principles of *p'ungsu*.[20] Most traditional geographical literatures and maps reflect both approaches. This is demonstrated in the examination of two materials: *Taengniji* (1751)[21] and *Taedongyojido* (1861).[22] *Taengniji*, a geographic work from the Chosŏn period (1392–1909), was written by Yi Jung-hwan, a literary aristocrat in the eighteenth century. Yi reveals the way in which indigenous geographical knowledge was institutionalised and represented in the early modern period. The book consists of two major sections: 'Discourse on the eight provinces' and 'Discourse on the selection of habitable places'. The former is a chorographic description, and the latter, a systematic geography, divided into *Chiri* (geomancy and topography), *Saengni* (livelihood; transportation and trade), *Insim* (social characters and customs) and *Sansu* (landscape and scenery). Broadly, two major sections of *Taengniji* could be said to correspond to two approaches in Western geography: regional and systematic.[23]

As the title of the first section 'Discourse on the eight provinces' indicates,[24] the territory of Chosŏn was explicitly delimited, with the exception of the north-east region around the Tumen River, and it was indicated to be under the administrative control of the central government of Chosŏn. This illustrates, according to Schmid, a modern concept of territoriality, assuming 'people might choose to move to any location within the realm.'[25] He goes further in saying that it even reflects the 'homogeneous space' of a modern nation.[26]

Interestingly, Yi Jung-hwan regards *p'ungsu* as part of the official geographical discourse that makes up the second section of *T'aengniji-Chiri*.[27] Since the early twentieth century, *chiri* (literally, the theory of earth or land) has usually defined (modern) geography, but in the pre-modern era, it implied principles of *p'ungsu*. That is why contemporary geographer, Inshil Choe Yoon, in her translation of *T'aengniji* into English, understood *chiri* as geomancy. Yi's explanation of topography through the entire book of *T'aengniji* is a reflection of the idea of *p'ungsu* in that he considers the Korean territory to be the extension of the mountain chain originating from Paektusan. There was thus a history of continuing interactions between *p'ungsu*, popular geographical ideas and official geographical knowledge–administrative discourse. Schmid explains the interpenetration of administrative discourse and *p'ungsu* as follows,

> Instead of following each mountain chain and describing landmarks along its natural course, Yi divided the peninsula into its eight provinces and then discussed each county, always returning to the geomantic principles as they related to the mountain. In this way both spatial visions were mutually supportive, offering a hybrid approach to both the entire peninsula and individual localities.[28]

Such implicit, but highly interdependent relations can also be demonstrated in other important maps from the Chosŏn period. *Taedongyojido*, the most technically refined pre-modern map of Chosŏn, expresses the influence of *p'ungsu* more strongly than previous maps, especially in representing the mountain system. Examining *Taedongyojichondo* [Fig. 12.5a and Fig. 12.5b] shows rhetorical features very similar to *Taedongyojido*. *Taedongyojichondo* too is assumed to have been made in 1860 by Kim Chong-ho.[29] Whereas *Taedongyojido* is an integration of sixty individual wood-printing maps describing each region, *Taedongyojichondo* shows clearly the topography of the whole national territory in a single map sheet. *Taedongyojichondo* is much smaller than *Taedongyojido* (the integration of sixty maps) in its size. In *Taedongyojichondo*, Paektusan is more symbolically emphasised, even somewhat exaggerated, than in any other general map of Korea produced since the sixteenth century. The emphasis on Paektusan in a pictorial way sets it apart from most of the other, more jagged, mountain ranges and ridges.

Another important feature of *Taedongyojichondo* is the way in which the mountain ranges as such are represented. Using thick black lines, it expresses strong connections among the mountains. In the map, most of the regional mountain systems are connected into the Paektu range (Paektudaegan). The focus on Paektusan and the continuity of the mountain chain implies the dramatic expression of *p'ungsu* on a national scale, illustrating how the living energy, *Ki*, flowing through the entire mountain chain originates from Paektusan. It can be said that the map shows a body-politic of the territory through the hierarchical vision of *p'ungsu*.

Interestingly, through the use of such graphic devices based on *p'ungsu*, *Taedongyojichondo* claims a much more modernised conception of territory than any other preceding map in terms of its clear demarcation of territorial boundary as the spatial scope of administrative power. In maps of Chosŏn made before the sixteenth century, northern regions above Paektusan were described, showing the tendency to consider Manchuria as part of the national territory.[30] However, after 1712, when a stone stele (*Paektusan Chongyebbi*) marking the boundary with China was set up on Paektusan, the mountain had become the substantial border region of Chosŏn. Leaving Manchuria as a blank space, not even drawing in rivers, the map illustrates an exclusive sovereignty over the peninsula. It is then possible to say that *Taedongyojichondo* makes significant political claims regarding the expression of evolving national sentiments, as well as evidence of the technological proficiency in mapping at that time. It reveals how the tradition of *p'ungsu* and administrative discourse are mutually constitutive parts of traditional geographical knowledge.

The relationship between administrative discourse and *p'ungsu* also reflects a dualistic concept of nature and politics.[31] According to Yang Bo Kyong, the perception of nature in Korea since the sixteenth century has been geographically dualistic: 'Paektusan as our root', and 'Hanyang, the capital city of Chosŏn (Seoul), as the centre'.[32] This structure can be elaborated through an analysis of two geographical works written in the eighteenth century: *Sankyongpyo* (*Booklet of Korean Mountain Ranges*) and *Sansugo* (*An Investigation of Korea's Nature*).[33] Whereas the former is an anonymous account and contains popular understandings of territory, the latter was written as part of a governmental project. The similarities and

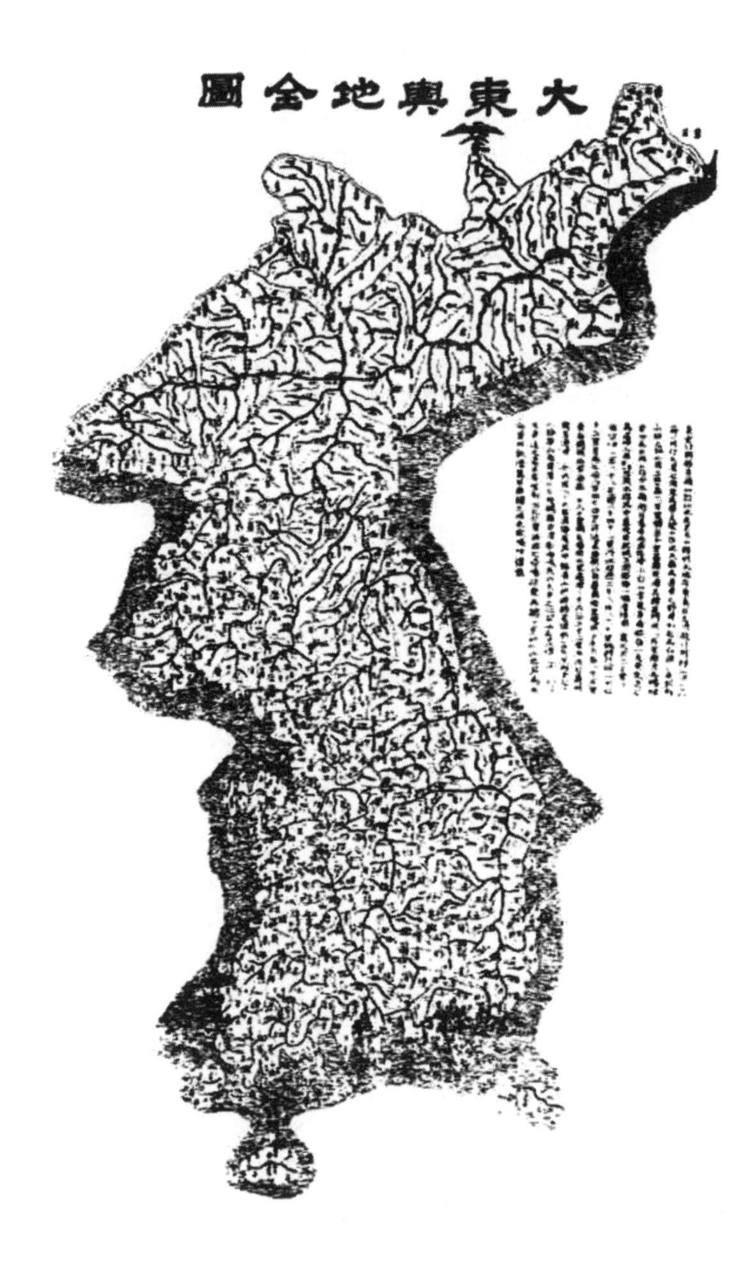

Figure 12.5a *Taedongyojichondo*, similar to a larger map, *Taedongyojido*. It was probably drawn by Kim Chong-ho. *Taedongyojichondo* makes it easier to appreciate the national geography of the mountain system (courtesy of National Central Library of Korea).

Figure 12.5b Representation of interlocking mountains and rivers in *Taedongyojido* (S. Cho, 1997, p. 78).

differences between the two are significant in showing how broadly circulated popular geographic discourse and official discourse of territory were.

Sansugo begins with the statement that Korea, as a natural space, is made up of twelve mountains and twelve rivers. Nature is configured in terms of yin and yang, and the number twelve has cosmological significance: the twelve months of the calendar year represented cyclical change in pre-modern time; thus, declaring twelve mountains and twelve rivers was a way to sanctify nature by the imposition of cosmic order onto the terrestrial world.[34] *Sansugo* lists Samgaksan, located in the capital, as the most important mountain and Paektusan as the second in the hierarchy. With the exception of Samgaksan all mountains are listed in the order of their geographic location, from north (Paektusan) to south (Chirisan). This means that the view of *Sansugo* is affected by not only the capital-centred view of territory but also the geomantic view of territory. In this sense, *Sansugo* negotiated administrative and geomantic geographical discourse in its depiction of Samgaksan and Paektusan.

Mountain representation in *Sankyongpyo* is somewhat different from that of *Sansugo*. In *Sankyongpyo*, the mountain hierarchy consists of one *Taegan* (Paektudaegan) at the top, one *Chongan* (Changbaeckchongan), and the thirteen *Chongmaek*.[35] This mountain system includes all the major mountain ranges and ridges of Korea [Fig. 12.4]. Unlike *Sansugo*, *Sankyongpyo* is not bound up in the cosmologically symbolic number twelve, but more focussed on the actual topographic features. The mountain system in *Sankyongpyo* is also hierarchical, representing a single stretch from north (Paektusan) to south (the mountain ranges extending to all parts of the territory). Paektusan is firmly situated as the symbolic centre (origin) of the national territory, symbolically impinging upon the authority of the 'capital centred view' represented in *Sansugo*. It claims a unity of territory, not by recourse to the authority of kingship or cosmological idealisation of nature, but by encouraging the poetic imagination of the *territory itself* as a living organism. In spite of some differences, these two works represents both administrative and geomantic ways of reading Korean geography in Chosŏn.

Reclaiming traditional geography in the early twentieth century

Some nationalists such as Chang Chi-yŏn at the turn of the last century were not antagonistic to Western science in general. They were Enlightenment thinkers as well as nationalists, meaning that their attitude toward traditional geographical knowledge was contradictory. They criticised and discarded the tradition of *p'ungsu* from the viewpoint of Western scientific rationalism. This is explicitly revealed by another nationalist, Choe Nam-sŏn, in his view of geography.[36] Choe studied at Tokyo Imperial University in 1906. He became interested in geography as a modern science through the works of Koto and Yashi. The fact that he followed Koto's mountain system in his contribution to the journal *Youth* (*Sonyun*) suggests that he felt positive about the introduction of western geography through the Japanese scholars.[37] Choe himself played an integral role in the introduction of western geography, mostly physical geography, after he returned to Korea in 1907. He, too, argued that traditional geography, especially *p'ungsu*, should be replaced with modern geographical science.[38] He thought that modern Western geography, along with world geography and physical geography, was one of the most important concepts for the Korean Enlightenment.

However, in 1910, when Korea was officially annexed into Japan, Choe's interests changed, from an optimistic and abstract concept of national Enlightenment to a more realistic and concrete history of the nation, and from world geography to the political and historical condition of East Asia. He also recognised the significance of traditional geographical knowledge.[39]

An increasing interest in traditional geography was shared by other nationalists such as Chang Chi-yŏn, who strenuously resisted Japanese rule. The 1911 publication of the two-century-old *Sankyonpyo*, which was implemented by the Chosŏn Kwangmunhoe (The Association of Korean Culture) is one of the most important products of their collective effort on traditional geography.[40] The goal of its publication, 200 years after it was written, was to contest the newly established mountain system founded by Koto and to restore traditional epistemology. The publication of *Sankyongpyo*, with its detailed explanation of the topography of Paektudaegan, shows the nationalists' changing view of modern geographical knowledge.

In the early years of colonial rule other important geographical works written in the Chosŏn era besides *Sankyongpyo* appeared, such as *T'aengniji* (*Choosing Settlements*), published in 1911, and *Abangkangyoko* (*An Investigation on our Nation's Territory*) also published by Chosŏn Kwangmunhoe. Geographical knowledge was located at the heart of an ideological struggle against Japanese colonial rule and strove to revitalise the traditional view of the national territory. The attempt to restore geographical knowledge was one way in which the imagination of the modern nation in the colonial period became involved in debates over the historical origins of modern Korean territoriality.

Practice, science and the reworking of the lost epistemology

As discussed at the beginning of this chapter, female alpinist Nam Nan-hee and climber poet Kwon Kyung-up walked the full length of Paektudaegan in 1990 and 1991. Since the planned destination of the journey was Paektusan, across the De-Militarised Zone (DMZ), they had to apply to the South Korean government for the permission to visit North Korea. The Ministry of Unification, on the basis of national security laws, denied their application. Therefore, after almost one year of climbing, their journey came to an abrupt halt at the DMZ, at the extreme northern point of the range within South Korea. In 1984, Nam Nan-hee had travelled the T'aebaeck range for 48 consecutive days, establishing a record in the history of modern climbing in Korea. Before the popular revival of Paektudaegan in the late 1980s, the T'aebaeck range had been accepted as the backbone mountain within the popular geographical knowledge, based on Koto's geomorphology. In response to the increasing interest in Paektudaegan and its promotion as the 'true' national backbone, thus devaluing the accomplishment of her previous climb of the T'aebaeck range, Nam decided to meet the challenge of the reclaimed national backbone and walk length of the Paektudaegan range.[41]

For the two alpinists, climbing Paektudaegan signified the dream of a unified national landscape through the corporeal engagement with Korea's topography. Climbing the numerous peaks and valleys along the ridge of Paektudaegan aroused in them a corporeal sensation, revitalising the buried body-politic of the nation. The climb was a pilgrimage, a 'search for the missing range' of history.

Whereas the T'aebaeck range climb had been a great physical challenge, in the tradition of testing the indomitable climber's spirit, the Paektudaegan *jongju* was imbued with a constant emotional struggle that took her far beyond the scope of normal athletic practice and experience. Her emotional upheaval (and Kwon's, too) reaches a climax in the last section of the journey, as they wrote,

> Everything comes into view, a tree, and a flower, even a small stone. Divided Paektudaegan, this land makes me sad. We, who have to stop here, feel sad.[42]

> Only reunification! I am ardently waiting for reunification. If it comes true, I will climb the rest of Paektudaegan![43]

Recovering Paektudaegan is therefore not just about the restoration of traditional geographical knowledge. It also gives possibility to the poetic imagining of 'a new national landscape'. Korea had rarely been given a chance to be a unified modern nation over the past century, rendering the claim of 'reunification' almost a dream or fantasy, but one which was now being reactivated through the imaginative construction of modern territoriality. At the very site where their travel was cut short in front of barbed wire, the claim to inherited geographical knowledge is suddenly transformed into a collective desire for reunification and for the imagined national landscape. Land as the object of science is replaced with the embodiment of a collective vision of the nation, which is the reworking of the nation's lost body-politic. In this sense, Paektudaegan is an imagined space where national identity is constantly articulated.

The revival of Paektudaegan was initiated by the enthusiasm of Lee Uh-hyung, an independent cartographer, climber and publisher. His challenge to existing scientific understanding of Korea's mountain system began with his rediscovery of *Sankyongpyo* in 1980.[44] He found the text by chance in a second-hand bookstore in Seoul. The book had been forgotten since its publication almost seventy years earlier. Lee had been working on the restoration of *Taedongyojido*[45] for a long time, and he had some trouble interpreting the map. He tried to identify the mountain ranges inscribed in *Taedongyojido* with modern topographical maps. Those lines did not match the lines of the modern mountain range formulated through Koto's geomorphology. The discovery of *Sankyongpyo* suggested a way to solve the problem caused by the discrepancy between the actual topography described in the map and the existing, geologically constructed mountain system. This led to his pioneering work in restoring the idea of Paektudaegan and traditional geography, with his ultimate goal being the reinstatement of Paektudaegan itself as the national backbone, as described in *Taedongyojido* by Kim Chŏng-ho. In the mid-1990s, Lee began to spread his newly discovered knowledge on Paektudaegan, *Taedongyojido* and *Sankyongpyo*, through public lectures and interviews in newspapers. His first contribution to *Chosŏn-ilbo*, a daily paper, 'Japanese imperial power changed our own mountain names', created a sensation.[46]

His work became known to, and reinforced by, amateur climbers and their practice of *jongju*. Climbers' interest in Paektudaegan had grown because of the difficulties presented to them by discrepancies between the officially recognised mountain system and the actual topography of ridges and valleys.[47] This discordance prevented many amateur college climbers from following the ridge of the Sobaeck mountain ranges (the southern part of Paektudaegan) using existing maps. They did their *jongju* hiking based on an academic geography text based on Koto's geology, seeking to travel along the ridge line without crossing rivers, only to get lost when they encountered the Sŏmjin River and finally being forced to give up the hike. The geography text did not offer an accurate representation of the material topography of the mountain ranges. Their difficulties were no different from the trouble Lee Uh-hyung had encountered.

The breakthrough came with the translation of *Sankyongpyo* into Korean by Park Yong-su in 1990. Also, Cho Sok-jun, doctor and amateur climber, who had succinctly recognised the discrepancies of the official description of existing mountain system from his climbing experiences, translated the Chinese version into Korean, while adding rich annotations and showing where it agreed with the modern topography of Korea.[48]

Sankyongpyo suggested a way for climbers to follow most of mountain ridges without crossing rivers. According to *Sankyongpyo*, the river system in the Korean peninsula is directly related to the mountain system as seen in the modified *Taedongyojichondo* [Fig. 12.5b]. The river system is seen as the negative imprint of the mountain system.[49] This interlocking system represents the body politic of the whole peninsula, with the rivers serving as arteries of a human body, so that the practice of climbers going along the ridges embraces the whole national territory. With all these collective endeavours from climbers, freelance writers and independent cartographers, the concept of Paektudaegan was disseminated through television programs and newspaper articles, thus entering public discourse. The Paektudaegan *Jongju* has become more and more popular since the mid 1990s.

Predictably, there was a reaction from official or academic geography. Geography textbooks began referring to Paektudaegan and *Sankyongpyo*, as well as the idea of *p'ungsu*, in the late 1990s, but the status of Koto's theory remained unchallenged, and Paektudaegan was largely treated as national cultural heritage, complementary but inferior to scientific knowledge of landforms. Most academic geographers did not say anything publicly about Paektudaegan until recently. Some historical geographers continued to work on the *Sankyongpyo*, *Sansugo* and Paektudaegan, but they did not actively criticise Koto's geological system.

The scientific knowledge initiated by Koto Bunjiro was only challenged by the embodied practice of climbing and the rediscovered discourse of traditional geographic knowledge. The rediscovery of Paektudaegan reveals how discourse, practice and science are interrelated in the representation of Korea's national landscape. The role of popular practise is integral to the construction of knowledge. The comparison of Koto's work and the two climbers' experience shows how this works. Above all, Koto's goal was to represent a 'new modern landscape', whether it is called geological or geomorphologic, and he was willing to erase existing forms of knowledge, which he regarded as imbued with layers of memory, myth and legend. His path was that of 'crossing and re-crossing the peninsula from one shore to the other',[50] systematically from east to west rather than north to south, following the course of Paektudaegan. His goal was to free nature from the barriers of culture and history and to place it within the realm of objective science.

By contrast, the two climbers followed the ridge line and by physically engaging it were able to make tangible an imagined geography of the mountain chain. Climbing, as a modern practice, helped transform Paektudaegan from 'barrier'[51] into 'path'. As barriers, mountain chains remained sanctified and untouchable, outside the realms of everyday practice and political contestation. This allowed the mountain chain to be employed as part of a cosmological ordering that mandated the rule of the king. Such mythic beliefs were systematised and reinforced by the idea of *p'ungsu*.

The modern practice of climbing combines with traditional epistemology, resulting in *jongju*, a particular form of climbing or hiking. *Jongju* climbing started in Chirisan[52] and Sŏraksan, and eventually expanded over the entire mountain range. In the beginning, *jongju*, like other types of Western mountaineering, was about the challenge, the adventure, of pitting human against nature. It differed explicitly from traditional mountain travelling practiced by aristocrats in Korea, especially during the Chosŏn period, whose goal was to visit the highest peaks and explore the cultural heritages, like Buddhist temples, in the surrounding mountains. *Jongju* still implied the subjugation of nature under human control when Nam Nan-hee travelled the T'aebaeck Range in 1984, before the term Paektudaegan became popularised. However, as the practice overlapped into the discursive context of recovering traditional geography, *jongju* became imbued with a sanctifying mission of nation-building.

Traditional geography was revitalised, critically questioning the role and scope of geographical practice in the formation of geographical knowledge. The rediscovery of Peaktudaegan was not initiated by professional geographers and scientists, but by the cooperative practice of amateur climbers and cartographers seeking to revive the meaning to Korea's high places.

Conclusion

The rediscovery of Paektudaegan emphasises the role of popular geography, its practise, knowledge and institution, in the production and circulation of knowledge. It challenges and negotiates with the official, academic, geographical science and imagination in Korea, founded during Japanese rule. The nationalist forces of popular geography are enabled through the regeneration of a pre-colonial, indigenous geographical knowledge connected to the Chosŏn dynasty. As in other nations, such as Ecuador, indigenous geographical knowledge can play a key, but often underestimated, role in the geographical imagination in post-colonial societies.[53]

> Inherited colonial imagined geographies of the world often marginalised Third World countries, colouring them through racist, 'imperialist eyes'. Such colonial

> images are currently being reassigned and reworked by individuals and groups within postcolonial societies, where the stress is on active engagement by postcolonial subjects with the legacies of colonial geographical imagination.[54]

Reflections on the traditional geography in Korea challenge the conventional assumption that indigenous knowledge in colonised society is homogenous and unitary, and contains a distinctively pre-modern sense of place and space. The intricate features of traditional geography have been selectively mobilised for the imagination of a modern nation. In particular, the publication (1911) and translations (1990–7) of *Sankyongpyo* by nationalists imply that traditional geographical knowledge has remained a recurrent theme in nationalist imaginings.

The recovery of traditional geographical knowledge, and the controversy with Koto's modernist and colonial scientific knowledge, reinforces the discursive nature of geographical knowledge, while also emphasising the practical engagement in the construction of geographical knowledge. In Driver and Rose's words, 'to argue that geographical knowledge is discursively constructed is to insist on the importance of practices and institutions as well as concepts.'[55] In addition, the examination of the specific historical context of Koto's project confirms the 'social and located nature of knowledge making',[56] and problematic questions about the spatiality of knowledge production come to the fore, such as Koto geology's privileged claims to universal and disinterested scientific knowledge and the fixed distinction between science and non-science. Challenging such claims lies at the core of the recent disputes over the high places of Korea.

13

Afterword

'The Unhandselled Globe'

J. Nicholas Entrikin

Preceding chapters have told in numerous and intriguing ways of how place making at the extremities of the globe encounters forms of natural resistance.[1] Their authors have examined the mediating role of narrative and map making as tools for overcoming such resistance by making it comprehensible in relation to human projects. They are keenly aware that the process of place making involves the representation of place through tales of scientific discovery, exploration, travel and personal growth, and of the extent to which these representations bring the relatively unknown edges of the globe into view. These texts illuminate the human experience of the physical world by drawing together its disparate elements, by mingling the aesthetic, the cognitive, the sensory and the affective.

This representational quality of place making is very much in evidence in this volume, but it is not the central motif. Rather, a more important theme is the reconnection to the material, or, in geographical terms, the point of contact between meaning and the physical environment. To those unfamiliar with the disciplinary debates of the last several decades, this would seem to go without saying about a geographical text. Would not this point of contact be at the centre of all geographic forms of representation? Yet those who are conscious of the recent strength of social constructionism recognise that the return to materiality carries, for some contemporary geographers, almost a revolutionary spirit of liberation.[2] The danger now, however, becomes a pendular swing to the other extreme. There are even signs of a turning away from theory altogether, as in the call for an oxymoronic 'non-representational theory', which expresses a hope of somehow reconciling the representational with the actual. At this particular moment in the field of human geography, this regressive turn toward naïve realism could only be seen as a conceit, *une fausse naïveté*.

KTAADN, AND THE MAINE WOODS.

BY HENRY D. THOREAU.

No. IV.

THE ASCENT OF KTAADN.

Figure 13.1 Henry Thoreau, 'Ktaadn and the Maine Woods', *The Union Magazine*, October 1848, p.177.

At either end of this pendular swing, the understanding of place making is diminished, since one of its essential elements is its bringing together of the symbolic and the material. Successful place making transforms this point of contact to appear as part of a seamless web. The extreme natural environments described in this volume pose special challenges to place making. Indeed, many are in fact stories about the failure of place making, the incompleteness of the places presented. The conceptual difficulties of this project can be seen at a variety of levels from social and political theory to literature and art. Since many of the authors frame their essays in terms of the latter, I will do the same by briefly considering one of the most creative and examined masters of such narratives of place, Henry David Thoreau.

Lack of reference to Thoreau's work could be viewed as a notable absence in this collection. However, such an omission seems minor when one considers the natural environments described in the preceding chapters and how they make Thoreau's native New England appear civilised and tame by comparison. Also, Thoreau's writings would not fit neatly with the volume's emphasis on various types of scientific writing and representation. The New Englander had a great appreciation and a self-taught understanding of natural history, but his writing about excursions into natural landscapes did not have a scientific intent. In spite of these differences, however, high places carried a special significance for Thoreau as he explored the edges of his world of mid-nineteenth-century New England. Interpreters of Thoreau cite one particular mountain, Mount Katahdin in Maine, as having had a profound effect on the naturalist by challenging his taken-for-granted assumptions about the relations of humans to the natural world.[3] Here he encountered the 'unhandselled globe', a place where humans did not belong, or more literally, where no 'gift' had been left. This unusual phrase describes an experience at the centre of discussions over the representation of the human encounter with extreme environments, discussions that seek clarity on the murky relation between narrating the sublime and the actual.

'Ktaadn'

Mount Katahdin is the highest peak in the state of Maine at 5,256 feet of elevation. By the standards of the high places described in this volume, this monadnock is neither very high nor is it an important site of scientific exploration and discovery. Its value is cultural, measured in terms of its role as a site of recreational tourism and as a literary monument to the writing of the noted American transcendentalist and environmentalist. 'Ktaadn', Thoreau's spelling of the Native American name, is an essay that describes one of approximately twenty climbs about which Thoreau wrote, spanning the time from his first and highest climb, New Hampshire's Mount Washington in 1839, to his ascent of Mount Monadnock in 1860.[4] His journey to Mount Katahdin occurred in the late summer and early fall of 1846.

Thoreau translates Ktaadn as meaning 'highest land'. His textual representation of the mountain, especially in its final dramatic pages, contrasts greatly with the romantic representations of this place in the visual arts. For example, Hudson River School painter Frederic Edwin Church painted Mount Katahdin (1853) several years after Thoreau's ascent, portraying a beautiful view of the mountain from a distant hill overlooking an imagined pastoral setting of harmonious, cultivated nature. Thoreau, in contrast, wrote about mountain peaks as 'among the unfinished parts of the globe'.[5] One way to interpret this statement is that these extreme areas of the Earth's surface are unfinished or incomplete as places. The extreme physical conditions of such spaces of nature thwart all but the most evanescent and tenuous attempts at human place making. Indeed, for Thoreau, humans did not belong in such spaces.

This belief is most dramatically expressed in the 'Burnt Lands' section of the 'Ktaadn' essay. Thoreau encountered the Burnt Lands area during his descent from the mountain. It was a descent that followed an unexpectedly arduous climb to a point near the summit, where Thoreau, leaving his party behind, made a solo excursion toward the top. He climbed through a difficult and craggy landscape. It appeared to him as if it had 'rained rocks' on the mountain, and these were left as they fell.

Figure 13.2 Frederic Edwin Church, *Mount Ktaadn*, oil painting, 1853 (courtesy of Yale University).

> They were the raw materials of a planet dropped from some unseen quarry, which the vast chemistry of nature would anon work up, or work down, into the smiling and verdant plains and valleys of earth. This was an undone extremity of the globe ...[6]

He was forced to stop by a dense cloud of mist, which hid the hoped-for reward of a vista of the valleys below and which conjoined with the craggy rock surface to create a 'Titanic' landscape, 'such as man never inhabits'.[7] This landscape exists outside the ordered world of places and on the edge of 'Chaos'. It has a physical, bodily effect on the unwelcome visitor.

> Some part of the beholder, even some vital part, seems to escape through the loose grating of his ribs as he ascends. He is more lone than you can imagine. There is less of substantial thought and fair understanding in him, than in the plains where men inhabit. His reason is dispersed and shadowy, more thin and subtile like the air. Vast, Titanic, inhuman nature has got him at disadvantage. ... She does not smile on him as in the plains. She seems to say sternly, why came ye here before your time? This ground is not prepared for you.[8]

This moment of uncomfortable and humbling presence near the peak informs the later description of Burnt Lands, an open area previously cleared through naturally caused fire. At first, Thoreau saw this area as a familiar landscape, similar to the meadows that he knew in

Concord. This sense of belonging was gradually eroded, however, by the growing recognition of its resistance to human habitation and its challenge to familiar categorisation.[9] This was the 'unhandselled globe'.

> It is difficult to conceive of a region uninhabited by man. We habitually presume his presence and influence everywhere. And yet we have not seen pure Nature, unless we have seen her thus vast, and drear, and inhuman, though in the midst of cities. Nature was here something savage and awful, though beautiful. I looked with awe on the ground I trod on, to see what the Powers had made there, the form and fashion and material of their work. This was the earth of which we had heard, made of Chaos and Old Night. Here was no man's garden, but the unhandselled globe. It was not lawn, nor pasture, nor mead, nor woodland, nor lea, nor arable, nor waste-land. It was the fresh and natural surface of the planet Earth, as it was made forever and ever – to be the dwelling of man, we say – so Nature made it, and man may use it if he can. Man was not to be associated with it. It was Matter, vast, terrific – not his Mother Earth that we have heard of, not for him to tread on, or be buried in – no, it were being too familiar even to let his bones lie there – the home this of Necessity and Fate. There was there felt the presence of a force not bound to be kind to man. It was a place for heathenism and superstitious rites – to be inhabited by men nearer of kin to the rocks and to wild animals than we. We walked over it with a certain awe, ... here not even the surface had been scarred by man, but it was a specimen of what God saw fit to make this world.[10]

Similar to his experience near the summit, it was a time of awareness of, and separation from, his own physicality, his body as physical matter.

> I stand in awe of my body, this matter to which I am bound has become so strange to me. I fear not spirits, ghosts, of which I am one – that my body might – but I fear bodies, I tremble to meet them. What is this Titan that has possession of me? Talk of mysteries! – Think of our life in nature – daily to be shown matter, to come in contact with it – rocks, trees, wind on our cheeks! the solid earth! the actual world ! the common sense! Contact! Contact! Who are we? where are we?[11]

Literary critics divide over the meaning of this passage. For some it is the recognition of an unadorned, unmediated, natural world and for others it is the Romantic Thoreau writing of the sublime.[12] However, as Lawrence Buell concludes, both interpretations imply each other: 'The one must acknowledge that reported contacts with particular settings are intertextually, intersocially constructed; the other must acknowledge that the nonbuilt environment is one of the variables that influence culture, text, and personality.'[13]

The chapters in this volume move between these two poles. The geographer's world is the world 'in-between'. It is a culturally constructed world of meaning that encounters and seeks to assimilate Thoreau's 'Wild', which Jane Bennett describes as 'a surplus that escapes our categories and organisational practices', a surplus to this culturally constructed world.[14]

Where the drama of the passage is most evident is in the strangeness and unwelcoming quality of the landscape. Thoreau describes it as not intended for him or for other humans. In doing so, however, he is not simply reporting experience, but he is also constructing and helping to complete a narrative. Parts of his essay were written at an extended interval from the actual journey and reflect carefully chosen rhetorical strategies and techniques. For example, Buell discusses Thoreau's use of the 'aesthetics of the not there', a means of describing another world in terms that are literally the opposite of one's own.[15] It involves a rhetorical emptying and re-filling of place and landscape:

> on the one hand, he executes the America-as-nature reduction, clearing the rugged interior of all traces of human history; on the other hand, he imports the language of the sublime.[16]

As the above paragraphs indicate, 'Ktaadn' is an essay that touches on many of the main themes of the preceding essays on high places. Yet for all of these similarities, a discussion of Thoreau seems oddly out of place amongst these chapters. Thoreau is now studied as part of the American literary canon, or as one of the pantheon supporting modern environmentalism. He is not in the intellectual universe of those described in discussions of nineteenth-century explorers or twentieth-century scientists. Even the Romantically-inspired Alexander von Humboldt seems to belong to a different category of nature writer. However, Thoreau demonstrates the aesthetic nature of the enterprise of giving meaning and order to the human experience of the natural, and the limits of human place making. As the editors note, writing on high places draws upon and contributes to an 'aesthetic reservoir best described by the parameters of sublime landscape'. At least one interpretation of Thoreau's 'Ktaadn' suggests that writing about these unhandselled edges of the globe illuminates those limits.

Modern geography

In recent years, human geographers have closely examined the role and position of the active subject interpreting the world through narrative and graphical representation, a perspective in fact much closer to that of a writer such as Thoreau than to the traditional academic geographer. The image of geographers remotely gazing from above or as disembodied observers in the field has changed to geographers as subjects in the world narrating their experiences. The dominant meaning of place has changed from a location of a cultural assemblage or a position in space to a complex relation of self and environment. Within this more recent perspective cartography and regional geography have become modes of representation as opposed to mirrors of nature, and as a result the line separating actual and imaginative geographies has become less clear. The monstrous figures that occupied the frames of ancient maps shift in meaning from curiosities that reflect a pre-modern, pre-scientific mind to windows that reveal the cultural and political frameworks that shaped ancient worlds.

This reorientation of human geography has led to more substantial links with disciplinary perspectives in the humanities and the humanistic social sciences. Contemporary interest in constructed and contested places demonstrates a shift from a seemingly static geography of the mid-twentieth century to a geography of process and change and to a concern with cultural imagination and practices. As the editors of this volume note in their introduction, places are about the multiple relations between human experience and location.

This linkage is most evident in many of the current interpretations of place and landscape. Places may be thought of as the paradigmatic and original form of what Bruno Latour refers to as 'hybrids'.[17] They are primitive junctures of nature/culture and subject/object, as well as being the basic tools for human projects and creative adjustments to the environment. Humans have always made places, given them value and meaning, used them to achieve goals and accomplish projects, and in the process they have transformed natural environments.

Robert Sack has argued that one of the primary means of transforming the space of nature is in the creation of places, through which worlds are created out of natural environments through the infusion of social rules and meanings.[18] Homes, cultivated fields, national territories, sacred sites, urban parks and wilderness preserves are all places created as tools. Their variable geometries or fluid spatial scales are adapted to such projects and in an ideal world are unmade and remade as these collective projects change. Such projects do not occur in empty space; they are frequently altered or undermined by natural processes. Such processes remain the unpredictable 'other' of human projects, sometimes simultaneously serving as altruistic benefactor and merciless foe.

It is in putting together the social and the natural environment that the role of place as a tool becomes evident. The world may be characterised as a dynamic composite of places that undergo continuous adjustment and change. Places may be made through habit and custom or through planning and forethought. They may be made through authoritarian decree or through collective discussion, planning and participation. They are made as tools to achieve various ends. Such ends may be relatively fleeting or stable, shared or contested. Places facilitate some plans, but in doing so, necessarily impede and block others.

In spite of their inherent contingency, places are a means of providing order and stability to the flux of experience. As cultural beings, humans tend to experience places as having permanence and historical depth and not as ephemeral intersections of natural and social processes. The fact that places are composed to varying degrees of non-human elements contributes to their appearance of historical depth and naturalness, as illustrated by the way in which the continuity of places may be imagined by contemplating their ruins.

Place, the geographer's object of study and the agent's object of manipulation, by definition involves borders. However, these borders and their borderlands need not be impenetrable barriers and impermeable spaces. They may instead be multi-scaled, overlapping, porous, and fluid. When guided by a cosmopolitan spirit, place making becomes a basic tool for building inclusive communities. Such an ideal, however, cannot overcome a fundamental dualism that is built into the geographical project, the divide between nature and culture and the ways in which the natural world both surprises and resists human desires and ambitions. It has become common among human geographers to make pronouncements about the overcoming of traditional conceptual dualisms in the field. However, the mostly implicit ontological commitments of geographers associated with these earnestly expressed intentions prove difficult to sustain in practice.

High places

The authors whose work is presented in this volume examine such points of surprise and resistance, a choice that reflects interests associated with a particular moment in geographic and environmental thought. They have recognised both the novelty and contingency of such encounters as well as the importance of representational strategies, e.g. narration and mapping, which give meaning to human experience of extreme parts of the globe. The kind of places identified, 'high places', is an intriguing choice because, as the editors correctly note, such areas of the globe mark the margins of humanised worlds and the boundaries of human projects. However, these boundaries are continually challenged and occasionally transgressed in attempts at human dominion over the globe, whether through the universalism of religious faith and scientific reason, or the more particular motives of nationalism and cultural chauvinism.

As places on the margin, high places are invested with varied and often contradictory meanings, from landscapes of fear to morally valued, 'pure' and natural landscapes. They have offered people sites of escape, reverence, physical challenge, discovery and learning, but at the same time have been sources of evil, human failure and death. They have challenged both the imagination and the body. High places are where heaven and earth meet and where people encounter a natural world not easily accommodated to human intentions and desires.

The term 'place' is used throughout much of this volume, but it would appear that the most notable quality of these high places is their incompleteness, except for their powerful role in shaping imaginative geographies. Indeed what many of the authors describe is the failure to make place, except of the most temporary kind, in the space of nature. Their incompleteness is evident in the ways that the natural remains stubbornly outside of this humanised place ordering. All places consist of natural elements, but in many of the high places described here some aspects of nature remain external to the weave of place making and often function as barriers to such efforts. With the notable exception of Mount Athos and other regions long settled by indigenous groups, and only recently 'discovered and explored' by western Europeans, the regions of the globe that remain on the edges of human experience remain spaces of nature rather than places. The incursion of wealth seekers or truth seekers into these marginal areas is less an instance of place making than it is a sojourn into the space of nature for material, intellectual or spiritual gain.

This feature of place making, the encounter with a resistant nature, is often lost in the discussion of the social construction of place, a reversal of early twentieth-century geography in which the social was submerged by the natural. Indeed, forms of theoretical and methodological reductionism have constantly challenged and undermined the geographer's broadly synthetic vision. The relatively recent disciplinary emphasis on the primacy of the social construction or social production of knowledge has been so enthusiastically pursued that its geography seems almost totally devoid of material elements. Evidence of this intellectual shift may be implied from the sudden silence between the traditionally bickering disciplinary siblings, physical geography and human geography. Physical geographers work within the paradigms of natural science, which the religiously-inspired geologist Joseph Le Conte once remarked required the scientist to put on the 'work-clothes' of materialism.[19] Human geographers, who emphasise the social rules of meaning production and the power relations behind those rules in relation to the natural realm, help to create a sense that the material relations to the world are inconsequential.

It is not surprising that such an extreme reductionism would eventually engender its opposite, especially in a field such as geography where the experiential qualities of one's material environment have been such strong motivational forces for choosing geography as a professional calling. Yi-Fu Tuan's experience of the vastness of the New Mexican desert sky; Torsten Hägerstrand's youthful exploration in the Swedish forest, or Peter Haggett's experience of confinement to an iron lung, which required him to view the world around him reflected through a mirror, are well-known moments of embodied sensation that left indelible imprints on the young imaginations of future geographers and that had consequences for the collective enterprise of geographical research.[20] These moments of transformative experience, however, are often submerged by theoretical currents that sweep away fundamental aspects of the relation between sensate creatures and the material universe. Various reductions sunder this core relation of an existential human geography. Frequent acknowledgement of the importance of this relation seems insubstantial in the face of the theoretical currents that direct disciplinary research. Such theories emphasise one of several possible analytic starting points, ranging from the creative subject or the social bases of meaning to the material sources of meaning.

The extreme environments described here share this same potential for personal transformation. Many of the authors dwell on the sensate, bodily response to these environments as a source of meaningful experience. Some ask to what extent did bodily struggles in extreme circumstances lead to particular meanings associated with these areas. Another addresses the neural mechanisms of perception, for example questions of spatial disorientation associated with the lack of identifiable landmarks. Still others follow the path of the geography of science, a path that has taken two directions, one close to environmental determinism and the other centred on the places of science.[21] It is the latter of these two directions that receives the greatest attention in this volume. Emphasis is given to the challenging of boundaries, those between scientific and everyday practice, the laboratory and the field, between materiality and meaning, male and female, native and non-native, and so on. They put back together what the analytic traditions of scientific philosophies had sought to disassemble. In the process, however, what often is lost is the understanding of how places matter. How exactly does place influences science?

One sees the difficulty of making the role of place in science explicit in David Livingstone's rich and colourful portraits of the places of scientific practice, such as laboratories, clinics and museums.[22] The accumulation of case studies gives the impression of the power of place, but how this power functions is not made explicit. What is place and what are the actual 'mechanisms' by which place influences human activity? How specifically does place work to influence science? The essays in this volume do a good job of suggesting directions but they, too, address only indirectly the causal role of place. It is one thing to describe how high winds, cold temperatures and high altitudes affect human perception and bodily function, but quite another to explain how place affects human action. One of the key stumbling blocks has been to 'hold together' place in relation to its parts, especially the material objects that help compose it. Place, like its disciplinary relative, landscape, is more than simply a collection of various objects, people and events. It is also the relational elements that draw these components together through the active agency of a knowing subject. Thus, understanding place as a relational concept suggests that the meaning of place is more than the sum total of the meanings of its contents.

What Thoreau experienced on his ascent of Mount Katahdin, and what many of the subjects of the earlier essays also encountered in various ways, was an occasionally dramatic recognition of the limits of these relational 'wholes'. Accounts of place making in the extreme latitudes and elevations of the globe vividly illuminate natural resistance to human projects. As in all good geographical writing, however, such insights are not as environmentally limited as the title of this volume might suggest. Even in long-occupied areas of human settlement nature's compliance with place-making projects is often more apparent than real.

Endnotes for chapter 1

1 B. Lopez, *Arctic Dreams*, Toronto, New York, etc., 1986, p. xxii.

2 F. Driver and L. Martins (Eds.), *Tropical Visions in an Age of Empire*, Chicago, 2005.

3 See the special issues of the *Journal of Historical Geography, The Historical Geography of Islands*, 29 (2003) and *Historical Geographies of the Sea*, 32 (2006).

4 M. Bravo and S. Sörlin, *Narrating the Arctic*, Canton, MA, 2002.

5 The Russian botanist Wladimir Köppen (1846–1940) initiated the global system of climatic classification, which was completed in 1936. The American geographer C.W. Thornthwaite elaborated on this classification for the American Geographical Society (American Geographical Society of New York, *World Climatic Atlas,* New York, 1957). The British geographer A.J. Herbertson used a classification similar to Köppen's to map what he called 'natural regions', connecting climate to geology and vegetation and human settlement, A. J. Herbertson, 'The major natural regions: an essay in systematic geography', *The Geographical Journal* 25 (1905) pp. 300–10.

6 Fleure's classification appears in his first book *Human Geography of Western Europe*, London, 1918. Regions of difficulty occur in the great central mountain belts stretching through the Alps for the Pyrenees to the Carpathians and in the northern forests and Arctic parts of the continent. South of the mountain belt, in the Mediterranean basin, are 'regions of increment' whose natural productivity allows latitude for the early development of intercommunication and intellectual culture, while to the north in the temperate forests and grasslands are 'regions of effort' that require a large investment of physical labour but eventually yield high increments. To a contemporary reader, Fleure's scheme has distinct deterministic overtones but was 'possibilist' in intent, seeking to relate the physical geography of Europe to its cultural expressions in a not dissimilar way to a writer such as John Ruskin.

7 E. Burke, *Philosophical Inquiry into the Origin of Our Ideas of the Sublime and Beautiful,* Dublin, 1756; M.H. Nicholson, *Mountain Gloom and Mountain Glory*, Seattle and London, 1997 (1959).

8 See, for example, Captain George Vancouver's journal descriptions of the Inland Passage and coastal ranges of British Columbia in 1794: 'The most remarkable mountain we had seen on the coast of New Albion, now presented itself. Its summit, covered with eternal snow,

was divided into a very elegant double fork, and rose conspicuously from a base of lofty mountains clothed in the same manner, which descended gradually to hills of a moderate height', available at: http://beyondthemap.ca/english/explorer_vancouver_journal.html.

9 Recent geographical essays on place that debate these perspectives include A. Pred, 'Place as historically contingent process', *Annals of the Association of American Geographers* 74 (1984), pp. 279–97; D. Massey, *Space, Place, and Gender,* Minneapolis, 1994, pp. 145–56; D. Harvey, *Justice, Nature and the Geography of Difference,* Cambridge, MA, 1996, pp. 291–326; N. Thrift, 'Steps to an ecology of place', in D. Massey et al. (Eds), *Human Geography Today*, 1999, pp. 295–322; N. Entrikin and V. Berdoulay, 'Pyrenees as place: Lefebvre as guide', *Progress in Human Geography* 29 (2005), pp. 129–47.

10 On the Estonian ascent of Everest, see Estonia Embassy in Sweden *Estonian Review* 3/10–16/2003,
On Estonian scientific interest in Antarctica see *The Antarctic Sun* 11/23/03
http://antarcticsun.usap.gov/oldissues2003-2004/Sun112303/aroundTheContinent.htm
Thanks to Helen Soovali for bringing these events to our attention.

11 F. Nietzsche, *On the Genealogy of Morals. A Polemical Tract*, Leipzig, 1887.

12 E. Casey, *Representing Place: Landscape and Maps*, Minneapolis, 2002, p. 106.

13 A. von Humboldt and A. Bonpland, *Personal narrative of travels to the equinoctial regions of America, during the years 1799–1804*, London, 1852–3.

14 K. Dodds, *Pink Ice*, London, 2002.

15 R. Macfarlane, *Mountains of the Mind: A History of Fascination,* London, 2003, p. 5.

16 P. Matthiessen, *Snow Leopard*, New York, 1978.

17 M. Helms, *Ulysses' Sail: An Ethnographic Odyssey of Power, Knowledge, and Geographical Distance*, Princeton, 1988; M. Robinson, *The Coldest Crucible: Arctic Exploration and the American Culture*, Chicago, 2006.

18 D. Livingstone, 'The moral discourse of climate: historical considerations on race, place and virtue', *Journal of Historical Geography* 17 (1991), pp. 413–34; Driver and Martins, *op.cit.*

19 W. Gallagher, *Power of Place: How Our Surroundings Shape our Thoughts, Emotions, and Actions,* New York, 1993, pp. 66–7. On the Denali laboratory see also:
http://www.jinxmagazine.com/denali.html.

20 W. Fox: *Driving to Mars*, Emeryville, CA, 2006.

21 S. Radstone and K. Hodgkin, *Regimes of Memory*, London and New York, 2003, p. 47; Macfarlane, *op.cit.*, p. 49.

22 On 'twinning' of mountain communities see G. Rudaz, 'Mountain sisters, gaining local legitimacy through international partnerships' delivered at the conference *Women of the mountains*, 2006, text available at:
http://www.womenofthemountains.org/files/Microsoft%20Word%20-%2007-02-17-Full-Paper_Rudaz_G.pdf.

23 G. Palsson, 'Arcticality: gender, race, and geography in the writings of Vilhjalmur Stefansson', in Bravo and Sörlin, *op.cit.* pp. 275–310.

Endnotes for chapter 3

1 R. Calasso, *The Marriage of Cadmus and Harmony*, London, 1994, p. 34.
This chapter is a reworked and extended version of my article 'Becoming icy: Scott and Amundsen's South Polar voyages', *Cultural Geographies* 9 (2002), pp. 249-265.
2 M. De Certeau, *The Practice of Everyday Life*, Berkeley, 1984, p. 112.
3 R. Amundsen, *The South Pole*, London, 1913, p. 102.
4 E. Wilson, *Diary of the Terra Nova Expedition*, London, 1972, pp. 35, 60.
5 R. Huntford, *The Last Place on Earth*, London, 1985, p. 309.
6 G. Deleuze and F. Guattari, *A Thousand Plateaus: Capitalism and Schizofrenia*, London, 1998, p. 4.
7 S. Pyne, *The Ice: A Journey to Antarctica*, Iowa City, 1986, p. 7.
8 H. Hanssen, *Voyages of a Modern Viking*, London, 1936, p. 122.
9 F. Nansen, *Farthest North*, London, 1900, p. 38.
10 F. Spufford, *I May Be Some Time: Ice and the English Imagination*, London, 1996, p. 5.
11 A. Cherry-Garrad, *The Worst Journey in the World*, London, 1939, p. 448.
12 R. Scott, *Scott's Last Expedition*, Vol. I, London, 1913, p. 284.
13 Amundsen, *op. cit.*, p. 57.
14 *ibid.*, p. 179.
15 Pyne, *op. cit.*, p. 152.
16 Amundsen, *op. cit.*, p. 214.
17 Pyne, *op. cit.*, p. 133.
18 W. Rees, 'Polar mirages', *Polar Record* 24 (1998), p. 193.
19 *ibid.*, p. 194.
20 C. Bertram, *The Techniques of Polar Travel*, Cambridge, 1939, p.75.
21 'Sastrugi are irregularities formed by the wind on the surface of the snow', Huntford, *op.cit.*, p. 12.
22 Amundsen, *op. cit.*, p. 212.
23 M. Serres, *Hermes*, Baltimore, 1982, p. 23.
24 H. Ponting, *The Great White South*, London, 1921, p. 192.
25 D. Thomson, *Scott's Men*, London, 1977, p. 48.
26 Wilson's lectures on drawing as summarised in G. Taylor, *With Scott: The Silver Lining*, London, 1923, p. 253.
27 *ibid.*, p. 199.
28 Wilson, *op. cit.*, p. 215.
29 Taylor, *op. cit.*, p. 174.
30 *ibid.*, p. 194.
31 Quoted in R. Huntford, *The Amundsen Photographs*, London, 1987, p. 114.
32 Amundsen, *op. cit.*, p. 79.
33 *ibid.*, p. 181.
34 Scott, *op. cit.*, p. 325.
35 F. Debenham, *The Quiet Land*, Denton, 1982, p. 101.
36 R. Scott, *The Voyage of the Discovery*, London, 1905, p. 226.
37 Scott, *Scott's Last Expedition*, p. 385.
38 R. Amundsen, *The North-West Passage*, Vol. I, London, 1908, p. 154.
39 B. Riffenbaugh, *The Myth of the Explorer*, Oxford, 1993, p. 160.
40 Amundsen, *The South Pole*, p. 84.
41 *ibid.*, p. 31.
42 Thomson, *op. cit.*, p. 254.
43 R. Amundsen, *My Life as an Explorer*, London, 1927, p. 236.
44 *ibid.*, p. 260.
45 Amundsen, *The South Pole*, p. 56.
46 T. Griffiths, *Judgement over the Dead*, London, 1986, p. 246.

47 Letter to his mother by Lt. H. Bowers, quoted in Spufford, *op.cit.*, p. 307.
48 Wilson, *op. cit.*, p. 213.
49 L. Bloom, *Gender on Ice*, Minneapolis, 1993, p. 127.
50 Scott, *The Voyage of the Discovery*, p. 467.
51 *ibid.*, p. 454.
52 Quoted in Cherry-Garrad, *op.cit.*, p. 10.
53 Bertram, *op. cit.*, p. 76.
54 Hanssen, *op. cit.*, p. 113.
55 Pyne, *op. cit.*, p. 2.
56 Deleuze and Guattari, *op. cit.*, p. 474.
57 Thomson, *op. cit.*, p. 283.
58 Amundsen, *The South Pole*, p. xvii.
59 *ibid.*, p. 121.
60 *ibid.*, p. 203.
61 Spufford, *op. cit.*, p. 331.
62 K. Holt, *The Race: A Novel of Polar Exploration*, New York, 1976, p. 243.
63 Scott, *Scott's Last Expedition*, p. 572.
64 Holt, *op. cit.*, p. 244.
65 Scott, *Scott's Last Expedition*, pp. 564–84.
66 Spufford, *op. cit.*, p. 337.
67 Amundsen, *The South Pole*, p. 1.
68 Spufford, *op. cit.*, p. 337.
69 Scott, *Scott's Last Expedition*, p. 607.
70 T. Gran, *The Norwegian with Scott*, London, 1984, p. 216.
71 Cherry-Garrad, *op. cit.*, p. 81.
72 Cherry-Garrad, *ibid.*, p. i.
73 M. Merleau-Ponty, *Essential Writings*, New York, 1969, p. 253.
74 R. Amundsen and L. Ellsworth, *The First Flight across the Polar Sea*, London, 1926, p. 176.

Endnotes for chapter 4

1 A. Upshur, Navy Department, Eleven charges and additional charges and thirty-five specifications, 20 July 1842.
2 *Proceedings of a General Court Martial, Charge 6. Scandalous Conduct…*, Washington Navy Department 1842, United States Courts: Court Martial Wilkes, Charges and Specification of Charges preferred by the Secretary of the Navy 1842, upon information of Asst. Surgeon Charles F. B. Guillon of United States Navy / A. Upshur. The charge was one of six including cruelty pertaining to the wounding of natives at Clermont Tonnerre; venna Lebre; and the killing of natives of Malola.
3 D. Henderson, *Hidden Coasts*, New York, 1953, pp. 97–8.
4 *ibid.*, pp. 97–8.
5 *ibid.*, pp. 99–100.
6 *ibid.*, p. 101.
7 The expedition began 18 August 1838 and reached Antarctic seas in 1839.
8 The events of the first United States Exploring Expeditions are contained in five volumes, C. Wilkes, *Narrative of the U. S. Exploring Expeditions 1838–42*, published by the US government with an additional sixteen volumes of scientific results.
9 Antarctica was the last of the continents to be discovered.
10 Hendesron, *op.cit.*, p. 102.
11 J. Ross, *A Voyage of Discovery and Research in the Antarctic Regions During the Years 1839–43*, Vol 1, London, 1847, pp. 218–9.
12 Henderson, *op.cit.*, p. 128.
13 This thesis is elaborated on in K. Yusoff, 'Arresting vision: a geographic theory of Antarctic light', PhD dissertation, Royal Holloway, University of London, 2005.
14 W. Hobbs in Henderson, *op.cit.*, p. 137.
15 The most famous mirage is probably Crocker Land in the Arctic. In June 1906, Arctic explorer, Robert E. Peary claimed to have discovered a new land and named it 'Crocker

Land' after one of his financiers. Seven years later, the Museum of Natural History outfitted an expedition to explore Crocker Land. On 13 April 1906, the expedition reached Peary's original point of sighting and set off in the direction he had speculatively mapped. Once the weather had cleared, the expedition spotted the land Peary had described. The Inuit travelling with the expedition were unimpressed and said that the vision was *'poo-jok'* – in other words, 'mist'. The group travelled one more day and took their position using a sextant and the sun. Shocked, they realised they were 150 miles onto the polar ice cap. According to Peary's calculations, they should have been 30 miles inland on Crocker Land at that point. It was then they realised that they and Peary had been fooled by a mirage. They started to return, with the mirage still persisting at their back, a mocking reminder of their mistaken visibilities. One of the leaders of the expedition, Donald MacMillan writes: 'our almost constant travelling companion, the mirage. We were convinced that we were in pursuit of a will-o'-the-wisp, ever receding, ever changing, ever beckoning'. On the return trip, 'throughout the day the mirage of the sea ice, resembling in every particular an immense land, seemed to be mocking us. It seemed so near and so easily attainable if we would only turn back'. They stand on 'the very spot' where Peary 'saw what resembled land. The day was exceptionally clear, not a trace of a cloud or mist; if land could ever be seen, it could be now. Yes, there it was! It could even be seen without a glass extending from southwest true to north-northeast. Our powerful glasses, however, brought out more clearly the dark background in contrast with the white, the whole resembling hills, valleys, and snow-capped peaks to such a degree that, had we not been out there for one hundred and fifty miles, we would have staked our lives upon it. Our judgment then as now is that this was a mirage or loom of the sea ice,' D. MacMillan, 'In search of a new land', *Harper's Magazine* (1915), pp. 925, 927, 928. See also: T. Young, Annotated bibliography of mirages, green flashes, atmospheric refraction, available at: http://mintaka.sdsu.edu/GF/bibliog/bibliog.html (02/02/2007); W. Hobbs, 'Visibility and the discovery of Polar lands', *Geografiska Annaler* 15 (1933), pp. 217–224. Anonymous, 'The Crocker Land Expedition', *Bulletin of the American Geographical Society* 44 (1912), pp. 189–93; Anonymous, 'The Crocker Land Expedition under the auspices of the American Museum of Natural History and the American Geographical Society', *Science* 35 (1912), pp. 404–8; Anonymous, 'The Crocker Land Expedition', *Scientific American* 111 (1914), p. 489; W. Hobbs, *Peary*, New York, 1937; E. Mills, *Romance of Geology*, New York, 1926, pp. 21–2.

16 In communication technologies, snow or noise is a description of the interference in the communication of information.

17 See K. Yusoff, 'Visualizing Antarctica as a place in time: from the geological sublime to "real time"', *Space and Culture* 8 (2005), pp. 381–98.

18 Hobbs' arguments contributed to a more wide-ranging discussion between American and British geographers in the 1920s and 1930s as to the legitimacy of the naming of the western area of Wilkes Land. See W. Hobbs, 'The discoveries of Antarctica within the American sector, as revealed by maps and documents', *Transactions of the American Philosophical Society* 31 (1939), pp. 1–71.

19 R. Weiss, 'Antarctica and concepts of order: two installations', *Leonardo* 17 (1984), p. 95.

20 R. Smithson, 'A sedimentation of the mind: Earth projects', in J. Flam (Ed.), *Robert Smithson: The Collected Writings*, Berkeley, 1966, p. 108.

21 Renzo Dubbini comments, 'The atmosphere's effect on visibility became a matter of great importance because meteorological conditions to a great extent determined the accuracy of the description of objects and the perception of relative positions.' R. Dubbini, *Geography of the Gaze: Urban and Rural Vision in Early Modern Europe*, Chicago, 2002, p. 177.

22 See M. Jay, *Downcast Eyes: The Denigration of Vision in Twentieth-century French Thought*, Berkeley and Los Angeles, 1993, pp. 1–2.

23 G. Rose, 'Geography as a science of observation: the landscape, the gaze and masculinity', in F. Driver and G. Rose (Eds), *Nature and Science: Essays in the History of Geographical Knowledge*, Historical Geography Research Series, 1992, p. 28.

24 See F. Driver, *Geography, Empire and Visualisation: Making Representation, Department of Geography*, Royal Holloway Research Papers General Series, 1995.

25 N. Bryson, *Vision and Painting: The Logic of the Gaze*, New Haven, 1983; Jay, *op.cit.*; T. Brennan and M. Jay, *Vision in Context: Historical and Contemporary Perspectives on Sight*, New York and London, 1996; J. Crary, *Suspensions of Perception: Attention, Spectacle and Modern Culture*, Cambridge, MA, 1999 are cognisant of emerging work in the field of visual culture/art theory that highlight the complexity and frequent failure of visual perception, as well as the distinct conditions of its emergence. Alongside this work that has been a consideration of a vision of affect, most notably in James Elkins' work: J. Elkins, *On Pictures and the Words that Fail Them*, Cambridge, 1998; J. Elkins, *Pictures and Tears: A History of People who Have Cried in Front of Paintings*, New York and London, 2001. The author describes seeing as searching, desirous and irrational, something 'like hunting and like dreaming' and entangled 'in the passions – jealousy, violence, possessiveness; and it is soaked in affect – in pleasure and displeasure, and pain', J. Elkins, *The Object Stares Back: On the Nature of Seeing*, London, 1996, p. 11. Arguably, what geography could bring to this discussion of vision is a consideration of how perception has emerged out of located practices and specific environmental conditions.

26 For an excellent exposition of the geographies of mountains see, M. H. Nicolson, *Mountain Gloom and Mountain Glory: The Development of the Aesthetics of the Infinite*, Cornell, 1959.

27 See N. Bryson, 'The gaze in the expanded field', in H. Foster (Ed.), *Vision and Visuality*, New York, 1988, p. 91.

28 J. Nourse, *American Explorations in the Ice Zones*, London, 1884, p. 489. The spectroscope was actually able to bring the physical condition of the moon and other nearer planets closer that the use of optical instruments in the Antarctic could facilitate.

29 H. Lamb, 'Topography and weather in the Antarctic', *The Geographical Journal* 111 (1948), pp. 48–62.

30 See chapter 4, 'Problems of Antarctic navigation and perception: the compass, longitude and mirages', in P. Simpson-Housley, *Antarctica: Exploration, Perception and Metaphor*, London, 1992, pp. 38–50.

31 While not the first to 'discover' Antarctica, Wilkes was the first explorer (apart from his contemporary rival d'Urville) to explore extensively a large stretch of coast, long enough to prove the continental character of the Antarctic. The 'continental character' of the Antarctic was difficult to discern because landfall was difficult to make. Stranded icebergs frozen into the inland ice, the off-shore ice, island ice and the ice shelves all presented the difficulty of ascertaining a continent, rather than a series of islands such as that which had been identified in the Arctic. Speculation as to Antarctica's continental character, and whether there were in fact 'two continents' connecting the permanent ice shelves of the Ross and Weddell sea as proposed by glaciologists such as Griffith Taylor in 1914, was not finally resolved until remote sensing began to reveal what lay under the ice.

32 W. Hobbs, 'Conditions of exceptional visibility with high latitudes, particularly as a result of superior mirage', *Annals of the Association of American Geographers* 27 (1937), p. 233.

33 See Jay, *op.cit.*, p. 7.

34 Norman Bryson's concept of a 'glance' in the *Logic of the Gaze* (1983) in contrast, describes a respectful and self-reflexive way of looking that keeps vision in motion, unfixable and tentative.

35 Considering the relationship between sight and other senses, the sketch is a touch-dependent activity that is led as much by the desire for a material object as by the desire of the eye. Here we might contend that images have just as much to do with practices of touching as practices of vision.
36 U. Wråkberg, 'Delineating a continent of ice and snow, cartographic claims of knowledge and territory in Antarctica in the 19th and early 20th century', in A. Elizinga, T. Nordin, D. Turner and U. Wråkberg (Eds), *Antarctic Challenges, Historical and Current Perspectives on Otto Nordenskjöld's Antarctic Expedition 1901–1903*, Göteborg, 2004, pp. 123–43.
37 Wråkberg, *ibid.*, p. 130.
38 P. Levi, *The Periodic Table*, Harmondsworth, 2000, p. 190.
39 R. Barthes, *Camera Lucida*, London, 2000, p. 93.
40 Wråkberg, *op.cit.*, p. 123.
41 In fact, Antarctica's first appearance on global maps was a kind of mirage, a hypothetical continent posited by the ancient Greek geographers to 'balance' the northern hemisphere. It was called Antipodean (meaning other footed) or Antarctikus (opposite the bear). The theory of the Antarctic continent was based on supposition alone, not geographical exploration.
42 Even the objects collected from the expedition were received as a doubtful accumulation. The original Act of Congress 1846 to establish the Smithsonian Institute stipulated that the Wilkes' collection was to become part of Smithsonian Institute, but Joseph Henry, the first secretary of the Smithsonian, was concerned that 'filling a costly building with an indiscriminate collection of objects of curiosity' would dull the Institute's purpose of advancing knowledge. He rejected Wilkes' objects and images as a disordered assemblage of suspect materials. After much debate, the specimens and objects that had lingered for nearly 20 years in the Patent Office, were included as founding objects in the National Museum of Natural History at the Smithsonian Institute in 1858.
43 Note that Melville's first chapter of *Moby Dick* is called 'Loomings' and this sets up the thematic symmetry of the novel as Ishmael and Ahab struggle to contend with the mirages of their own characters in the formless whiteness of the whale. As matter is accounted for, and Ahab pursues the whale, it simultaneously cannot be accounted for, in that Ishmael cannot comprehend the boundaries of it. In this failure to grasp the whale's dimensions, a sense of geography is lost – and space is dissolved into whiteness and mass rendered devoid of navigation.
44 See 'Appendix, the earliest sources', in H. Melville, *Moby Dick*, Harmondsworth, 1986, pp. 991–1011.
45 The theory of Hollow Earth was first proposed by Edmund Halley – of comet fame – in 1692.
46 In G. Murray (Ed.), *The Antarctic Manual: For the Use of the Expedition of 1901*, London, 1901, the two sections under the heading 'Geography' are 'Cartography' and 'Narration'.
47 Symmes wrote and lectured tirelessly on Hollow Earth Theory, even though he was considered an indifferent writer and poor speaker (he suffered from stage fright, which eventually killed him). Despite this, Hollow Earth captured the popular imagination as an inverted heaven on earth, and still has many followers today.
48 D. Tyler, *The Wilkes Expedition: The First United States Exploring Expedition (1838–1842)*, Philadelphia, 1968, p. 5.
49 Poe actually reviewed Reynold's *Address*, on the subject of a surveying and exploring expedition to the Pacific Ocean and the South Seas in *The Southern Literary Messenger* in January 1837; E. Poe, *The Narrative of Arthur Gordon Pym of Nantucket*, New York, 2002, p. 188.
50 See particularly, J.G. Ballard, *Terminal Beach*, London, 2001; J.G. Ballard, *The Drowned World*, London, 2001.
51 R. Smithson, *Slideworks*, Verona, 1997, p. 80.
52 A. Shipley, 'Zoology: on the abysmal fauna of the Antarctic region', in Murray, *op.cit.*, pp. 243–4.
53 Shipley, 'Zoology' (note 53), p. 245.

54 M. Bravo and S. Sörlin, *Narrating the Arctic*, Canton, 2002, p. 24.

55 Charles Baudelaire translated Poe's narrative into French, and it was read by Jules Verne. He combined his own interests in scientific discourse and exploration with Poe's new forms of literary expression to write a sequel to *The Narrative of Arthur Gordon Pym* entitled, *J. Verne, An Antarctic Mystery; or, The Sphinx of the Ice Fields: A Sequel to Edgar Allan Poe's The Narrative of Arthur Gordon Pym*, Philadelphia, 1899.

56 See K. Robinson, *Antarctica*, London, 1997 and *Imagining Abrupt Climate Change: Terraforming Earth*, Amazon, 2007.

57 See F. Jameson, *Archaeologies of the Future*, New York, 2005, p. xii.

58 J. Kneale and R. Kitchin (Eds), *Lost in Space: Geographies of Science Fiction*, London, 2002, pp. 3–4.

Endnotes for chapter 5

1 Written in fall 1993, this is the initial diary entry to the third and final official notebook kept during GISP2's extraction. All three notebooks can be viewed at: www.gisp2.sr.unh.edu/GISP2/NOTEBOOKS

2 The above quote refers to GISP2 as '100,000 years of the earth's climate history'; even though GISP2's deepest ice is around 200,000 years old, annual strata remain true to their original depositional order to only ≈110,000 years ago. At the time research for this study began, GISP2 was the world's longest ice core ever drilled; in July 2003 the NGRIP (North Greenland Ice Core Project) ice core was completed and surpassed GISP2 in length.

3 See, for instance, K. Knorr-Cetina, *Epistemic Cultures: How the Sciences Make Knowledge*, Cambridge, 1999. In *How Scientific Practices Matter*, Chicago, 2002, pp. 135–40, J. Rouse details the scholarly lineage of what has been called 'the 'Strong Programme' for the sociology of scientific knowledge and its sociological successors and competitors'. Another branch of sociological interest in scientific practices can be found in the work of Bruno Latour; see, for example, B. Latour, 'When things strike back: a possible contribution of 'science studies' to the social sciences', *British Journal of Sociology* 51 (2000), pp. 107–23; B. Latour, *Pandora's Hope*, Cambridge, 1999; and B. Latour and S. Woolgar, *Laboratory Life: The Social Construction of Scientific Facts*, Princeton, 1986. Also see I. Stengers, *Power and Invention: Situating Science*, Minneapolis, 1997.

4 Rouse, *op.cit.*, p. 140; he also argues for the centrality of what he terms 'postepistemological' aspects: 'Scientists are involved with their objects of study rather than aspiring to detachment; scientific understanding is situated and intra-active rather than totalising and explanatory; the telos of scientific work is transformative and futural rather than representational and retrospectively reconstructionist. … Such a postepistemological conception of scientific knowing takes scientific practices as the primary focus of interpretation and recognises that the sciences are ongoing ways of dealing with the world practically and discursively,' p. 160. See also J. Wylie, 'Becoming-icy: Scott and Amundsen's South Polar voyages, 1910–1913', *Cultural Geographies* 9 (2002), pp. 249–65.

5 For a discussion of this usage see K. Barad, 'Agential realism: feminist interventions in understanding scientific practices', in M. Biagioli (Ed), *The Science Studies Reader*, New York,

1998, pp. 1–11. Non-Western conceptualisations of how (high-latitude) places harbour matter-based forms of knowledge are interesting to consider in this context; see for instance, I. Krupnik and D. Jolly (Eds), *The Earth is Faster Now: Indigenous Observations of Arctic Environmental Change*, Arctic Research Consortium of the U.S., Fairbanks, 2002 as well as J. Cruikshank, *Do Glaciers Listen? Local Knowledge, Colonial Encounters, and Social Imagination*, Seattle and Vancouver, 2005.

6 The distinction between human and nonhuman has been widely contested: see C. Barron (Ed.), 'A strong distinction between humans and nonhumans is no longer required for research purposes: a debate between Bruno Latour and Steve Fuller', *History of the Human Sciences* 16 (2003), pp. 77–99. For discussions about the distinction between 'natural' and 'social', see: B. Braun and N. Castree (Eds), *Remaking Reality: Nature at the Millennium*, London, 1998; and N. Castree and B. Braun (Eds), *Social Nature*, Oxford, 2001. See also L. Daston (Ed.), *Biographies of Scientific Objects*, Chicago, 2000.

7 P. Mayewski and F. White, *The Ice Chronicles: The Quest to Understand Global Climate Change*, London, 2002, p. 82.

8 D. Livingstone, *Putting Science in its Place*, Chicago, 2003, pp. 13–14.

9 C. Helfferich, Old times in air, Alaska Science Forum (1998) Article #1370, available at: http://www.gi.alaska.edu/ScienceForum/ASF13/1370.html

10 H. Fischer et al., 'Ice core records of atmospheric CO_2 around the last three glacial terminations', *Science* 283 (1999), p. 1712.

11 Particulate matter such as methane gas from the tropics, volcanic ash from the Pacific Northwest, and continental dust from the Saharan desert.

12 For an historical discussion of these geographically polarised regions, see G. Hartwig, *The Polar and Tropical Worlds: A Popular and Scientific Description of Man and Nature in the Polar and Equatorial Regions of the Globe*, Chicago, 1878.

13 The idea of time as a crucial factor in making places in the pre-modern world is discussed by A. Scafi, *Mapping Paradise*, Chicago, 2006.

14 E. Brook, T. Sowers and J. Orchado, 'Rapid variations in atmospheric methane concentration during the past 110,000 years', *Science* 273 (1996), p. 1087.

15 P. Mayewski and M. Bender, 'The GISP2 ice core record – paleoclimate highlights, U.S. National Report to the International Union of Geodesy and Geophysics (1991–1994)', *Reviews of Geophysics* 33 (1995), available at: http://www.agu.org/revgeophys/mayews01/node2.html.

16 Rouse, *op.cit.*, p. 263.

17 Mayewski and Bender, *op.cit.*

18 *ibid.*

19 The NGRIP (North Greenland Ice Core Project) core surpassed GISP2 in length in July of 2003. Although GISP2 was the world's longest core at the time of its extraction (and provided the oldest, most continuous annual deposition record to date), it did not produce the oldest ice ever cored; the Vostok core from Antarctica, for instance, is comprised of ice nearly 400,000 years old.

20 On why such temperatures are valuable see R. Alley, *The Two-Mile Time Machine*, Princeton, 2002, p. 67.

21 An excerpt from NSF press release #93–57 (July 15, 1993): 'World's deepest ice core yields unique climate archive'. This press release also included the following logistical information: 'The Greenland Ice Sheet Project Two was carried out by technicians, researchers and scientists from: the US Army Cold Regions Research and Engineering Laboratory in Hanover, NH, Carnegie Mellon University, the Desert Research Institute in Reno, Nevada, The Massachusetts Institute of Technology, Ohio State University, Pennsylvania State University, the New York State Department of Health, the State University of New York at Albany, the State University of New York at Buffalo, Lamont-Doherty Geological Observatory of Columbia University, University of Arizona, University of Colorado, University of Miami, University of New Hamp-

shire, University of Rhode Island, University of Washington, the US Geological Survey in Tacoma, Washington, and the University of Wisconsin. GISP2 drilling was funded by the US National Science Foundation Division of Polar Programs as a part of the Arctic System Science Initiative (ARCSS). The Science Management Office of the University of New Hampshire developed an on-site core-processing facility and still coordinates GISP2 scientific activities. Logistical and drilling support was provided by the Polar Ice Coring Office (PICO) at the University of Alaska in Fairbanks'.

22 Alley, *op.cit.*, pp. 23–4.

23 GISP2 core was shipped from Greenland aboard LC–130 aircraft of the 109th Air National Guard, out of Scotia, New York. US Air Force Military Airlift Command from McGuire Air Force Base in New Jersey also provided air transport. Support at Sondrestrom Air Base in Greenland was provided by the US Air Force Space Command.

24 This text appears on the cover of a visitor information leaflet produced by the NICL (updated August 2002). The following information about NICL ice-core curation was collected during interviews I conducted there in October 2003.

25 Contemporary art curator, Laura Heon, comments on this aspect of Western scientific environments in *Unnatural Science*, Massachusetts, 2000, p. 59, 'Even though many of these medicines may come from natural materials, the Western pharmacy gives little evidence of this; Western medicine has refined and regimented the natural into invisibility'.

26 P. Galison and C. Jones, 'Trajectories of production: laboratories/factories/studios', in H. Obrist and B. Vanderlinden (Eds), *Laboratorium*, Germany, 2001, p. 205.

27 A scanned image of a 13-centimetre by 1-metre-long core can be enlarged to a 2-foot-high, 12-foot-long image without significantly losing resolution. At full resolution each core metre yields 480 megabytes of visually-imaged data. To keep these image files properly (digitally) stored and safely backed up the NICL will run its own server for the images, and has also begun talks with the EROS Data Center located in Sioux Falls, South Dakota. EROS Data Center is responsible for the maintenance of huge data files (such as remote-sensed images) and will eventually work with the NICL in archiving GISP2 images.

28 It bears mentioning that viewing GISP2 digitally does not erase issues of materiality; the material issues simply shift. In media design and new media studies it is generally understood that data and data storage mechanisms are just as thoroughly matter-based as whatever they are recording; after all, data are stored in material apparatuses that exist in physical locations.

29 Such as the GRIP (Greenland Ice Core Project) and NGRIP (North Greenland Ice Core Project) cores.

30 Rouse, *op.cit.*, p. 25. See also M. Bravo and S. Sorlin, 'Narrative and practice – an introduction', in M. Bravo and S. Sorlin (Eds), *Narrating the Arctic: A Cultural History of Nordic Scientific Practices*, Canton, 2002, pp. 3–32.

31 Rouse, *op.cit.*, p. 165. Also see, P. Galison and E. Thompson, *The Architecture of Science*, Cambridge, 1999, for more on how scientific spaces are integral to scientific practices.

32 The NICL regularly receives experimental cold-protective gear from private companies doing research on product design and new fabrics. Due to spending extended hours in such a cold environment, NICL technicians and scientists are the perfect candidates for testing such gear. They are asked to rate things like warmth, mobility and how design features might be improved.

33 The Milan-based InterICE conference took place in August 2003. This text was sent to me (pre-publication) upon request, after an interview with Todd Hinkley in October 2003.

34 D. Livingstone, *Putting Science In Its Place*, Chicago, 2003, p. 13. 'Consider the laboratory as a critical site in the generation of experimental knowledge. … Attending to the micro-geography of the lab … takes us a long way toward appreciating that matters of space are

fundamentally involved at every stage in the acquisition of scientific knowledge. What is known, how it is obtained, and the ways it is secured are all intimately bound up with the venues of science', p.12.

35 For examples of data-based GISP2 research papers see R. Alley, 'Ice-Core evidence of abrupt climate changes', *Proceedings of the National Academy of Sciences of the United States of America* 97 (2000), pp. 1331–4; E. Brook, T. Sowers and J. Orchado, 'Rapid variations in atmospheric methane concentration during the past 110,000 Years', *Science* 273 (1996) pp. 1087–91; see also Fischer et al., *op.cit.*, pp. 1712–4.

Endnotes for chapter 6

1 Buache's biography is well developed in three texts: L. Drapeyron, 'Les deux Buache et l'origine de l'enseignement géographique par versants et par bassins', *Revue de géographie* (1887) pp. 6–16; N. Broc, 'Philippe Buache: un géographe dans son siècle', *Dix-Huitième siècle* 3 (1971) pp. 223–35; L. Lagarde, 'Philippe Buache: cartographe ou géographe?' in D. Lecocq, A. Chambard (Eds), *Terre à découvrir, terres à parcourir*, Paris, 1998, pp. 147–66. The commemorative address given at the Academy can be of some help: 'Eloge de Monsieur Buache par Grandjean de Fouchy', *Histoire et Mémoires de l'Académie Royale des Sciences* (1772), pp. 135–50. English texts are fewer: G. Kish, 'Early thematic mapping: P. Buache', *Imago Mundi* 28 (1976), pp. 129–36; L. Lagarde, 'Philippe Buache (1700–1773)', *Geographers Biobibliographical Studies* 9 (1985), pp. 21–7; A. Godlewska, *Geography Unbound: French Geographic Science from Cassini to Humboldt*, Chicago, 1999.

2 P. Buache, 'Essai de Géographie Physique, où l'on propose des vues générales sur l'espèce de Charpente du Globe, composée des chaînes de montagnes qui traversent les mers comme les terres, avec quelques considérations particulières sur les différents bassins de la mer, et sur sa configuration intérieure', *Mémoires de l'Académie Royale des Sciences*, 1752.

3 Quoted in A. von Humboldt, *Voyage aux régions équinoxiales du nouveau continent, fait en 1799, 1800, 1801, 1802, 1803, et 1804,* Vol. II, Paris, 1819, p. 538.

4 About this travel and, more generally Humboldt's work, see C. Minguet, *A. de Humboldt: historien et géographe de l'Amérique espagnole (1799–1804)*, Paris, 1969; M. Dettelbach, 'Global physics and aesthetic Empire: Humboldt's physical portraits of the tropics', in D. Miller and P. Reill (Eds), *Visions of Empire: Voyages, Botany and Representations of Nature*, Cambridge, 1996, pp. 258–92; M. Dettelbach, 'Humboldtian Science', in N. Jardine, J. Secord and E. Sparry, *Cultures of Natural History*, 1996, pp. 287–304; H. de Terra, *Humboldt: The Life and Times of A. Von Humboldt*, New York, 1955.

5 Humboldt, *op.cit.*, p. 490.

6 *ibid.*, p. 515.

7 *ibid.*, pp. 537–8.

8 *ibid.*, p. 515.

9 *ibid.*, p. 517.

10 *ibid.*, p. 515.

11 D. Diderot and J. d'Alembert (Eds), *Encyclopédie ou dictionnaire raisonné des sciences, des arts et des métiers par une société de gens de lettres*, Vol. X, Paris and Neuchâtel, 1751–65.

12 M. Clozier, *Mémoires de mathématique et de physique présentés à l'académie royale des sciences*, Vol. II, Paris, 1755.

13 B. Debarbieux, 'The mountain in the city: Social uses and transformations of a natural landform in urban space', *Ecumene* 5 (1998), pp. 399–431.

14 See for example '*Angles correspondants des montagnes*' in Diderot and d'Alembert, *op.cit.*, Tome 1, Paris, 1751–1765, p. 464

15 Jaucourt, '*Montagnes*', in Diderot and D'Alembert, *op.cit.*

16 It is the case of Saussure; see H.B. de Saussure, *Voyages dans les Alpes,* Vol. IV, Neuchâtel, 1796, pp. 14–5.

17 B. Farrington, 'Words as new as the hills: concept formation in the field of high altitude topography (1750–1850)', *French Language Studies* 10 (2000), pp. 45–70.

18 Henceforth the word will be written without quotation marks. However, one should regard the word not as a description of geographical reality, but a discursively produced category.

19 G.-L. Leclerc, *Histoire et théorie de la terre,* Paris, 1749, p. 69.

20 Buache, *op.cit.*, p. 401. Writing this way, Buache uses one of the two recurrent analogies developed in response to the continuity of mountain chains, the other being the skeleton. The latter, very common during the Middle Ages, was still in use in the eighteenth century, for example in Diderot et d'Alembert's *Encyclopédie* where one can find in d'Holbach's text on '*montagne*': 'Mountains can be compared to bones, which support the globe and makes it solid, as bones in the body support flesh and other parties …', Vol. X, 1751–1765, p. 672.

21 Buache, *Essai de géographie physique*, p. 402.

22 'Planisphère Physique centré sur le pole septentrional', in *Cartes et tables de la géographie physique ou naturelle, présentées au roi le 15 mai 1757*, Paris.

23 As a Royal Geographer, Philippe Buache taught geography to the royal family children. See L. Drapeyron, *Les deux Buaches et l'éducation géographique de trois rois de France, Louis XVI, Louis XVIII, Charles X avec documents inédits*, Paris, 1888.

24 P. Buache, 'Sur une nouvelle disposition de mappemonde', *Histoire de l'Académie Royale des Sciences* (1755), pp. 121–4.

25 P. Buache, *Cartes et tables*, Paris, 1754. The phrase – '*premier coup d'œil*' (at first glance) – is used at least four times in Buache's writings. It underlines his belief in the pedagogic and heuristic qualities of tables and maps.

26 H. Blais and I. Laboulais (Eds), *Géographies plurielles: Les sciences géographiques au moment de l'émergence des sciences humaines*, Paris, 2006, p. 29.

27 'It would be appropriate for sailors to note, according to the concepts I have mentioned here, small phenomena that may be neglected, but which, when gathered, could lead to the discovery of a general cause …' Buache, *Essai de géographie physique*, pp. 415–6.

28 P. Buache, '*Carte et coupe du canal de la Manche et d'une partie de la Mer d'Allemagne*', in Buache, *Cartes et tables.*

29 P. Buache, '*Parallèle des fleuves des quatre parties du Monde, pour servir à déterminer les hauteurs des montagnes de Globe physique de la Terre qui s'exécute en relief au dôme du Luxembourg*', *Mémoires de l'Académie Royale des Sciences* (1753), pp. 586–8.

30 Buache, *Essai de géographie physique*, p. 402.

31 *ibid.*, p. 408.

32 A. Miquel, *La géographie humaine du monde musulman jusqu'au milieu du 11e siècle*, Paris, 1980.

33 Contrary to contemporary books which belong to the so-called natural theology theory, such as John Woodward's books on physical geography of the Globe: J. Woodward, *Géographie physique ou essai sur l'histoire naturelle de la terre*, Paris, 1735.

34 P. Buache, 'Observations géographiques et physiques où l'on donne une idée de l'existence des Terres Antarctiques et de leur Mer glaciale, avec quelques remarques sur un globe physique en relief, d'un pied de diamètre, qui sert de modèle pour celui de neuf pieds',

Mémoires de l'Académie Royale des Sciences (1757), pp. 190–204. He details the reasoning which allows him to deduce the morphology of the continent from the quantity of icebergs recorded by sailors.

35 I. Laboulais, 'Le système de Buache: une nouvelle façon de considérer notre globe et de combler les blancs de la carte', in I. Laboulais-Lesage (Ed.), *Combler les blancs de la carte: modalités et enjeux de la construction des savoirs géographiques, XVIIe-XXe siècle*, Strasbourg, 2004, pp. 93–115.

36 In French geography, Nicolas Buache de la Neuville, nephew of Philippe Buache, and Edme Mentelle, both members of the Institute, were the main promoters of this idea. See F. Labourie and D. Nordman, 'Introduction aux leçons de géographie de Buache et Mantelle', in D. Nordman (Ed.), *L'Ecole Normale de l'an III: leçons d'histoire, de géographie, d'économie politique (Edition annotée des cours de Volney, Buache de La Neuville, Mentelle et Vandermonde)*, Paris, 1994, pp. 137–61. Among German geographers, Johann Christoph Gatterer (1727–99) borrowed the most from Buache's ideas and adopted his natural borders theory.

37 On this topic, see, for the French context, D. Nordman, *Frontières de France: de l'espace au territoire, XVI-XIXe siècle*, Gallimard, Paris, 1999.

38 For his contribution to the mapping of Mexico, Buffon is mentioned 233 times, and Riccioli, the Italian astronomer famous for his numerous, but approximate, measurements of altitude during the seventeenth century, 79 times.

39 N. Desmarets, 'Géographie physique', in Diderot and D'Alembert, *op.cit*. The following quotations are from the same text.

40 I. Laboulais, 'Voir, décrire et combiner: les méthodes de la géographie physique selon Nicolas Desmarets', *Revue d'histoire moderne et contemporaine* 51 (2004), pp. 38–57. On geography in *l'Encyclopédie*, see C. Withers, 'Geography in its time: Geography and Historical Geography in Diderot and d'Alembert's *Encyclopedie*', *Journal of Historical Geography* 19 (1993), pp. 255–64 ; I. Laboulais, 'La géographie dans les arbres encyclopédiques de la seconde moitié du XVIIIe siècle', in H. Blais and I. Laboulais (Ed.), *Les sciences géographiques au moment de l'émergence des sciences humaines*, Paris, 2006, pp. 63–93 ; A. Godlewska, *Geography Unbound: French Geographic Science from Cassini to Humboldt*, Chicago, 1999.

41 Though faithful to Buache's theory, he mentions the case of the Cassiquiare: 'I see only one exception to this general arrangement, it is the communication between Orinoco and a river which merges with the Amazon river', N. Desmarets, 'Géographie physique', in Diderot and d'Alembert, *op.cit.*, p. 622.

42 R. de Vaugondy, 'Géographie', in Diderot and d'Alembert, *op.cit.*

43 He happens to mention 'this *massif* that one calls vaguely *le plateau de Tartarie*'; but, immediately after mentioning it, he discusses its topography since many parts are of little height. Humboldt, *Sur l'élévation des montagnes de l'Inde*, Paris, p. 13.

44 A von Humboldt, *Asie Centrale: recherches sur les chaînes de montagnes et la climatologie comparée*, Paris, 1843, p. 155.

45 *ibid.*, p. 51.

46 A von Humboldt, *Cosmos: Essai d'une description physique du monde*, Paris, 2000 (1844), p. 57.

47 Humboldt, *Asie Centrale*, p. 210.

48 'Letter of 2 October 1845', A von Humboldt, *Lettres de Alexandre de Humboldt à Varnhagen von Ense (1827–1858)*, Genève, 1860. *Cosmos* contains the same idea: 'Science begins for human beings when the spirit grasps the matter, when it strives to submit a collection of experiences to rational combinations'. Humboldt, *Cosmos*, p. 87.

49 A Von Humboldt, *Essai politique sur le royaume de la nouvelle Espagne*, Paris, 1811.

50 Humboldt, *Voyage*, pp. 490–518.

51 On the role of scientific instruments and of measure in Humboldt's work, see: S. Provost, 'Les instruments de Humboldt et de Borda au volcan des Canaries', *Revue du Musee des arts et metiers*, 39–40 (2003), pp. 112–4.

52 According to C. Minguet in his introduction of Humboldt, *Essai sur la géographie des plantes*, Nanterre, 1990.
53 A von Humboldt, 'Lettre à Caroline von Wolzogen: 14 May 1806', in *Lettres américaines d'Alexandre de Humboldt (1798–1807),* Paris, 1904.
54 Humboldt, *Cosmos*, pp. 651–66.
55 A von Humboldt, *Expériences sur le galvanisme et en général sur l'irritation des fibres musculaires et nerveuses,* Paris, 1799. For a detailed analysis, see W. Reise, 'The Impact of Romanticism on the experimental method', *Studies in Romanticism* 2 (1962) pp. 12–22 and M.-J. Trumpler, 'Questionning Nature: Experimental Investigation of Animal Electricity in Germany (1791–1810)', PhD thesis, Yale, 1992.
56 Humboldt, *Voyage*.
57 The climb took place on 23 June 1802. Humboldt and Bompland reached the altitude of 18,000 feet, and were interrupted by a 'defile' located a few hundreds metres below the summit.
58 In the first pages of his text, he recalls how scientifically poor was such a climb: barometric measures were less reliable than trigonometric calculus made at a distance; rocks were hidden to geognostic observations; organic life was 'dead in these high solitudes'. However, by publishing this narrative, he seeks to answer the curiosity of his time : 'Chimborazo has become the continuous object of questions addressed to me since my first return to Europe ... I will pick up from the still unpublished materials of my dairies the very simple narrative of an excursion in mountains ... which cannot offer any dramatic interest...' A von Humboldt, *Notice de deux tentatives d'ascension du Chimborazo*, Paris, 1838, pp. 7–8. See also *Lettres*.
59 Humboldt, *Notice* , p. 21.
60 *ibid.*, p. 21.
61 *ibid.*, p. 24.
62 *ibid.*, p. 25.
63 A. Godleweska has shown how innovative he was in this respect: 'From Enlightenment vision to modern science? Humboldt's visual thinking', in D. Livingstone and C. Withers, *Geography and Enlightenment*, Chicago, 1999, pp. 236–75; see also N. Rupke, 'Humboltian distribution maps: the spatial ordering of scientific knowledge', in T. Frängsmyr (Ed.), *The Structure of Knowledge: Classification of Science and Learning since the Renaissance*, Berkeley, 2001.
64 Humboldt, *Cosmos*, p. 46. A few pages later, he writes that on equatorial mountains 'it is given to human beings to observe all plant families and stars at the same time'.
65 Among very numerous possible examples, once again Chimborazo is paradigmatic: 'On the shore of the South Sea, when the long winter rains are over, when the transparency of the air has suddenly increased, Chimborazo appears, like a cloud on the horizon; It isolates itself from the neighbouring peaks; it rises above the whole Andes cordillera, like that gorgeous dome – Michel-Angelo's genial work – rising above the ancient monuments encircling the Capitol,' A von Humboldt, *Sites des Cordillères et monuments des peuples indigènes de l'Amérique*, Paris, 1869, p. 76.
66 A von Humboldt, *Volcans des Cordillères de Quito et du Mexique*, Paris, 1854, p. 6.
67 S. Briffaud, 'Le temps du paysage: A. de Humboldt et la géohistoire du sentiment de nature', in H. Blais and I. Laboulais (Eds), *Les sciences géographiques au moment de l'émergence des sciences humaines*, Paris, 2006, p. 279.
68 *ibid.*, pp. 278–9 and immediately after he writes: 'The human subject of *Cosmos* is man considered as a spectator of nature, thus as a being who, in so far as he is impressed by the spectacle, in so far as he feels and sometimes reflects on it, bears within himself the unity of nature,' p. 280.

Endnotes for chapter 7

1 A. Strid, *Mountain Flora of Greece*, Cambridge and New York, 1986, p. xv.

2 'Also inaccessible mountain summits and remote deserts and all the guts of the earth', R. Buxton, 'Imaginary Greek mountains', *Journal of Hellenic Studies* 62 (1992), p. 5.

3 Quoted in W. Hyde, 'The development of the appreciation of mountain scenery in modern times', *Geographical Review* 3 (1917), p. 113.

4 R. Grove, *Green Imperialism: Colonial Expansion, Tropical Island Edens and the Origins of Environmentalism, 1600–1860*, Cambridge and New York, 1995, p. 325.

5 S. Diamantes, *Fysē kai periballon sto Agion Oros, in: Kentro Diafylaxēs Agioretikēs Klēronomias, Odoipōriko sto Agion Oros,* Thessalonica, 1999, p. 115.

6 S. Dafis, 'Anthrōpines drastēriotētes kai fysiko perivallon', in S. Dafis *et al.* (Eds.), *Fysē kai Perivallon sto Agion Oros,* Thessalonica, 1998; G. Sideropoulos, *Agion Oros: anafores stēn anthrō pogeōgrafia,* Athens, 2000, p. 28; O. Rackham, 'Our Lady's Garden: the historical ecology of the Holy Mountain', *Friends of Mount Athos, Annual Report* (2000), p. 50; D. Babalonas, 'Chlōrida kai endemismos tou Agiou Orous', in M. Parcharidou and M. Fountoulēs (Eds), *Agion Oros: fysē, latreia, technē*, Vol. I, Thessalonica, 1999, p. 119.

7 J.C. Larchet, 'La funzione profetica del monachesimo athonita nel mondo moderno', *Le Messager Orthodoxe* 131 (1998), p. 44; S. Schama, *Landscape and Memory,* New York, 1998, p. 537.

8 The *Geoponika*, an agricultural and horticultural encyclopedia aimed at presenting an accumulated practical lore of the ancients, is the work most representative of this tradition. See R. Rodgers, '*Kepopoiia*: garden making and garden culture in the Geoponika', in A. Littlewood and H. Maguire (Eds), *Byzantine Garden Culture,* Washington, DC, 2002, pp. 159–76. Herbalists, trained in the writings of Dioscorides (*ca.* AD 70), and herb gardens are attested in the monasteries at least since the post-Byzantine period. See A.M. Talbot, 'Byzantine monastic horticulture: the textual evidence', in Littlewood and Maguire, *op.cit.*, p. 55.

9 Talbot, *op.cit.*, p. 56.

10 D. Cosgrove, 'Gardening the Renaissance world', in D. Cosgrove, *Geography and Vision: Imagination, Landscape, Mapping*, London, 2008, pp. 51-67.

11 D. Livingstone, *Putting Science in its Place,* Chicago and London, 2003, p. 5.

12 Quoted in K. Dodds and S. Royle, 'Introduction: rethinking islands', *Journal of Historical Geography* 29 (2003), p. 487.

13 Pomponius Mela, *Description of the World*, ii, 31; Pliny, *Natural History*, vii, 35.

14 '... And the other hill that men call Athos is so highe, that the shadow of him stretcheth unto Olymphus and it is neare lxxvii myle between, and above that hill is the aire so cleere, that men may fele no wynde there, and therefore may no beast live there the ayre is so drye, and men say in the country that Philosophers somtyme went up to these same hilles and helde to their noses a sponge wet with water for to have ayre, for the ayre was so drye there & above in the pouder of the hill they wrote letters with their fingers, and at the yeares ende they came againe and found those letters which they had written the year before without any defaute, and therefore it seemeth well that these hilles passe the cloudes to ye pure ayre.' J. Maundeville, *The Voiage and Travayle of Sir John Maundeville Knight which Treateth of the Way toward Hierusalem and of*

Marvayles of Inde and Other Islands and Countreys, London, 1887 (1356), pp. 15–16.

15 J. Golinski, *Making Natural Knowledge: Constructivism and the History of Science,* Cambridge and New York, 1998, p. 81.

16 P. Belon, 'A description of Mount Athos, commonly called Monte Santo', in J. Ray (Ed.), *A Collection of Curious Travels and Voyages,* London, 1693, p. 11.

17 F. Lestringant, *Mapping the Renaissance World: the Geographical Imagination in the Age of Discovery,* Berkeley and Los Angeles, 1994, p. 26.

18 D. Cosgrove, *Apollo's Eye*, Baltimore, 2001.

19 "Contained garden", P. Belon, *Voyage au Levant. Les observations de Pierre Belon du Mans de plusieurs singularités & choses mémorables trouvées en Gréce, Turquie, Judée, Égypte, Arabie & autres pays étranges*, Paris, 2001 (1553), p. 150; Livingstone, *op.cit.*, p. 49.

20 Cosgrove, 'Gardening the Renaissance world'.

21 See Lestringant, *op.cit.*

22 P. Fortini-Brown, *Venice and Antiquity: The Venetian Sense of the Past*, New Haven and London, 1996.

23 Grove, *op.cit.*, pp. 14, 221.

24 From John Sibthorp's diary, 19 September 1794, in R. Walpole, *Travels in Various Countries in the East,* Vol. I, London, 1820, p. 54.

25 C. Withers, 'Geography, natural history and the eighteenth-century Enlightenment: putting the world in place', *History Workshop Journal* 39 (1995), p. 138.

26 R. Walpole, *Travels*, p. x; R. Walpole, *Memoirs Relating to European and Asiatic Turkey,* London, 1818, p. 233; W. Lack, *The Flora Graeca Story: Sibthorp, Bauer, and Hawkins in the Levant,* Oxford, 1999, p. 200.

27 Apollonius Rhodius, *Argonautica*, I, pp. 601–6; Herodotus, *Istoria*, vii, 22–4.

28 N. Imrie, *A Catalogue of Specimens Illustrative of the Geology of Greece, and Part of Macedonia,* Edinburgh, 1817, p. 6, my emphasis.

29 From John Sibthorp's diary 4 October 1794, in Walpole, *Travels*, p. 63.

30 Lack, *Flora Graeca*, pp. 108–9; B. Latour, *Science in Action: How to Follow Scientists and Engineers through Society*, Milton Keynes, 1987; D. Miller, 'Joseph Banks, empire, and "centres of calculation" in late Hannoverian London', in D. Miller and P. Reill (Eds), *Visions of Empire: Voyages, Botany, and Representations of Nature,* Cambridge, 1996, p. 23.

31 Withers, *op.cit.*, p. 154.

32 Sibthorp in Walpole, *Travels*, p. 40.

33 Sibthorp in Walpole, *Travels*, p. 40. According to Rackham, 20 out of Athos' 28 endemics are limited to the 'rock-garden' of the alpine zone, O. Rackham *op.cit.,* p. 54.

34 Imrie, *op.cit.*, p. 11; Sibthorp in Walpole, *Travels*, pp. 76, 80.

35 Lack, *op.cit.*, p. 179.

36 Withers, *op.cit.*, p. 138.

37 M. Nicolson, 'Humboldtian plant geography after Humboldt: the link to ecology', *British Journal for the History of Science* 29 (1996), p. 289.

38 M. Dettelbach, 'Global physics and aesthetic empire: Humboldt's physical portrait of the tropics', in Miller and Reill, *op.cit.*, p. 258.

39 D. Livingstone, *The Geographical Tradition,* Oxford, 1992, p. 138.

40 Quoted in Dettelbach, *op.cit.*, p. 261.

41 Nicolson, *op.cit.*, p. 297.

42 A. von Humboldt, *Cosmos: A Sketch of the Physical Description of the Universe,* vol. I, Baltimore, 1997 (1858), p. 8.

43 A. Grisebach, *Reise durch Rumelien und nach Brussa in Jahre 1839,* vol. I. Göttingen, 1841, p. iv.

44 Bougainville, for example, named Tahiti '*La Nouvelle Cythère*'. Similarly, Mauritius was compared by the physiocrat Bernardin de Saint-Pierre to the island of Samos. See Grove, *op.cit.*, pp. 237, 249.

45 G. Bachelard, *The Poetics of Space,* Boston, 1998 (1954).

46 Quoted in Dettelbach, *op.cit.*, p. 268.

47 Grisebach, *Reise durch Rumelien*, pp. 260, 245.

48 *ibid.*, p. 245; Dettelbach, *op.cit.*, p. 268.

49 Von Humboldt, *op.cit.*, p. 33.

50 Grisebach, *op.cit.* p. 269.

51 Grisebach, *op.cit.* p. 302; A. Grisebach, *La vegétation du globe d'après sa disposition suivant les*

climats esquisse d'une géographie comparée des plantes, vol. I, Paris, 1875, p. 482. In Grisebach's travel account, the Parisian foot is employed as the measure unit.

52 Quoted in E. Bunkse, 'Humboldt and aesthetic tradition in geography', *Geographical Review* 71 (1981), p. 145.

53 Grisebach, *op.cit.*, pp. 314–15.

54 Bunkse, *op.cit.*, p. 146.

55 Humboldt, *op.cit.*, p. 79.

56 Grisebach, *Vegétation du globe*, p. xiii.

57 Humboldt, *op.cit.*, p. 25.

58 Grisebach, *op.cit.*, p. 316.

59 *ibid.*, p. 317.

60 *ibid*, pp. 317–18.

61 *ibid*, p. 319.

62 *ibid*, p. 323.

63 *ibid*, p. 329.

64 W. Rauh, *Klimatologie und Vegetationsverhältnisse der Athos-Halbinsel und der ostägäischen Inseln Lemnos, Evstratios, Mytilene und Chios*, Heidelberg, 1949, p. 57.

65 K. Ganiatsas, *E blastesis kai e chlwris tes chersonesou tou Agiou Orous*, Mount Athos, 2003.

66 Humboldt, *op.cit.*, p. 29; emphasis added.

67 Cosgrove, *Geography and Vision*.

68 A. Ogilvie, 'A contribution to the geography of Macedonia', *Geographical Journal*, 55 (1920), pp. 10, 12, 14. The originator of this idea was George Perkins Marsh.

69 A. Grove and O. Rackham, *The Nature of Mediterranean Europe: An Ecological History*, New Haven and London, 2001, pp. 8–9.

70 W. Turrill, 'A contribution to the botany of Athos peninsula', *Bulletin of Miscellaneous Information, Royal Botanic Gardens, Kew* 4 (1937), p. 207.

71 W. Turrill, *The Plant Life of the Balkan Peninsula: a Phytogeographical Study*, Oxford, 1929, p. xiii; Rackham has recently shown the limits of this theory and revisited 'floristic Athos' in terms of a cultural landscape, a product of the interaction between monks and environment, rather than 'a prelapsarian paradise withdrawn from the corrupting effects of human activities', Rackham, *op.cit.*, p. 55.

72 L. Cameron and D. Matless, 'Benign ecology: Marietta Pallis and the floating fen of the delta of the Danube, 1912–1916', *Cultural Geographies* 10 (2003), pp. 253–77.

73 W. Turrill and V.S. Summerhayes, 'Ecology and taxonomy: the taxonomist's viewpoint', *Journal of Ecology* 27 (1939), p. 424.

74 F. Golley, *A History of the Ecosystem Concept in Ecology: More than the Sum of the Parts*, New Haven, 1993, p. 8.

75 Turrill, *Plant Life*.

76 W. Turrill, 'Some problems of plant range and distribution', *Journal of Ecology* 39 (1951), p. 206; Turrill, *Plant Life*, p. 213.

77 A.G. Tansley, 'Editor's preface', in Turrill, *Plant Life*, p. viii; Turrill, 'Plant range', p. 206. That such a mix depended on the geographical location and undefined form of the Balkan peninsula was a driving argument also among European and American geopoliticians of the time; see for example F. Kovacs, *The Untamed Balkans*, New York, 1941.

78 Turrill, 'A contribution to the botany of Athos', *The Plant Life of the Balkan Peninsula: a Phytogeographical Study*, p. 208.

79 Turrill, 'Plant range', p. 215.

80 Cameron and Mattless, *op.cit.*

81 A. Hill, 'A botanist on the Holy Mountain', *Blackwood's Magazine* 236 (1934), p. 81.

82 Turrill, 'Botany of Athos', p. 202; Hill, *op.cit.*, p. 81.

83 *ibid.*, p. 83.

84 G. Speake, *Mount Athos: Renewal in Paradise*, New Haven and London, 2002, p. 34.

85 B. Latour, 'How to be iconophilic in art, science, and religion?', in A Slaton (Ed.), *Picturing Science, Producing Art*, New York and London, 1998, p. 433.

86 *ibid.*, p. 422.

87 Y.F. Tuan, 'Introduction: cosmos versus hearth', in P. Adams, S. Hoelscher and K. Till (Eds.), *Textures of Place*, Minneapolis, 2001, p. 320.

88 Bachelard, *op.cit.*, p. 151.

Endnotes for chapter 8

1 A spectroscope records the wavelengths of light reflected or emitted from a celestial body. Because different chemical elements produce different spectral signatures in reflected solar light, an observer on Earth can determine and characterise – by virtue of the exaggeration or dullness of various wavelengths captured by the spectroscope – the existence and composition of an atmosphere. Because the effects of Earth's own atmosphere must always be accounted for, spectroscopic studies often involve the comparison of two or more celestial bodies, which allows for any common anomalies to be discounted as due to Earth's atmosphere.

2 W. Campbell, 'The spectrum of Mars as observed by the Crocker expedition to Mt. Whitney', *Lick Observatory Bulletin* 169 (1909), p. 149.

3 *ibid.*, 152.

4 *ibid.*, 152.

5 *ibid.*, 152.

6 Campbell's plates showed the spectra of the Moon and Mars to be identical. Because they were observed at virtually the same time, under the same atmospheric conditions, this finding indicated that Mars must have an extremely thin atmosphere, or none at all, just like the Moon.

7 Campbell did not conclusively reject the possibility that Mars had water vapour, but clearly stated that the new data 'put the burden of proof' on those who claimed this to be true. Campbell, *op.cit.*, p. 155. For a discussion of Campbell's role in the controversial history of Mars spectroscopy, see D. DeVorkin, 'W.W. Campbell's Spectroscopic study of the Martian atmosphere', *Quarterly Journal of the Royal Astronomical Society* 18 (1977), p. 37–53. For a more detailed discussion of the Mount Whitney expedition, see D. Osterbruck, 'To climb the highest mountain: W.W. Campbell's 1909 Mars Expedition to Mount Whitney', *Journal for the History of Astronomy* 20 (1989), pp. 77–97.

8 Campbell, *op.cit.*, p. 153.

9 Early work in science studies showed that the emergence and institutionalisation of experimental science, for example, was dependent on the gathering of 'witnesses' who could vouch for the legitimacy of experimental observations and phenomena. S. Shapin, 'The house of experiment in seventeenth-century England', *Isis* 79 (1988), p. 373–404; S. Shapin and S. Schaffer, *Leviathan and the Air-Pump: Hobbes, Boyle and the Experimental Life*, Princeton, 1985. Furthermore, the uniquely local laboratory sites in which witnesses were typically assembled are now understood to have reflected and replicated social geographies of privilege. S. Schaffer, 'Physics laboratories and the Victorian country house', in C. Smith and J. Agar (Eds.), *Making Space for Science: Territorial Themes in the Shaping of Knowledge*, New York, 1998, pp. 149–80; G. Gooday, 'The premisses of premises: spatial issues in the historical construction of laboratory credibility', in *ibid.*, pp. 216–245. This spatial expression of a social geography importantly allowed for the cultivation of 'trust' in the truth of scientific claims, even among those who had not witnessed the reported empirical phenomena in person. Ophir and Shapin helpfully suggest that the 'irremediably local dimension' of scientific knowledge should be seen not as a damaging critique but as a methodological point of entry. A. Ophir and S. Shapin, 'The place of knowledge: a methodological survey', *Science in Context* 4 (1991), p. 4. See also Livingstone's summary work on this theme: *Putting*

Science in its Place: Geographies of Scientific Knowledge, Chicago, 2003. Despite these early acknowledgements of spatial influences in the practice of science, the 'geographical turn' in this literature is just now coming into full swing.

10 Arguing 'Scientific notions like discovery, the challenge to authority, natural knowledge and so on both produce and are produced by geography,' Livingstone called for attention to 'the role of the spatial setting in the production of experimental knowledge, the significance of the uneven distribution of scientific information, the diffusion tracks along which scientific ideas and their associated instrumental gadgetry migrate, the management of laboratory space, the power relations exhibited in the transmission of scientific lore from specialist space to public place, the political geography and social topography of scientific subcultures, and the institutionalisation and policing of the sites in which the reproduction of scientific cultures is effected.' D. Livingstone, 'Geography, tradition and the scientific revolution: an interpretative essay', *Transactions of the Institute of British Geographers* 15 (1990), p. 338; D. Livingstone, 'The spaces of knowledge: contributions towards a historical geography of science', *Environment and Planning D: Society and Space* 13 (1995), p. 16.

11 For an overview of spatial approaches to the study of science, see R. Powell, 'Geographies of science: histories, localities, practices, futures', *Progress in Human Geography* 31 (2007), pp. 309–29, and S. Shapin, 'Placing the view from nowhere: historical and sociological problems in the location of science', *Transactions of the Institute of British Geographers* 23 (1998) pp. 5–12. See also Smith and Agar, *op.cit.*, for a collection of early work in this vein, and M. Bourguet et al., *Instruments, Travel and Science: Itineraries of Precision From the Seventeenth to the Twentieth Century*, London, 2002, for more recent treatments.

12 N. Thrift et al., 'The geography of truth', *Environment and Planning D: Society and Space* 13 (1995), p. 2.

13 The constructivist critique of science has usefully focussed our attention on the relationship between knowledge and power. B. Latour and S. Woolgar, *Laboratory Life: The Construction of Scientific Facts*, Princeton, New Jersey, 1986; D. Haraway, 'Teddy bear patriarchy: taxidermy in the Garden of Eden, New York City, 1908–1936', in *The Haraway Reader*, New York, 2004, pp. 151–98; F. Driver, 'Geography's empire: histories of geographical knowledge', *Environment and Planning D: Society and Space* 10 (1992), pp. 23–40. But it has also often tended to obscure the ways that individuals engage with real phenomena in unique places and reach conclusions with some hesitation. For a discussion of the ultimate failure of an antirealist stance, see K. Bassett, 'Whatever happened to the philosophy of science?: some comments on Barnes', *Environment and Planning A* 25 (1994), pp. 337–42. For a discussion of the problem of treating science as a monolithic entity, see D. Pedynowski, 'Science(s) – which, when and whose? Probing the metanarrative of scientific knowledge in the social construction of nature', *Progress in Human Geography* 27 (2003), pp. 735–52.

14 These themes, first outlined in 'The spaces of knowledge', are fully elaborated in Livingstone, *Putting Science in Its Place*.

15 For an overview of these contributions, see S. Naylor, 'Introduction: historical geographies of science – places, contexts, cartographies', *British Journal for the History of Science* 38 (2005), pp. 1–12. Anne Secord's oft-cited 'Science in the pub: artisan botanists in early nineteenth-century Lancashire', *History of Science* 32 (1994), pp. 269–315, laid the foundation for much of this work.

16 Naylor, *op.cit.*, p. 6.

17 D.A. Finnegan, 'Natural history societies in late Victorian Scotland and the pursuit of local civic science', *British Journal for the History of Science* 38 (2005), pp. 53–72.

18 L. Dritsas, 'From Lake Nyassa to Philadelphia: A Geography of the Zambesi Expedition, 1858–64', *British Journal for the History of Science* 38 (2005), pp. 35–52; D. Livingstone, 'Science,

text and space: thoughts on the geography of reading', *Transactions of the Institute of British Geographers* 30 (2005), pp. 391–401; J. Topham, 'A view from the industrial age', *Isis* 95 (2004), pp. 431–42. Although these geographical themes have become commonplace in the history-of-science literature, historical geographers are just beginning to apply them to their own discipline. For a review of their relevance for geographers, see C. Withers, 'History and philosophy of geography, 2002–2003: Geography in its place', *Progress in Human Geography* 1 (2005), pp. 64–72. See also a recent special issue of the *Journal of Historical Geography*, which takes up many of these ideas. D. Lambert, et al. (Eds.) *Special Issue: Historical Geographies of the Sea*, *Journal of Historical Geography* 32 (2006).

19 See R. Kohler, *Landscapes and Labscapes: Exploring the Lab–Field Border in Biology*, Chicago, 2002, for his theorisation of a border zone between field and lab that operates much like a cultural border zone. Kohler argues that the negotiation of fundamental differences between the two spatial spheres – like the acceptance of amateurs and the emphasis on physical action in the field, both of which would be considered unacceptable in a lab setting – gave rise to new and vibrant sciences like ecology, which tries to integrate elements from both sides of the border. See also T. Gieryn, *Cultural Boundaries of Science: Credibility on the Line*, Chicago, 1999.

20 F. Driver, 'Making space', *Ecumene* 1 (1994), pp. 386–90.

21 For a collection of essays that explore the role of fieldwork in bringing different types of science together, see H. Kuklick and R.E. Kohler (Eds.) 'Science in the field', *Osiris* 11 (1996). See especially the article by McCook for views on the complicated intertwining of reputations and legitimacy among scientists working in different sites and with different standards.

22 I am indebted to Margaret Pilkington's review of Kohler for noting that his neat distinction between lab and field is perhaps insufficient in contemporary contexts, as a more relevant distinction has emerged between observational and experimental practice. M. Pilkington, 'The ecologist's very own ecotone: exploring the lab–field border', *Journal of Biogeography* 31 (2004), p. 516.

23 For a collection of now-classic approaches to representation in science, see M. Lynch and S. Woolgar, *Representation in Scientific Practice*, Cambridge, MA, 1990.

24 On the representation of naturalists as world travellers, see Dritsas, *op.cit.* On the shifting portrayals of geological science as heroic, manly, and sporting, see B. Hevly, 'The heroic science of glacier motion', *Osiris* 11 (1996), pp. 66–86. On the popularity of meteorological science among audiences that associated high-altitude ballooning with adventure and spectacle, see J. Tucker, 'Voyages of discovery on oceans of air: scientific observation and the image of science in an age of "Balloonacy"', *Osiris* 11 (1996), pp. 144–76.

25 D. Osterbruck *et al.*, *Eye on the Sky: Lick Observatory's First Century*, Berkeley, 1988.

26 E.C. Pickering, 'Mountain observatories', *Appalachia* 3 (1883), p. 100.

27 Osterbruck *et al.*, *op.cit.*

28 The road was built in 1876, but an official test of 'seeing' conditions was not conducted until 1879. E. Holden, 'The Lick Observatory', *The Sidereal Messenger* 7 (1888), p. 47–65.

29 'The Lick Observatory', *The Sidereal Messenger* 4 (1885), p. 49.

30 E. Holden, *A Brief Account of the Lick Observatory of the University of California*, Sacramento, 1895. Of the pamphlet's fifteen images, four of the first six depicted the mountaintop site – as remote, overgrown, menacing, or sublime. The pamphlet contained only one image, near the end, of the great equatorial telescope, then the largest in the world.

31 'Mountain Observatories', *Publications of the Astronomical Society of the Pacific* 1 (1889), p. 123. The Astronomical Society of the Pacific and its journal were founded in 1889, one year after the Lick Observatory opened. Lick's director Holden was its first president, and all of the Lick astronomers were members.

32 D. Osterbruck, *Yerkes Observatory, 1892–1950*, Chicago, 1997.
33 Yerkes Observatory's first director, George Hale, used the occasion of Chicago's coming-out party – the 1893 World's Fair – to organise the first international astronomical congress ever held in the United States. The Yerkes Observatory, which was still in the planning stages at that time, featured prominently at the congress and showcased the promise of American astronomy and of the University of Chicago. Osterbruck, *Yerkes Observatory*.
34 *ibid.*, p. 15.
35 *ibid.*, p. 16.
36 Hale publicised the fact that he had sent a questionnaire to many prominent astronomers and reprinted their verbatim responses to questions he had asked about the effects on astronomical research of proximity to urban areas, to lakes and to railroads. He thus relied on the stature and credibility of others to support his view that Lake Geneva posed no major detriment to the observations planned for the new observatory. Interestingly, however, Hale's transcription of questionnaire responses includes the following comment by Simon Newcomb (then considered the leading American astronomer): 'To be of the greatest benefit to science the telescope should be mounted at some such point as Mt. Hamilton, California; Arequipa, Peru; or the Peak of Teneriffe.' G. Hale, 'The Yerkes Observatory of the University of Chicago: 1. Selection of the Site', *Astrophysical Journal* 5 (1897), p. 177.
37 G. Hale, 'The aim of the Yerkes Observatory', *Astrophysical Journal* 6 (1897), pp. 310–21.
38 Hale tried in vain to convince readers that 'notwithstanding a widespread impression to the contrary, the excellent atmospheric conditions enjoyed at the Lick Observatory do not seem to be common to all mountain summits'. Hale, 'The Yerkes Observatory', p. 168. He also drew attention to his colleague Edward Barnard's experience conducting nebula observations at both Yerkes and Lick, reporting that 'Professor Barnard has found that the best nights here are fully as good as the best nights at the Lick Observatory ... and he assures me that he now sees [certain nebulae] better than he could see them with the Lick telescope.' Hale, 'The Aim of the Yerkes Observatory', p. 317.
39 Sherburne Burnham, a respected double-star observer at Lick who had also performed the official atmospheric testing for Lick Observatory in 1879, wrote in 1900, 'There is probably no place in the world, where an observatory has been established, which can compare favourably with Mount Hamilton', cited in Osterbruck, 'Yerkes Observatory', p. 30. Hale announced the establishment of his new mountain observatory in G. Hale, 'The development of a new observatory', *Publications of the Astronomical Society of the Pacific* 17 (1905), pp. 41–52.
40 P. Lowell, *Mars*, Boston, 1895, p. v.
41 P. Lowell, 'New photographs of Mars: taken by the astronomical expedition to the Andes and now first published', *Century Magazine* 75 (1907), p. 303.
42 According to Lowell, 'A steady atmosphere is essential to the study of planetary detail: size of instrument being a very secondary matter.' Lowell, *Mars*, p. v.
43 S. Newcomb, 'Astronomy', in D. Wallace, *et al*. (Eds.), *The New Volumes of the Encyclopaedia Britannica: Constituting in Combination with the Existing Volumes of the Ninth Edition the Tenth Edition of that Work, and also Supplying a New, Distinctive, and Independent Library of Reference Dealing with Recent Events and Developments*, Edinburgh, 1902, p. 728.
44 C. Flammarion, 'Recent observations of Mars', *Scientific American* 74 (1896), p. 133.
45 A. Douglass, 'The Lowell Observatory and its work', *Popular Astronomy* 2 (1895), p. 395.
46 D. Strauss, 'Percival Lowell, W.H. Pickering and the founding of the Lowell Observatory', *Annals of Science* 51 (1994), pp. 37–58.
47 J. Lankford, *American Astronomy: Community, Careers, and Power, 1859–1940*, Chicago, 1997.
48 When the professionalisation of astronomy began in the mid-nineteenth century, amateurs were seen as a major asset. It was widely accepted and often commented that the tasks of observation were best performed by amateurs, while theoretical work or work requiring

advanced instrumentation was better done by professionals. By the end of the nineteenth century, however, the two groups were in conflict. Amateurs were trying to organise their own societies, push their own agendas, and garner public interest through popular publications, rather than disciplinary journals. In a debate over telescope size, amateurs began arguing that their small telescopes were actually better than the professional observatories' large telescopes. As a result, the peaceful coexistence between amateurs and professionals had largely come to an end by the first decade of the twentieth century. Professionals forwent the benefits of amateur labour for the higher goal of establishing the legitimacy of astronomy among American sciences. Though amateurs continued to be involved in astronomy (as they still are to this day), they were no longer in a position to drive new developments in the discipline. J. Lankford, 'Amateurs versus professionals: the controversy over telescope size in late Victorian science', *Isis* 72 (1981), pp. 11–28; J. Lankford, 'Amateurs and astrophysics: a neglected aspect in the development of a scientific specialty', *Social Studies of Science* 11 (1981), pp. 275–303; M. Rothernberg, 'Organization and control: professionals and amateurs in American astronomy, 1899–1918', *Social Studies of Science* 11 (1981), pp. 305–25.

49 For a discussion of the geometrical maps that emerged as dominant representations of Mars, see M. Lane, 'Mapping the Mars canal mania: cartographic projection and the creation of a popular icon', *Imago Mundi* 58 (2006), pp. 198–211.

50 For a discussion of the ways that geographical narratives were embedded in astronomers' representations of Mars as an inhabited world, see M. Lane, 'Geographers of Mars: cartographic inscription and exploration narrative in late Victorian representations of the Red Planet', *Isis* 96 (2005), pp. 477–506.

51 Strauss, 'Percival Lowell'; W. Hoyt, *Lowell and Mars*, Tucson, Arizona, 1976; Lankford, *American Astronomy*. For extended treatments of the early debates over life on Mars, see S. Dick, *The Biological Universe: The Twentieth-Century Extraterrestrial Life Debate and the Limits of Science*, Cambridge, 1996; M. Crowe, *The Extraterrestrial Life Debate 1750–1900: The Idea of a Plurality of Worlds from Kant to Lowell*, Cambridge, 1986; K. Guthke, *The Last Frontier: Imagining Other Worlds, from the Copernican Revolution to Modern Science Fiction*, trans. H. Atkins, Ithaca, 1983; W. Sheehan, *Planets and Perception*, Tucson, AZ., 1988.

52 E. Holden, 'What we really know about Mars', *The Forum* 14 (1892), pp. 359–68. It should be noted that most of this article was an attempt to defuse the popular sensation over Martian inhabitants. Holden insisted that the only question of value was whether Mars was habitable, as it would be impossible to determine whether the planet was actually inhabited.

53 W. Campbell, 'The spectrum of Mars', *Publications of the Astronomical Society of the Pacific* 6 (1894), p. 230.

54 'The Lick Observatory of the University of California', *Scientific American* 58 (1888), p. 162.

55 See, for example, his 1894–95 articles in *Astronomy and Astro-physics*, *Popular Astronomy*, and *Atlantic Monthly*, as well as his 1895 book, *Mars*.

56 Hale and Newcomb, of Chicago and Washington, DC respectively, both suffered Lowell's sarcasm regarding their eastern, near-urban locations. According to Lowell, no one was qualified to criticise his research unless they were working in similar or better atmospheric conditions. He found it especially easy to attack his British critics on the basis of known atmospheric impurities throughout the British Isles, as in this biting suggestion to Walter Maunder of the Royal Observatory, Greenwich: 'if England would only send out an expedition to steady air ... it would soon convince itself of these realities [the canals]'. Lowell Observatory Archive, Correspondence Files, P. Lowell to W. Maunder, 28 November 1903.

57 P. Lowell, *Mars and Its Canals*, New York, 1906, pp. 7, 8.

58 R. Nash, *Wilderness and the American Mind*, New Haven and London, 1967. See particularly his discussion of John Muir's representa-

tions of the Sierra Nevada Mountains. In this parallel discourse, remote western mountains figured as perfect antidotes to dirty and over-large cities.

59 Lowell, *Mars and its Canals*, p. 15. For a discussion of how turn-of-the-century American enthusiasm for wilderness was rooted in a desire to police national identity in an age of immigration and was also dependent on the mythology of the Western frontier, see D. Cosgrove, 'Wilderness, habitable earth and the nation' in *Geography and Vision: Seeing, Imagining and Representing the World*, London, 2008.

60 E. Holden, *Mountain Observatories in America and Europe*, Washington, DC, 1896, p. iii.

61 *ibid.*, p. 14.

62 See, for instance, Lowell's discussion of telescope size and use in his book, *Mars*.

63 The following passage provided a subtle but damaging critique of Lowell's deputy, Slipher, implying that he made critical scientific errors because of his lack of understanding of mountain atmospheric conditions: 'What assurance have we that the air columns through which Mr. Slipher observed Mars immediately after dark and the Moon from two to eight hours later were carrying equal quantities of aqueous vapour? ... Air masses at high altitudes may and usually do change rapidly. ... It is a common occurrence for clouds to form in the afternoons in high and mountainous regions, chiefly because of convection currents which carry moisture up, for the clouds to clear away about dark.' Campbell, 'The spectrum of Mars as observed by the Crocker expedition', p. 161.

64 For discussions of the ways that mountaineering – as a science and a sport – became embedded in Western notions of masculinity, heroism and nationalism, see Hevly, *op.cit.*; K.M. Morin, *et al.*, '(Troubling) spaces of mountains and men: New Zealand's Mount Cook and Hermitage Lodge', *Social and Cultural Geography* 2 (2001), pp. 117–39.; R. Macfarlane, *Mountains of the Mind*, New York, 2003.

65 A. Pang, 'The social event of the season: solar eclipse expeditions and Victorian culture', *Isis* 84 (1993), pp. 252–77.

66 'Mapping the southern sky from a mountain peak 14,000 feet high', *Scientific American* 64 (1891), p. 36. For more detail than the following discussion provides, see B. Jones and L. Boyd, *The Harvard College Observatory: The First Four Directorships, 1839–1919*, Cambridge, MA, 1971; H. Plotkin, 'Harvard College Observatory's Boyden Station in Peru: origin and formative years, 1879–1898', in A. Lafuente, et al. (Eds.), *Mundialización de la ciencia y cultura nacional. Actas del Congreso Internacional 'Ciencia, descubrimiento y mundo colonial'*, Madrid, 1991; S. Bailey, 'Expeditions and foreign stations', in: *The History and Work of Harvard Observatory, 1839–192: An Outline of the Origin, Development, and Researches of the Astronomical Observatory of Harvard College together with Brief Biographies of its Leading Members*, New York, 1931.

67 W. Pickering, 'Mars', *Astronomy and Astro-Physics* 11 (1892), p. 675.

68 S. Bailey, 'Harvard Observatory in Peru', *Scientific American* 76 (1897), p. 329.

69 Solon Bailey, cited in Jones and Boyd, *op.cit.*, p. 291. See also 'Harvard Observatory in Peru – The Highest Meteorological Station in the World', *Scientific American* 70 (1894), p. 67.

70 Lowell telegraphed Todd from Flagstaff with the following: 'The world, to judge from the English and American papers, is on the qui vive about the expedition as well as about Mars. They send me cables at their own extravagant expense and mention vague but huge (or they won't get 'em) sums for exclusive magazine publication of the photographs'. Lowell Observatory Archive, Correspondence Files, P. Lowell to D. Todd, 26 July 1907.

71 Lowell, 'New photographs of Mars'; D. Todd, 'The Lowell expedition to the Andes', *Popular Astronomy* 15 (1907) 55, pp. 1–53; D. Todd, 'Professor Todd's own story of the Mars Expedition: first article published from the pen of the leader of the party of observation', *Cosmopolitan Magazine* 44 (1908), pp. 343–51.

72 Campbell, 'The spectrum of Mars', p. 152.

Endnotes for chapter 9

1 B. Messerli and J. Ives (Eds), *Mountains of the World: A Global Priority*, New York, 1997, p. 456.
2 P. Viazzo, 'Le paradoxe alpin', *l'Alpe* 1 (1998), pp. 28–33.
3 There are attempts to establish a 'mountain science', which means to 'build an interdisciplinary and intersectoral mountain discipline'. Messerli and Ives, *op.cit.*, p. 460.
4 J. Blache, *L'homme et la montagne*, Paris, 1950 (1933), p. 7.
5 Messerli and Ives, *op.cit.*, pp. 2–3.
6 B. Debarbieux and F. Gillet (Eds.), *Mountain Regions: A Research Subject?*, Brussells, 2002; M. Price and D. Funnel, 'Mountain geography: a review', *Geographical Journal* 169 (2003), pp. 183–90.
7 I. Sacareau, *La montagne, une approche géographique*, Paris, 2003, p. 9.
8 *ibid.*, p. 283. '*Territorialités*' which she describes as 'individual and/or collective relationship to the territory'.
9 O. Dollfus, 'Réalités et perceptions comparées des Andes au Pérou et en Colombie', in B. Debarbieux (Ed.), *Quelle spécificité montagnarde?, Revue de géographie alpine* 1 (1989) p. 172.
10 *ibid.*, pp. 171–85.
11 Debarbieux and Gillet, *op.cit.*, p. 140.
12 A. Turco, 'Géographie, ordre symbolique et cycle de l'information', in J.P. Guérin and H. Gumuchian (Eds.), *Les représentations en actes: actes du Colloque de Lescheraines*, Grenoble, 1985, p. 78.
13 *ibid.*, p. 79.
14 Sacareau, *op.cit.*, p. 15.
15 J.P. Bozonnet, *Des monts et des mythes: l'imaginaire social de la montagne*, Grenoble, 1992.
16 Debarbieux and Gillet, *op.cit.*
17 F. Gerbaux, *La montagne en politique*, Paris, 1994.
18 B. Poche and J.P. Zuanon, 'Les collectivités de montagne: image externe et représentation propre', *Actes du XIe colloque franco-italien d'études alpines: spécificité du milieu alpin?*, Grenoble, 1986, p. 5.
19 Six of them are half-states.
20 E. Mévillot, 'Une image identitaire alpine à travers les récits de voyages, XVIIIe-XIXe siècles: l'exemple du Valais (Suisse)', *Revue de géographie alpine* 1 (1995), pp. 67–87.
21 P. Guichonnet (Ed.), *Histoire et civilisations des Alpes*, Vol. II, Lausanne, 1980, p. 213.
22 J. Brunhes and P. Girardin, 'Les groupes d'habitations du Val d'Anniviers comme types d'établissements humains', *Annales de géographie* 82 (1906), pp. 329–52.
23 Quoted in M. and S. Praplan, *Icogne*, Sierre, 1991, p. 23.
24 Samivel, *Hommes, cimes et dieux*, Paris, 1984 (1973), p. 35.
25 M. Troillet, *Le génie des Alpes valaisannes*, Genève, 2005 (1893), p. 69.
26 ProClim, 'Tourisme d'hiver: les conséquences du réchauffement climatique peuvent-elles être compensées par des investissements?', *Climate Press* 15 (2003), pp. 1–4.
27 T. Cerf, 'Le Glacier du Trient a connu les meilleurs restaurants parisiens. Il se meurt', *Le Temps* (27 July 2002).
28 J. Eschasseriaux, *Lettre sur le Valais, sur les mœurs de ses habitans*, Paris, 1806, p. 32.
29 C. Tombet and M.T. Wenner, *De la nature et des rapports de l'homme à la nature: quelques aspects, du XVIIIe au XXe siècle. Un exemple: Vallée de Bagnes*, Lausanne, 1980, p. 20.
30 M. Kilani, 'Les images de la montagne au passé et au présent, l'exemple des Alpes valaisannes',

Archives suisses des traditions populaires 1 (1988), p. 36.
31 *ibid.*, p. 37.
32 F. Walter, *Les Suisses et l'environnement : une histoire du rapport à la nature, du XVIIIe siècle à nos jours*, Carouge, 1990, p. 82.
33 A. Guex, *Le demi-siècle de Maurice Troillet*, Vol. I, Martigny, 1971, p. 239.
34 *ibid.*, p. 239.
35 *ibid.*, p. 272.
36 Kilani, *op.cit.*, p. 43.
37 The historian, Anselm Zurfluh, finds the premises in the fourteenth and fifteenth centuries. A. Zurfluh, 'L'Arc alpin, l'Europe et l'Homo Alpinus', in G. Dumont, *Histoire et géopolitique d'un espace européen*, Paris, 1998, p. 117.
38 Walter, *op.cit.*, p. 131.
39 A. Clavien, 'Valais, identité nationale et industrie des étrangers, 1900–1914', in Groupe Valaisan de Sciences Humaines, *Le Valais et les étrangers, XIXe–XXe*, Sion, 1992, p. 264.
40 B. Crettaz, *La beauté du reste: confession d'un conservateur de musée sur la perfection et l'enfermement de la Suisse et des Alpes*, Carouge, 1993, p. 92.
41 M.-C. Morand, 'Notre beau Valais: le rôle de la production artistique étrangère dans la construction de l'identité culturelle valaisanne', in Groupe Valaisan de Sciences Humaines, *op.cit.*, pp. 191–246.
42 *ibid.*, p. 209.
43 *ibid.*, p. 227.
44 Federal Office of Industry, Arts and Professions and Work, *Mesures de la Confédération en faveur des populations montagnardes*, Bern, 1956, pp. 5–6.
45 B. Debarbieux, 'The symbolic order of objects and the frame of geographical action: An analysis of the modes and effects of categorisation of the geographical world as applied to the mountains in the West', *Geojournal* 60 (2004), p. 402.
46 Speech of the President of the General Assembly of the GPMVR, 13 October 1963.
47 *ibid.*
48 GPMVR, *Annual Report*, Sion, 1960, p. 6.
49 J. Moulin, 'Quelques considérations sur l'évolution de la situation dans les régions de montagne et les conséquences à en tirer', 8 May 1964, p. 2.
50 GPMVR, *Etude d'un programme d'activité*, 14 January 1965, p. 2.
51 R. Gex-Fabry, 'Revitaliser l'agriculture de montagne', *Terre valaisanne*, 30 March 1995, p. 19.
52 GPMVR, *Annual report*, Sion, 1993, p. 17.
53 D. Sierro, '*La montagne en action*', *Montagna* 9 (1993), p. 17.
54 Speech of the President of the GPMVR, 'Politique de la montagne en Europe', Brussells, 25 June 1992, p. 28.
55 E. Bourgeois and J. Nizet, *Pression et légitimation*, Paris, 1995, p. 11.
56 GPMVR, *Annual Report*, Sion, 2002, p. 13.
57 Letter, 7 March 2000.
58 Speech given during the European Conference, 'Les massifs de montagne et la coopération territoriale en Europe', Chambéry, 8–9 June 2006.

Endnotes for chapter 10

1 This essay is also intended as a contribution to the International Polar Year (2007–9) project: Sea Ice and Knowledge Use: Assessing Arctic Environmental and Social Change (Project ID: 166) directed by Igor Krupnik and Claudio Aporta. The author acknowledges the generous support of awards from the Managers of the Cambridge University

Smuts Fund and the Scott Polar Research Institute's B.B. Roberts Fund, as well as a Research Leave Award Grant AH/E001106/1 from the Arts and Humanities Research Council. The author would also like to acknowledge information, advice and comments given generously by Claudio Aporta, Paul Crowley, Franklyn Griffiths, John MacDonald, and Lynn Pelplinski. The views expressed in this article do not imply their endorsement.

2 'Petition to the Inter American Commission on Human Rights Seeking Relief from Violations resulting from Global Warming Caused by Acts and Omissions of the United States'. Submitted by Sheila Watt-Clouthier, with the Support of the Inuit Circumpolar Conference, on behalf of all Inuit of the Arctic Regions of the United States and Canada, 7 December 2005. The quotation is from the 'Petition', p. 1.

3 *Arctic Climate Impact Assessment*, Cambridge, 2005. The 140-page summary report was published several months earlier under the title *Impacts of a Warming Arctic*, Cambridge, 2004.

4 'Petition', p. 1.

5 These measures are stated in the 'Petition', pp. 7–8.

6 Inter-American Commission on Human Rights. Text available at: http://www.cidh.org/what.htm, last accessed 21 March 2007.

7 For aesthetic responses to ice amongst British and Canadian travellers, see for example I. MacLaren, 'The aesthetic map of the North, 1845–1859', *Arctic* 38 (1985), p. 89–103.

8 See E. Wilson, *The Spiritual History of Ice: Romanticism, Science and the Imagination*, New York and Basingstoke, 2003.

9 See Chapter 5.

10 C. Aporta, 'Life on the ice: understanding the codes of a changing environment', *Polar Record* 207 (2002), pp. 341–54.

11 T. Berger (Ed.), *Northern Frontier, Northern Homeland: The Report of the Mackenzie Valley Pipeline Inquiry*, Toronto, 1977.

12 Quoted from a letter from the Inter-American Commission on Human Rights to the chief petitioner, Sheila Watt-Clouthier, cited in *Nunatsiaq News*, 15 December 2006.

13 Sheila Watt-Cloutier met with the IACHR on 1 March 2007. Media coverage of her visit eclipsed the launch events for International Polar Year on the same day.

14 Personal communication, 22 May 2007.

15 Author's interview with P. Crowley, 27 September 2006.

16 Aporta, *op.cit.*; R. Nelson, *Hunters of the Northern Ice*, Chicago, 1969; G. Wenzel, 'Archaeological evidence for prehistoric Inuit use of the sea-ice environment', in A. Cooke and E. Alstine (Eds.), *Sikumiut: People Who Use the Sea-ice*, Ottawa, 1984, pp. 41–59.

17 Aporta, *op.cit.*

18 A number of classic studies drew attention to the importance of sea ice for Inuit. Amongst these were H. Brody, *Living Arctic: Hunters of the Canadian North*, London, 1987; Nelson, *op.cit.*

19 S. Watt-Cloutier, 'The right to be cold: ice is not all that's going to disappear as the climate warms', *Orion*, July/August 2005. Text available at:
http://www.oriononline.org/pages/om/05-4om/Watt-Cloutier.html, last accessed 21 March 2007.

20 On Inuit astronomy, John MacDonald opened up an entirely new vocabulary of stargazing for non-Inuit students of astronomy: J. MacDonald, *The Arctic Sky: Inuit Astronomy, Star Lore, and Legend*, Toronto and Iqaluit, 1998. On Inuit zoology, see: V. Randa, *L'ours polaire et les Inuit*, Paris, 1986. This text offers a highly detailed knowledge of the natural history of polar bears, in which distinctions between movements such as running and walking differ from those understood in the discipline of academic zoology. On Inuit geography, spatiality, and toponymy, B. Collignon, *Les Inuit: ce qu'ils savent du territoire*, Paris, 1996, is amongst a number of works that explore the spatial structure of Inuit mobility. On climate change, see Gita Laidler's PhD dissertation-in-progress, 'Ice through Inuit eyes: contributions of Inuit Qaujimajatuqangit to sea ice and climate sci-

ence in the Canadian Arctic', Department of Geography, University of Toronto. On Inuit law, see W. Rasing, 'Too Many People: Order and Nonconformity in Iglulingmiut Social Process', *Recht En Samenleving* n.8, Nijmegen, 1994. On the topic of ice, Claudio Aporta's 2002 study of sea ice broke new ground in establishing that Inuit name sea ice features, a fact that previously was not widely understood.

I played a relatively modest role compared to some other university-trained researchers like John MacDonald and Wim Rasing in contributing to the Oral History Project. Nevertheless I spent five months in Igloolik learning from elders about a range of subjects including cartography, navigation, and sea ice, as well as many less tangible lessons from collaborations with younger Inuit. It is a privilege to be able to draw on interviews created through a collective effort by people whose company and insights I have enjoyed.

21 MacDonald, *op.cit.*; Rasing, *op.cit.*

22 Aporta, *op.cit.*; G. Laidler, 'Inuit and scientific perspectives on the relationship between sea ice and climate change: the ideal complement?', *Climatic Change* 78 (2006), pp. 407–44; Nelson, *op.cit*.

23 M. Bravo, 'Geographies of exploration and improvement: William Scoresby and Arctic whaling, 1782–1822', *Journal of Historical Geography* 32 (2006), pp. 512–38 ; D. Finnegan, 'The work of ice: glacial theory and scientific culture in early Victorian Edinburgh', *British Journal for the History of Science* 37 (2004), pp. 29–52.

24 T. Lodwig, 'The ice calorimeter of Lavoisier and Laplace and some of its critics, *Annals of Science* 31 (1974), p. 1–18.

25 E. Wilson, *op.cit.*

26 T. Porter, *Trust in Numbers: The Pursuit of Objectivity in Science and Public Life*, Princeton, 1995.

27 Germane to my argument is Theodore Porter's important historical study, *Trust in Numbers*, in which he examines why quantitative evidence is so readily and uncritically accepted as reliable knowledge.

28 A. Innuksuk, IE-038, Subject of Ice Conditions, interviewed by M. Bravo and P. Irngaut, trans. L. Tapardjuk, Igloolik, November 1988.

29 A. Innuksuk, IE-035, Subject of Ice Conditions, interviewed by P. Irngaut, trans. P. Irngaut, Igloolik, January 1988.

30 A somewhat dated but still very useful introduction to the geography of Igloolik can be found in K. Crowe, 'A Cultural Geography of Northern Foxe Basin, N.W.T', *Canada Northern Science Research Group* n. 69–2, Ottawa, 1970.

31 R. Gagné, 'Spatial concepts in the Eskimo language', in V. Valentine and F. Vallee (Eds.), *Eskimo of the Canadian Arctic*, Toronto, 1968, 38; MacDonald, op.cit., p. 162.

32 Aporta, op.cit., p. 341.

33 MacDonald, op.cit., pp. 173–80.

34 A. Qunnut, IE-321, Subject of Survival and Seal Hunting, interviewed by Maurice Arnattiaq, trans. L. Tapardjuk, Igloolik, February 1992; T. Ikummaq, IE-466, Subject of Navigation and Place-names, interviewed by C. Aporta, Igloolik, December 2000; G. Qulaut, IE-476, Subject of Place-names, Hunting, Navigation, and Ice Conditions, interviewed by C. Aporta, n.d.; L.A. Utak, IE-477, Subject of Sea Ice, Wayfinding, and Adolescence, interviewed by L. Tapardjuk, trans. L. Tapardjuk, Igloolik, April 2001.

35 Aporta, *op.cit.*

36 Qulaut, IE-476.

37 Utak, IE-477.

38 Qunnut, IE-321.

39 Utak, IE- 477.

40 Sea Ice and Knowledge Use (SIKU): Assessing Arctic Environmental and Social Change (Project ID: 166) directed by I. Krupnik and C. Aporta.

41 A. Innuksuk, IE-004, Subject of Traditional Knowledge, interviewed by W. Rasing and P. Irngaut, trans. L. Tapardjuk, October 1986.

42 Utak, IE-477.

43 One of the strengths of the Anijaarniq project, and the Igloolik Oral History Project, is the majority of interviews are conducted by Inuit

researchers. Without taking anything away from the very productive collaborative work of visiting university-based researchers, local interviewers belonging to the local community are privileged participant-observers and often elicit more textured responses to their questions.

44 V. Aqatsiaq, IE-376, Subject of Igloolik History and Traditions, interviewed by L. Otak, translated by L. Otak, Igloolik, July 1996; A. Innuksuk IE-324, 1995, in: MacDonald, *op.cit.*, p. 20.

45 A. Spalding, 'Doctor Faust and the woman in the sea', *Artscanada* 28 (1972), p. 102; cf. MacDonald, *op.cit.*, p. 35.

46 Aqatsiaq, IE-376.

47 G. Kappianaq, IE-273, Subject of Wind, Ice, Walrus Hunting, and Mushing, interviewed by Maurice Arnattiaq, trans. L. Tapardjuk, Igloolik, April 1993.

48 Personal communication, MacDonald, 27 May 2007.

49 Kappianaq, IE-273.

50 F. Alaralak, IE-229, Subject of Snow Conditions, Igloo Construction and Ice Conditions, interviewed by Maurice Arnattiaq, trans. L. Tapardjuk, Igloolik, March 1992.

51 Kappianaq, IE-273.

52 Personal communication, July 1988.

53 Alaralak, IE-229.

54 *ibid.*

55 *ibid.*

56 *ibid.*

57 *ibid.*

58 W. E. Parry, 'Iligliuk's Chart No. 2', in *Narrative of Parry's Second Voyage*, London, 1824, p. 198.

59 Innuksuk, IE-038.

60 *ibid.*

61 *ibid.*

62 C. Aporta and E. Higgs, 'Satellite culture: global positioning systems, Inuit wayfinding, and the need for a new account of technology', *Current Anthropology* 46 (2005), pp. 729–53.

63 *ibid.*

64 The ice forecasts can be seen at: http://www.glacesice.ec.gc.ca/app/WsvPrdCanQry.cfm?subID=2003&Lang=eng last accessed on 4 January 2007.

65 Royal Proclamation of 1763. The full text can be found in the Solon Law Archive online at: http://www.solon.org/Constitutions/Canada/English/PreConfederation/rp_1763.html, last accessed 5 April 2007; C. Calloway, *The Scratch of a Pen: 1763 and the Transformation of North America*, Oxford, 2006.

66 Minister of Supplies and Services Canada, *Inuit Land Use and Occupancy Project: A Report*, Ottawa, 1976.

67 F. Griffiths, 'Safe and sound', *Globe and Mail*, 8 November 2006.

68 P. Steinberg, *The Social Construction of the Oceans*, Cambridge, 2001.

Endnotes for chapter 11

1 D. Gregory, *The Colonial Present: Afghanistan, Palestine, Iraq*, Oxford, 2004.

2 *Qallunaat*, translated literally, means the 'big, high (eye)brows' in Inuktitut. It is therefore used to refer to non-Inuit. See F. Laugrand and J. Oosten, 'Inuit and Qallunaaq perspectives: interacting points of view', *Études/Inuit/Studies* 26 (2002), pp. 13–15.

3 S. Ortner, *Life and Death on Mt. Everest: Sherpas and Himalayan Mountaineering*, Princeton and Oxford, 1999, p. 17. See also S. Ortner, *Anthropology and Social Theory: Cul-*

ture, Power, and the Acting Subject, Durham, NC, and London, 2006.

4 R. Paine's Preface, in his *The White Arctic: Anthropological Essays on Tutelage and Ethnicity*, St John's, Newfoundland, 1977, pp. xi–xiii.

5 H. Brody, *The People's Land: Eskimos and Whites in the Eastern Arctic*, Harmondsworth, 1975. Iqaluit is the territorial capital of Nunavut and was known as Frobisher Bay until 1987.

6 This essay draws from field notes and interviews collected during ethnographic fieldwork in Resolute, Iqaluit, and field sites across the Canadian Arctic during 2001 and 2002. As well as the use of pseudonyms, conversational notes recorded during fieldwork are used so as to protect the identity of informants. This participant observation was supplemented by structured, tape-recorded interviews. These are recorded by date and location, with identities of informants revealed only when requested.

7 On the history of the Manchester School, see L. Schumaker, *Africanizing Anthropology: Fieldwork, Networks, and the Making of Cultural Knowledge in Central Africa*, Durham, NC, and London, 2001.

8 V. Turner, *From Ritual to Theatre: The Human Seriousness of Play*, New York, 1982, p. 11, original emphasis.

9 *ibid.*, p. 11.

10 V. Turner, *The Anthropology of Performance*, New York, 1987.

11 M. Bakhtin, *Rabelais and His World*, Bloomington, IN, 1984.

12 P. Stallybrass and A. White, *The Politics and Poetics of Transgression*, Ithaca, 1986.

13 S. Ortner, *Sherpas Through their Rituals*, Cambridge, 1978.

14 C. Lewis and S. Pile, 'Woman, body, space: Rio Carnival and the politics of performance', *Gender, Place and Culture* 3 (1996), pp. 23–41; P. Jackson, 'The politics of the streets: a geography of Caribana', *Political Geography* 11 (1992), pp. 130–51.

15 V. Turner, *Dramas, Fields, and Metaphors: Symbolic Action in Human Society*, Ithaca, 1974.

16 R. Powell, 'Resolute Base', in M. Nuttall (Ed.), *Encyclopedia of the Arctic*, Vol. III, New York and Abingdon, 2005, pp. 1760–1.

17 F. Tester, 'Resolute Bay', in Nuttall, *op.cit.*, pp. 1761–2.

18 *ibid.*

19 For more on this history of the adoption of Resolute as a centre for High Arctic research activities, see R. Powell, *op.cit.*; D. Bissett, *Resolute: An Area Economic Survey*, Ottawa, 1967; R. Gajda, *Radstock Bay, NWT, Compared With Resolute Bay, NWT, as a Potential Airbase and Harbor*, Ottawa, 1964; W. Kemp, G. Wenzel, N. Jensen and E. Val, *The Communities of Resolute and Kuvinaluk: A Social and Economic Baseline Study*, Montreal, 1977.

20 G. Robertson, *Memoirs of a Very Civil Servant: Mackenzie King to Pierre Trudeau*, Toronto, 2000.

21 For full accounts of the relocations to Resolute, see the discussions in F. Tester and P. Kulchyski, *Tammarniit (Mistakes): Inuit Relocation in the Eastern Arctic 1939–63*, Vancouver, BC, 1994; and A.R. Marcus, *Relocating Eden: The Image and Politics of Inuit Exile in the Canadian Arctic*, Hanover, NH, 1995.

22 Interview with Ralph Alexander, Hamlet Council offices, Resolute, 23 July 2002.

23 Interview with Graham Rowley, Ottawa, 18 April 2002; Robertson, *op.cit.*

24 Tester, *op.cit.*

25 2001 Census of Canada, Available online at: http://www12.statcan.ca/english/profil01/CP01/details/Page.cfm?Lang=E&Geo1=CSD&Code1=6204022&Geo2=PR&Code2=62&Data=Count&SearchText=RESOLUTE&SearchType=Begins&SearchPR=01&B1=All&Custom=.

26 C. Taylor, *The Ethics of Authenticity*, Cambridge, MA, 1991; W. Kymlicka, *Politics in the Vernacular: Nationalism, Multiculturalism, and Citizenship*, Oxford, 2001; W. Kymlicka, 'Being Canadian', *Government and Opposition* 38 (2003), pp. 357–85; C. Harris, 'Postmodern patriotism: Canadian reflections', *The Canadian Geographer / Le Géographe canadien* 45 (2001), pp. 193–207.

27 R. Hulan, *Northern Experience and the Myths of Canadian Culture*, Montreal and Kingston, 2002; R. Powell, 'Northern cultures: myths, geographies and representational practices', *Cultural Geographies* 12 (2005), pp. 371–8.
28 J. Saul, *Reflections of a Siamese Twin: Canada at the End of the Twentieth Century*, Toronto, 1997.
29 *ibid.*, p. 508.
30 J. Amagoalik, 'Wasteland of nobodies', in J. Dahl, J. Hicks and P. Jull (Eds), *Nunavut: Inuit Regain Control of Their Lands and Their Lives*, Copenhagen, 2000, pp. 138–9.
31 For a full account of the history of the creation of Nunavut, see J. Hicks and G. White, 'Nunavut: Inuit self-determination through a land claim and public government?', in J. Dahl, J. Hicks and P. Jull (Eds), *Nunavut: Inuit Regain Control of Their Lands and Their Lives*, Copenhagen, 2000, pp. 30–115.
32 For more on the process of becoming a hunter in Inuit societies, see T. Takano, 'Connections with the land: land-skills courses in Igloolik, Nunavut', *Ethnography* 6 (2005), pp. 463–86; and M. Nuttall, 'Becoming a hunter in Greenland', *Études/Inuit/Studies* 24 (2000), pp. 33–45.
33 Interview with Ralph Alexander, Hamlet Council offices, Resolute, 23 July 2002.
34 *ibid.*
35 *ibid.*
36 *ibid.*
37 J. Kobalenko, *The Horizontal Everest: Extreme Journeys on Ellesmere Island*, Toronto, 2002, pp. 5–6.
38 Where I stood in this cultural space was obviously complicated. Among natural scientists at Resolute, I was positioned as outsider by being a social scientist. Among Inuit, all researchers are held to be outsiders. This situation was further complicated by my English identity – my country of origin has been historically connected with colonial practices in the Canadian Arctic. However, at the time of conducting fieldwork, I had recently graduated, after 24 months of study, with a Masters degree from a leading western Canadian university and had been resident in Ottawa for a further 18 months. This moderated my status somewhat. For fuller development of this point, see R. Powell, 'Intemperate spaces: field practices and environmental science in the Canadian Arctic, 1955–2000', Unpublished PhD thesis, University of Cambridge, 2004.
39 J. England, A. Dyke and G. Henry, 'Canada's crisis in Arctic science: the urgent need for an Arctic science and technology policy; or, "Why work in the Arctic? No one lives there"', *Arctic* 51 (1998), pp. 183–90; J. England, 'An urgent appeal to the Government of Canada to proclaim our northern identity', *Arctic* 53 (2000), pp. 204–9.
40 Interview with Bruce Rigby, Nunavut Research Institute, Iqaluit, 25 June 2002.
41 Interview with Mary Ellen Thomas, Nunavut Research Institute, Iqaluit, 25 June 2002.
42 Interview with Bruce Rigby, Nunavut Research Institute, Iqaluit, 25 June 2002.
43 Bakhtin, *op.cit.*, p. 10.
44 *ibid.*, p. 10.
45 J. Briggs, *Never in Anger: Portrait of an Eskimo Family*, Cambridge, MA and London, 1970. Nicole Stuckenberger has made similar observations in her recent account of Christmas celebrations in Qikiqtarjuaq, see N. Stuckenberger, *Community at Play: Social and Religious Dynamics in the Modern Inuit Community of Qikiqtarjuaq*, Amsterdam, 2005.
46 P. Stern, 'Land claims, development, and the pipeline to Citizenship', in P. Stern and L. Stevenson (Eds), *Critical Inuit Studies: an Anthology of Contemporary Arctic Ethnography*, Lincoln, 2006, pp. 105–18; L. Stevenson, 'Introduction', *ibid.*, pp. 1–22.
47 I would like to Sandra Mather for preparing the maps. Assistance from Ian Qualtrough was valuable in the preparation of the other illustrations.

Endnotes for chapter 12

1 *Jongju* is not a traditional form of climbing. The archetype of *jongju* began in Chirisan, at southern end of Paektudaegan, in the early twentieth century and became popular over the last few decades.

2 B. Koto, 'An orographic sketch of Korea', *Journal of the College of Science* 19 (1903), pp. 1–61.

3 Since around 1890, many geological surveys, especially for the purpose of mining, had been done by the Japanese, but there is little research of the land-form of the whole peninsula before Koto Bunjiro.

4 Koto Bunjiro divided Paektudaegan into four geologically distinctive mountain ranges; Macholyong range and Hamkyong range in the north and T'aebaeck range and Sobaeck range in the south. Refer to Figure 12.2.

5 The Kangwha treaty eventually put an end to the stubborn isolation policy of Chosŏn dynasty, and as a result of it, Chemulpo, a port near the capital city, Seoul, was opened. It is analogous to the Maiji treaty (1867) between Japan and the US in that it is a rather coerced and unequal one.

6 B. Braun, 'Producing vertical territory: geology and governmentality in late Victorian Canada', *Ecumene* 7 (2000), pp. 7–46.

7 *ibid.*, p. 7.

8 'The moderns think they have succeeded in such an expansion only because they have carefully separated Nature and Society (and bracketed God), whereas they have succeeded only because they have mixed together much greater masses of humans and nonhumans, without bracketing anything and without ruling out any combination! The link between the work of purification and the work of mediation has given birth to the moderns, but they credit only the former with their success.' B. Latour, *We Have Never Been Modern*, Cambridge, MA, 1993, p. 41.

9 According to Braun, 'geological landscape', which was visualised by George Dawson in the enframing nature of the western coast of Canada, is altogether a different way of seeing nature by eighteenth-century travellers such as Cook and Le Pérouse. Geological vision made it possible to see 'the depth of the landscape as well as its surface'. This difference, Braun argues, 'cannot be explained through appeals to "nature", "reason", or "economy" but instead must be understood in terms of much more mundane historical and spatial practices that gave rise to particular modalities of "seeing" and "knowing" nature.' Braun, *op.cit.*, p. 16. In this way, Braun attempts to historicise Dawson's 'geological vision' by analysing it in the context of 'specific historical geographies of "seeing" and "ordering" nature.'

10 Latour, *op.cit.*

11 Koto, *op.cit.*, pp. 7–11.

12 It means Chosŏn dynasty.

13 Koto, *op.cit.*, p. 8; italics in the original text.

14 D. Stoddart, *On Geography and its History*, New York, 1986.

15 Koto, *op.cit.*, pp. 53–54.

16 M. Park, 'The Classification of Mountain Systems and its Changes in Korea'. MA Thesis, Koryo University, Seoul, 1996, p. 81.

17 A. Schmid, *Korea Between Empires, 1895–1919*, New York, 2001, p. 201.

18 The idea of *p'ungsu* (*feng shui* in Chinese) has been one of the fundamental Korean geographical concepts. The Chinese ideogram *p'ungsu* means wind and water, reflecting a holistic world-view under the historical conditions of an agricultural society. Controlling wind and water necessitated both an ideological instru-

ment for maintaining social order as well as for the technological understanding of topographical features and climatic elements and their management. Thus, *p'ungsu* emerged not only as a practical form of geographical thought for the purpose of finding good places, but also as part of the moral rhetoric of a society. Specifically, Korean *p'ungsu* placed emphasis on feasible and practical methods for realising interdependence and co-existence between humans and the natural environment within a local setting, rather than the general principle, theory, and the absolutely cosmological logic of Chinese *feng shui*. As a result, Korean *p'ungsu* reflects specific climatic and morphological features in the Korean Peninsula, and there are a variety of indigenous local traditions of *p'ungsu* related to the particular environment of regions therein.

19 Schmid, *op.cit.*, pp. 216–23.

20 *ibid.*, p. 217.

21 The English version is titled *Yi Chung Whan's Taengniji: The Korean Classic Choosing Settlements* (trans. I. Yoon). It was written in Chinese, and translated into Korean and English. It is assumed that the book was originally written in 1751 by a high-ranking official during his exile.

22 *Taedongyojido*, a famous woodcut map, was made in 1861 by independent cartographer Kim Chong-ho and its scale is 1:216,000. Very little was known about Kim Chong-ho's life. This map is the most outstanding and largest (4 metres wide by 6.6 metres long) old map of Korea. Its representation is very accurate, even as compared to a modern map of Korea. See B. Yang, 'Taedongyojido', *Citizen's forum on Korean History* 23 (1998), pp. 45–59; C. Lee, *Old Maps of Korea*, Seoul, 1991.

23 Yi, *op.cit., p. 2.*

24 It is composed of Pyongan-do, Hamkyong-do, Whanghae-do, Kangwon-do, Kyongsang-do, Cholla-do, Chongchong-do, Kyongki-do, which are the same as modern administrative boundaries except some subdivisions within some of the provinces (for example, South Kyongsang-do, North Kyongsang-do).

25 Schmid, *op.cit.*, p. 203.

26 *ibid.* However, it may be questionable whether the modern concept of space can be applied to the Chosŏn period in that the implosion (encroachment) of place by space happened with the establishment of modern transportation systems, such as the railway toward the end of the nineteenth century. Before then, Korea was based on a pre-modern territorial concept hierarchically centred on Seoul. Furthermore, it should also be noted that the search for a desirable place to live is exclusive to upper-class scholars, which makes it essential to differentiate *Taengniji* from modern Western geographical concepts, Yi, *op.cit.*, p. 15. Yi Jung-whan evaluated local characters in terms of the perspective of a Confucian scholar gentry not from any working people, which is especially clear in the four elements of the latter part of *Taengniji – Sansu* (*Landscape and Scenery*) as well as other parts of the book. According to key lessons of Confucianism in the Chosŏn period, nature and its scenic beauty give the literary upper class an opportunity to reflect on their lives in a secular world and re-discover moral and ethical principles from the orderliness of nature. In the introductory chapter, 'Four classes of people', the author explicitly shows the stand taken by a particular class, the scholarly gentry, in pre-modern Chosŏn.

27 *P'ungsu* is here considered as a factor with livelihood, social characteristics and scenery, Yi, *op.cit.*

28 Schmid, *op.cit.*, p. 218.

29 There is no evidence though that Kim made *Taedongyojichondo*. See H. Yoon, 'A preliminary study of "The Preface" to Taedongyojichondo (The whole map of Korea)', *Journal of Cultural and Historical Geography* (*MunhwaYoksaChiri*) 4 (1992), pp. 97–107.

30 It also demonstrates that the boundary of the state was not delineated at that time.

31 B. Yang, 'Perceptions of nature in the Chosŏn period', *Korea Journal* 4 (1997), pp. 134–55.

32 *ibid.*, p. 138.

33 It is certain that *Sansugo* was written by Shin Kyong Joon (1712–81), but the author of

Sankyongpyo is unknown. Some people argue that both were written by Shin, because *Sankyongpyo* seemed to be based on *Sansugo*. However, I do not accept the argument, because the categorising systems of mountains and epistemological assumption are fairly different, even though the two works share other similarities.

34 Yang, *op.cit.*, p. 138.

35 Mountain ranges are categorised into three hierarchies in terms of their significance: *Taegan*, *Chogan* and *Chongmaek*.

36 He is one of the most famous nationalists, poets, novelists, and 'Enlightenment' thinkers in early twentieth-century Korea. However, he did not receive the attention and respect he deserved in the postwar period because of his collaboration with the Japanese colonial government in his last years. He is thus remembered as national traitor by many Korean nationalists.

37 J. Kwon, 'The early writing of Nam-sun Choi (1890–1957) and his geographical concern: Geography as the science of global knowledge and the impact of Meiji physiography on his cultural movement', *Journal of Applied Geography (UnyongChiri)* 13 (1990), pp. 1–34.

38 *ibid.*, p. 12.

39 He identified traditional geography with *p'ungsu* alone in the past.

40 It was established in 1910 by nationalists to stimulate concern about the traditional culture and history of Korea. It collected and published many ancient texts written in the Chosŏn period. *Sankyongpyo* was one of the traditional geography books edited and published by the association. Very few people could access and understand the book before its publication, because the number of Chinese manuscripts was very limited.

41 She even confessed in her travelogue that she was ashamed of not previously knowing about Paektudaegan.

42 N. Nam and K. Kwon, *Saramkwa San* 9 (1991), p. 169.

43 *ibid.*, p. 169.

44 S. Cho, *There Is No T'aebaeck Mountain Range*, Seoul, 1997, p. 47.

45 Kim Chong-ho successively made three important maps; *Chonggudo*, *Tongyodo*, *Taedongyojido*. *Tongyodo* is a developed version of *Chonggudo*, and *Taedongyojido* is a woodcut of *Tongyodo*. However, he could not represent all the content of *Tongyodo* because of the difficulty of inscription and the limit of the size of the wood plate. For example, there are around 5,600 mountain place-names in *Tongyodo*, but he eliminated 1,180. Lee put all the original place-names in *Tong-yodo* and published a modern version of *Taedong-yojido*: U. Lee, *Reading Tasedong Yojido, Kwangudang*, 1990, p. 24.

46 24 July 1986; Cho, *op.cit.*, p. 48.

47 *ibid.*, pp. 100–1.

48 *ibid.*

49 On the historical dependency between river system and mountain system, see B. Yang, *op.cit.*.

50 Koto, *op.cit.*, p. 2.

51 One of the main reasons why Paektudaegan was culturally so important in the past is that it worked substantially as a material barrier, causing cultural, political, historical difference particularly between the Yongnam (located east of Paektudaegan) and the Honam region (west of Paektudaegan). Historically, the Korean War (1950–3) and Donghak rebellion (1894), show what role Paektudaegan played in the patterns of the diffusion of political uprising and military defence. In the case of Tonghak rebellion, see Cho, *op.cit.*, pp. 152–5. The role of an old map describing the mountain/river system in detail is similar to that of the street map of a modern city: how to get to a distant place easily and fast.

52 According to a map produced in 1920s, it is assumed that *jongju* in Chirisan began during the colonial era.

53 S. Radcliffe, 'Imaginative geographies, postcolonialism, and national identities: Contemporary discourses of the nation in Ecuador', *Ecumene* 3 (1996), p. 23.

54 *ibid.*, p. 23.

55 F. Driver and G. Rose, 'Introduction: towards new histories of geographical knowledge', in F. Driver and G. Rose (Eds.), *Nature and Science: Essays in the History of Geographical Knowledge*,

Historical Geography Research Group Publication Series 28, Cheltenham, 1992, p. 4; C. Withers, *Geography, Science and National Identity: Scotland since 1520*, Cambridge and New York, 2001.
56 Withers, *op.cit.*

Endnotes for chapter 13

1 I would like to thank Nicolas Howe and the editors of this volume for their assistance and critical commentary.
2 N. Entrikin, 'Place and region 2', *Progress in Human Geography* 20 (1996), pp. 215–21; N. Entrikin, 'Hiding places', *Annals of the Association of American Geographers* 91 (2002), pp. 694–9.
3 H. Thoreau, 'Ktaadn', in J. Moldenhauer (Ed.), *The Maine Woods*, Princeton, 1972, pp. 3–83.
4 J. Huber (Ed.), *Elevating Ourselves: Thoreau on Mountains*, New York, 1999, p. 3.
5 Thoreau, *op.cit.*, p. 65.
6 *ibid.*, p. 63.
7 *ibid.*, p. 64.
8 *ibid.*, p. 64.
9 D. Robinson, *Natural Life: Thoreau's Worldly Transcendentalism*, Ithaca, 2004, p. 135.
10 Thoreau, *op.cit.*, pp. 70–71.
11 *ibid.*, p. 71.
12 L. Buell, *The Environmental Imagination: Thoreau, Nature Writing, and the Formation of American Culture*, Cambridge, MA, 1995, p. 423, note 33.
13 *ibid.*, p. 13.
14 J. Bennett, *Thoreau's Nature: Ethics, Politics, and the Wild*, Thousand Oaks, 1994, p. xxi.
15 Buell, *op.cit.*, pp. 70–1.
16 *ibid.*, p. 71.
17 B. Latour, *We Have Never Been Modern*, Cambridge, MA, 1993.
18 R. Sack, *Homo Geographicus*, Baltimore, 1997.
19 J. Le Conte, *Evolution: Its Nature, its Evidences, and its Relation to Religious Thought*, New York, 1897, pp. 301–3.
20 Y.-F. Tuan, *Who am I? An Autobiography of Emotion, Mind, and Spirit*, Madison, 1999; T. Hägerstrand, 'In search for the sources of concepts', in A. Buttimer (Ed.), *The Practice of Geography*, New York, 1983, pp. 238–56; P. Haggett, *The Geographer's Art*, Oxford, 1990, pp. 1–20.
21 H. Dorn, *The Geography of Science*, Baltimore, 1991; D. Livingstone, *Putting Science in its Place: Geographies of Scientific Knowledge*, Chicago, 2003.
22 Livingstone, *op.cit.*

Index